Wallace Stevens and Literary Canons

Wallace Stevens
AND
Literary Canons

John Timberman Newcomb

UNIVERSITY PRESS OF MISSISSIPPI
Jackson & London

Passages from *Collected Poems of Wallace Stevens.* Copyright © 1954. Reprinted by permission of Alfred A. Knopf, Inc.

Passages from *Letters of Wallace Stevens.* Copyright © 1966 by Holly Stevens. Reprinted by permission of Alfred A. Knopf, Inc.

Copyright © 1992 by University Press of Mississippi
All rights reserved
Manufactured in the United States of America
Designed by Sally Hamlin

Library of Congress Cataloging-in-Publication Data

The paper in this book meets the guidelines for permanence and durability of the Committee on Production Guidelines for Book Longevity of the Council on Library Resources.

Newcomb, John Timberman.
    Wallace Stevens and literary canons / John Timberman Newcomb.
      p. cm.
    Includes bibliographical references and index.
    ISBN: 978-1-60473-872-8
    1. Stevens, Wallace, 1879-1955—Criticism and interpretation—
  History. 2. Canon (Literature) I. Title.
PS3537.T4753Z694   1992
    811'.52—dc20   91-31930
                                                               CIP

British Library Cataloging-in-Publication data available

Children picking up our bones
Will never know that these were once
As quick as foxes on the hill;

And that in autumn, when the grapes
Made sharp air sharper by their smell
These had a being, breathing frost;

And least will guess that with our bones
We left much more, left what still is
The look of things, left what we felt

At what we saw.
>—Stevens,
> "A Postcard from the Volcano,"
> 1935

If you talked about the writings of some minor American novelist or short-story writer or poet—by *minor*, here, I mean anybody but the immediately fashionable six or eight—your hearer's eyes began to tap their feet almost before you had finished a sentence.
>—Randall Jarrell
> on American literary culture, 1953

Contents

	Acknowledgments	ix
1.	**Introduction:** The Shadow of His Fellows	3
2.	**New York Circles:** Stevens and the Little Magazine Avant-Garde, 1914–1923	23
3.	**The Lutanist of Fleas:** Stevens and *Harmonium* in the 1920s	48
4.	**It Must Change:** Stevens in the 1930s	81
5.	**Life Anywhere But on a Battleship:** The Poet's Wartime and Postwar Reception, 1941–1953	128
6.	**A Shaping Spirit:** Stevens and the Canons of Modernism, 1954–1966	172
7.	**Afterword:** His Own Best Critic?	236
	Notes	245
	Works Cited	270
	Index	287

Acknowledgments

I am grateful to the staffs of the following libraries for their aid and comfort: Davis Library, University of North Carolina; North Carolina State University Library; Green Library, West Chester University; Emory University Library; the New York Public Library; the Library of Congress; and especially Perkins and East Campus Libraries, Duke University. This book was finished with the aid of a Faculty Development Grant from West Chester University. West Chester's English Department and its former and current chairs, Kostas Myrsiades and Claude Hunsberger, also granted me release time to help complete this project. The office staff at West Chester, especially Roxana Liberace, Barbara Bottoms, and Anne Rayburn, were enormously helpful as I tried to finish a book and start a new job simultaneously.

Special thanks are due to the following people for reading substantial parts of the manuscript, and for making unfailingly helpful suggestions: Bernard Duffey, Frank Lentricchia, Louis Budd, Barbara Herrnstein Smith, Martin Danahay, Laura Severin, Alan Filreis, and most of all, Lori Newcomb. I am also grateful to John Bassett, Brad Christie, Hugh Crawford, Leigh DeNeef, Richard Fusco, Sheri Gravett, Jeff Hendricks, Doug Lanier, Christine Levanduski, Elaine Orr, Susan Poznar, Regina Schwartz, and Susan Walsh for their conversations, their canny suggestions, and for their faithful friendship and occasional commiseration over the years. Milton J. Bates, Cary Nelson, and Alan Wald supplied inspiration and courteous assistance.

Parts of chapter one originally appeared in different form in *South Atlantic Review;* some of chapter two in *Essays in Literature;* and parts of chapter five and six in *Criticism* (© 1990, Wayne State University Press). Grateful acknowledgment is made to those journals for supporting my work and for allowing it to be reprinted here.

This book is dedicated to my exemplary parents, and to my wife, for whom no adjective suffices.

Wallace Stevens and Literary Canons

ONE

Introduction

The Shadow of His Fellows

> What was the purpose of his pilgrimage,
> Whatever shape it took in Crispin's mind,
> If not, when all is said, to drive away
> The shadow of his fellows from the skies,
> And, from their stale intelligence released,
> To make a new intelligence prevail?
> —Stevens,
> "The Comedian as the Letter C," 1923

> A work of poetry is not a thing or an object, nor should criticism conceive it as such; it is the result of an interactive network of productive people and forces.
> —Jerome J. McGann,
> *The Beauty of Inflections*, 1985

In September 1914, a series of eight lyrics by Wallace Stevens, then thirty-five, appeared in an obscure New York magazine, marking his first attempt at postgraduate publication. In 1966, eleven years after the poet's death, a monumental volume of letters culminated Stevens's body of work. During the intervening half-century, extremely selective canons of modernist poetry gradually formed, and the reputations of most of the hundreds of poets active in the period peaked and declined; however, after a slow start Stevens's status continued to rise steadily, to become perhaps more secure than that of any American poet of this century. Those involved in literary studies have usually treated such events as the unproblematic reality of literary history, viewing the centrality of certain authors as reflections of intrinsic qualities of their work. This study, however, is grounded in the belief that to analyze and historicize evaluative phenomena such as these constitutes one of the preeminent uses of the activity of literary history itself. The goal of this book is to use the particular question of Stevens's rise to examine questions fundamental to the conjunction of cultural history and cultural value in twentieth-century America: why do we read Stevens and not his early associates, many of whom continued to publish throughout their lives as he did? What institutional practices, processes, and discourses made it possible for Stevens's advocates to promote his "majority" at the expense of various other writers and their advocates? Under what changing criteria of evaluation, and what changing conditions of reading, could Stevens first not be seen as a major writer, and eventually not be seen as anything else?

That conditions of literary evaluation do change, continuously and often drastically, should be clear from the quickest of glances at the history of American literary culture: yesterday's unknown is today's Melville; yesterday's Amy Lowell is today's nobody. Yet few have actually been willing to examine the specific historical factors that have operated in this state of persistent canonical instability. Tracing the development and institutionalization of aesthetic axiology in Western rationalist culture, Barbara Herrnstein Smith's "Contingencies of Value" has offered a seminal critique of the dilemma that has largely paralyzed the American literary academy's understanding of cultural evaluation. Smith has shown that judgments of literary works have been seen either as ontologically true or false, or, following Northrop Frye's pseudoscientific rejection of evaluation in 1957, as "only" subjective matters of "the history of taste," with no place in the discipline of criticism (*Anatomy*, 9). To counter this impasse Smith has developed a relativist theory of evaluation which accounts for the historical presence of both evaluative continuity and discontinuity. In her argument the status of a literary work is contingent in multiple ways upon specific and variable conditions of reading, using, and valuing such works; as those conditions change, the cultural meaning of many "canonical" works will be rearticulated by interested users so as to make them effective, and therefore valued, under those emergent conditions. Other works will not survive the changed conditions, while some previously ignored or devalued texts or authors may be resurrected and newly perceived as central ("Contingencies," 14). By sketching a typology of evaluative actions ranging from the "innumerable and unspoken acts of approval and rejection" performed by the individual author during a work's creation, to "highly specialized institutionalized forms of evaluation" such as academic scholarship and pedagogy, Smith has further indicated the ubiquity and complexity—but also the accessibility—of the concept of literary evaluation ("Value/Evaluation," 450–51). Though she seldom applies her principles to specific historical situations, Smith's theoretical account of the contingency of cultural value has mapped out a direction for the study of literary canons which promises to enhance greatly our understanding of the action of institutional and ideological processes in modern culture.

Even though some form of evaluative relativism is now taken as a commonplace in many critical circles, the concrete cultural processes by which resurrections and deaths of reputation occur are still largely ignored. The widespread attention to canons in the past decade has yet done little to get us past Frye's interdiction on evaluation. The evaluations of those who once thought Melville unimportant, or Lowell important, are still usually dismissed by those who think otherwise as the defective taste, absolute error, or ideological sin of a benighted era or group. Secure in their intellectual and institutional positions, both traditionalists and revisionists have been content simply to assume the absolute value of the evaluative configurations and criteria which comprise their canons. In 1979, for example, J. Hillis Miller came out squarely and self-consciously on the side of canonical tradition with a famous announcement that began: "I believe in the established canon of English and American literature and in the validity of the concept of privileged texts" ("The Function of Rhetorical Study," 12). On the other hand, in perhaps the most influential polemic on behalf of canonical revisionism, *Sensational Designs* (1985), Jane Tompkins rejected a mostly male-dominated and male-defended canon of American literature centered around Hawthorne and Melville for one of "subversive" female writers simply by means of an "embrace of the conventional [that] led me to value everything that criticism had taught me to despise: the stereotyped character, the sensational plot, the trite expression" (xv).[1]

Both of these positions are inadequate. Since, as Smith argues, all such professions of intrinsic value are repressive in tending to shut off evaluative debate,[2] a liberating demystification of evaluative practice can be achieved neither by unproblematically maintaining established polarities of value, nor by simply reversing them by absolutely valuing alternative canons existing in their own institutional niches. Instead of either of these forms of absolute valuation, what is needed is the adaptation of a relativist theory of value to elaborate the historical development of specific canonical configurations.[3] By revealing and interrogating absolutist practices as they substantially—if often covertly—influence specific instances of cultural evaluation, relativist histories can help to erode the pseudo-ontological underpinnings of various cultural hierarchies and can work to portray evaluative divergences as productive bases of cultural interchange rather than as bogeys to be ignored or suppressed. This book is an attempt to do that.

A significant part of this process involves identifying the operation of absolute valuation and the sorts of "established evaluative authorities" that license it. As the ensuing analysis will detail, influential evaluators of Wallace Stevens, like his preening poetic comedian Crispin, have consistently sought to efface the shadow of the poet's fellows, portraying the development of his reputation not as a significant part of twentieth-century American literary history but as ideologically laden evidence of some essence of "Modernism." In their broadest outlines, dominant evaluations of Stevens have fallen into two stages, corresponding to steps in the advent of the cultural formation which came to be called "modernism," and the competition for control of its dominant discourses. For the first three decades of his career Stevens's reputation was retarded because he was widely seen as a representative of the ultramodern "decadence" which insidiously threatened to erode the cultural populism championed by many of the readers and critics who shaped the discourses of early twentieth-century American poetry; during these decades his reputation was sustained largely in the oppositional realm of the avant-garde. In the next three decades, as this avant-garde gradually achieved a dominant role in the very definition of modernist poetic value, his reputation grew wider, and his work became a major tool in the propagation of a postwar view of modernism as a central element of elite culture, excellent exactly *because* it appeared successfully to withstand debilitating social or political entanglements.

The details of these processes will of course form the body of this book's analysis. Before beginning that discussion, however, a more thorough discussion of the persistence and the consequences of the unreflective absolutism which has characterized evaluation in twentieth-century American criticism is in order. Though a comfortable consensus of opinion about Stevens's centrality has reigned for the past two decades, it has been broken notoriously in one clash of critical titans which will serve an illustrative case for discussion. In perhaps the most prominent history of poetic modernism, *The Pound Era* (1971), Hugh Kenner barely mentioned Stevens, dismissing his work as the result of "an Edward Lear poetic pushed toward all limits" (516–17). As a measure of Stevens's importance to many literary scholars of the day, this omission—or insult—drew fire from another canonical critic of modernism. Beginning in *A Map of Misreading* (1975), and especially in his important study of Stevens (1977), Harold Bloom replied to Kenner's evaluation in kind, explicitly denying that Pound could be seen as "Stevens's true twentieth-century rival" and eventually suggesting that we "might begin to call [modernism] the Age of Stevens (or shall we say the Stevens Era?)" (*Wallace Stevens* 68, 152). The rhetoric of this first round of the exchange indicates the extent to which both critics have expressed their sweeping evaluations of modernist poetry in facetious analogies, parenthetical asides, and barbed allusions, rather than engaging in substantial intellectual discussion with those who disagree with them.

At least as significant as the low level of argument in this feud, however, is the exclusive superlativism that grips both critics equally. In an essay in *Critical Inquiry*'s *Canons* volume (1984), Kenner rejoined in similar terms: "The absence of Wallace Stevens from *the canon I use* has somehow been made to seem notorious. I account for it by his unassimilability into *the only story that I find has adequate explanatory power*: a story of capitals, from which he was absent. Like Virginia Woolf of Bloomsbury or Faulkner of Oxford, he seems *a voice from a province*, quirkily enabled by the International Modernism *of which he was never a part*, no more than they" ("The Making of the Modernist Canon," 373; emphases added).

Declining to refer to his adversary by name, Kenner at first appears to be backpedaling from his earlier stance, indulgently agreeing to disagree with those who believe otherwise about Stevens. But by the second sentence he begins to use the controversy over his evaluation of the poet to justify the rise of the writers in his pantheon (Pound, Yeats, Eliot, Joyce, Lewis). By appearing to cede his considerable institutional authority into mere subjectivity ("the canon I use"), Kenner liberates himself from the bother of accounting for the evidence that the canons used by many others are almost totally excluded from the "story of capitals" he has successfully promulgated throughout Anglo-

American literary culture. Despite a cursory acknowledgement that "other people have seen it quite differently" (371), Kenner's absolutist rhetoric leaves him only two ways to see these other people. Either they are simply airing their own subjectivities as he is, in which case everyone is thrust into a struggle to see who can get more publishing space (not a promising situation when one is up against Hugh Kenner), or, as he suggests two pages later, these "other people" are just plain wrong, valuing academic poets such as Stevens "fully half of [whose] work is rhythmically dead" (373) — whatever that means. Intentionally or otherwise, Kenner's remarks suggest a remarkably narrow conception of the power of interchange between artists and their cultures, between writers and readers, between critics and history. Unwilling to rearrange his life around the physical presences of Joyce, Pound, or Eliot, Kenner implies, Stevens was forever stranded in the (noncanonical) United States. That Kenner is content to dismiss out of hand the multiplicity of cultural strands involved in twentieth-century culture for the "story" of one superlative coterie which defines for him the essence of modernism is clear from the title of his essay: "The Making of the Modernist Canon."

Bloom's latest salvo can be found in the introduction to his Chelsea House volume on Pound (1987), where he becomes more explicit (though no more constructive) in his animosity, portraying Kenner as "the greatest of antiquarian Modernists," whose justification of Pound's archaism, employing the same tortuous paradox and obfuscation as its subject, has become "doubtless unassailable" (1).[4] Employing a trope notably similar to Kenner's phrase "the canon I use," Bloom affects an obviously false deference that travesties the whole idea of a serious evaluation of either poet: "I in any case would not care to dispute any critic's Pound. They have their reward, and he has them" (1). In the next paragraph, Bloom notes rather opaquely that such "differences in poetic taste" might be due to "accidents," or to "irreconcilable attitudes concerning the relation of poetry to belief," or, in what is suddenly the clear point of his attack, to "judgments as to value that transcend literary preferences": specifically, the fact that "*The Cantos* contain material that is not humanly acceptable" to him (1). Not content merely to play this trump card, Bloom ends his discussion ad hominem, insinuating a link between critics who would advocate Pound's work and the poet's own reprehensible opinions: "if that material is acceptable to others, then they themselves are thereby less acceptable, at least to me" (1). In other words, critics value Pound because their natures are fundamentally and invariably in sympathy with the poet's own objectionable political attitudes; Bloom thus glosses over complicated historical, ethical, and philosophical issues in favor of a "transcendent" moral notion of value which happens to damn Pound and his whole critical tradition.

One might think that this feud had achieved a level of stylized ferocity which would render it little more than a piquant footnote to the careers of these individual critics and to the histories of their poetic idols. But in a twist that demonstrates the influence of unreasoning absolutism in shaping versions of literary history, another well-known scholar of modernism, Marjorie Perloff, has since 1982 waged a campaign to use these ill-considered evaluations of Stevens and Pound as a Manichaean historical model for comprehending the essence of American modernist poetry. In her article "Pound/Stevens: Whose Era?" (which became the opening chapter in her book *The Dance of The Intellect*), Perloff began this process by rehearsing the course of the Kenner/Bloom feud through 1977, concluding from it, "The split [between Stevens and Pound] goes deep, and its very existence raises what I take to be central questions about the meaning of Modernism—indeed about the meaning of poetry itself in current literary history and theory" (486). The assumption that there must be a single "meaning of Modernism" is only the first of many instances in Perloff's attempt to reduce all of modernism to a mutually exclusive choice between these two poets and their critical traditions.

At the beginning of the next paragraph, Perloff continues this dualizing strategy by asking, "What prompts those who believe in the Stevens Era to ignore or dismiss Pound?" (486). The very phrasing of such a question attempts to institute and normalize a radically exclusive dichotomy: one might reasonably ask about all those people who have high regard for both poets and about those who value other modernists as or more highly? Since Perloff sees her questions about Stevens and Pound as central enough to determine "the meaning of Modernism"—and later to call them "the Modernist debate" (501)—it seems that these other people are simply to be ignored. Near the end of the essay, Perloff once again delineates the Manichaean contest over "what . . . we mean when we talk of Modernism in poetry," and "more important, what are our present norms for the 'great poem'?" (504). Even were the objectified notion of "the great poem" the most useful focus for the literary critic, and even could we somehow determine "norms" for such a poem, it still would not follow that the Stevens/Pound showdown she has constructed could give us an adequately comprehensive view of such a question. The use of "we" in such sweeping pronouncements is also deeply problematic, implying that the custody of modernist canons is held by a small circle of critics (who all know each other) tending a very few writers.

Even more importantly, perhaps, it follows that anyone who believes in the priority of any single poet so exclusively as to posit "the X era" would tend to devalue ("ignore or dismiss") pretenders with their own critical advocates. In other words, what Perloff presents as a central ideological choice that critics have had to make between Stevens and Pound may be more usefully seen as a problem of evaluative intolerance and absolutism among advocates of both poets. Such superlativists number among them Perloff herself, who, if she has not quite ignored or dismissed Stevens in this essay and other recent work, has persistently attacked him in her quixotic attempt to promote the Pound Era as a politically progressive version of modernism.

Perloff's own values are heavily weighted towards one of the two poetic camps she purports to analyze; therefore the distinctions she employs turn into a series of dichotomies—fact vs. invention, form vs. content, outwardness vs. inwardness, the political vs. the personal, the historical epic vs. the lyric, Pound vs. Stevens—primarily designed to attack Stevens and his critical tradition to the benefit of Pound and his. Not only does Perloff unproblematically present these loosely sketched binaries as the only two possible courses for critics of modernism, but she apparently sees one set as being always politically correct, the other as always politically evasive or reprehensible. Though I cannot take the space to critique all of these oppositions, I will point out a few of them in order to call into question the oversimple binary model of modernism this essay employs and advocates.[5]

Perloff's valorization of Poundian poetics rests on a fundamental and untenable separation of fact and invention. She quotes D. S. Carne-Ross on the "cardinal principle" of *The Cantos* as follows: "that the materials it presents must be presented exactly as they are or were. A man's actual words, and as far as possible even the sound of his words, must be reported, the date, location, etc. must be given. As Pound sees it, this is part of the *evidence*" ("Pound/Stevens," 493; emphasis in original). Surely in poststructuralist discourse, "evidence" is not a concept that can bear much weight in evaluating the political rectitude of such a heavily mediated and individualized form of cultural discourse as a poem. Perloff, however, appears to endorse uncritically this aspiration to capture "real" events and words, citing Pound's own description of his poetic aim as the "constatation of fact" and adding that this goal obtains "however disjunctively those 'facts' are structured in a given Canto" (493). In view of the drastic level of such disjunction to be found in most of the *The Cantos*, how much can we make of the presence or absence of "factual" signifiers such as dates, locations, and ostensibly verbatim quotations? In what sense is any element of *The Cantos* unmediated "evidence" of anything except the activity of imaginative reconstruction constantly being performed by the poet? One hopes that American criticism is over its once-pathological aversion to dates, names, places, and immediate topical references in poetry, but to suggest that the presence of such elements makes for automatic historical or political engagement, or that their absence demonstrates a lack of such engagement, is equally rigid and foolish.[6]

This tendency to seize on polysignificant attributes of poetic texture such as the use of "actual" geography and specific names, to make them into political litmus tests, is part of Perloff's larger effort to recuperate Pound's poetics as the basis for a progressive modernism. But the politically embarrassing elements of Pound's life and work mean that to do so she must reinstitute an old-fashioned dualism between content ("what the poet is saying") and form ("how he says it") (489), and then she must radically sever the two, valorizing Pound's "open form" as an immanent, exclusive embodiment of social engagement in poetry. The logical extension of this argument is that a poem based on collage technique, no matter what its content—even an epic sympathetic to fascism— is politically enlightened compared to a lyric poem in a traditional form expressing any political position whatsoever. This approach is self-defeating in that it ultimately impoverishes the idea of poetry as a concrete activity in the sociopolitical world; even as Perloff marshals broad arguments for valorizing the historical scope of Poundian poetics, she must completely obscure or ignore Pound's relationships to political ideologies and power structures which existed outside *The Cantos*. A consideration of the circumstances of the poem's gestation, creation, and publication as a cultural product and the avowed sociopolitical intentions of its author are nowhere to be found in her discussion because they would erode the artificial boundaries that make her paradoxical assertions conceivable. Despite Perloff's good intentions to reclaim a social efficacy for poetry, ultimately this fetishizing of poetic form as autotelic, and the consequent dismissal of poetry's subject matter and the sociopolitical events and relationships that affected it constitutes yet another (belated) incarnation of high-modernist elitism.

All of these more specific binaries participate in Perloff's ambitious attempt to establish an essential fissure between the two poets and their critical traditions, an assertion that is itself a highly debatable and complicated issue. She notes only one late instance of Pound's and Stevens's lack of enthusiasm for one another, a wariness that is unexceptionable in itself between canonically competitive poets. The main basis for what she calls "the very real gap" between the two poets' versions of modernism is the critical feud between Kenner and Bloom, buttressed by the much less directly opposed expressions of several other critics, which she shapes into apparent mutual exclusivity: if you do significant work on (or if you value) Stevens, you cannot value Pound, and vice versa. Yet Perloff herself notes that the critical generation of the mid-century — including Blackmur, Tate, Winters, Jarrell, O'Connor, and others — wrote substantially on both poets. When Perloff says that by the 1960s "the alliance posited by the critics but never by the poets themselves was falling apart" (485), she begs the question of the development and significance of the "gap" by assuming that it is normative and that the mid-century critics had merely obscured it temporarily. I suggest that she has it backwards: that there is no inherently greater fissure between these two poets than between any other two poets with differing cultural backgrounds, life experiences, and temperaments, that earlier generations wrote about both poets because conditions of reading and critical writing did not suggest that they need do otherwise. Only in the 1950s did any substantial split between these critical traditions develop, and then it was due to historically specific changes in those conditions: the increasing and still strong pressure for author-centered specialization within academic criticism which has also separated the critics of many other prominent twentieth-century writers from one another; the adoption by some younger poets and critics of a Pound-influenced avant-gardism that generated substantial oppositional energy to the academic establishment even as some of them entered it;[7] the advent of forceful and idiosyncratic individual critics such as Kenner and Bloom whose intellectual and institutional identities were inextricably bound up with their respective authors; and not least, the gradual shift of the evaluative climate of modernist poetry from the more disordered and tolerant *contemporary canon* of recent and still living writers into a reverential pantheon of great authors, a *modernist canon* for the ages. The gap between Stevens and

Pound, if it can be said to exist, is a function of the conditions of postwar criticism, is neither intrinsic nor necessarily permanent, and does not explain the essential questions of modernism.

Perloff's reliance on the priority of the poets' opinions of one another as the source of this gap points out yet another basic analytical problem with her argument which has a bearing on my own project: the critics of each poet become little more than puppets mouthing the views of their idols. She approaches an acknowledgement of this when she notes, "Pound critics . . . are just as likely as are the Stevensians to adopt the vocabulary of their master. The close relationship of Pound's terminology to that of his critics becomes apparent no matter what critical text of Pound's we choose to look at" (497).

True, no one expects that Pound critics will start using terminology closer to Stevens's own critical lexicon, or vice versa, but this passage, and indeed the whole article, gives no indication that what critics do, if they are to be seen as forceful and distinctive critics, is not merely to "adopt" but to *adapt* selected portions of the poets' thought and terminology for their own purposes, an appropriation over which poets have a variable (but never total and always decreasing) level of control. Perloff's insistence on the poets' unshakable mastery over their critics is a rather disingenuous strategy for enlisting all of the distortions and reductions made by Stevens critics over the years into the campaign to discredit the poet himself. In contrast, this book assumes that critics have a primary constitutive role in shaping the perceived character of the poets they discuss and must take responsibility for the importance of that role.

Ultimately "Pound/Stevens: Whose Era?" is an exemplary illustration of what Frank Kermode in *History and Value* describes as the development of ostensibly analytic historical models that are shaped first and foremost by a critic's desire to hierarchize one author or group or authors over another. Referring to a critic's specious differentiation of "two types of fragment" in order to valorize Pound over Eliot, Kermode notes: "Here we have a simple illustration of the way a period description can be used to give apparent objectivity to opinions and discriminations. Modern fragments in a poet you like are Modernist, in a poet you don't like merely modern. In one case you require the parts to be related to some conceptual or imaginative scheme, in the other you don't" (143–44).

The historical models that result from such strategies, based on an unreasonably exclusive or absolute level of evaluation, can nevertheless have substantially shaping effects on institutional frameworks. Kenner's version of Pound, as Bloom points out, may as well have been "*the* Pound" over the past two or three decades and has clearly influenced Perloff's position to a great degree. The argument of "Pound/Stevens: Whose Era?" has itself met with general approbation, having been described as "nicely contrast[ing] . . . two opposing tendencies in contemporary criticism," "dazzling," "penetrating and magisterially synoptic," "provocative and clarifying . . . carry[ing] considerable force and effect."[8] The force of this synoptic argument about modernism has generated explicitly evaluative effects at least in one commentator, who concludes a discussion of the essay by judging, "To be both a Stevensian and a Poundian may involve not an admirable but a muddled catholicity of taste" (Sherry, 427). Indeed, despite my desire to reject almost all of the premises and conclusions of "Pound/Stevens: Whose Era?", by making it the focus of a lengthy discussion, I run the risk of unwittingly furthering the canonical exclusivity and ideological rigidity it endorses.

In one sense, no less than anyone else's, my own study is itself an evaluative act that cannot be called disinterested or neutral, in that I do not seek to challenge the "canonical" view that Stevens is of central importance to American poetry in this century. Canon-busting is not my aim here, nor, for that matter, is canon-buttressing. Clearly I find great value in reading and studying Stevens; but unlike Kenner, Bloom, and Perloff, I would not consequently seek to convince people that Stevens or anyone else embodies the essence of American modernism. Indeed, I must risk a "muddled catholicity" by saying that I find significant value in reading and studying many other modernist poets, including Pound, and am not obsessed with quantifying or ranking that value. Rather than pushing for a superlative judgement on behalf of any poet, I proceed under the assumption that to call into question some of the taken-for-granted evaluative activities that have surrounded Stevens criticism is in itself a useful historicizing operation. The constant goal of such interrogation will not be to disagree with anyone's evaluations of a given author, though I may do so, but continually to reject the characterization of those opinions as intrinsically *correct* (or incorrect) and therefore beyond debate, rather than as *historically produced*.

In seeking to contest the ostensible self-evidence of Stevens's importance or unimportance, I have based my account of his rise not on the widely held view of American poetic culture as consisting of a few giant figures who were radically alienated from the world of commerce but instead on a materialist view of culture *as* a type of commerce.[9] The activity of evaluation implies selection and hierarchization and thus a state of competition among various possible alternatives. Literary activity in early twentieth-century America can therefore be seen as a spectrum of cultural economies in which a writer, editor, publisher, or magazine developed a reputation to the extent that he, she, or it was more or less favorably received and evaluated in relation to any number of identifiable competitors. In almost every instance, supply exceeded both demand and economic resources—more aspiring magazines than readers and advertisers could support, more submissions than a magazine or publisher could print, more poets published than reviewers and critics could assimilate. The evaluative selections made and not made were functions of the multiple and sometimes contradictory values and interests of the parties involved, which suggests that the fortunes of institutional entities such as magazines or publishing houses and the reputations of individual writers were highly interdependent.

This economistic model of cultural activity is not, however, meant as a simple superstructural relationship in which the perceived value of a writer was completely or uniformly a function of emotionless market forces. The modernist cultural marketplace obviously did not run only on the motivation of quickest and largest monetary profit but was constituted by a variety of interests ranging from strictly financial benefit to nebulous "aesthetic"—but still profitable in some way or other—criteria such as "prestige," "enthusiasm," "cultural leadership," "patronage," or "innovation." The reputations of certain writers, once established in various circles, functioned as a currency for the benefit of themselves and others; individuals and groups competed to publish their latest work, or wrote articles and books about them, because the prestige already associated with them could help gain a circulation or solidify a critical or publishing reputation. Thus the nature of the competition continually varied, but the competitive state itself remained, and underlies my analysis of twentieth-century literary history.

Three key terms I employ throughout this book are *reception, canonization,* and *modernist*; each could use some initial exposition to clarify the methodological and historiographical principles underlying my analysis. The fundamental ramifications of *reception* should be largely familiar. Over the past two decades various theorists and critics, particularly Hans Robert Jauss and Jerome McGann, have demonstrated that the character of the literary work is inextricably linked to dynamic cultural conditions—intellectual, aesthetic, institutional, political—of reading and writing at particular historical moments. In reconceiving the "literary work as a complex event in sociohistorical space, the always particularized interchange of a present with a past," McGann has offered a valuable revision of the concept of literary meaning as "the process by which literary works are produced and reproduced" (5, 10). These fundamental redefinitions of the elements of literary study rely for both their methodological grounding and their empirical value upon the development of specific *reception histories*: analytical accounts of the ways in which past readers have read a given work and related works, which constitute the range of possible present perceptions and evaluations of those works. The foremost institutional potential of these illuminations, as McGann sees it, is "to collapse the schism . . . between the traditional forms of scholarship [such as literary history] and the new modes of interpretation" (6). Clearly contemporary reception history can be linked to what have been seen as ultratraditional methodologies such as textual criticism, biography, and the old-style reputation study; but it must also be informed by an understanding of the textuality (in the poststructuralist sense) fundamental to the very fabric of culture and language. In such a work the insights generated about the history of a text, an author, or a canon are thus irreducibly interpretations—which is not to say that they are not literary history, since literary history can be nothing but a series of interpretations.

This book is a diachronic account of the practices of literary reception and evaluation in the modernist period, with Stevens as an illustrative but by no means always exemplary figure. The body of each chapter will analyze his reputation in a specific chronological interval in which a further portion of his work was received and evaluated. Unlike Melita Schaum's *Wallace Stevens and the Critical Schools* (1988), however, which focuses on Stevens's reception in the criticism of but a few representatives of various critical paradigms, my analysis uses a broader definition of cultural reception, which includes the writer's position not only in formal literary criticism but in a variety of discursive practices, institutional sites, and ideological affiliations: the work of other poets and artists; letters, biographies, and histories of the period; anthologies, surveys, and textbooks; prize-giving and subsidizing bodies; academic pedagogy; and patterns of literary publishing. I will also pay some attention to attributes of Stevens's life and personality which, as they were perceived by his readers, also shaped his developing reputation. What I offer, then, is not a reading of Stevens's poetry as such, but an interpretation of contemporary commentary on the poet and his work to describe the conditions under which readers found it possible and desirable to read him, and the light that those patterns of reception shed both on his own position and, more broadly, on the changing status of modernist poetry in American culture.

A viable model of literary reception cannot treat the interchange between text and reader in an ahistorical vacuum (as such theorists as Stanley Fish and Wolfgang Iser have sometimes done) but must trace processes of evaluation through changing temporal circumstances as they shape the evaluative configurations we call canons. Any history of literary reception thus requires a working definition of *canonization*. My definition will begin negatively by noting that in their legion of current usages, the word *canon* and its derivatives float weightlessly through innumerable levels of specificity, temporality, and evaluative intensity. Social or institutional entities at many levels, any number of individual commentators, and groups based on socioeconomic, ethnic, regional, sexual, stylistic, institutional, generic, theoretical, ideological, and other commonalities are all said to have their own canons: the canons of *The New Yorker* and *Diacritics*, "the academic canon," "the high school canon," "the Afro-American canon," "the deconstructionist canon," the canons of Hugh Kenner and Harold Bloom. To acknowledge the full import of this institutional fact is to give up the usage of *canonization* as a measure of absolute valuation and to see it instead as merely a continuum of relative consensus on the value of given works or authors at a particular time at a particular evaluative site or group of sites. There is no defensible threshold at which a writer can be unproblematically "in" or "out" of "the canon" of an entire culture. There can be only marshalings of evidence that can describe and possibly alter the status of a given reputation in given canons, evidence that will always be subject to further critique and amendment.

To define the concept of *canon* narrowly and reverentially, as has most of postwar literary criticism, has been an ideologically charged stratagem for shrinking the range of acceptably canonical authors and preserving that exclusivity. The more rigid the standards for membership in a canon—or especially "the canon"—become, the more mystified the ideological implications of processes of literary evaluation will be. As I have suggested above, the effect of absolutely valorizing a very few works or authors—of positing either a Pound Era *or* an Age of Stevens—over preserving the multiple and often contradictory operations of a cultural field has been to constrict the range of writers and texts that could be valued as the subjects of useful discussion, to retard the cultural enfranchisement of various social groups, and to rarefy and circumscribe ever further the social scope of literature.[10]

There is no single "canon" of American literature, nor is there a single canon within an institution as heterogeneous as today's literary academy (nor should there be). To act as if there were is to distort the multifarious forces of cultural valorization and exclusion into a monolith of orthodoxy, which has at least two undesirable consequences. Such totalizations make the possibility of effecting significant local changes seem that much more difficult; they also threaten to paralyze rather than advance our understanding of the ways in which oppositional forces have had broad effects on institutional practice.[11] All descriptions of canonicity should therefore be specified with reference to particular cultural phenomena: a canon *of* some defined person, group, genre, institution, period of time, or combination of these; no discussions of cultural evaluation should claim or represent themselves to be comprehensive and sufficient explanations of "the canon." Indeed, some of the most basic tenets of poststructuralist thought make it nonsense to describe a canon as if it were an object; a canon is not the thing explained but the explanation itself.

With these caveats in mind, I will use *canonization* to refer to a specialized way of describing processes of reception and evaluation as they intensify to a state (always volatile, never uniform throughout a culture) in which, for a relatively large number of readers in a more or less describable culture at a given time, the importance of a writer or work seems natural or inescapable, a basis upon which other cultural assumptions, values, and models depend. Most of the incremental changes that constitute the naturalizing processes we call canonization will remain shadowy, individually unremarkable, often occurring in unnoticed or unrecorded contexts. Despite this—indeed, because of it—an adequate analysis of literary evaluation cannot be accomplished by a reliance on the few spectacular acts of evaluation which leap out at the historian but by the collation, contextualization, and interpretation of as many evaluative actions in various sites as possible. If we assume (as I do) that no single author, text, or event can substantially alter patterns of cultural valuation without acting in concert with emergent, latent, or otherwise favorable historical conditions, then to identify and analyze those conditions becomes one of the central tasks of contemporary literary history.

As the character and the reception of literary works (which are not finally separable from one another) are shaped by a multitude of historical practices and interests, changes in a literary culture come partially as the works of certain authors—and critics—produce or help to produce alterations in conditions and practices of reading and writing (Jauss, 27). Eventually the reception of Stevens's work became a significant moving force in the changing fabric of American modernist and postmodernist culture. The development of such power of alteration at some level is very likely a necessary attribute of what we call canonicity, but it is not a sufficient one; reception theory has often acted as if it were, focusing on the power of alteration exerted by "great works" at the expense of an analysis of adequate historical breadth. Jauss, for one, appears to afford an a priori privilege to authors or works that produce a "horizon change," using the "aesthetic distance" between existing reader expectations and the defamiliarizing strategies of a new work as a master criterion for assigning aesthetic value (14). The dangerous consequence of overemphasizing this side of the interchange between works and readers is that canons have often appeared to spring full-blown from the very brows of the great authors, as in this remark by Kenner: "[T]he Modernist canon has been made in part by readers like me; in part . . . by later writers choosing and inventing ancestors; chiefly though, I think, by the canonized themselves, who were apt to be aware of a collective enterprise, and repeatedly acknowledged one another" ("The Making of the Modernist Canon," 374).

The major failure of most recent discussions of canons has been a similarly narrow concentration on a few great canonizers at the expense of an analysis of diffused and often conflicting historical processes. Canons, like the creation of literary works themselves, have been portrayed as deriving from a small group that looks too much like the table of contents of *Critical Theory Since Plato*. After reading, say, John Guillory on T. S. Eliot and Cleanth Brooks, or Jonathan Arac on F. O. Matthiessen, we understand better the ideological impulses that motivated these critics' own revisions of Milton and Donne, or Melville and Whitman. Still very little systematic attention has been paid to the institutional and cultural contexts of the 1920s, 1930s, and 1940s which enabled some of their judgments to persuade so strongly and caused others to sink almost without trace. This great-man approach to the study of canons has largely kept intact the longstanding myth that literary opinion consists mainly of the freely construed judgments of titanic individuals. The persistence of this narrow focus is demonstrated in what remains the authoritative collection for canon study, the *Critical Inquiry* volume *Canons*, in which only two essays (those by Alan Golding and Richard Ohmann) attempt the analysis of a broad historical field rather than resting content with close readings of a very few selected texts. Thus far even many of those arguing against rigid canons have knuckled under to a New-Critical emphasis on a small number of authors and their "major" texts.

Rather than laying the responsibility for Stevens's canonization on a small number of commentators, collapsing temporal, intellectual, and ideological distinctions into a "tradition" or "essence" of modernism, then, I will seek to preserve the multiplicity of aesthetic, ideological, and generational emphases that have been instrumental in receiving his work and gradually situating it as central to the modernist period. One of the ways I hope to promote the loosening of evaluative rigidity is by defusing the ideologically laden term *modernist*. As Kermode suggests, especially in its capital-M form, *Modernist* often offers a dangerous ambiguity—apparently historical, effectively judgmental—for exploitation by exclusively minded critics. Recently, Daniel Singal has argued sensibly that modernism, far from being limited to "the philosophy and style of life of the artistic avant-garde at the turn of the twentieth century . . . deserves to be treated as a full-fledged historical culture much like Victorianism or the Enlightenment, and . . . supplies nothing less than the basic contours of our current mode of thought" (8). Certainly anyone who wished to dispute this assertion would have difficulty finding a viable terminological alternative: if you are not a "modernist" in the first half of the twentieth century, you might as well be nobody. It follows that the competition for control of the definition and use of the term "modernism" is one of enormously high ideological stakes. Narrower usages of the term such as Kenner's and Perloff's, in referring to the work of but a few ideologically or stylistically congruent writers, employ this ambiguity to normalize those writers as expressing *the* conditions of twentieth-century literary culture and to efface all other writers from positions of importance.

To counter this tendency I will adapt McGann's useful distinction between "Romanticism"—which he calls "a critical concept with a more or less ideological component"—and "The Romantic Period," "a critical concept that defines an historic reality" (9). Though I will continue to use *modernist,* I do not mean it as a qualitative indicator of any particular poetic or ideological attributes but instead as a purely temporal designation. In this study a modernist poet, analogous to McGann's "Romantic," is any poet who emerged into the literary culture between about 1910 and 1945. Throughout this study, when I wish to refer to the various aesthetic, intellectual, institutional, and ideological strands of modernism, I will use what I hope will be clearly defined descriptive terms: "popular modernist," "avant-garde modernist," "high modernist," "progressive modernist."

Though I deal in detail with only one literary reputation as it changed and grew in the cultural marketplace of American modernism, I trust that establishing connections between the specific historical problem of Stevens's reception and the broader literary culture will suggest the fruitfulness of an approach to literary history based on the analysis of evaluation. The reputation of each modernist poet has experienced a distinctive trajectory from immediate reception to current canonization, marginalization, or neglect. Most of these trajectories can be said to continue, and the future directions of many reputations are by no means certain. Despite the uniqueness of each of these routes, to trace one is to make more accessible the conditions that shaped, and were shaped by, the fortunes of others. It is also to begin to take up one of the major challenges of Smith's work: that we investigate processes of literary evaluation as extensively as we now understand the processes and variables of literary interpretation. Much as original and even contradictory readings of a single text are seen to enrich our understanding of that text and its author, an ever-changing network of histories of evaluation—each with a necessarily distinct perspective, each working at a different level of chronological and institutional specificity, producing a multiplicity of accounts of various canonical configurations—would offer us a richer and more sensitive historical understanding of those cultural fields than literary history has yet been able to provide.

Rather than creating a tidy teleological account of a writer's inevitable rise, I have sought to keep in view the contingency of Stevens's canonical status, acknowledging that neither he nor any other currently "major" writer possesses an intrinsically privileged status. Conditions of cultural evaluation are changing continually and perhaps radically within and among various cultural forms and institutions. Whether the status of a given writer will grow or dissipate will depend on the evaluative actions of individuals and groups working under those changing conditions. The shadows of a writer's fellow—past, present, and future—will not only persist but will determine the degree and quality of light in which he or she may be seen. Thus it is necessary to acknowledge that my own evaluations are, like all evaluations, historically contingent, and it is sufficient to hope that my conclusions will for a time have satisfactory explanatory power for the similarly contingent views of other readers.

This is not to say that I have no interest in interrogating prevailing characterizations of Stevens and his meaning to American culture. The question of what poetry has meant or might mean to twentieth-century American culture is more important than the future prominence or obscurity of a single writer's reputation. For too long the study of Stevens, and of modernist poetry as a whole, has been dominated by an antipolitical formalism that has circumscribed the social potential of poetry in which apparent opponents such as Bloom and Kenner can be situated equally. Every theoretical principle embraced in this introduction presupposes that the way in which any writer's work will be viewed is largely dependent on the ways in which critics and readers find it in their interests—intellectual, professional, political, moral—to view that work. Stevens is no more intrinsically politically irrelevant than he is intrinsically anything else. To increase the social resonance of any body of texts therefore requires only one prerequisite: that someone believe it is possible and desirable to do so. From that belief, however provisional we may take it to be, much may follow.

TWO

New York Circles

Stevens and the Little Magazine Avant-Garde, 1914–1923

> As I was gathering these together, I wondered whether you understood how I came to contribute to all these things. I always contributed because somebody asked me to do so, and never by way of sending things round. This is just the opposite of the common experience and is, of course, due to the fact that one is always running round in circles in New York.
> —Wallace Stevens, 1938

> Quite free of literary allegiances to period or place, he distils [sic] into a pure essence the beauty of his own world.
> —Harriet Monroe on Stevens, 1924

Of the broadly canonical poets of American literature, Wallace Stevens has long been the least situated within the historical contexts of American modernism. The character and status of Stevens's work have largely been explained in rarefied intellectual terms, in one of two ways: as embodying theories of poetry which derive from various philosophical orientations (aestheticism, naturalism, phenomenology, existentialism, pragmatism) or as descending in a mysterious intertextual process through various poetic "traditions" (Mallarméan, Paterian, Keatsian, Emersonian, Whitmanian). The heavy reliance in Stevens criticism on philosophical and phenomenological abstractions—beauty, reality, imagination, fiction, disinterestedness, perception, process, decreation, crossings, cure—has been both symptom and cause in the removal of the poet from the sociocultural milieu in which his poetic powers and his canonical reputation developed. Until the mid-1980s, the nearly unchallenged critical view of Stevens was ahistorical, one that saw him, in Dana Gioia's summarizing phrase, as a poet "sui generis, an inexplicable hybrid of two seemingly irreconcilable sides of the American experience" (13).

Gioia's linkage of a supposed bifurcation at the heart of American experience to the popular mythology of Stevens is extremely apt. Though his critics (and many of his business colleagues) knew all along that Stevens was both poet and businessman, they have mostly emphasized the inexplicability, the irreconcilability of this "double life," instead of treating his two careers as a conjunction that might add to our understanding of the character and potentials of literary activity in America. Indeed, the first chapter of the first critical book devoted to Stevens, William Van O'Connor's *The Shaping Spirit* of 1950, rather than approaching its subject in a conventional way, was entitled "Stevens as Legend." Though O'Connor purported to treat the view of Stevens as a literary mystery man critically, noting, "There is nothing especially strange about a poet like Stevens dividing his life between insurance and poetry," ultimately he too perpetuated it by concluding without irony, "In his own person, [Stevens] dramatizes the opposition between the world of business and the alienated artist" (4, 21)[1]

Rooted in Stevens criticism from the beginning, this assumption has come under attack in the last few years, as a number of fine studies have helped to reconnect this seemingly disconnected poet to his immediate environment.[2] Unprecedented in the history of American literature scholarship, this sudden biographical boom is conclusive evidence both of Stevens's centrality to current academic canons and of the previous inattention to his concrete historical origins. Though readers of Stevens are indebted to them all for their many insights, these works all focus primarily on Stevens as a titanic poetic mind, the cynosure of the cultural contexts in which his reputation emerged and grew. In complement to their more or less biographical accounts, this chapter will provide a context for early readings of Stevens by situating him as a member of a late-blooming literary generation that came to prominence in the 1910s.

A major part of the "legend" of Stevens which has made him seem a self-canonized olympian untouched by concrete historical circumstances is the notion that he was an extraordinarily late starter; he did not publish significantly until he was thirty-five years old. On the contrary, his "late start" is a sign that he was not isolated from the cultural matrix of his times but tangibly situated in it. Like nearly all Americans born between 1869 and 1885 or so, Stevens entered adulthood as part of a generation that possessed almost no opportunity for participating in a world of vital contemporary literature.[3] While a standard generational conceptualization would place Stevens in a high-modernist group born between 1879 and about 1889, which makes some sense in terms of his aesthetic kinship, on this important issue of career genesis, he shared more with those older writers who came of age in the nineteenth century and whose twenties were spent entirely in the literary wasteland before 1912.[4] When Stevens left Harvard in 1900, he faced adulthood with literary prospects no better than Edwin Arlington Robinson's upon leaving Harvard a decade earlier. The chance that the poets who eventually became most canonical were still in their twenties when the first landmarks of modernism were established has led historians to neglect the fact that most of those central to the initial development of a vigorous avant-garde in the 1910s—Robinson, Edgar Lee Masters, Amy Lowell, Carl Sandburg, Vachel Lindsay—belonged to this excluded generation of the 1870s.[5]

Would-be writers born in the 1870s were in a highly precarious position. Not only the careers but the very lives of many promising writers who came to adulthood in the 1890s—Stephen Crane, Jack London, Frank Norris, David Graham Phillips, William Vaughn Moody, George Cabot Lodge, Trumbull Stickney—were swallowed up early in a commercial culture in which little provision was made for the impracticalities and inaccessibilities of innovative literature.[6] As a twenty-year-old cub reporter, Stevens left an account of Crane's tawdry funeral in June 1900 which offers a poignant gloss on the contemporary lack of interest in what we now consider the major literary loss of the generation. That Crane—only eight years older than Stevens and not even thirty when he died—was so quickly celebrated and forgotten was to Stevens forlorn proof of the impossibility of cultural accomplishment: "As the hearse rattled up . . . with not a single person paying the least attention to it and with only four or five carriages behind it at a distance[,] I realized much that I had doubtfully suspected before—There are few hero-worshippers. . . . Therefore, few heroes (L, 41). The detached tone of his remarks suggests that Stevens himself could not generate much hero-worship either—making his realization all the more discouraging.

The situation for poets was especially bad between 1890 and 1910. During that period the opportunity for younger American poets to achieve periodical publication was squeezed between the small group of established magazines which had led American genteel culture for decades and new mass magazines that had developed into vigorous commercial and cultural forces by the mid-1890s. The established magazines, which had long conceived of themselves as "civilizing" forces and more recently as preservers of standards against the influx of cultural mediocrity, wanted no poetry that might challenge or disturb their respectable, comfortable readership.[7] On the other hand, although the mass magazines represented a democratizing of overall cultural opportunity, it was an expansion that, in its strongly "nonfictional emphasis" and its ethos of antiliterary professionalism, had constricted opportunities for poetry publication even further (C. P. Wilson, 45–57). Such leaders of the mass magazines as Edward Bok, publisher of *Ladies' Home Journal,* tended to view the idea of "literary style" as "foolish," "since it often means nothing except a complicated method of expression which confuses rather than clarifies thought" (quoted in C. P. Wilson, 58). Here Bok treated words as simple utilitarian counters for ideas rather than as the elements that constituted the texture of ideas themselves. The descent of this opposition of verbal form and content would also appear in widely held assumptions of poetry-reading in the early modernist period. For now it is enough to note that, as the literary form closest to pure "style," poetry was drastically marginalized in the 1890s.[8]

The early difficulties of the poets who lingered on until they could find an avant-garde that appreciated them were gravely discouraging. Robinson's efforts to find space between 1896 and 1905 became the stuff of modernist legend. He placed barely more than a dozen poems in all, in two minor literary magazines and the *Boston Evening Transcript*. In 1902 a publisher's representative misplaced the manuscript of his *Captain Craig* in a Boston whorehouse (Ziff, 329). It took a review of the reissue of his second book in 1905 by no less than the president of the United States before Robinson, then thirty-six, could place a poem in a widely read literary magazine (Hogan, 102). By 1894 Frost had found one periodical that would occasionally print his work, but he still placed fewer than a dozen poems in magazines before 1912, when he was thirty-eight (Clymer and Green). Lowell finally published her first magazine poem in the *Atlantic* in 1910, when she was thirty-six. Masters vainly attempted to write plays between 1900 and 1914. Under these circumstances, one understands the fatherly reason for Garrett Stevens's discouraging his son's literary ambitions in 1901 (*L*, 52–53).

When it came, the establishment of a modernist avant-garde in the 1910s in both poetry and the visual arts was not carried out by the very young with whom the concept of the avant-garde is associated but, as Alfred Kreymborg noted in 1925, mostly by men and women approaching middle age (*Troubador*, 201). Harriet Monroe was 52 when the first issue of *Poetry* appeared in 1912. In 1914, when Stevens began publishing at the age of 35, Robinson was 45, Masters 45, Frost 40, Lowell 40, Sherwood Anderson 38, Sandburg 36, Lindsay 35, and William Carlos Williams 31. Stevens's late entry into an identifiable literary field was thus quite consonant with many others of his generation. Furthermore, biographical evidence and the *Letters* both indicate that Stevens had written poetic compositions from at least 1906.[9] The "June Books," presented to his fiancée on her birthday in 1908 and 1909, suggest that Stevens was capable of conceiving of collections or sequences of his poems; but where in the 1900s could he have published them? Stevens was not so much an enemy of the established magazine culture as a conscientious objector. Others of his age and unconventionality might land an occasional publication somewhere or have their books privately printed and largely ignored; Stevens did not even find it worthwhile to try. Instead, through the decade, he attempted to develop and preserve a single reader whose approbation, if not exactly assured, was at least not dependent on contemporary editorial attitudes and market pressures.

Only after the critical period of cultural ferment between 1911 and 1914 did it become feasible for such poets as Stevens to try to publish their work. The suddenly successful development of a little magazine avant-garde in these years consisted of, among other things, the establishment of basic systems of modern publication and reception of poetry which had until then been substantially attenuated in American culture. Understanding this, in their first issue in 1912, the editors of *Poetry* expressed their goals not uncertainly in terms of the material aspects necessary for cultural accomplishment: "The arts . . . have need of each an entrenched place, a voice of power, if they are to do their work and be heard" ("The Motive for the Magazine," 26). Through admirable fortitude, and a healthy dose of inside connections, the editors had brought that voice into existence by cajoling, flattering, and abashing members of the Chicago elite into the patronage of poetry. With great optimism, but also with a sure sense of the growing reader demand for poetry, they emphasized the crucial function of literary reception in the motto from Whitman they adopted for their magazine: "To have great poets there must be great audiences too."

The entrenchment of *Poetry* was perhaps the most important single breakthrough, but other, more broadly operative cultural trends were equally central to the avant-garde successes of these years. As *Poetry*'s motto suggested, Whitman, long a cult figure in this country and in England, was already in the process of emerging as a major cultural force; within a few years he would be a sort of universal parent for the new poetry, uncritically accepted by Sandburg and Untermeyer, reluctantly acknowledged by Pound. As Christopher Wilson has pointed out, some of the same technological advances in printing and papermaking that made possible the mass magazines of the 1890s also made the production of magazines on a shoestring budget more feasible.[10] Between 1911 and 1915 at least sixteen significant "little" magazines containing poetry began in America—a small number by later standards, but a dramatic increase over the three that had appeared in the previous decade.[11] *Poetry* itself had to rush into print early to beat a competitor from Boston to the use of its name.[12] The growth of the mass-circulation magazines and newspapers had meant an enlarged opportunity for quasi-literary employment such as journalism and editing, which gave some technological and professional knowledge to writers who were temperamentally unsuited to commercial culture but who were able to use that knowledge to establish their own means of literary production such as little magazines or publishing ventures.[13] Since the 1890s, but with renewed vigor after 1910, the influence of British and continental avant-gardism, both in literature and the visual arts, had helped to foster among some younger Americans a sense of revolt against what they saw as genteel conventionality and in many cases had offered models for the styles and subjects those revolts would adopt—naturalism, symbolism, decadence, cubism, dada. This relationship between American writers and artists and manifestations of European modernism was dramatically crystallized by the Armory Show of 1913.[14]

There were also events that bore more specifically on changes in the control of the production and distribution of poetry. Though it had been steadily expanding since 1880, the number of total books published in the United States leapt to new plateaus in 1900 and again in 1907. In sharing proportionately in this increase, the market for books of poetry and drama expanded significantly even before 1905 (the total for the years 1900–1904, for example, represented a 52 percent increase over the figures for 1895–99).[15] After 1907, poetry and drama publication took off even faster, far outstripping the general increase in book production and averaging over seven hundred titles a year for the next ten years—a figure that would not be surpassed before the end of World War II.

In book publishing as in magazines, a reaction to the duality of old genteel culture vs. new commercial mass culture had begun by the mid-1910s, with the advent of a young, adventurous group of publishers who hoped to produce not only profits but innovative literature, among them Mitchell Kennerly, B. W. Huebsch, Albert Boni, Horace Liveright, Alfred Harcourt, and Alfred A. Knopf.[16] In 1912 Ferdinand Earle's *The Lyric Year*, published by Kennerly, proved that the United States contained a vast amount of poetic aspiration, garnering ten thousand entries by two thousand poets for its contest (viii). Though *The Lyric Year* did not survive as an ongoing enterprise, within three years its descent would germinate in such annual publications as the *Anthology of Magazine Verse, Some Imagist Poets*, and the *Others* anthologies. During that three-year period the principles of Imagism and free verse, propounded most forcefully by Pound in the early issues of *Poetry*, gave aspiring verse writers a vigorous and accessible methodology for innovation rather than convention.[17] Taking up the Imagist banner in America, the uniquely entrepreneurial Amy Lowell quickly made herself and the poets she sponsored into causes célèbres whose work was disseminated with remarkable success in the Imagist anthologies beginning in 1915.

By the second half of 1914, then, Stevens had before him the encouraging example of newly burgeoning careers of poets his own age or older, several little magazines that prominently featured poetry, and a New York intelligentsia galvanized by European artistic innovation. To his good fortune he also had at his disposal a network of personal acquaintance stretching back to Harvard. If, as recent biographers have posited, Stevens had thought of himself as a poet since the beginning of his adult life, the specific developments of 1911–14 and these figures of early New York modernism in the arts, education, and literature—Walter Arensberg, Pitts Sanborn, Carl Zigrosser, Carl Van Vechten, Walter Pach, Allen Norton, Donald Evans, Alfred Kreymborg—were mainly responsible for making it possible for him to see writing and publishing poetry as a practicable and desirable possibility. The willingness of his first readers and editors to allow Stevens to set the terms of his relationship to his audience meant that the retiring poet could remain in a position of relative security by offering his work mainly to those who were already his friends or acquaintances.[18] He avoided as far as possible the unpleasant position of throwing his work on the mercy of editors of unfamiliar magazines in unfamiliar places. By 1921, when a new wave of little magazines began, his policy of hard-to-get reticence had meant that Stevens was already in demand in New York avant-garde circles. New magazines such as *Contact, Broom, Secession,* and *The Measure* saw the publication of his poems as distinctive advertisements and solicited them through their already existing connections with him.

Stevens's supposed inability or unwillingness to form close friendships with other literati has often been used as evidence of the alienated life of the businessman-poet. Far from suggesting Stevens's isolation or alienation from the cultural activity around him, the chummy circumstances of his debut into little magazines suggest both that he was already well enough placed in social class and educational background to achieve publication with relative ease and that even in the first years of avant-garde activity there was a mutually reinforcing network of editors, poets, and readers from which fledgling poetic reputations could benefit. Milton Bates has pointed out that the September 1914 issue of *The Trend*, in which Stevens first appeared in print in that decade, carried items from no fewer than seven Harvard alumni, including several who became fairly well-known poets (*Wallace Stevens*, 70). Similarly, in a review article in the August issue, Pitts Sanborn began by remarking, "It is a coincidence that four Harvard Class Poets of reasonably recent years [Witter Bynner, Arthur Davison Ficke, John Hall Wheelock, and Hermann Hagedorn] have emerged in the last twelvemonth each with a book of verse" (Sanborn, 570). Perhaps; but given all the magazine's school connections, it is hardly coincidental that the books of these four succeeded in being reviewed in *The Trend*. Nor could it have been purely a coincidence of aesthetic orientation that in the *Spectra* hoax, the literary stunt of the decade, "Emanuel Morgan" and "Anne Knish" (Bynner and Ficke) had the impulse to single out Stevens as the only contemporary poet "who can be regarded . . . as a Spectrist" (quoted in W. J. Smith, 67). This web of evaluative events certainly suggests the operation of what Joan Richardson has called "the old Harvard boys' network," and contrasts starkly to the experiences of the self-educated east-sider Kreymborg.[19]

This pattern of publishing opportunity through a network of personal acquaintance and class congruence continued throughout the decade before *Harmonium*. Soon after his first publications in Sanborn's and Van Vechten's magazine, *The Trend*, those friends led him to more publishing opportunity in Norton's *Rogue*, whose first issue in March 1915 carried the earliest publications Stevens saw fit to include in *Harmonium*. In suggesting that Stevens's *Rogue* poems carried the strong flavor of 1890s decadence that Norton's "Patagonian" group strove for, McLeod has indicated the sort of power an already existing group could have over the development of a new entrant into the field (3–18), but the process of forming a reputation is highly reciprocal: as early readers shape the course of poets' work, poets—some, at least—may alter the attitudes and values of those readers. The first issue of *Rogue* demonstrated the neophyte Stevens's ability to beguile avant-garde readers by singling him out respectfully in a mock "letter not yet received" from the genteel versifier "Richard Sir Vallienne," who effused: "I never knew there was such a thing as poetry before. I just thought it was something we were all doing. However, Wallace Stevens has shown us. I am going to take up painting" (3). In this earliest documentary instance of Stevens's critical reception, he was already seen by at least a few readers as an exemplar of the true poet who put dilettantes to shame.

All told, despite his (legendary) fastidiousness of acquaintance, Stevens was personally acquainted with the editors of over half of the fourteen periodicals he published in between 1914 and 1924 even *before* each magazine first published him: Sanborn of *Trend* and *The Measure*; Norton of *Rogue*; Kreymborg of *Others, The Chapbook*, and *Broom*; William Carlos Williams of *Others* and *Contact*; Zigrosser of *The Modern School*; and possibly Scofield Thayer of *The Dial*. Indeed, the kind of faithful advocacy of a small number of well-connected editors which was suggested by the *Rogue* remarks on Stevens was the most important single way by which his reputation, such as it was, survived through the end of the 1920s.

Though it was largely determined by circumstances of his temperament and his circle of acquaintance, this initial movement into the little magazines of the New York avant-garde served as an important evaluative selection for Stevens. Had his earliest poems instead been submitted to and accepted by the *Atlantic Monthly* or another mainstream magazine, his career might well have taken a very different course and his chances for later canonization might have been drastically reduced—as happened with his friend and *Harvard Advocate* successor, Witter Bynner. Bynner's family connections (a newspaper editor grandfather and novelist uncle) may have helped get him the posts of assistant editor and literary advisor for *McClure's* magazine and publishing house after graduation in 1902. Bynner soon became a well-known poet, publishing seventy-seven poems in established magazines between 1903 and the end of 1912 (Lindsay, 19–23), but he paid for this early success. The momentousness of the new poetry in the 1910s was such that, despite his mainstream reputation, Bynner felt the pull of his generation, making rather wistful gestures towards the radicals: the *Spectra* hoax, publication in *Others* and *The Little Review*, and extensive translations of Chinese poetry. By that time the avant-garde did not really want him; Harriet Monroe, no radical herself, harshly dismissed his work in 1920 as "the effort of a conventional mind to express itself unconventionally; achieving merely artificial conceits" ("Others Again," 150–51). To a great extent, there was a mutually exclusive choice in this conflict of cultural values; if one was perceived as a friend of established magazine forces, one was not easily accepted into a little magazine set when the revolution came.

The one important exception to Stevens's policy of letting editors come to him was his unsolicited submission to *Poetry*, in the autumn of 1914, of the series called "Phases," which thoroughly impressed editor Monroe, with whom the poet soon began a long and cordial relationship. The eventful first year of his career culminated with the ambitious debut in mid-1915 of another new Manhattan poetry magazine, *Others*, financed (at first) by Arensberg and edited by Kreymborg, both fervent Stevens admirers. As Stevens's "magazine period" continued through the end of 1910s and into the 1920s, his network of acquaintance and his occasional appearances in scattered magazine numbers became less important to his reputation than a more concentrated quality of affiliation with these two magazines. Between them *Poetry* and *Others* captured over half of the poems Stevens published before *Harmonium* (60 of 118). Together they offered Stevens an unusual dual structure of evaluative support. Contrary to impressions left by later accounts of the origins of modernism, however, *Others* and *Poetry* were not interchangeable parts of a monolithic literary avant-garde of the 1910s. The specific reputation of each was important in shaping the character and magnitude of Stevens's early reputation. The evaluative power of *Poetry* consisted in its solidly established position as the front-runner of the new poetry, which meant for poets such as Stevens a relatively wide audience and the possibility of a long-term critical advocacy. On the other hand, the more radical avant-gardism of *Others* offered Stevens the editorial approval to extend his innovative wings, giving him notoriety as an intriguing mystery man while, in the short run, also helping to confine his influence to the margins of modernist culture.

Poetry had been nearly the first little poetry magazine of modernist America; with each passing year, it further proclaimed its position as the longest lived. By appearing reliably every month, always paying its contributors, awarding regular prizes, engendering a standard anthology, and adopting a pose of beneficent (if sometimes lukewarm) advocacy of American poetic activity, *Poetry* was acknowledged, by itself and nearly everybody else, as the steward of the field of modernist poetry.[20] Reaching a broader readership than any other little literary magazine during the 1910s, *Poetry* offered approvals and disapprovals that meant much for contemporary reputations. Unable to get published there, a poet such as Kreymborg could feel he had to start his own magazine, to break *Poetry*'s too-tight hold on the field: "I have never doubted the general policy of *Poetry*, even though my particular breed of poetasting was politely rejected for three consecutive years, so that Uncle Bill Reedy once ejaculated that I had to publish my own magazine to see my stuff in print" ("As Others See Us," 223). Kreymborg's efforts to overcome his exclusion resulted first in *The Glebe* and then in *Others*.

Very quickly *Poetry* had become the first institution of American literary modernism. Its relative security and cultural respectability also produced some important institutional limitations. It was subsidized by rich Chicagoans, most of whom presumably cared little about the course of contemporary poetry but liked the idea of cultural patronage. Some of Monroe's conservatism against which avant-garde radicals like Pound raged was no doubt produced or exacerbated by indirect effects from this institutional situation: her not unreasonable fears that if enough of these patrons were offended, the magazine's life would end (E. Williams, 18). The resultant tendency towards inoffensive eclecticism meant that *Poetry* found it hard to benefit fully from its many discoveries; as they would with Stevens, early commentators tended not to associate poets primarily with *Poetry* when there was an alternative that seemed to characterize the poet more vividly, such as *Others* or *The Little Review*.

Thus the mere fact that Stevens published a good deal in *Poetry* does not distinguish him from many of his peers, since almost everyone of later canonical importance, and hundreds of current unimportance, published there at least a few times, but between 1916 and 1923, at Monroe's instigation, *Poetry* portrayed Stevens as one of the central figures in its advocacy of the new verse. In 1916 his *Three Travelers Watch a Sunrise* was awarded the prize in *Poetry*'s competition for best one-act play; *Poetry* called the play "a strange and fantastic work of original genius" with "extraordinary poetic beauty" ("Prize Announcement," 160). In 1920 Stevens's fourteen-poem group *Pecksniffiana* was awarded the Levinson Prize, the magazine's most important annual honor, which placed him in the company of the highest poetic reputations of the new poetry; two years later he received honorable mention in the Levinson competition. When Stevens finally published a book in 1923, the magazine ran two entirely favorable reviews. Stevens seemed genuinely surprised and flattered by the honors and support from the leading magazine of the field.[21] If he suffered the kind of chafing dissatisfaction with Monroe's timidity which was felt by Pound, Williams, and Kreymborg, he kept it to himself. After initial evasions, Stevens rewarded the persistent Monroe with his elusive friendship. In the early 1920s, the poet was comfortable enough with her to joke at the expense of her competitors.[22] By the early 1920s, *Poetry* was quite evidently the major outlet for his favorite work.[23]

Poetry was thus undeniably an outstanding supporter of Stevens's early career. In later accounts of the poet's early years, however, *Poetry* and Stevens as discoverer and protégé often seem to go together as exclusively and unproblematically as, say, *The Dial* and E. E. Cummings.[24] By the summer of 1915, however, the crucial period of Stevens's earliest major work, *Poetry* had a legitimate competitor, both for Stevens's allegiance and for the leadership of the cutting edge of the new poetry, in *Others*. *Others* had as much claim as *Poetry* to "discovering" Stevens, publishing his first long, critically successful, and widely known poem, "Peter Quince at the Clavier." His contributions in *Others* remained some of his most popular work for years. In this smaller pond, Stevens was seen as a bigger, stranger, and more distinctively colored fish, and his overall reputation stayed strongly associated with *Others* or fellow *Others* poets until *Harmonium* and beyond.

Others was conceived by Kreymborg and Arensberg as an explicit rejection of and alternative to the more conservative interest in innovation that *Poetry* represented. According to Kreymborg, after "courteous notes from Miss Monroe endeavoring to correct his peculiarities" and similar rejections from other editors, "he was once more determined to have recourse to a magazine of his own and collect therein the rejected work of men and women who deserved at least a small audience" (*Troubador*, 199).²⁵ In its first year of publication in July 1915, this champion of the rejected scored successes by having its existence remarked upon by such important publications as *The New Republic, Poetry, Life, The Literary Digest, The Review of Reviews*, and the *Anthology of Magazine Verse*. Clearly, its circulation—around three hundred, according to Kreymborg—did not reflect the extent of its impact (circulation figures from Kreymborg, "An Early Impression," 12). Those behind *Others* were supplied generously enough with the avant-gardist's antagonism towards the literary mainstream that they counted any publicity, any stir in the torpid surface of conventional literary discourse, as a measure of their success.²⁶

Others was positioned immediately and almost unanimously as the most radical entrant in the field, as the side of the new poetry which was "revolutionary" or "queer."²⁷ Many saw its aims only as a cacophonous inversion of ideals of poetic beauty: "*Others* is the medium of the ultra-realists, the ultra-impressionists and the ultra-imagists. At present much of the new verse presents unrhythmic jangle to the ear of the untrained reader and kaleidoscopic convulsions of nothingness to the mind" (Review of *Harmonium*, *Springfield Republican*, 17).

William Stanley Braithwaite's remarks in his 1916 *Anthology of Magazine Verse* delineated the various camps of contemporary poetry as they were widely perceived: "At the beginning of the present year one could define four separate groups of poets. The fixed and firm traditionalists, the social-revolutionists, the Imagists, and the Radicals of the *Others, A Magazine of the New Verse* group" (xv). For the conservative Braithwaite to name it as one group of only four indicates an *Others* of distinctive and forceful reputation. Thus for a time *Others* seemed to be achieving its goal of prominently supporting poetic innovation, an instigation that promised trouble for *Poetry*'s stewardship.

The allegiance of Wallace Stevens was one point of the unspoken conflict between the two magazines—and that allegiance was in doubt throughout the lifetime of *Others*. Despite the always cordial, respectful relationship between Stevens and Monroe, which has obscured the rift from historians, Stevens did in fact transfer his primary poetic allegiance to *Others* between 1915 and 1918. Importantly, at the time of the founding of *Others*, he was one of *Poetry*'s rejected. After the acceptance of "Phases," Stevens's next submission to Monroe, in January 1915, was met with warm encouragement ("I don't know when any poems have 'intrigued me' so much as these") but rejection nonetheless: "They are weirder than your war poems, and I'll be blamed if I'll print them" (quoted in E. Williams, 113). Three poems (perhaps among those Monroe had rejected) would appear in the first issue of *Rogue* in March and "Peter Quince at the Clavier" in the second number of *Others,* before Stevens submitted to *Poetry* again. When he did, in the summer of 1915, he gave Monroe just what she seemed to want: "Sunday Morning," a poem more conventionally beautiful than any he would ever write again, but even then the editor was not satisfied, wanting to chop up that remarkable work as if it were a series of rearrangeable little poems like "Phases."[28]

Given his high opinion of Stevens's work and his later comments on "Sunday Morning," it is safe to say that Kreymborg would have jumped at the chance to publish the entire poem in *Others*. Though Stevens's docility in allowing Monroe's surgery suggests that he was still courting her and the magazine, her reluctance had an important effect: between the fall of 1915 and the fall of 1918, Stevens published seventeen poems in *Others* and none in *Poetry*. In 1917 and 1918 Stevens also made contributions to the New York little magazine *Soil,* to *The Little Review,* and even to Carl Zigrosser's journal of progressive education, *The Modern School,* rather than to *Poetry*. Although practically moribund in late 1918, *Others* still received the biggest plum Stevens yielded during that year, "Le Monocle de Mon Oncle." In keeping with his career-long pattern of behavior, Stevens had not allowed anyone to put him in the position of frustrated author for long; after only one actual rejection, his stance toward *Poetry* quickly gravitated towards a characteristic hard-to-get mode. The only connection Monroe was able to cultivate with Stevens in these years was with his plays, those odd mummeries that she advocated with curious insistence. The editor's wish to keep Stevens in the *Poetry* fold at a time when he was not sending her poems may well have been one reason she worked to quell the reservations of the prize committee in 1916 to give the One-Act Play Prize to *Three Travelers*.[29]

For Monroe in 1915 and 1916, *Others* presented a threat on two levels. In a general sense it threatened to usurp *Poetry*'s position as the front-running little poetry magazine, if not in resources and history, at least in immediate attention; but because *Poetry*'s insistently nonsectarian rhetoric had always held that, the more poetic activity there was, the better for American culture, Monroe could not too clearly disparage the existence of any such competitor without appearing petty or hypocritical. More specifically, since Monroe could not be sure how much identification poets such as the reticent Stevens felt with the *Others* crowd, by openly attacking *Others* she risked driving fence-sitters into the other camp. For a while, however, the need for her magazine to assert itself took precedence despite these risks. Nearly everything *Poetry* said about *Others*, whether broadly humorous or subtly patronizing, suggests that the Manhattan magazine was perceived as a troublesome competitor.

In May 1916, at the peak of the reputation of *Others*, as its first anthology was appearing, *Poetry* disdained a serious review and instead fired the harshest salvo in the feud from associate editor Alice Corbin Henderson. Her parody "A New School of Poetry" reduced the contents of *Others for 1916* to an absurd solipsistic collage by telescoping together phrases beginning with "I," including part of Stevens's "Six Significant Landscapes." (Henderson, 103–5).[30] As the only time Stevens was mentioned negatively by *Poetry* in the twenty-four years of Monroe's tenure, this abuse of the poet served not as dispassionate evaluation of a specific poem but as a bit of retribution for his defection to *Others*, suggesting that the support he enjoyed from *Poetry* was at least partially contingent upon his own support of the magazine. More broadly, the strategy of *Poetry* clearly lay in portraying *Others* as a marginal coterie—"the I-am-it school"—rather than as the open-ended clearinghouse for any experimental poetry that Kreymborg wanted it to be.

The threat of *Others* dissipated through 1917 as the impoverished Kreymborg gradually found it impossible to sustain financial backing and editorial energy. *Poetry*'s review of *Others for 1917*, a generally serious and favorable summary by Helen Hoyt, one of only a few poets to be significantly associated with both magazines, betokened the weakening of oppositional tension between the two magazines. *Poetry* could afford once again to adopt its familiar role of slightly smug materfamilias, portraying the *Others* revolution as a successful—but now rather obsolete—instigation that could be safely incorporated into its own version of poetic modernism: "A 'regular absolute humpty-dumpty business' expresses well the general verdict [in the summer of 1916] on the *Others* magazine and group; but those who shook their heads are now growing used to the new verse, and they will feel less bewildered with this volume than with the first one. Many of . . . the poems are directly enough in line with the accepted traditions for anyone to like them who has come into sympathy with the new verse at all" (Hoyt, 277–78).

As it became plainer that *Others* would not survive *Poetry*, Monroe grew more intent on reclaiming Stevens's poetic allegiance and reputation for her magazine. In *Poetry*'s later remarks about *Others*, Stevens's name arose repeatedly, always in highly laudatory remarks insisting to readers that, despite his frequent presence in *Others*, his primary allegiance was to *Poetry*. The Levinson Prize for Stevens's *Pecksniffiana*, a series published in the autumn of 1919 just after the final demise of *Others*, can be seen as a sort of reward for his strong return to the fold of *Poetry* contributors. By 1920 Monroe was willing to call Stevens "the peer of any poet now living" ("Others Again," 155), but even this striking praise was not pure awestruck appreciation; it too was shaped by its competitive context, *Poetry*'s review of the final *Others* anthology, which Monroe found useful if only in providing her "at last a chance to say a word about this reticent poet" (155). Even though the necessity of attacking *Others* as a competitor was now completely gone, "the magazine . . . having apparently come to the end of its gay career" (150), in praising Stevens, Monroe repeatedly asserted *Poetry*'s claims to his discovery and allegiance, which plainly she could not assume. In the review's first paragraph she named Stevens as one of the four poets whose *Others* anthology entries had actually been first published in *Poetry*. (This part of the reclamation was somewhat weakened by the fact that Stevens had given Kreymborg permission to reprint some of his prize-winning work, suggesting his continued support of the *Others* enterprise.) Later in the review Monroe evoked her long history of advocacy of Stevens's work by recounting her first encounter with "Phases" in 1914 and then again reminded readers of *Poetry*'s Levinson sponsorship of Stevens: "If you want some of his most perfect poems, read these few *Pecksniffiana* [in the *Others* anthology], and then turn to the whole group in *Poetry* of October 1919" (157). Such persistent claims suggest Monroe's perception that, despite the fact that Stevens published earlier and often in *Poetry*, she needed to repossess the poet's reputation even after the dissolution of *Others*.

Critical commentary from across the contemporary literary spectrum until well past the publication of *Harmonium* in 1923 justifies Monroe's belief that Stevens had become associated more closely with *Others*. For example, the poet and critic Conrad Aiken, writing in the conservative magazines *The Poetry Journal* and the old *Dial*, repeatedly identified Stevens as an outstanding member of the group or evaluated him in the same breath with favored *Others* poets.[31] In the field-defining 1919 debate in the *New Republic* between Aiken and Louis Untermeyer on the merits of "aesthetic" poetry, both principals linked Stevens equally with a strain of "absolute" poetry which Untermeyer called "the mere verbal legerdemain of the Pound-Stevens-Arensberg-*Others*" ("The Ivory Tower II," 60). Probably the most influential American poetry critic and anthologist of the early modernist period, Untermeyer repeatedly grouped Stevens with such prominent *Others* poets Williams and Moore, and he would for decades view Stevens through his disdain for *Others* "decadence"—an evaluation that formed a substantial obstacle to a broader readership for Stevens at least through the 1920s ("Among the New Books," 159–60).

The American Imagists, with whom Stevens was sometimes to be linked by commentators, saw him primarily as a member of *Others* as well. In an August 1915 letter to Kreymborg, Amy Lowell twice asked about the identity of the impressive author of "Peter Quince" and "The Silver Plough-Boy," published in the July *Others* (quoted in Damon, 316). She also spoke of including Stevens in the influential Imagist anthology of 1916. This never happened, not because Lowell soured on Stevens, whose work she continued to admire, but probably because she quickly soured on *Others*—and she may have felt that she could not help Stevens without helping *Others*.[32] John Gould Fletcher's 1920 survey of American poets for a British magazine distinguished between the work of Aiken and a "younger school" consisting of Stevens and Kreymborg—even though Aiken was actually younger than Stevens by ten years and Kreymborg by six ("Some Contemporary American Poets," 28–30). Fletcher's confusion indicates the extent to which *Others* had stamped such fortyish poets as Kreymborg and Stevens with labels of youthful, wild-eyed radicalism.

Even in reviews of *Harmonium* in 1923–24, with *Others* four years dead, Stevens was remembered as a primary member of the group. Mark Van Doren's important review in the *Nation* began "Mr. Stevens's most famous poem 'Peter Quince at the Clavier' appeared in *Others* as long as seven years ago" (eight, actually); Kreymborg was prominent for Van Doren mainly for "introduc[ing] Mr. Stevens to *Others*" (Van Doren, 400). Even if *Others* was not always named in such remarks, it often functioned implicitly as the genesis of a recognizable, influential group of poets to which Stevens was integral, as in this version of recent literary history by *Broom*'s editor Harold Loeb in 1923: "The poetry revival first attracted public attention with the vitriolic denunciations of Masters, but broadened as it developed, and includes among its representatives several writers, such as Marianne Moore, Williams, Stevens, and Kreymborg, who, by their concentration on aesthetics, may be considered precursors of the latest movement" ("Comment—*Broom*, 1921–23," 56).

As late as 1925, Clement Wood's reactionary estimate of Stevens was shaped by his strong association with *Others*. Despite finding "flashes of poetic ability," Wood dismissed Stevens as explicitly a part of a "totality [of *Others* that was] less than nothing" (Wood, 303). And the next year, from the avant-garde side, Yvor Winters was still naming Stevens, with Moore, Williams, and Mina Loy, as "the outstanding members" of a "set" that he explicitly identified with *Others* (Winters, "Mina Loy," 496; also see Munson, "The *Others* Parade," 226–32).

Whether by his choice or not, then, *Others* became Stevens's major literary association during this entire decade.[33] Readers and critics could easily see him as a central member of the *Others* canon, as they could not with *Poetry*. The reputational consequences of this association were both immediate and long-term. Over the shorter run, the quick rise of *Others* in the little magazine field was closely linked to the success of Stevens's "Peter Quince at the Clavier," and vice versa. From the second issue of *Others*, the poem went into the 1915 *Anthology of Magazine Verse* edited by Braithwaite, who was no fan of *Others* but who nonetheless rated "Peter Quince" as one of the five best magazine poems of the year. This decision moved Stevens's work from the crackpot avant-garde that many felt would publish any outlandish thing, into an established site of mainstream literary culture. When in December *The Literary Digest* reprinted Braithwaite's five best poems, a Stevens poem was exposed to a national audience for the first time, and *Others* had some national publicity.[34] The poem was then chosen for the first *Others* anthology, from which it was singled out for mention in *The Review of Reviews* and in 1917 was reprinted in the prominent Monroe-Henderson anthology *The New Poetry*.[35]

By virtue of this progression into wider literary circles, "Peter Quince" became Stevens's best-known and best-liked poem for many years. It evoked numerous critical discussions of Stevens through the mid-1920s: Aiken in several of the essays in *Scepticisms*; Monroe and Fletcher in 1920; Wood in 1925; and in many *Harmonium* reviews.[36] The anonymous *Springfield Republican* reviewer of *Harmonium* said less about the unique brilliance of "Peter Quince" than about its secure position within contemporary literary consciousness by predictably singling it out as an "exquisite poem," for which he or she "would give all the rest [of *Harmonium*] and more" (7a). In 1922 Amy Lowell even immortalized its impact in the verse of *A Critical Fable* ("Looking back, I don't know that anything since/ Has delighted me more than his 'Peter Quince' ") (97). In 1925, Kreymborg felt comfortable calling "Peter Quince" a "now famous poem" and thought the episode in which Stevens furtively submitted it to *Others* worth recounting in his own autobiography (*Troubador*, 239). Through 1940 the poem was anthologized at least eleven times, more, for example, than any single poem by T. S. Eliot.[37] "Peter Quince" was clearly the first Stevens poem to become part of a contemporary poetic canon.

As Stevens and "Peter Quince" had helped provide impetus to *Others*, the magazine's position as a hardy pioneer within the literary avant-garde, and the developing reputation of its prominent poets, strongly shaped views of Stevens through the 1920s. The geographical and personal convenience offered by *Others* enabled Stevens to become associated with a vigorous center of cultural energy without forcing him to engage in hobnobbing or self-promotion, which he was always unwilling to do. Despite the efforts of *Poetry* and others to belittle its impact, and despite continual financial difficulties from early 1916, *Others* earned points for durability by surviving for four years, a quite respectable life span for a little magazine. Within its first year, *Others* had managed to escape the trap of being just one of many fugitive magazines by generating its own anthology, brought out by Alfred Knopf in 1916 and 1917 and by Nicholas L. Brown in 1920. An anthology led to the possibility of reviews in major periodicals instead of fleeting mentions in departments of literary "news."[38] Reviews meant publicity within larger reading markets and accessibility to libraries and universities through such clearinghouses as *Book Review Digest, The Literary Digest*, and *The Review of Reviews*, all of which mentioned *Others*. Book publication also offered the chance to present to all these sources the best of the magazine rather than the motley assortment of material faced by the editor of a monthly periodical. All these effects meant the potential for continued impact even after the magazine itself ceased publication.

Furthermore, the assertiveness of *Others* meant immediate easier access for Stevens, Kreymborg, and other *Others* poets within the field of little magazines, both in existing ones such as *Poetry* and in the new ones they were to be involved with. After 1915 *Poetry* became a faithful Stevens advocate. After enduring those years of rejection slips from *Poetry*, Kreymborg first appeared there only eight months after the beginning of *Others*; he even won a minor *Poetry* prize in 1922. Though Williams consigned *Others* to oblivion in the vitriolic valediction "Belly Music" in 1919, Lola Ridge resuscitated the group through a series of poetry-reading parties through late 1919 and early 1920 (Williams, "Belly Music" 25–32; Kreymborg, *Troubador* 330–31). Kreymborg's goal—that *Others* could be "a starting point wherein these folk might express themselves independently of one another"—had been successfully realized and would be sustained in the 1920s and beyond (*Troubador*, 331).

The impetus that Stevens's avant-garde reputation received from *Others* carried him into a position of respect in the burgeoning modernist mainstream of the 1920s that was exemplified by the eclectic New York magazine *The Dial*. The very fact that such an established magazine as *The Dial* had been taken over by owners as sympathetic to the avant-garde as were Scofield Thayer and James Sibley Watson indicated the movement of modernist discourse from the fugitive antagonism of *Others* into more central positions within American literary culture in the 1920s. Eighteen of the thirty-seven poets included in the first two *Others* anthologies went on to publish in *The Dial*.[39] There were also concrete relationships forged between the *Dial* and the *Others* remnant as they met to read their work in 1919–20. In *Troubador*, Kreymborg remembered a gathering at which Thayer, newly enthroned editor of this powerful magazine, was observed (and presumably courted) by the "expectant" *Others* poets in attendance. According to Kreymborg, Stevens and others read aloud late that evening, though this is unsubstantiated. Thayer was so impressed by Marianne Moore's offering that he persuaded her then and there to part with it for *The Dial* (*Troubador*, 330–33). Moore's association with *The Dial* grew until in 1925 she became managing editor, eventually replacing Thayer in one of the most important editorial positions of the decade.

Others and *The Dial* evidently overlapped across far-reaching evaluative networks that during the 1920s came to shape conceptions of accomplishment in the field of avant-garde modernism. Perhaps the most impressive descent of *Others* to *The Dial* developed gradually through the 1920s and has never been sufficiently noted: of the five recipients of the ballyhooed *Dial* award who were primarily poets, four had published significantly in *Others* (T. S. Eliot, 1922 award; Moore, 1925; Williams, 1926; and Pound, 1927).[40] According to William Wasserstrom, Stevens very nearly won the final award in 1928, losing out to Kenneth Burke only because he had sent *The Dial* nothing for years (Wasserstrom, 126). This list of winners suggests that *The Dial* award functioned as an evaluative counterforce to *Poetry*'s Levinson Prize, several of whose early winners defined a group of somewhat older poets who are still convenient to consider together: Robinson, Frost, Lindsay, Masters, and Sandburg. In this folksy company, Stevens seems an anomalous hothouse flower as a Levinson winner. In a pattern that strongly suggests the interdependence of magazine reputation and poetic reputation, *Poetry*'s prize poets had by the end of the 1910s formed a canon of popular modernism, while *The Dial*'s would, in the coming decades, form the center of an avant-garde modernist canon. This latter canon derived largely from *Others*, which a decade earlier had offered its poets a locus of avant-garde support after they had proved unacceptably radical to the editorial sensibilities of *Poetry*.

Notable also in the *Others* legacy, both for Stevens specifically and for modernism more generally, was the ability of many of the *Others* mainstays to find major publishers for their books of poetry. Of the thirty-seven poets chosen for either the 1916 or 1917 *Others* anthologies (the 1920 edition was taken mostly from other magazines), thirty had not published a volume of poems by 1915. Sixteen of these thirty aspiring poets successfully moved from the little magazine field into book publication between 1916 and 1925. Most of the publishers who furthered this infiltration were part of the new breed: Mitchell Kennerly, B. W. Huebsch, Edmund Brown of the Four Seas Company, and most of all, Alfred A. Knopf, called by a competitor "the most original American publisher of our day" (Huebsch quoted in *Alfred A. Knopf, 1915–1940*, 36–37). Though in general he published quite sparingly in the field of contemporary American poetry—around twenty volumes by 1920[41]—Knopf served as the best opportunity for *Others* poets to break into the book field and thus to gain the potential for wider recognition. One of Knopf's most adventurous moves upon setting up his own firm in 1915 was to undertake the first *Others* anthology. Between 1915 and 1924, he published books by no fewer than ten contributors to *Others*, including five in the magazine's inner circle (Maxwell Bodenheim, Orrick Johns, Kreymborg, Stevens, and Pound).[42] For five of these ten poets, Knopf enabled their first commercially produced book of poetry in the United States, demonstrating an extraordinary willingness to take chances on poets with untried and in some cases highly radical reputations. Despite his firm's size and inexperience, Knopf immediately commanded a position of respect within the mainstream literary world; nearly all of his volumes by *Oth-*

ers contributors were reviewed by at least four major periodicals. For the reluctant Stevens, the opportunity to be successfully cajoled into publishing a book by Knopf's confidante Carl Van Vechten was a long-overdue prerequisite to the possibility of canonization.

From their immediate offers of publishing space in the mid-1910s to an indirect legacy decades later, *Others* and *Poetry* and their moving forces Monroe and Kreymborg provided Stevens with an exceptionally strong base of support, one enjoyed by very few other poets. As mentioned earlier, a reputation at *Poetry* and one at *Others* were quite different things; for a poet to have had both was surprisingly unusual. Only seven poets managed to publish five items in *Others* (1915-19) and ten items in *Poetry* between 1912 and 1920: Bodenheim, Helen Hoyt, Kreymborg, Pound, Sandburg, Stevens, and Williams.[43] Except for Hoyt, these poets would all have modernist "careers," and four of them would develop substantial canonical reputations. To have been long in the good graces of both magazines, then, was mainly the privilege of poets who were to become thought of as "important." This pattern is not arbitrary or coincidental; *Poetry* and *Others* were able to help position poets so that they could be considered important.

In her position in the mainstream of modernist discourse, Monroe continued to promote Stevens for the next two decades. Her anthology *The New Poetry* (1917, 1923), more catholic in scope than the *Others* efforts, Lowell's Imagist anthologies, or the Untermeyer series begun in 1919, and published by the large mainstream house of Macmillan, became nearly as standard to the field of the modernist anthology as *Poetry* was to the little magazine. Through its comprehensiveness and respectability, *The New Poetry* took modernist poetry and Stevens poems a long way towards both the library shelves and the bestseller lists. In general, the anthologists' choices offered large chunks of the popular side of the new verse (even to the extent of including Joyce Kilmer's "Trees"); the exercise of their power of selection on Stevens's behalf was their primary attempt to form rather than to reflect current fashions. The three Stevens poems in the 1917 edition included the two longest works he had yet published and represented about one-ninth of his entire published output. In the 1923 edition, in which Stevens was given 19 poems on 16 pages, only five poets filled more pages (Lindsay 22, Lowell 18, Masters 27, Pound 19, Sandburg 19), only three placed more poems (Masters 24, Pound 20, Sandburg

35). Each of these other poets had published at least four books of poetry. Stevens had published none. Clearly the space allotted to him in this important book was massively disproportionate to the common estimate of his importance. This anthological advocacy had a strong impact on such a young reader and writer as Louis Zukofsky, who remembered half a century later that *The New Poetry*, a book he had "saved for" as a teenager, rewarded him with much of Stevens's early work.[44] Although right after *Harmonium*, Stevens's writing abruptly stopped for seven years, Monroe kept praising him — always in a tone that assumed his centrality to the period — in an article written for teachers in the *English Journal*, in her collection of poetry reviews, and in her posthumous autobiography *A Poet's Life*.[45]

The trajectory of Kreymborg's advocacy of Stevens was symptomatic of the infusion of the forces behind *Others* into increasingly mainstream contexts through the 1920s. Kreymborg's *Others* anthologies were followed by a hand in Stevens's contributions to *The Chapbook* and *Broom*; in 1925 came the engaging autobiography *Troubador*, whose anecdotes of Stevens's imposing demeanor offered the literary public a sense of the poet's soon-to-be-legendary authority. In 1927 Kreymborg became a coeditor of *The American Caravan* (a mainstream modernist journal to which Stevens would contribute in the 1930s), and he ended the decade as a comprehensive surveyor and anthologist of American poetry. Both *Our Singing Strength* (1929) and the companion anthology *Lyric America, 1630–1930* (1930) continued his unflagging advocacy of Stevens. Still associating Stevens with *Others* writers, but frustrated at the poet's utter silence, Kreymborg was moved to call Stevens's poems "among the most perfect things in any literature" (*Our Singing Strength*, 501). In the anthology, Kreymborg placed Stevens near the top, giving him 8 pages; among twentieth-century poets, only Frost (11), Fletcher (10), Robinson (10), and the editor himself (8) had as many.

In no sense were Monroe and Kreymborg responsible for "canonizing" Stevens; what they did manage to do was to keep his name alive for a sizable period of time in the significant arenas of discourse over which they had some control. Their lofty opinions of him could not produce much of a discernible ripple in the literary field as a whole and would have almost no apparent effect on the disappointing sales of *Harmonium* in 1923. In contrast, Stevens was largely dismissed by the most popular strain of contemporary poetry in these years, the self-consciously vigorous and unbookish descent from Whitman which was represented most typically by the anthologies and criticism of Untermeyer. In these circles, Stevens's association with other *Others* poets was a hindrance; he was seen as a hyperaesthetic formalist obsessed with quirks of language and mood, "the laureate of the intellectual gymnasts" ("Recent Books in Brief Review," 483). Through the 1920s Stevens was associated with a strain of aesthetic poetry that was considered, even by many commentators sympathetic to avant-gardism, to be "minor."[46]

One must not lose sight of the fact that these mostly intangible or inarticulate responses and evaluations of Stevens before *Harmonium* were quite important in helping his work not only to be preserved but to possess certain marks of distinction as his career entered its second decade. Indeed, the greater part of literary evaluation is accomplished almost simultaneously with a work's production or publication. Without a certain minimum level of immediate interest evinced by other poets, editors, publishers, and reviewer-critics, a poet's career could scarcely even continue, much less become central to a period. The later poetic careers of the contributors to *Others*, for example, followed varied but classifiable patterns towards, and mostly away from, canonical potential.[47] Only a few—including Stevens—provoked enough interest in editors and readers (or in themselves) to continue publishing or ever to be evaluated by anyone as a serious poet. This elementary selectivity may seem obvious or mundane, but it is important to canon study as an instance of what Barbara Herrnstein Smith calls *pre-evaluation*, which is usually obscured in considering patterns of evaluation ("Contingencies of Value," 27). It is seldom acknowledged that the present field of evaluation of modernist poetry was mostly chosen in the 1910s and 1920s by these poets' contemporaries. If several hundred poets had aspired to establish careers in the little magazines of the 1910s, their first readers had cut the number of vigorous survivors to perhaps thirty by 1930, of which Stevens was definitely one.

In his publication before 1923, then, Stevens had attained a notably advantageous position within the field of avant-garde poetry. He had developed intellectual and institutional relationships with centrally situated allies from his own literary generation and social class. *Others* had given the producers of literary discourse an aesthetic cohesion that helped them place his spectacularly individual discourse in the galaxy of contemporary poetry. The divergences of evaluation of Stevens from the rest of the *Others* circle nearly always fell in his favor and provided indications of the level to which he had, without even seeming to try, made an equally deep impression upon such varied contemporaries as Williams, Monroe, Kreymborg, Aiken, Moore, and Knopf, poets, critics, editors, and publishers who were playing significant roles in the production and reception of modernist poetry. Furthermore, in 1924 Monroe would assert that Stevens had become a central influence on a group of younger poets, an observation borne out by the comments of Harold Loeb and Gorham Munson, and also by Josephson writing in *Broom*.[48] The early interest in Stevens manifested in such varied younger modernists as Winters, Josephson, and Zukofsky suggested that the poetic and personal authority he had established in the avant-garde magazine scene would find through the 1920s and 1930s a broadening curve of advocacy.

THREE

The Lutanist of Fleas

Stevens and Harmonium *in the 1920s*

> Exit the mental moonlight, exit lex,
> Rex and principium, exit the whole
> Shebang. Exeunt omnes. Here was prose
> More exquisite than any tumbling verse:
> A still new continent in which to dwell.
> —Stevens,
> "The Comedian as the Letter C," 1923

> The playing of a Chinese orchestra. On a gong a bonze creates a copper din. The most amazing cacophony amid dissolving labials and silkiest sibilants. Quirks, booms, whistles, quavers. Lord, what instruments has he there? Small muffled drums? Plucked wires? The falsetto of an ecstatic eunuch?
> —Paul Rosenfeld on Stevens, 1925

In the literary milieu of 1923, when *Harmonium* was published, Stevens's canonical potential is barely detectable. Unlike the great majority of poets publishing in little magazines in the 1910s, Stevens had the advocacy of some centrally situated editors, a number of poets from his own generation, and an innovative and respected publisher; nearly all of them would prove loyal to an extent virtually unknown in modernist alliances. Of more importance for his immediate reputation, however, were three attributes Stevens lacked: articulate critics to discuss his poems, a reading public to buy them, and the overriding desire to keep writing them. The failure of *Harmonium* reveals much about the conditions of publishing, reading, and evaluating poetry in the 1920s.

The myriad of poets who published regularly in little magazines, and the shortage of intelligent critics of contemporary poetry, meant that, especially for a poet such as Stevens who would not engage in outright self-promotion, a book was prerequisite to any sustained critical reputation. As well as achieving wider dissemination and a better chance at preservation, the publication of a book carried a less tangible but no less important mark of authority, a sign that the writer was not a magazine dilettante but a serious person whose work might be seen as having a coherent artistic philosophy. Without this stamp of authorial self-assertion, no commentator needed to feel obligated to deal with a given poet's work. For example, of the forty poets from across the aesthetic spectrum who were represented in the bibliography of Aiken's 1919 collection of essays *Scepticisms*, Stevens was the only one who had not published a volume (297–300).[1] Aiken's interest was extraordinary. More typical of the rough critical treatment of work culled from magazines rather than books was Howard Cook's 1918 survey *Our Poets of Today*, which, although not hostile to some innovators such as Amy Lowell's Imagists, curtly dismissed the verse published in such places as *The Little Review* as the "things [for which] writers of free verse must blush," calling the writer of "Depression Before Spring" "a misnomered poet" without even bothering to attribute authorship to Stevens (10–11). For Cook, this work was inconsequential magazine charlatanry that quite literally carried no authority at all.

Furthermore, in the cultural marketplace of the 1910s and 1920s, before the onset of any institutionally subsidized journals that would recognize the existence of modernism, criticism of individual contemporary poets largely meant the format of the book review. Even many of the critical essays that did appear in little magazines, and less often in cultural magazines, were, as Gorham Munson remarked in 1925, semireviews dependent on the recent publication of a book: "there are three or four critics who would delight in telling as large an audience as they can reach that Hart Crane is probably the most richly endowed of our younger poets, but what editor will permit them to do so until some publisher brings out Crane's first volume?" ("Hart Crane," 160–61).[2]

Even for those with no reputation, the process of publishing a book of poetry was not particularly difficult as long as they had the hundred dollars or so necessary to engage a vanity press, but the dominance of the book review format was shaped by the magazines' desire not only to serve as a useful guide to their readers' aesthetic choices but also to sell advertisers' and supporters' books. Consequently, then as now, major publishers and advertisers had the inside track on serious reviewing in periodicals. For example, despite his longstanding and intense involvement with *Poetry, Others,* and numerous other magazines, William Carlos Williams's fourth book, *Kora in Hell,* published by the Four Seas Company of Boston, a decent vanity press, received not a single major review in 1920. Despite the dramatic opening up of the markets for poetry publishing in books since 1905 and in magazines since 1912, the mechanisms for generating criticism, less directly connected to any financial returns for anyone, were still quite rudimentary, leading to intense competition for the critical attention that was available.

Unwilling to risk the disappointment of putting his work in front of this highly competitive system of critical reception, Stevens had procrastinated for nine years, accumulating enough material for at least two books. His extraordinarily long delay in taking this step greatly retarded his reputation by helping to shape a perception that was widespread at least through the mid-1930s—that he was not a serious poet. One immediate result of his refusal to publish a volume was that through 1923 critical discussion of him had been practically nil. There had been not a single article primarily about Stevens, not in *Poetry* or *Others,* not by Aiken, Monroe, Kreymborg, or anyone. Even his most laudatory notices had come in incidental contexts—little magazine "news," announcements of prizes in *Poetry,* passing remarks in discussions of other poets, or brief mentions in anthologies, in reviews of them, and in surveys of the American poetic scene. In other words, until he published a book, not even his strongest supporters were economically able to justify any space for the express purpose of advocating Stevens.

Once the book finally emerged, it did make possible some elementary steps toward canonical potential. Finally allowed a sustained focus on Stevens rather than fleeting glimpses in magazines, readers could now see Stevens as having produced a substantial body of work in these nine years. They could now trace central characteristics and concerns of his work by examining it for such elements as verbal mannerisms, recurrent images, favorite scenes, themes, influences, and tonal shadings. It was also possible to assimilate Stevens's more important efforts, especially the newly published opus, "The Comedian as the Letter C," into the context of his day-in, day-out poetic work, seeing the less remarkable works as part of a generally coherent whole. A distinctive space of discourse, a "world" of Stevens, could now be perceived.

This catalog of what *Harmonium* made possible is worth noting because of the often untraceable but evident effects the book would eventually have on younger modernist critics and poets in the next three decades, some of whom, like Blackmur, Winters, and Zukofsky, were aware of Stevens even by 1923. But in the explicit responses to the book which constituted and shaped the reception of Stevens in this decade, these advances of reputation did not often occur. The pattern of review response to *Harmonium* faithfully traced the major divisions in American literary culture of the mid-1920s. The most solidly established and culturally conservative literary periodicals—*The New York Times Book Review, The North American Review, The Atlantic, The Saturday Review, The Independent, Scribners', The Century, The Literary Digest International Book Review*, and all academic journals—were still generally hostile to most or all contemporary innovation and did not acknowledge the book at all. Even within the aesthetically progressive arenas of the literary culture, where Stevens could not be ignored, the response clearly indicated two fundamental evaluative divisions. Reviews of *Harmonium* in more institutionalized organs of cultural commentary—*The Nation, The New Republic, The Freeman, The Yale Review*— were lukewarm at best. Only the little magazines of the aesthetic center and left—*Poetry, The Dial, Broom, The Measure*—were willing to praise Stevens wholeheartedly, and even they could not do so in a form that was forceful or persuasive.

Given the fact that some people had been waiting for Stevens to publish a book for nine years, *Harmonium* also produced truly dismal sales, which was obvious and surprising to the poet and his supporters. Despite serious reviews in eight magazines with a combined circulation of perhaps fifty thousand, the first edition sold very poorly and was quickly remaindered. A year after its publication, R. P. Blackmur and Aiken ran across copies of *Harmonium* in a Filene's Christmas sale in Boston. They bought all there were at a bargain price of eleven cents apiece, and sent them to friends as Christmas cards (Fraser, 99). Amy Lowell, who had never helped Stevens as she had promoted so many poets, expressed surprise and disappointment that *Harmonium*, "a good book," had not sold at all (Damon, 656). In 1954 Louise Bogan was proud of being one of the few people who had actually bought a copy of the first edition, at the Old-Corner Bookstore in Boston ("*Harmonium* and the American Scene," 18).

There are a number of interrelated reasons for this remarkably flat response. Stevens may have waited too long to publish his book, won too many fleeting magazine accolades that were not consolidated and were half-forgotten. By 1923, like his generation as a whole, Stevens was no longer news. Even given the exigencies of their commercially motivated format, most reviews of *Harmonium* took the form of impressionistic, disjointed remarks with little attempt to describe in detail the book's functions, intentions, or antecedents, and they paid little attention to the question of Stevens's more permanent value. In many of them Stevens was considered in the same omnibus evaluation with a number of other poets.[3] Constant references to Stevens's "obscurity" showed clearly that most commentators struggled unsuccessfully to understand much of what they read.

Within two years of *Harmonium*, true to Munson's analysis of the critical situation, three brief essays on Stevens appeared, but through the decade *Harmonium* produced very little articulate response. Though in most of his letters Stevens ostentatiously appeared to expect nothing from the book, he must still have been surprised by the utter lack of sales and enthusiasm it generated after he had been highly lauded by such seemingly influential people as Monroe, Kreymborg, and Aiken. It is fairly safe to say that Stevens saw its reception as a fiasco; a book of poems, he had confided with uncharacteristic candor to Williams in 1918, was "a damned serious affair."[4] The failure of his book to make a stronger showing was undoubtedly one of the things that destroyed Stevens's desire to write for the next six years. Nevertheless, the ways in which these reviews and critical essays evaluated the poet's perceived strengths and limitations revealed much about conditions of reading poetry in the 1920s.

Two perceptions of Stevens's poetry transcended otherwise fundamentally opposed evaluations and made their way into nearly all commentary on *Harmonium*: its formal brilliance and its obscurity. The perception of Stevens's impregnable formal ability was no doubt aided by the evidence of that skill from virtually the first poem he published. Monroe's account in 1920 of the excitement she felt at the appearance of "Phases" in her office in 1914, indicated the suddenness and mystery with which Stevens seemed to emerge as a finished poet.[5] Within a year of his debut, in two tour-de-forces that became classics of early modernism, "Sunday Morning" and "Peter Quince at the Clavier," Stevens demonstrated a mastery of long poems in both traditional and free verse. Unlike many poets of his age, he had apparently undergone no apprenticeship, no series of failed attempts at publication, and little association with other writers.

By the time of *Harmonium*, few readers, even of the least sympathetic group, were willing to dispute Stevens's virtuosity. In the early 1920s Stevens was called: the master of "a delicate, sensual perception of loveliness" (Seiffert, 160); "a rare talent" (Squire, 657); "the most accomplished . . . of modern American poets" (Fletcher, "The Revival of Aestheticism," 356). His poetry was "very fine art" (Holden, 16), full of "delicately enunciated melody . . . [and] gentle excellence" (Van Doren, 401), which carried "the authority of a superb virtuoso" (Josephson, 237). Yvor Winters, twenty-two years old, called Stevens "the greatest of living and of American poets," but could not develop this passing remark made in a review of a book by E. A. Robinson ("A Cool Master," 287). Louis Untermeyer, Stevens's most important detractor during this period, admitted that he was "a stylist of unusual delicacy," which was apparent to "even the least sympathetic reader" (*American Poetry Since 1900*, 327). The immediate consensus was that Stevens was "master of a style" (E. Wilson, "Wallace Stevens and E. E. Cummings," 102).

Rather than encouraging much analytical understanding, *Harmonium*'s stylistic authority usually manifested itself in odd or indirect ways, one of which was its appearance in the reviewer's own style as an ornateness of rhetoric that seemed to want to surpass the poetry itself. The opening of Paul Rosenfeld's 1925 essay on Stevens, with its spectacular conglomeration of chinoiserie, onomatopoeia, assonance, and synaesthesis, formed an effete critical echo of the poet's own verbal textures: "The playing of a Chinese orchestra. On a gong a bonze creates a copper din. The most amazing cacophony amid dissolving labials and silkiest sibilants. Quirks, booms, whistles, quavers. Lord, what instruments has he there? Small muffled drums? Plucked wires? The falsetto of an ecstatic eunuch?" (Rosenfeld, 35). This echoing also occurred in the work of detractors, as in the anonymous *Bookman* review of *Harmonium*: "Mr. Stevens has a highly individual argot, a unique pungency in conveying sense impressions, and a gay diablerie in arranging grotesque word patterns which seem quite liberated from time and space and prosody and all other ills to which the flesh is heir" ("Recent Books in Brief Review," 483).

Even Untermeyer's plain-spoken vocabulary strayed into ornament in considering Stevens's method: "Unable to effect simple illusions, [Stevens] endeavors to bemuse with elaborate prestidigitation, plucking shining phrases out of a vacuum" (*American Poetry Since 1900*, 325). These negative judgments were meant to devalue the importance of form by showing that anyone could come up with overblown rhetoric for any purpose. Collectively these imitations indicated the widespread assumption that form was an overlay to communicable content; without a strongly perceived "meaning," many critics saw nothing of substance left except frivolous linguistic preciosity, but what this mimicry also suggested was that even in disparagement commentators acknowledged the power of Stevens's formal textures in shaping its own discourse of reception.

Many of those who did not explicitly mimic the poet's own mannerisms fell back on terms borrowed from other genres, like the equation of poetry with music, as in Van Doren's "delicately enunciated melody" or in the title of Holden's review, "The Word of Music." More trendy, if not necessarily more illuminating, were a number of comparisons of Stevens's work with visual arts such as "modern abstract painting" (Josephson, 237).[6] For want of a comfortable terminology to discuss Stevens, J. C. Squire threw in both painting and music: "[He] does give something peculiarly his own: the vision of an original painter, new light on new things, and faint humming in a faint music" (657).

These vague synaesthesic descriptions, descendants of symbolism, were to be found throughout the reviews of *Harmonium*. What they suggest is that verbal form as such was widely perceived as indescribable. The "obscurity" of Stevens's poetry, which meant a lack of paraphraseable content for the critic, left nothing but the evocation of tonal nuance. There was not yet any of the critical terminology specifically attuned to structural and rhetorical strategies that would enable critics fifteen and twenty years later to articulate "meaning" in poetry as opaque as Stevens's.

However vague or silly in their expression, these early laudatory citations must not completely discounted. *Harmonium* did forcefully assert a important stylistic authority to Stevens's long-term benefit. Even in an inhospitable evaluative climate, the poet's work was strong enough to force from nearly all commentators concessions that were often uncomfortable to their evaluative preconceptions. Some of the most influential of these reader-critics, such as

Untermeyer and Wilson, would never alter their early views enough to see Stevens as a major poet, and Winters would come explicitly to reject Stevens's poetics. In a sense this is exactly the point; the estimate of Stevens as a formal virtuoso had quickly become a consensus independent of the evaluative vagaries of any particular critical ideology. As criteria of evaluation turned more in the direction of formal excellence in the next two decades, instead of appearing as a concession in an overall disparagement of Stevens, these acknowledgements would form the bases of highly favorable evaluations.

In the 1920s, however, the consensus on Stevens's formal gifts was not sufficient for a viable advocacy of his majority. Though by no means deaf to his seductive Peter Quincean virtuosity, his earliest commentators simply could not fit it comfortably into existing frames of poetic reference. Acknowledgements of Stevens's virtuosity nearly always went hand-in-hand with objections to his incomprehensibility. The most common type of response entailed a reader's acknowledgement of incomprehension, which he or she ascribed entirely to the poet's innate obscurity of expression, concluding in a disparagement of his ultimate importance. The anonymous reviewer in the conservative *Bookman* gave backhanded kudos to Stevens as "the laureate of the intellectual gymnasts," who "will not be in the least disgruntled" at the reviewer's complete inability to make intelligible sense out of the poems ("Recent Books in Brief Review," 483). Despite her enthusiasm, Marjorie Allen Seiffert in *Poetry* had to admit that "after all, there is a lot that one never quite 'gets' " (155). Van Doren's review in *The Nation* was most representative of all in attempting to be positive, noting that the future would have a different conception of real obscurity, but it ultimately reached the negative conclusion that Stevens "will never be much read" and consequently assumed that the poet's work would date severely, to end by "drifting permanently, like frozen chords, through certain memories—the overtone of our droll, creedless time" (160).

This perception of Stevens was so widespread that in *Our Singing Strength* (1929) Stevens's old advocate Alfred Kreymborg felt compelled to plead for a fair and careful reading of the poet—despite his acknowledged obscurity. The work he particularly cited as being "a great poem, though obscure," was one that may well be considered among Stevens's most direct, "Sunday Morning" (503). Kreymborg here echoed Fletcher's comments of nine years earlier, which cited a "magnificent" passage but then called "Sunday Morning" "deliberately cryptic" ("Some Contemporary American Poets," 30). In both statements there was an implicit apology for an acknowledged shortcoming and only vague suggestions of the compensations to be found. A few years later, despite his liking for Stevens's "delightful connoisseurship in verse," New Humanist Stanley P. Chase concluded from his inability to make a coherent system of symbolic content from "Anecdote of the Jar" that Stevens represented a "decline in what has been called 'communicative efficacy.' " Because no definite symbolic value could be assigned to the jar, Chase objected that it was "not only like nothing else in Tennessee but like nothing else in the universe" and hence artistically valueless (211–12).

In the short term, this combination of formal virtuosity and obscurity led toward two basic conclusions in estimating Stevens's value, seemingly quite opposed but with similar underlying assumptions about poetic meaning. For one type of early reader, such as Harriet Monroe, decorative formal virtuosity regardless of content was sufficient to warrant the highest praise if the final product could be seen as "beauty" (as it usually could with Stevens but not with, say, Eliot). On the opposite side, for such readers as Louis Untermeyer, formal mastery was seen as something subordinate to, and indeed often inversely proportional to, a significant content that contained the profoundest meaning of poetry; for them, Stevens offered little of communicative substance. These groups of readers shared a dualistic opposition of formal refinement and profound content that was crippling to Stevens's reputation throughout the decade.

An unequivocal but reductive and mostly ineffectual advocacy of Stevens's creation of "beauty" was presented most prominently in *Poetry* by Monroe and Seiffert. As an editor, Monroe often realized her limitations as a reader, agreeing to print things she considered positively ugly ("Prufrock," for example), but as a commentator on Stevens, she felt no such compulsion to tough-mindedness; she largely ignored the darker elements of *Harmonium*'s world and wholeheartedly praised Stevens's depiction of "the ineffable serenity of beauty." Her reading habits provided a built-in emotional supplement that meant "beauty," when recognized, did not need a basis in idea, hardly needed a "content" at all, but was a reassuring, satisfying emotional end in itself: "Beauty's imperishable perfection among shifting mortal shows is the incongruity at the heart of life which this poet accepts with the kind of serene laughter that covers pain" ("A Cavalier of Beauty," 327). Seiffert drew similar links between beauty and emotional consolation, concluding that "there is a background of gracious beauty behind Mr. Stevens' art that causes one to believe he is as happy as a poet is permitted to be" (160). If "gracious beauty" offered a satisfying consolation, however, it also substantially reduced the scope of poetry. Thus, even by his strongest supporters, Stevens was rendered less serious, more "minor," than he would come to be seen in later decades.

Readers such as Monroe and Seiffert were drawing their terms and criteria of evaluation largely from a genteel Paterian aestheticism. For them, the world of *Harmonium* was softened so much by its decorative exoticism that its harsher side could be overlooked. In her review, for example, Monroe portrayed Stevens's Florida as an overblown decorative idyll: "I should like to take my copy to some quiet sea-flung space in Florida, where a number of the poems were written. The sky, perhaps, is cobalt, with mauve-white clouds; the sea is sapphire, flicking into diamonds under the wind; the sand is a line of purplish rose, and there are gaudy bathers and loiterers on the beach. And here is a poet as sure of delight as nature herself, as serenely receptive of beauty" ("A Cavalier of Beauty," 323–24).

Monroe's easy identification of nature with delight and decoration derived from an aestheticist valorization of beauty over the darker Romantic sublime. In their characterization of Stevens, Monroe and Seiffert both chose to emphasize the Florida presented by his "Fabliau of Florida," a vividly observed but statically imagistic depiction of an exotic and beautiful landscape. Such readers were largely deaf to the voice of Stevens who, in another poem, called Florida "venereal soil" and spoke to its goddess thus:

> Lasciviously as the wind,
> You come tormenting,
> Insatiable,
>
> When you might sit,
> A scholar of darkness,
> Sequestered over the sea,
> Wearing a clear tiara
> Of red and blue and red,
> Sparkling, solitary, still
> In the high sea-shadow. [*CP,* 47]

Monroe and her Pateresque fellow readers obviously tried to become the elegant "scholars" of darkness that the lascivious goddess of Florida disorder refused to become for the poet.

Their fondness for decorative aestheticism somewhat incongruously made these genteel-modernist readers into Stevens's most wholehearted advocates through the 1920s. The strong emotional response they themselves supplied when confronted with poetic "beauty" carried them through modernism's revolutionary reconception of the principles of poetic form. As important as they were in the formation and maintenance of such institutions of modernist literature as *Poetry*, it is not too much to say that these readers were necessary for the remarkable success of contemporary poetry in the 1910s. Unlike professors of literature, they could articulate the continuity between nineteenth-century poetic values and poets like H.D., Pound, Lowell, and Stevens who used the newest formal tools. But by the mid-1920s, this mild-mannered fetishizing of beauty looked backward, not forward, and was gradually ceasing to function as a viable critical position. These readers' "persistent etherealizing"[7] of Stevens as the poetic "cavalier of beauty" was undoubtedly instrumental in engendering the widespread view of the poet's basic inconsequentiality among younger critics who, by the mid-1920s, had little interest in the rather old-fashioned poetics represented by Monroe and *Poetry*.[8]

Instead of the unqualified but limiting support of a Monroe, the most prevalent responses to *Harmonium* acknowledged Stevens's formal gifts but then hastened to add the important caveat that such a poetry, devoid as it was of emotion, power, directness, or passion, could only ever be "minor," to be enjoyed by aesthetes. The reviews of Untermeyer, Wilson, Fletcher, Van Doren, and Squire connected a central lack—of communicable emotion, typically— to their ultimate evaluations of Stevens: that formal perfection by itself was not enough to sustain first-rate poetry. Not coincidentally, these five represented the magazines with the widest influence and readership of those that reviewed *Harmonium* (except, perhaps, *The Dial*). For reviewers and readers of cultural magazines, as opposed to the little magazines, the quality of emotional and verbal accessibility in poetry was a canonical category, an element on which canonicity necessarily depended. Such preconceived valorizations of emotional expressiveness in poetry subordinated the value of sensory and intellectual stimulation to "the poignant utterance of . . . a moral passion" (Untermeyer, "The Ivory Tower II," 61). In these reviews the ultimate emphases of evaluation were shifted from primarily formal or decorative grounds to criteria of thematic accessibility, emotional expressiveness, or moral intensity, which produced their estimations of Stevens's ultimate insignificance: "Mr. Stevens, who is so observant and has so distinguished a fancy, seems to have emotion neither in abundance nor in intensity" (E. Wilson, "Wallace Stevens and E. E. Cummings" 102). This sort of review generally did not acknowledge the necessity of reaching a fuller understanding of Stevens's work, seeing him less as a poet who was there to stay than as a slightly frivolous curiosity of the times.

As the central critical representative of popular modernism, Untermeyer's responses were the most influential in the short run and the most revelatory of these canonical criteria. That Untermeyer's approach to the poet was a defensive counterattack against a discomfiting mode of art is suggested by his early and unrevised opinion of Stevens as a prototypical hyperaesthete in his debate with Aiken in the *New Republic* in 1919. There Stevens functioned as an example for Untermeyer's main theoretical argument, which disparaged the importance of form and drew direct links between ultraformalism and moral decadence:

> [The artist's] manner of expression is usually *fortuitous* and *always secondary*. When it assumes ... primary importance, it is accompanied by work that is technically adroit, fastidious, often sensitive but more often precious. . . . This is the *true minor note* and it is here that decadence begins. The overnice preoccupation with shades, the elaborate analysis of a spent emotion, the *false* emphasis on half-lights or a novel technique lead *inevitably* to The Yellow Book, to the mere verbal legerdemain of the Pound-Stevens-Arensberg-Others. ["The Ivory Tower II," 61; emphases added]

Stevens's evident rejection of this crude and defensive humanism meant that Untermeyer would dismiss his work as having "much for the eye, something for the ear, but nothing for that central hunger which is at the heart of all the senses" ("Among the New Books," 159).

Most readers involved in poetry in a professional capacity, as these mainstream reviewers were (and Stevens was not), could not accept their incomprehension as the result of a formal virtuoso straining for virtuosic effects or, more alarmingly, as a strategic effect of alienation of reader from author. Instead, they saw themselves as representatives of a "common" reader to whom a poet had the duty of communicating fairly directly. In light of their acknowledgements of Stevens's formal virtuosity, however, readers' objections to his obscurity produced an unusual set of problems, because it could not be dismissed as the product of artistic incompetence. Whether or not they liked the world of *Harmonium*, readers could see that Stevens had the verbal means to create a world exactly as he wanted it to be: "Even when you do not know what he is saying, you know that he is saying it well"; "This, I confess, beats me. . . . But . . . Mr. Stevens must always know what he means and what he is trying to do" (E. Wilson, "Wallace Stevens and E. E. Cummings," 102; Squire, 656). The result was a perceived disparity between the poet's formal accomplishments and what seemed to be a meaningless, cryptic, or iconoclastic substance inside the form. The magnitude of his formal authority meant that, with some of the most refined aesthetic tools the national literature had ever seen at disposal, Stevens seemed to be scoffing at the very idea of value in art. How to deal with this contradiction became the central problem for would-be Stevens critics, at least for the first two decades of his career; until it could be resolved, Stevens could not generally be seen as important.

In responding uneasily to the contradiction between form and function produced by *Harmonium*'s elegant obscurity, detractors and supporters alike perceived in Stevens's discourse a disturbing or threatening quality of radical otherness, to the extent that the poems seemed to be written in a completely different language: "Upon deliberate examination it appears Stevens's matter is the perfectly grammatical arrangement of an English vocabulary. . . . But so novel and fantastic is the tintinnabulation of unusual words . . . that you nearly overlook the significations, and hear outlandish sharp and melting musics" (Rosenfeld, 35).

There was thus no "real" emotion or human situation in Stevens's work: "It is an 'absolute' poetry . . . of syllabic tone and color which, separate from any relation to the human element, aims to exist and blossom by itself in a pure aestheticism" (Untermeyer, *American Poetry Since 1900*, 324). This otherness was closely related to the observation that the poet was engaged in an alienating and obsessive quest for what Squire called "complete individuality and detachment": "he will repeat no creed mechanically, look at nothing through another man's eyes, use no clichés, be drugged by the easy melody of no established form." Unable to accept a redefinition of poetry in Stevens's terms, commentators projected their own alienated exhaustion onto the author: "It is a superhuman task; and the struggle . . . leaves him, as it must leave all who undertake it, a little exhausted" (Squire, 657). Unlike Squire, Van Doren understood that the effects of this quest were felt more by the audience than by the author but still concluded with a disparagement of Stevens's importance:

"What public will care for a poet who strains every nerve every moment to be unlike anyone else who ever wrote?" (Van Doren, 159).

Most explicitly damaging was the perception that, in view of his verbal command, the poet's obscurity had to be deliberate. For readers like Untermeyer, being "deliberately cryptic" made Stevens ethically deficient in not upholding his end of the communicative contract between writer and reader. He was guilty of "a determined obscurity, an obscurity of intention as well as an uncertainty of communication," which suggested a complete disregard for the well-being of an audience: "many pages . . . lead one to doubt whether its author even cares to communicate in a tongue familiar to the reader" ("Among the New Books," 159). This "caring" was the most important revelation of the aesthetic moralism of the 1920s; a poet was supposed to "care" about, and for, his audience's "hunger," and it was exactly this overt ministration to an imagined audience that the poetics of *Harmonium* rejected.

For most readers of the 1920s, then, *Harmonium* remained a jumble of suave sounds, uninhibited wordplay, and disturbing but oblique sentiments that fit neither traditional conceptions of poetry nor any familiar avant-garde model. Together these poems presented an antihumanistic redefinition of the poetic subject that readers of the 1920s could not accept. Further, the poems made their challenge not with stridency but with a cool equanimity, as a kind of cosmic first principle about which their creator simply refused to debate. Many poems seemed to demand implicitly that readers stop looking for meaning and just enjoy the sensuous impressions produced by the words. These subversive stylistic strategies suggested that art was no longer a transmission of intelligible meaning between creator and reader but an affective formal occurrence whose total uniqueness was more likely to produce a disconcerting sense of alienation from the poet.[9] Stevens's poetry appeared repeatedly to undermine the usefulness and importance of poetic utterance itself, asking readers to put into question the period's dominant evaluative criterion for artistic endeavor: that it address that central emotional "hunger" Untermeyer had posited as the ground of all great art. Readers whose intellectual and institutional identities were bound up in assumptions of the value of art were bound to reject what seemed to be a continual search in *Harmonium* for "new leaf and shadowy tinct" to amuse oneself with and then to discard.

The most fundamental of these subversive mannerisms, a hyper-formalistic delight in the play of "suave sounds" seemingly for their own sake, troubled early detractors, who often turned defensively to patronizing: "Stevens displays an almost childish love of alliteration and assonance (one can only smile indulgently at 'Chieftain Iffucan of Azcan in caftan')" (Untermeyer, "Among the New Books," 160). As Untermeyer suggested here, Stevens's characteristic play of dazzling sonorities was experienced most spectacularly of all in "Bantams in Pine-Woods," where it completely overwhelmed the poem's ostensible philosophical content:

> Chieftain Iffucan of Azcan in caftan
> Of tan in henna hackles, halt!
>
> Damned universal cock, as if the sun
> Was blackamoor to bear your blazing tail.
>
> Fat! Fat! Fat! Fat! I am the personal.
> Your world is you. I am my world.
>
> You ten-foot poet among inchlings. Fat!
> Begone! An inchling bristles in these pines,
>
> Bristles, and points their Appalachian tangs,
> And fears not portly Azcan nor his hoos. [CP, 75–76]

Untermeyer's disparagement of this poem was highly indicative of the period's widespread evaluative preconceptions. Because for Untermeyer form and content were separable, the overwhelming assonance of the first lines, which had little to do with the "content" of the chieftain's costume, emptied the poem of meaning. For Stevens, these sonorities constituted the invention of linguistic colors and thus a fusion of form and content, which asserted that meaning and value were to be found in the internal play of the poem as a linguistic whole.

The poems of *Harmonium* were difficult enough for readers to understand; if anything, their titles were even more obscure and bizarre: "Jasmine's Beautiful Thoughts Under the Willow," "Tea at the Palaz of Hoon," "The Paltry Nude Starts on a Spring Voyage," "Homunculus et la Belle Etoile," "The Emperor of Ice-Cream," "Le Monocle de Mon Oncle," "Anecdote of Men by the Thousand," "Gubbinal." A glance over the table of contents, at the full range of titles, still brings home to beginning readers the difficulty of access into Stevens's poems; on a reader accustomed to the "Songs and Sonnets" of the 1910s, their impact must have been even more intense. Far from being guides to what followed, these wild titles announced that the reader was entering a world ruled by a mind that would do exactly as it liked regardless of poetic convention: even title a fifteen-line poem with a four-sentence bit of doggerel, complete with a-b-c-b rhyme and a predominantly regular meter ("Frogs Eat Butterflies. Snakes Eat Frogs. Hogs Eat Snakes. Men Eat Hogs"). Van Doren, Untermeyer, Fletcher, Squire, and Wilson all expressed irritation or wonderment at the titles in their reviews. The only way most commentators could resolve the problem of Stevens's titles was again to resort to counterattacks against their ostensibly pointless obscurity. The most common objection to the titles was that they willfully refused to have anything to do with the poems themselves.[10] Early readers were forced to dismiss the titles as yet another nonsensical color mannerism of the sort they saw everywhere in Stevens. To judge from a 1935 anecdote in which a bemused Stevens remarked that a Wesleyan student had once arrived for a visit "under the impression that there was no relation whatever between the titles and the poems," this view was actually being taught to students (L, 297).

The titles of *Harmonium* asserted the rejection of the conventions and traditions of communicative poetry most comprehensively, perhaps, in continually signifying new formal structures that the poet, unfettered by poetic tradition, had simply invented at will. In *Harmonium* there were five "anecdotes," a "colloquy," an "inscription," an "anatomy," a "meditation," a "sonatina," an "invective," an "explanation," "landscapes," a "theory," a "cortege," a "fabliau," a "hymn," "metaphors," and "nuances of a theme." Stevens's formal terms tended to come from regions so far removed from lyric poetry—from philosophy, art, science, religion, baroque music, oratory—that they travestied not just particular existing forms but the whole notion of a conventional poetic form with mutually referring and reinforcing attributes that had made such genres of lyric poetry as the sonnet and the ode into important cultural forms.[11] Few of Stevens's "forms" had a conventional length, foot, meter, or anything else. It is little wonder that they seemed to early critics to have no relation to the poems that followed, since they existed in no prior frame of poetic reference. By inventing forms rather than using existing ones, Stevens remained in a realm of his own generic creation, which could be directly set against no one else's poetry because no one else had used them. He had made his poetry literally incomparable, and this was not conducive to the development of an assured or articulate critical reception.

The poems of *Harmonium* thus offered to readers an avant-garde creator-persona who rejected existing poetic models, implicitly claiming unlimited authority to remake the genre. Much of Stevens's later work was to attempt a synthesis of this poet-figure intent on his own interactions with a dynamic and challenging environment, making it easier for readers to read him in terms of a more or less conventionally romantic creative subject. Here, however, the prevailing drift of this poetic world was entropic: *Harmonium* encouraged no recourse to a "supreme fiction," rage for order, or other such consolatory solution but often seemed purposely to invoke and enjoy the chaos of the universe. The disconcerting unconventionality of *Harmonium* did not stop with a celebration of the creator as an individual mind who became his own world and its omnipotent god as well, the sort of Pateresque solipsism with which the Seiffert/Monroe reader was happy to remain content.[12] With characteristic rigor, *Harmonium* rejected the notion that even the poet could control the workings of his own chaotic native land and language. Poems large and small extended the collapse of belief in the seriousness of poetic expression seen in "Bantams in Pine-Woods" to its logical conclusion by presenting personae who found in sudden moments of clear-headed detachment that whatever imaginative satisfactions they could produce would be evanescent and often illusory, threatening to dissolve into radically self-conscious parody. These subversions were particularly strong in the weird little ditties that seemed to deal with poetry such as "Ploughing on Sunday," "The Plot Against the Giant," "Metaphors of a Magnifico," "Negation," and "Explanation." For example, using the conventional figure of poet as metaphysical creator, "Negation" acknowledged the rage for order which kept the creative imagination going, yet asserted the inevitable failure of this "incapable master" to circumscribe the world with his mind. There was no "harmonious whole," only "his" version of it, incomplete, even illusory (*CP*, 97–98). Most drastically, "Explanation" acknowledged the Gallicism of Stevens's poetic descent and orientation, but its weird conversational Teutonism and its total disregard for the conventions of the poetic line would have given readers an understandably difficult time in accepting its creator as a serious poet:

> Ach, Mutter,
> This old, black dress,
> I have been embroidering
> French flowers on it.
>
> Not by way of romance,
> Here is nothing of the ideal,
> Nein,
> Nein. [CP 72]

None of these poems was assimilated by early commentators, who relegated them to the margins of Stevens's oeuvre in favor of the more high-flown exploration of the subject found in "To the One of Fictive Music." Placed a page or two away from ostensibly serious, "valuable" utterances like "Le Monocle de Mon Oncle" and "Sunday Morning," poems such as "Negation" and "Explanation" helped to further the pervasive contradiction of form and function within *Harmonium,* but perhaps the most effective presentation of this contradiction came not in the totality of the volume but within a single poem which could not be marginalized or ignored. The great ode to the earth "Sunday Morning" stood, as Stevens commentators knew, at the head of his career like a first, audacious declaration of principles. Though most early discussion found enough conventionally "poetic" material to approve of it in a general way, there are strong indications that it too posed difficulties for early readers.

First of all, *Harmonium* offered readers a very different version of "Sunday Morning" from the one they had seen in *Poetry* in 1915. In *Poetry,* the fifth and final stanza, now recognized as the seventh stanza, had expressed the exalted paganism of "a ring of men" chanting "Their boisterous devotion to the sun" (*CP,* 69–70). This ecstasy of human physical feeling, the only divinity of humankind, would then be recreated and sustained by echo throughout the environment.[13] In *Harmonium,* however, this ringing affirmation of human and natural coexistence was no longer the poem's final emphasis. It was followed by an eighth stanza in which Stevens's persona massively qualified his own construction and brought his divine concept of death down to earth with a resounding thud. Just as the tomb of Jesus was only a cave "where he lay" in physical death, the earth was merely a place where humans live and then die, "an old chaos of the sun" in which the processes of life, embodied by deer and "casual flocks of pigeons," went on oblivious to the echoing chants of human meaning.[14] The imposing position of "Sunday Morning" within Stevens's oeuvre made this subversive ending more than simply another assertion of the world's chaotic meaninglessness. The poem's subject matter, formal precision, and glorious blank-verse line all fostered the expectation of a strong affirmation of man's existence and artistry. The last stanza then functioned to do just the opposite, implying that such an affirmation was no more than an invention of the human mind which tended to vanish once the field of vision was broadened to include the inhuman realities of the earth.

To confront the poem's last stanza thus is to understand better why the eighth-stanza version of "Sunday Morning," submitted to *Poetry* in 1915 as it would appear in *Harmonium*, had disturbed Monroe into editorial butchery. It must have been incomprehensible to her that the poet would have meant to end on such an anticlimactic note. At that time, Stevens's extreme newness on the scene (and his personal unfamiliarity to her) no doubt enabled her to see his arrangement as the odd fruit of artistic inexperience. Following her own muse, which counseled ending with those triumphantly echoing human chants, she placed Stevens's seventh stanza last. By restoring the original stanzaic order in *Harmonium*, Stevens exerted a corrective authority on a misreading which was much unlike his usual diffidence and which demonstrated the emotional and intellectual stringency that separated him from the genteel aestheticism of Monroe. The disturbing effects of "Sunday Morning" also produced Arthur Davison Ficke's bizarre and often quoted remark: " 'Sunday Morning' tantalized me with the sense that perhaps it's the most beautiful poem ever written, or perhaps just an incompetent obscurity."[15] The total incommensurability of these two alternatives indicated Ficke's sense of the extent to which the poem challenged readers' conventional dualisms of form and meaning. Whatever else he meant by it, Ficke certainly implied, as Fletcher and Kreymborg later openly acknowledged, that "Sunday Morning" eluded the understanding—which a poem of spectacular affirmation should not do.

The poet's policy of singling out poetry as a source of ultimately trivial expression was cemented in *Harmonium* by the first appearance of "The Comedian as the Letter C," an apparently ludicrous poetic odyssey that many took as an expression of Stevens's own disinterest in his art, "an autobiographical confession of withdrawal," as Untermeyer claimed ("Among the New

Books," 160). In *Poetry*, Monroe's worried response to Stevens/Crispin's apparent threat to give up poetry shifted his lack of interest onto the more comprehensible ground of creative blockage: "We must hope that the poem is not strictly autobiographical, that Mr. Stevens, unlike his baffled hero, will get his story uttered" ("A Cavalier of Beauty," 327). Despite its obvious ambitions to centrality (length, genre, subject, autobiographicality), "The Comedian" checked early readers (and does so even now) through its thoroughgoing absurdity of language. The "nincompated pedagogue" that readers encountered seemed less an important poetic mind than the valet-clown his name implied. The clipped ending of Crispin's odyssey, "So may the relation of each man be clipped" (*CP*, 46), which sounded as if the poet had suddenly just gotten tired and walked away, perturbed readers like Seiffert who wanted more of a climactic closure to a "major" poem. This, she felt, was "a last line one might well resent, had last lines any significance in this poem" (Seiffert, 155). Unhappy with the feeling that the poet's deliberations over his endeavors suddenly seemed to him of little consequence, Seiffert stretched credulity with the implication that the poem was either so randomly constructed or frivolous that its last line could plausibly have no special significance.

With the publication of "The Comedian," there was now another major addition—the growth of the poet's mind—to the core of value-laden genres that Stevens had been subverting. Once again, his treatment of a conventional mode had violated readers' expectations of what an important poem about self-expression was to be, instead depicting the "disintegration of the artist's personality" (Fletcher, "The Revival of Aestheticism," 356). This remark by Fletcher is most interesting in its evocation of the strange, elusive "personality" that readers detected behind the gaudy linguistic surface of Stevens's poetry. Most obviously with "The Comedian," but with the rest of *Harmonium* as well, they tended to associate this poetry closely with a particular personality. That so little was known about the man meant that what was said in a Stevens poem was necessarily part of Stevens himself. In an unusual sense, then, all of Stevens's poems were seen as highly autobiographical. This narrowly autobiographical emphasis has persisted in the writing of such later Stevens critics as Harold Bloom and Helen Vendler, further obscuring the poet's engagement with his times and society. The more immediate consequence of this identification was that the avant-garde disturbances adduced in those poems were made more difficult to reconcile by what little was known or could be detected from the behavior and demeanor of Stevens the man, which further confounded serious evaluation of the poet. If Stevens seemed to take his own poetry so utterly lightly, how seriously could earnest critics take it?

Throughout the 1920s, Stevens seemed to most readers to be almost totally indifferent to, even contemptuous of, the notion of poetic activity or a poetic career as having any value. As early as 1920, Fletcher had noted Stevens's seeming disinterest in his art by detecting a link between the poet and the title character of his play *Carlos* [Wallace?] *Among the Candles*: "It is obvious that in the figure of this 'eccentric pedant of about forty' who lights candles in a darkened room in order to fill his life with magnificence, and then blows them out again because he prefers the darkness outside, Stevens has symbolised much of his attitude to life" ("Some Contemporary American Poets," 29).

In *A Critical Fable* in 1922 Amy Lowell put this prevailing view into verse, imagining that occasionally Stevens noticed that

> . . . he has a poem if he'll trouble to bale it,
> Address it to 'Poetry,' and afterwords mail it.
> His name, though the odds overbalance the evens
> Of those who don't know it as yet's Wallace Stevens,
> But it might be John Doe for all he seems to care—
> A little fine work scattered into the air
> By the wind, it appears, and he quite unaware
> Of the fact, since his motto's a cool '*laisser-faire.*'
> [*A Critical Fable*, 97]

In their remarks on *Harmonium*, Untermeyer, Kreymborg, Monroe, and Fletcher all mentioned Stevens's casualness, reticence, abstemiousness, lack of interest.

With individual poems such as "Sunday Morning," commentators generally could not articulate these subversions of the value of the creative process that were so problematic to them, but the dominant impression perceived by the readers of *Harmonium* was of a poet who exhibited an almost complete disinterest in the fate of his own creations—a self-portrayal that prevented even such impressive efforts as "Sunday Morning" and "Le Monocle de mon Oncle" from achieving the heights of the contemporary poetic canon. Especially those readers who knew Stevens, or knew of his personal manner, were pressured to acknowledge both his authority as a distinctively talented writer and, paradoxically, his authoritative assertions of the ephemerality of artistic utterance. The strategies Stevens used to defend his privacy emerged in a way that not only repelled possible invaders but often trivialized his own role as poet. Kreymborg's account of his first meeting with Stevens in 1915 showed that Stevens habitually rejected the pleasantry of receiving compliments on his work: "[Kreymborg] visualized a slender, ethereal being, shy and sensitive. The man he was introduced to was shy and sensitive, but so broad-shouldered and burly that Krimmie was overawed. He tried to refer to Tea [just published in Allen Norton's *Rogue*], but the tall man waved a deprecating hand and muttered something that sounded like 'Jesus.' Norton drew Krimmie aside and explained: 'Cornering Wallace about his own work isn't done,' " (*Troubador*, 219).

In his autobiography, Carl Zigrosser presented a remembrance of the late 1910s which extended Stevens's reluctance with the role of poet into a slightly obsessive fetish for privacy in all matters artistic: "Stevens was rather secretive in manner. He once said to me at the gallery, "Don't tell anybody that I come in here"; and I had the feeling that when he went out of the gallery door, he glanced up and down the avenue to make sure that no one caught him in the act.... It could be that the fear of being considered 'bohemian' was genuine at first, but later became a habit and a kind of pose" (84).

In these years Stevens's physical and social impenetrability was matched by a polite yet determined reticence towards his private life. Even to direct requests for personal details, Stevens would refuse or give the sketchiest of replies. Monroe's first attempt in November 1914 was met with this (false) reply: "My autobiography is, necessarily, very brief, for I have published nothing" (*L*, 182). Seven months later he broke down and revealed himself thus: "I was born in Reading, Pennsylvania, am thirty-five years old, a lawyer, reside in New York and have published no books" (*L*, 183). Even eight years later, when Stevens was relatively widely known in modernist circles, this miserliness continued. He wrote *Dial* managing editor Gilbert Seldes in 1922: "Do, please excuse me from the biographical note. I am a lawyer and live in Hartford. But such facts are neither gay nor instructive" (*L*, 227). For whatever reasons Stevens employed these strategies of extreme reticence, their function was to contribute to an image of the poet which did not make more palatable the strange subversions of the role of poetry detected in his work.[16]

Far from evincing interest in his own work or anybody else's, Stevens's reticence included an apparently complete lack of concern with any kind of literary notoriety. His refusal to bring out a volume of his work until nine years after he began publishing is only the most apparent neglect of his poetic "career." A revealing line from Amy Lowell's *A Critical Fable* explicitly connected this refusal with Stevens's self-created literary persona: "He has published no book and adopts this as pose" (97). In 1929 Kreymborg facetiously implied that Stevens had finally agreed to publish *Harmonium* only because he was too little interested in the issue even to refuse any longer: "bored with being the sole poet who had not published a book, [Stevens] permitted Carl Van Vechten to cajole Alfred Knopf into printing *Harmonium*" (*Our Singing Strength*, 500).[17] Unlike most ambitious poets, Stevens had written no prose to give his poetry any poetical or philosophical buttressing or to link his work with great traditions. He did no campaigning of any kind for attention, declining to see literary acquaintances often or intimately, refusing to make the trip to suburban Grantwood, New Jersey, for *Others* meetings, only attending when he could make a quick getaway into the sheltering streets of Manhattan, then leaving for Hartford in 1916. He simply sent his poems off, with little or no comment.

Furthermore, Stevens made certain choices that could only have been counterproductive to his reputation: for example, the poem he chose to send to Kreymborg's American compilation for London's *Chapbook* in 1923, to become his first poem originally published in Great Britain, was the hilariously effete "Mandolin and Liqueurs," which he did not favor enough to include in *Harmonium*. This poem's self-parody is apparent enough to those familiar with Stevens's work, but it must have created an impression of insufferable preciosity to those many British readers who had never encountered another line from this poet. In 1927 this selection rebounded against Stevens's British reputation when Laura Riding and Robert Graves published their astringent *Survey of Modernist Poetry* in London, ferociously dismissing Stevens as producing "frivolousness" in the company of such "so-called authors" as Aldington, Pound, and Williams. The main example of Stevens quoted in that condemnation was, of course, "Mandolin and Liqueurs" (Riding and Graves, 166, 216). No doubt partially as a result of this poem's prominence in Britain, and of the impact of the Riding/Graves book, the British suspicion that Stevens was a simpering lutanist of effete fleas lingered for decades.[18]

A significant neglect of his American reputation came in December of 1923, when, as Nicholas Joost reports, *Dial* editor Scofield Thayer invited Stevens to contribute new poems to form part of a package to commemorate the publication of *Harmonium* and to include a highly favorable review by Marianne Moore and a critical essay (the first ever on Stevens alone) by Llewellyn Powys. Stevens could not have been unaware of the success of *The Dial*'s efforts on Eliot's behalf one year before, when *The Waste Land* was published along with a laudatory essay by Edmund Wilson and the announcement that Eliot had won *The Dial* award. Now it was Stevens's turn to be feted, if he would let it happen, but he put the magazine off for several months, until finally Moore's piece was run by itself. The separation of her review, much more laudatory than the Powys essay, and the overall delay dissipated the impact of the plan. Stevens finally sent in "Sea Surface Full of Clouds," which appeared with Powys's "The Thirteenth Way" in July 1924, nearly a year after *Harmonium* had come out. Joost has described Stevens's behavior as a "rebuff" to *The Dial*, which is inaccurate in the sense that Stevens undoubtedly was genuinely distracted; but more importantly, it may well have been perceived by *The Dial* as a rebuff (199–200). That Stevens never published again in *The Dial* was his own doing, and in 1928 he missed out on a probable *Dial* award because he had not submitted anything for so long. According to William Wasserstrom, Stevens was Sibley Watson's "prime candidate"; but Moore, usually a strong Stevens advocate, acted a bit like a rebuffed editor and suggested Kenneth Burke instead, to whom the last award went (126).

Stevens's ultracasual attitude towards the fate of his work appeared not only in the poems themselves but, as Untermeyer suggested, in his apparent opinions of them. With what Ellen Williams calls, interestingly, "superhuman detachment," Stevens had let Monroe cut up "Sunday Morning" on its first publication (E. Williams, 158). This apparent unconcern for the fate of even his most significant work cannot be wholly dismissed as the timidity of a new man on the poetic scene, since by 1922, not only was he still sending disclaiming messages to editors, but he had even developed the form into an amusing subgenre in itself. To Seldes of *The Dial* he wrote: "I have no desire to be persnickety about the arrangement of the group, except to make a good beginning and a good end. Accordingly, it does not matter how you arrange the poems, if you begin with The Bantams and end with The Emperor [good audience-alienating strategy, by the way]. Do as you like about the hog poem; that is to say, you can include it as one of the group or publish it separately" (*L*, 227).

Manifesting a lack of interest in his work which allowed him to describe it in terms like "the hog poem" (why not "the frog poem," at least?), Stevens's actions continually forced his observers to ponder the position of a poet who considered his most brilliant works as nothing more than "crisp salad" plucked "from the garbage of the past" (L, 232). Reflecting in her autobiography on a quarter-century of close acquaintance with American poets, Harriet Monroe concluded that "of all the poets I have ever met, Stevens is the most indifferent to the fate of his works after they have emerged from his mind" (*A Poet's Life*, 391).

Stevens's meager comments about his poetry during this period furthered the confounding function it served for many early readers. In a 1928 reply to an anthologist who had asked for clarification of the meaning of some poems, and who thus functioned as a representative of his baffled audience, Stevens asserted explicitly that the meaning of a poem (in this case, "Domination of Black") inhered not in its ostensible ideas but only in the emotional and even physical effects conveyed by its verbal texture: "I am sorry that a poem of this sort has to contain any ideas at all, because its sole purpose is to fill the mind with the images & sounds it creates."[19]

In this same letter the poet's treatment of "Sunday Morning" functioned similarly to undercut the poem as an object of value when he reduced it to "simply an expression of paganism," but true to form, Stevens was not even content to leave himself in a position of control as a knowing celebrator of paganism. He continued that same sentence: "of course, I did not think that I was expressing paganism when I wrote it." Because the poem expresses nothing but paganism, and that only unintentionally, he seemed to imply that he had no intention of "expressing" anything at all. Stevens concluded his comment on "Sunday Morning" by dismissing the fundamental critical desire to understand and articulate a poem's "meaning": "Now these ideas are not bad in a poem. But they are a frightful bore when converted as above" (L, 250–251).

Stevens's unconcern for his own poetic stature reached a sort of perverse climax between 1924, just after "Sea Surface Full of Clouds" was published, and 1930, with his complete withdrawal from publication and the literary scene. *Harmonium* had quickly fallen out of print and, as Kreymborg saw it, Stevens would not "make the slightest effort to revive and reprint it" (*Our Singing Strength*, 504). For about six years he said to inquirers that he had nothing to send them, that his time was totally swallowed up by his insurance career. Commentators gradually came to feel that the creator of these "most perfect" things in poetry had decided that the world of business was not only equal to but more important than the world of poetry. As the poems themselves had done, his actions evoked the contradiction of that most accomplished of artists who seemed to care nothing for art, thus calling into question the whole complex of attitudes which had taken for granted the value of artistic endeavor as superior to worldly efforts.

Whether he had meant to or not, through the 1920s Stevens had portrayed himself as a man lacking all trace of interest in his poetic activity. By creating this mysteriously aloof yet authoritative persona in his life and in his poems, and then leaving unanswered the questions his existence raised—especially, "What, if any, is the value of poetry?"—Stevens denied readers any reassurance or resolution. During his hiatus through the rest of the decade, anthologists and editors from across the poetic spectrum felt compelled to urge Stevens to publish more, to reveal more of himself. Even unsympathetic commentators could not ignore the lack of resolution presented by Stevens's withdrawal. Untermeyer's puzzled discomfort was evident in his repeated descriptions of Stevens in the editions of *Modern American Poetry* as "a poet of peculiar reticences" whose "attitude to his work is, in itself, significant" (1925 edition, 326). Not only was he reticent but unnaturally so, Untermeyer implied; poets should not simply stop publishing for business. (After all, Untermeyer himself managed to make a business of poetry for sixty years.)

In 1929 Kreymborg was more obviously frustrated in the following remark, the last sentence of which switched into an elegiac past tense to lay Stevens's career to rest: "Formerly, it was impossible to get him to publish a book; now it is impossible to get him to publish a poem. Write him, wire him or visit him, one always receives the same answer: he has written nothing for years. . . . Continued self-deprecation has finally removed the man from the scene in which he had always refused to participate. He wrote purely for the pleasure of writing, as he has lived purely for the pleasure of living" (*Our Singing Strength*, 500). Kreymborg concluded forlornly that the poet had captured himself in these last lines of "The Wind Shifts":

> This is how the wind shifts:
> Like a human, heavy and heavy,
> Who does not care. (*Our Singing Strength*, 504).

By decade's end Stevens had finally succeeded in making his strongest early champions doubt his commitment to being a serious poet.

The astonishingly disinterested persona that Stevens had created for himself undoubtedly contributed to the difficulties encountered by supporters who attempted to reconcile his virtuosity with their own conceptions of what poetry should or could be. Mired in the reductive duality of genteel beauty vs. real human emotion, American criticism lacked a methodology or terminology that could bring forth an understanding of the richness of Stevens's methods. A widespread respect for this poetry's formal polish, coupled with a nearly universal lack of comprehension, did not add up to a viable criticism. Those few readers who openly acknowledged Stevens as important could not effectively articulate their evaluations. Only a few of them produced any significant commentary on him; none of that, at least in the 1920s, was useful in promoting a canon-shaping advocacy.

The only remotely argumentative defense of the poetics of *Harmonium* was attempted by Raymond Holden, a young poet writing in *The Measure*. Even in asserting Stevens's importance, Holden was forced to agree that "there will be much difference of opinion . . . as to the thickness of the strata in which Mr. Stevens's metal is to be found." Then he attempted, very tentatively, to "establish some *arbitrary* standard of measurement" for characterizing Stevens's words as "having a value *separate from their meaning in terms of human speech*" (emphases added). Holden put forward an argument that, like many early views of *Harmonium*, had recourse to the childlike or irrational sides of human experience and expression: "It is not, therefore, stretching the point to any dangerous degree, to say that there is, in syllables written and pronounced, a sense value different from, if not *entirely independent* of, their meaning to the literate mind. After all it is the *illiterate portion of the mind* which covets the subtler music of the world. I feel that Mr. Stevens had [sic] addressed himself to this covetousness with conspicuous success" (17; emphases added).

At the end of this self-disintegrating passage a reader might well have wondered exactly what Stevens had succeeded in doing, and what was the value of having done it. The obvious terminological strain encountered in Holden's attempt to praise Stevens and the solitariness of his defense show that in 1923 an honest effort to assimilate Stevens's work by defining a new conception of poetry was nearly inconceivable.

Of all the reviewers of *Harmonium*, only Marianne Moore, another poet long associated with Stevens, also "obscure" in prose as well as poetry, seemed really comfortable with the book, neither ignoring it, attacking it, distorting it, or apologizing for it. Moore was the only reviewer to see in Stevens's work a bristling, savage eloquence, figuring the poet as a successful lion among mice in her title ("Well Moused, Lion") and, in her last sentence, asserting Stevens's centrality in the redefinition of poetic value in a tougher, more concrete direction: "In the event of moonlight and a veil to be made gory, [Crispin/Stevens] would, one feels, be appropriate in this legitimately sensational act of a ferocious jungle animal" ("Well Moused, Lion," 91). Moore's approbation of Stevens's avant-garde methods was, however, itself a highly imaginative and opaque performance that could have had little impact on the unconverted.

Though the three critical essays on Stevens published in the mid-1920s did at least mean a new level of interest in him as a continuing presence who had produced a body of work rather than mere fragments, ultimately all they could do was to continue the ambivalent, listless approval of most of the *Harmonium* reviews. Their authors—Llewellyn Powys, Paul Rosenfeld, and Gorham Munson—were all young enough to suspect that Stevens was not to be dismissed but not young or intellectually rigorous enough to play a part in the development of analytical criticism of modernism that began in earnest in the early 1930s. Their pieces, like the reviews, were not so much analyses as impressionistic appraisals that exhibited a familiar enervating tension between form and content, between Stevens's impressive virtuosity and his discomforting triviality.

The essays of Powys and Rosenfeld, published in 1924, both gave high marks to Stevens as an "impeccable craftsman" (Rosenfeld, 40), but they eventually undermined their praise by drifting towards a view of the poet as an exemplum of a well-known, even clichéd, notion of the 1890s as a time of coy, precious, and excruciatingly self-conscious aestheticism. Rosenfeld portrayed the poet rather patronizingly as a Laforgueian "Pierrot," "leaning in evident boredom against the corner of a mantelpiece, or adjusting his monocle with a look of martyrdom," and summed up both pieces when he suggested that "*Harmonium* does not . . . entirely represent the day. . . . The characteristic note of 1890 was not outworn for us ten years ago; and yet, today . . . we have transcended it. . . . An impulse in us bids authors be more simple and direct, and give completely what they feel" (Rosenfeld, 40). Rosenfeld's contempt for the aesthetics of the recent past, and his attempt to situate Stevens firmly in that past rather than see him as having "transcended" it, boiled down, as with Untermeyer, to a valorization of emotional openness to the audience.

By the time of *Harmonium*, these critical values (and Rosenfeld himself as their most florid exponent) were under attack from young avant-gardists such as the publishers of *Secession* and *Broom*, including Matthew Josephson, Harold Loeb, Kenneth Burke, and Malcolm Cowley. Some of this crowd, and especially the "director" of *Secession*, Gorham Munson, had been consistently praising Stevens and a few of his *Others* compeers since the beginning of the 1920s.[20] A thoroughly radical aesthete, Stevens seemed to cut the kind of indomitably individual and detached swath through the cultural jungle that Munson wanted to achieve by publishing *Secession*.[21] Although they were able to see Stevens as perhaps the most accomplished poet of their age, among them only Munson would manage to do any significant work on Stevens through the decade. When it came time to wrestle with the ultimate value of such poets, even Munson could only go so far with Stevens's avant-garde play as a basis for poetry. Apparently the established evaluative patterns of even the avant-garde literary-critical mind of the 1920s simply would not allow the use of Stevens as a poetic or cultural model.

Nevertheless Munson's "The Dandyism of Wallace Stevens," published in *The Dial* in 1925 and revised for his 1928 volume *Destinations*, was the most important of the decade's essays on Stevens, both because of what it did accomplish and what it could not. Munson's work crystallized existing views of the poet in establishing a convenient term with which to label him. This epithet of "dandy," obviously implicit in Rosenfeld's essay as well, stuck to critical writing on Stevens for years. In 1929 Allen Tate felt that Munson had "ably described" Stevens's dandyism, but in the same year Kreymborg took issue with what he saw as a damaging label, insisting that "Stevens is more than a dandy, a designer, an aesthete" (Tate, 85; Kreymborg, *Our Singing Strength*, 500–501). Morton Zabel voiced similar objections in 1931 ("The *Harmonium* of Wallace Stevens," 153), while in reviewing *Ideas of Order* in 1936, F. O. Matthiessen asserted that Stevens's dandyism had by then disappeared ("Society and Solitude in Poetry," 606). Thirty-nine years after Munson's essay, Carl Zigrosser paid tribute to the accuracy of that formulation in the opinion of the age by remarking that "somehow the word dandiacal [sic] always turns up in my mind to sum up [Stevens's] character and presence" (84). In best summing up the ambivalent critical position on Stevens in the 1920s, Munson's essay also exemplified the general inability to grant the poet's majority. Clearly the term "dandy," supposedly conceived in sympathy with the poet, actually functioned as a judgment similar to the derogatory evaluations of Stevens as an amoral hedonist by Rosenfeld, Powys, and even Untermeyer: "Is there not fundamentally a kinship between the sensory discriminations and comfortable tranquility of Wallace Stevens' poetry and the America that owns baronial estates?" ("The Dandyism of Wallace Stevens," 44).

The other major evaluative distinction Munson developed in his essay on Stevens, between major and minor poetry, which was derived from Eliot's elevation of Dryden's minority over Milton's majority, provided another apparently affirmative description of Stevens's methods. But like "dandyism," the major/minor formulation carried considerable derogatory evaluative baggage that ultimately could not help but valorize Eliot himself at Stevens's expense:

> What is the distinction between major and minor? It appears to me that there exists none in detail or craftsmanship but that it is to be discovered in the pattern in which details are set and *the purpose for which craft is employed*. There is a difference in scope. The effort of the major poet is to be comprehensive *and* precise, whereas the minor poet values precision alone. There is a difference in purpose. The great poet's aim is to see *totalities*, to treat his experience, to treat *life*, as a whole. The minor poet is content with *fragments* of his experience, even with the *isolated* perception. [Munson, *Destinations*, 93; emphases added]

Once more the complex concepts of craft and form were reduced to being overlays to a deeper separate "purpose," involving "life, as a whole." The final result in Munson was a highly conventional evaluation of Stevens, along with his comrades Moore and Williams, as being "in the last analysis minor," with all of that term's usual pejorative connotations (*Destinations*, 9). Munson's failure to achieve an articulate and wholehearted advocacy of Stevens, despite having given off many indications that he was willing and able to do so, and his consistency in applying the same evaluative criteria to the other writers he associated with Stevens are indications of the general prevalence of the major/minor distinction as a canonical category. Despite their aversion to Eliot's Waste Land ethos, writers such as Munson still felt forced into acknowledging its majority as an attempt to take in and express "totalities" of experience.

By most of the decade's major critical evaluations, then, Stevens was seen, quite incorrectly according to later evaluations, as a poet of minor aspirations and as a consciousness of the genteel aestheticist past, rather than as one central to the development of modernism. Acceptance into the relatively narrow realm of the avant-garde little magazines, which Stevens had achieved with *Harmonium*, had not meant infusion into the wider streams of American cultural discourse in the 1920s, much less into a general readership. Having seemed to both Untermeyer and Aiken an exemplar of "pure" aesthetic poetry in 1919, Stevens was virtually shut out of the evaluative hegemony that had thrust such popular modernists as Robinson, Frost, and Sandburg to national prominence even before the end of the 1910s. Despite the inroads towards cultural centrality that the new poetry had made by 1923, through the decade a poet like Stevens could still be embraced only by an oppositional avant-garde. Yet there is very little evidence of any avant-garde embrace in the 1920s; indeed, Stevens's strongest early advocates—Monroe, Kreymborg, and Aiken—were becoming less, not more, centrally positioned within a vital avant-garde.

In a general sense, the playful hermeticism of *Harmonium* demanded a critical flexibility and patience that reader-reviewers of 1923 were unable to sustain, but within that same year the publication of *The Waste Land* had proved that hermeticism in itself was not a necessary stumbling block to widespread critical enthusiasm. It had quickly enabled Eliot to become the strongest avant-garde challenge to the prevalent popular modernism of the day. Here again, *Harmonium* was at an evaluative disadvantage under the conditions of contemporary reading. Eliot's hermetic poetry excluded the reader who did not follow its allusive textures, but it also clubbishly admitted those who did follow it into the priesthood of a prestigiously erudite tradition. On the other hand, Stevens's hermeticism primarily functioned not to exclude a reader who could not identify Azcan, an inchling, or a blackamoor but instead to promote a play of elusive "suave sounds" by not letting them take on meaning as conventional, skimmable words. Deriving not from Shakespeare or Sanskrit but merely from the dictionary and the poet's imagination, these obscurities offered no discernible cultural laurels to the winners, nor did they force a guilty acknowledgement from the losers that they should have remembered their Dante better. Stevens's hermeticism often seemed to assert the resistance of the poetic subject against all linguistic or conceptual systems that would attempt to circumscribe it ("Your world is you. I am my world") and did so through the use of alienating strategies that in the 1920s made it nearly impossible to articulate the problems and rewards of reading it.

Eliot's breakthrough helped Stevens indirectly in the long run by impelling avant-garde values towards a more central cultural position, but it certainly hindered his reputation in the short run by riveting the attention of young avant-gardists, some of whom might have expended critical energy on Stevens, onto what seemed newly and clearly marked boundaries of major cultural controversies. That the strident response to *The Waste Land*, both positive and negative, gave definition to ongoing generational and aesthetic conflicts was suggested by such chronicles of the 1920s as Waugh's *Brideshead Revisited*, whose "aesthete par excellence," Anthony Blanche, "in languishing, sobbing tones recited passages from *The Waste Land*" through a megaphone to a throng of Oxford undergraduates (32–33). Since *Harmonium*'s brand of avant-gardism did not explicitly attack existing cultural conventions so much as coolly ignore them, there were no clear and compelling battle lines drawn to push young writers into response of any kind.

For the "lost generation" of American modernists, born in the few years before 1900, the chill blast of Eliot's avant-gardism was a magnetic force through the 1920s. Edmund Wilson, one of Eliot's strongest early advocates, clearly expressed his sense of generational revolt in 1926: "As for poetry, the new movement of twelve years ago [when Wilson was nineteen] seemed at the time to assume impressive proportions. But who can believe in its heroes now?" ("The All-Star Literary Vaudeville," 85). This "new movement" that Wilson went on to disparage bitingly was, of course, the cataract of poets—Masters, Lindsay, Frost, Sandburg, Lowell, Fletcher—who had barreled down Spoon River in the mid-1910s. For Wilson, Eliot was a newer, more powerful movement in his own right, in comparison to whom Stevens seemed "a charming decorative artist" ("The All-Star Literary Vaudeville," 87). Thus when Wilson wanted to illustrate the emotionless "aridity" of *Harmonium* in 1924, he turned easily to Eliot's monumental agonism as a contrast: "Mr. Stevens . . . seems to have emotion neither in abundance nor in intensity. He is ironic a little in Mr. Eliot's manner; but he is not poignantly, not tragically ironic" ("Wallace Stevens and E. E. Cummings," 102). As with Munson's distinction between major and minor, the implicit damage to Stevens's value from his lack of this tragic irony is obvious. Through this generation of younger modernist critics and poets would eventually play a role in the beginnings of Stevens's canonization, in the second half of the 1920s, most were too much taken with *The Waste Land* to bother with *Harmonium*—especially since the completely silent Stevens did not appear to be capable of important future work.

FOUR

It Must Change

Stevens in the 1930s

And they said then, "But play, you must,
A tune beyond us, yet ourselves,

A tune upon the blue guitar
Of things exactly as they are."
—Stevens,
"The Man With the Blue Guitar," 1937

One . . . is a little surprised by the eminence of the poems. Not their excellence, for that is customary in Stevens, but a passionate sharpness of authority which I do not remember having felt before.
—Robert Fitzgerald, 1937

Considering Stevens's poetic output through these first two decades of American modernism, astonishingly meager by any conventional standard of importance, it is notable that he still had any influential advocacy left by 1930. Yet after seven years during which Stevens published exactly three poems, Knopf was willing to reissue *Harmonium* as if the whole enterprise had been quite satisfying to everyone. True to his highly disinterested form, the poet himself had little to do with the idea of reprinting. Knopf's initial query had come in the spring of 1930, but Stevens had apparently waited several months to agree, diffidently gathering the fourteen poems that would first appear in the 1931 edition.[1] Knopf's own liking of Stevens's work was not the only factor involved in the decision to reissue. Through the 1920s Stevens's reputation rose despite his indifference to it. For this to have happened there must have been forces of reception gaining strength which, though mostly unable to forge a general perception of Stevens's majority, were embracing emergent evaluative criteria that were more favorable to him.

The most immediately striking pattern about the reviews that emerged after the reissue of *Harmonium*—the complete lack of continuity between the reviewers of 1923–24 and those of 1931–32—indicates an important ongoing transition in the evaluative milieu of literary modernism. This wholesale changeover of Stevens's reviewers contrasts with later intervals and presages the development of an important group of critics who would faithfully follow Stevens's work as it emerged over the next decades. At least twice between 1930 and 1955, one could read Stevens reviews and essays by R. P. Blackmur, John Holmes, Eda Lou Walton, Ben Belitt, Ruth Lechlitner, Morton Zabel, Robert Fitzgerald, F. O. Matthiessen, Horace Gregory, Delmore Schwartz, Randall Jarrell, Gerard Previn Meyer, and Peter Viereck—all from an interwar generation of modernist critics and poets born between 1900 and 1920. Unlike commentators and readers born even five to ten years earlier (such as Edmund Wilson, Paul Rosenfeld, and Babette Deutsch), these critics had emerged as adults into an existing system of production and distribution of modernist writing. For them some variety of modernism was the ground of contemporary culture, which largely constituted their own developing aesthetic, intellectual, and ideological identities. Their enthusiastic responses to Stevens's development through these decades show that these writers followed him not only because it was their beat to review poets who produced new books but because he had come to occupy a place in their sense of what modern poetry had been and was.

Despite the long-term importance of these critics and poets, whose names will appear repeatedly in the following pages, the fact that they began to appear in 1931 did not mean a drastic or immediate change in perceptions of the poet. Indeed, the majority of the response to *Harmonium* 1931 fell into patterns familiar from the critical commonplaces found in mainstream magazines in the 1920s. In the 1931 reviews one no longer finds any pure Monrovian beautymongers; but there was a substantial contingent of reviewers (and, no doubt, a larger number of readers) who held to the accessible anti-avant-garde humanism, advocated most strongly by Untermeyer, which had become widely established in the literary culture by the mid-1920s. Values such as these Stevens could not fulfill: "poetry is founded in ideas; to be effective and lasting, poetry must be based on life, it must touch and vitalize emotion. . . . In poetry, doctrinaire composition has no place" (Hutchison, 4).[2]

Though none were strongly unfavorable, reviews in some of the same fairly conservative periodicals as before (*The Bookman* and *The Boston Evening Transcript*) and some new ones (*Commonweal* and *The New York Times Book Review*) could achieve no more than the familiar ambivalence between admiration and denigration, reiterating patterns of evaluation that stemmed from the three essays of the mid-1920s which had consolidated the dominant characterization of Stevens as a dandy of obscure, super-refined intellectual poetry. Here the terms of minority varied only slightly: Stevens's work, "its meaning often obscure," "errs . . . on the side of foppishness"; it constituted "not poetry . . . [but] a tour de force, a 'stunt' in the fantastic and the bizarre."[3] As before, the consequence of Stevens's mannered persona and his ultraformalist work was a banishment to ultimate insignficance: "the beau as poet" could only be "a minor poet" (Larsson, 640–41). While the existence of these reviews indicated Stevens's (or Knopf's) ability to get books reviewed in most of the major review forums, these discussions showed little rethinking of the previously and widely held opinions of the poet.

Notably, several of this group of reviews conveyed a patronizing attitude towards the period of early modernism, especially towards Imagism and the other poetic "schools." They tended to conclude smugly not only that that era was now over (the "isms" of the 1910s "have died the death which could have been prophesied for them") but also that "the bulk of what came of Imagism . . . will have value merely for the scholar, the pedant, the historian" (Hutchison, 4; Larsson, 641). In taking on the appearance of a historical rather than a contemporary phenomenon, early modernism had now become, among other things, a millstone of obsolescence to hang around poets' necks. Even though Stevens wore well in comparison to others of that era, some saw him as doomed by these associations to minority or obscurity, "a martyr to a lost cause" (Hutchison, 4). Such remarks about early modernism might have elicited agreement in principle from the reviewer-critics who aided Stevens's reputation in the next two decades. The difference, of course, was that for them

Stevens, unlike most of his early contemporaries, had transcended those limitations of Imagism to become a major writer, but until Stevens began publishing significantly once again, it was quite plausible to dismiss him as a relic of the avant-garde past.

Two reviewers of 1931, Eda Lou Walton and Morton Dauwen Zabel, did engage in some active revision of the conventional perceptions of Stevens. The importance of their efforts lay in their willingness to make evaluations on bases other than the major-minor, substantialist-formalist dualities that to this point had stymied not only praise but nearly all intelligent criticism of Stevens. Though they shared the view that early modernism was a phenomenon of the past, their animus was directed not against Imagism and its descendants as much as against what they saw as a slack and complacent popular modernism, in contrast to which Stevens became a figure of aesthetic integrity and precision. Walton portrayed Stevens not as a sensibility marginal to the course of modernist poetry but as a central figure capable of contesting Eliot's domination of avant-garde values. In his "deliberate deflations of the emotions," Stevens carried the "emotional ennui" mapped out by Eliot in *The Waste Land* to its logical and rigorous extreme of sincerity ("Beyond the Wasteland," 263). In his ironic evocation and rejection of all old-fashioned emotional outpourings in poetry, Stevens had achieved a kind of ultimate sincerity, since "to this mind no simple statement is possible, every word has innumerable associations. The poet is sincere in being insincere, since to be sincere for him would be ridiculous" (263). Walton's logic here was obviously a product of a later, far less ingenuous generation than the consolatory aestheticism of Monroe or the earnest humanism of Untermeyer. Walton's conception of aesthetic honesty as moral value was, in a broad sense, not unlike that of a score of older figures; but the particular moral values of poetry she emphasized—sincerity and fortitude in the face of an assumed emotional desiccation—suggested that Eliot and *The Waste Land* had done much to shift the intellectual starting points of younger critics.

For Walton, however, Eliot was ultimately inadequate as an exemplar of modernity since he had failed to sustain that necessary fortitude: having "merely defined the territory . . . he escaped from it into scholarship, into religion" (263). Contrasted to this position of "escape," Stevens could for the first time be seen as a poet who had courageously cast his lot, for better or worse, in the part of the human world that was most independent and distinctive—the individual imagination. And though it let the poet in for the contumely of the less sophisticated, his avant-garde stance was to be admired as a model in a world that threatened to make all ordinary men faceless drones to authority: "Moreover if Stevens is over-refined, it is only because we still measure refinement by the normal bluntness preserving the ordinary man for his mechanical world—not by the truer instrument of the sensitive imagination. Refinement is all we have today of exuberance and vitality" (263).

As this passage suggests, the vitality Stevens represented for Walton came at some cost, the same kind of cost Stevens would attempt to deal with later in the decade: the dismissal or neglect of the "ordinary man." Plainly, to Walton, the populist and humanist poetic values of the 1910s were no longer viable as they had been for Untermeyer. The danger, as she saw it, came from the other corner: Eliot had all the antidemocratic elitism Stevens did and more, with none of his "exuberance and vitality." If Eliot would remain unavoidably central for her generation of poets and critics, he would often be so not from their own freely conceived versions of poetic value but through a stern institutional and psychological authority. One way of rebelling against this authority was through the adoption of alternative poetic or cultural models; as adumbrated here, an advocacy of Stevens gradually became an important method of the rebellion against what Delmore Schwartz would later call "The Literary Dictatorship of T. S. Eliot."

In *Poetry*, Zabel's response to *Harmonium* 1931 further developed the position of authority, ethical as well as aesthetic, in which Walton placed Stevens, confidently asserting that a rigorous rather than a frivolous intelligence was working in these poems and that its thrust was serious both in method and intention. Attacking Munson's ubiquitous label of dandyism, which implied "style without significance motive or conviction," Zabel limned a Stevens whose imaginative flights were the product of a "disciplined individualism," an unwillingness to let any system of established authority weaken "the sole anchorage [that] is the private fortitude of conscience and personal will" ("The *Harmonium* of Wallace Stevens," 152–53). Zabel's treatment of the concept of "fortitude" against what Stevens would later call "the pressure of reality" conjoined well with Walton's evaluation of Stevens as brave man, not ineffectual beau. Importantly, Zabel also connected that moral advocacy to Stevens's formal distinction, which had previously been impossible despite his acknowledged virtuosity: "The poetic means whereby Mr. Stevens has sublimated this individualism has made his style in every detail the component of his convictions as they emerged from experience. This hair-line correspondence is at once the clue to the sensuous logic of his style, and to the realism which saves his imagery from imaginative extravagance, his wit from verbal exercise, and his morality from the illusory intellectual casuistry which has betrayed most of his colleagues" (154). More a triumph of rhetoric than an articulate analysis, Zabel's conjunction of formal value (Stevens's "creative virtuosity"), with quasi-ethical value ("a set of pure principles which make his work a unity") would prove to be a key to the widespread critical advocacy of Stevens and his fellow virtuosi of avant-garde modernism over the next two decades.

What Zabel did not do for Stevens in 1931 was to articulate the specific effectiveness of his technical virtuosity, but the development of such an explicative criticism was rapidly approaching by the time Zabel's review appeared. Stevens would be one of the first beneficiaries of it, in an exhaustive and brilliant analysis by R. P. Blackmur in *Hound and Horn* in 1932. Blackmur's "Examples of Wallace Stevens" superseded Munson's "Dandyism" essay as the standard critical text on Stevens and would be prominently evoked in several critical commentaries on the poet during the next decade. His essay was the first sign in Stevens criticism that respect for the poet's formal excellence could itself shape the terms of an enthusiastic and articulate response not only to his own poetry but to contemporary poetry as a whole. More broadly, Blackmur's work on Stevens, along with his other *Hound and Horn* pieces on Eliot, Cummings, and Pound, would help to steer the infant New Criticism towards an emphasis on articulating the formal attributes of the modernist lyric. Rich both in the ingenious ways it undertook to redefine the poet's position and in the seeds of explicative New Criticism it contained, Blackmur's essay merits extended treatment as canonical criticism. The canonical features it promoted were multiple and highly interdependent: Stevens within modern poetry canons; Blackmur within the canons of New Criticism; and New Criticism within the canons of American literary criticism.

Blackmur's essay was not only a brilliant defense of the poet but a labor of critical self-definition in which Stevens played an important role. In contrast to the quickly written reviews predominant in earlier evaluations of Stevens and of most modern poetry, "Examples of Wallace Stevens" took the better part of a year to complete. The project was on the calendar of *Hound and Horn* from at least April 1931, when editor Lincoln Kirstein and Stevens exchanged correspondence over it; Blackmur was still working on it in November, writing to Stevens apologetically, "I am timid of mistakes in a matter where I so wish to be correct" (*L*, 261; Fraser, 57). Even as early as February 1931, Conrad Aiken had replied to Blackmur's query for help on how to treat the poet by running through a litany of ways of seeing Stevens had been seen in the 1920's: "You can link him up, of course, with the Rimbaud-symbolist business—even with Valéry, and 'pure' poetry . . . the mere delight in verbal legerdemain etc. for its own sake . . . he's perhaps the most remarkable *humorist* in poetry. . . . Then, finally, there is of course the extremely keen critical awareness. . . . An aesthetic, and a pretty complete one, presented polychromatically piecemeal: now in terms of music now in colour. And often enough if not too often the colour-buffoonery for its own sake" (Aiken, *Selected Letters*, 170).

Whether or not Blackmur was seriously asking for Aiken's help, the finished essay revealed little of any of these older views of Stevens. Instead, Blackmur gave Stevens what his reputation needed: an advocacy free of no longer fashionable hyperaesthetic associations. Perhaps Blackmur asked Aiken about Stevens less for his critical views than for a simple reinforcement of Aiken's long-professed belief that Stevens was a major modern poet: "All I can add to this I've said to you before—that I think him as sure of a permanent place of importance as Eliot, if not surer" (Aiken, *Selected Letters* 170). It appears that Blackmur, who had known Aiken since the beginning of his adult life, had taken such repeated judgments to heart.

Both the thoroughness and the intellectual adventure suggested by the essay's long gestation period were realized in the finished piece, which Stevens himself found, for good reason, "extraordinarily interesting" (Fraser, 56). "Examples of Wallace Stevens" opened up at least two ways of viewing Stevens as central to the course, methods, and goals of modernist poetry. The most immediately influential was a fuller elaboration of the conjunction adumbrated by Zabel and Walton between formal excellence and a quality of ethical fortitude, a line of argument important to conceptions of poetic value during the New Critical period. The other posited the resistance of Stevens's formal integrity, his fortitude, and human language to such central New Critical concepts as order, resolution, unity, and authority. Long neglected, this more subversive line of interpretation would eventually come into play against the New Critical hegemony in future decades. The first would encourage but not exhaust Stevens's canonical potential in the short run; the second would help to keep his position critically fertile in the longer run.

For Blackmur, unlike most critics of the 1920s, Stevens's formal virtuosity could function as an unmixed good. Blackmur's opening sentence abruptly announced that his would be a formal approach to Stevens made without apology or trepidation: "The most striking if not the most important thing about Mr. Stevens's verse is its vocabulary" ("Examples of Wallace Stevens," 52).[4] Blackmur's determination to track down elements of poetic effect led him to use a terminology of poetic form—assonance, couplets, connotation—in distinct contrast to most contemporary discussions of poetry, which were limited to estimations of a poet's success or failure in achieving an emotional effect. This formalist self-positioning was crucial to Blackmur's advocacy of Stevens, and vice versa. One of Blackmur's ambitions for the essay was to wrest Stevens out of the clutches of his major supporters who would preserve him as an aestheticist cult figure. He moved right to the heart of the existing critical impasse that was deterring the rise of Stevens's reputation, identifying and rejecting the crippling dualism of antiformalist plain-speaking and precious ornamenting: "Mr. Stevens has a bad reputation among those who dislike the finicky, and a high one, unfortunately, among those who value the ornamental sound of words but who see no purpose in developing sound from sense. Both classes of reader are wrong. Not a word listed above is used preciously; not one was chosen as an elegant substitute for plain term" (52).

In pursuing the consequences of this critique through the essay, Blackmur used Stevens's integration of "sound" and "sense" as a basis for his avowal of the crucial importance of poetry to human expression. The equation of tone and meaning, which Stevens had been asserting for years, was one important suggestion of the poet's centrality to the critic's developing position.[5] Speaking of "Bantams in Pine-Woods," a poem that Untermeyer had repeatedly picked on, Blackmur concluded that the poem's rhetoric was integral to its purpose and that to think otherwise was massively to reduce what poetry could offer: "If the reader is deceived by the rhetoric and believes the poem is no more than a verbal plaything, he ought not to read poetry except as a plaything" (73). Explicitly contradicting Untermeyer's opinion of the poem as "childish," Blackmur asserted the seriousness that Stevens's behavior seemed to belie: "Mr. Stevens' rhetoric is as ferociously comic as the rhetoric in Marlowe's *Jew of Malta*, and as serious" (73). Under these premises, the strong formal authority exerted by Stevens's poetry was well situated to further a theoretical argument for the inseparability of content and form in poetry: "We have been considering poems where the light tone increases the gravity of the substance, and where an atmosphere of wit and elegance assures poignancy of meaning. It is only a step or so further to that use of language where tone and atmosphere are very nearly equivalent to substance and meaning themselves" (61).

This conviction that rhetoric and meaning were integrally related in a poem underlay all of Blackmur's lines of argument and indicated that this essay was conceived not only as a discussion of Stevens but as a full-scale advocacy of formal excellence in poetry: "There is nothing which has been said so far about Mr. Stevens' use of language which might not have been said, with different examples, of any good poet equally varied and equally erudite—by which I mean intensely careful of effects" (63–64).

A major part of Blackmur's vigorous formalism involved a redefinition of the dualistic assumptions and terminology under which poetic form was viewed by influential critics of the 1920s. Blackmur connected his conception of the centrality and seriousness of formal excellence to a view of language not as an inert material that contained a separable essence of content but as the recalcitrant and unique means of constituting human perception and understanding. The immediate stratagem in Blackmur's program was to generalize Stevens's methods into the universal methods of great poetry:

> Good poets gain their excellence by writing an existing language *as if* it were their own invention; and as a rule success in the effect of originality is best secured by fidelity, in an extreme sense, to the individual words as they appear in the dictionary. If a poet knows precisely what his words represent, what he writes is much more likely to seem new and strange—and even difficult to understand—than if he uses his words ignorantly and at random. That is because when each word has definite character the combinations cannot avoid uniqueness. [53; emphasis in text]

This deft passage evoked a number of central elements of New Critical modernism: originality, precision, difficulty, uniqueness, but less typical of New Criticism was the emphasized metaphoric connective *as if*, itself a Stevensian balancing of belief and skepticism, which formed the key to Blackmur's creation of a causal sequence defining the relation between the individual poet's idiom and the common language.[6] The "good" poet by no means spoke a private language but used the common one; that use became original in the depth, breadth, precision, and specificity of understanding which the poet brought to bear on the common linguistic reservoir. The poet's command of the resources of the common language, beyond what most readers had achieved, sometimes led to the difficulty, or perceived obscurity, of the communicative relation between poet and reader. This was both a reassurance and a challenge to the reader: the obscurity of modern poetry was conquerable, but only by hard work. Stevens's fidelity to the nuances of the common language, conveyed aptly by Blackmur's figure of the dictionary, implied a conception of the ideal poet's function: imaginative and ethical education. With careful attention, a reader could receive from a poet such as Stevens a sense of the inexhaustible richness of linguistic expression and human imagination; modern poet and reader *could* communicate. At the same time, through the difficulty of the reading activity, the reader would come to understand the inevitable imperfections of and obstacles to linguistic articulation and could consequently embrace the ethical imperative to infuse thought and expression with as much precision and integrity as possible.

Blackmur thus presented to the literary establishment a version of Stevens as a figure of poetic virtue, offering significant rewards to anyone willing to use a dictionary with patience and sensitivity—an evaluation that explicitly revised nearly every estimate of Stevens up to that time. It revised explicitly the dominant perception that Stevens's obscurity was deliberately alienating and incorrigible, that he spoke a whole different language from that of the reader of poetry. Unlike nearly all of the reviewers of the first *Harmonium*, Blackmur admitted no discomfort with Stevens's difficulty. One of the most important tasks his essay undertook was to demonstrate Stevens's accessibility by explicating several demanding short poems that had never been articulately discussed and some of which have since become standards: "The Emperor of Ice-Cream," "The Snow Man," "Bantams in Pine-Woods," "The Ordinary Women." As if this were not enough, Blackmur also provided intelligent glosses on such seemingly insurmountable longer poems as "Le Monocle de Mon Oncle," "Sunday Morning," and especially "The Comedian as the Letter C." Going against the later New Critical preference for the brief lyric poem, Blackmur called this long, daunting narrative Stevens's "most important poem"; where most reviewers had positioned "The Comedian" as some sort of admission of creative failure or disinterest, he found it to be vital to the development of Stevens's thought, "everywhere characteristic of [his] style and interests." In thriving on the poem's difficulty, the critic encouraged the reader to thrive on it as well: "it has the merit of difficulty—difficulty which when solved rewards the reader beyond his hopes of clarity" (74). Blackmur's explication of the poem moved smoothly between global narrative and linguistic nuance to suggest that this apparent conundrum was actually a brilliant, accessible description of a subject that would emerge as central to much modernist poetry: "the shifting of a man's mind between sensual experience and its imaginative interpretation" (74).

The advocacy of Stevens and other "difficult" modern poets on the evaluative basis of precision, originality, and integrity was already in the air in some of the 1931 reviews of *Harmonium*. Clearly the fetishizing of formal proficiency was an emerging idea, and, mostly in other hands than Blackmur's, it would further the reification of poetic form, at the expense of a sense of literature as a vital process, which was New Criticism at its most rigid. Despite his criticisms of Eliot's poetic method, Blackmur's work undeniably derived much from the critical doctrines developed in Eliot's early essays and would pass on much to New Criticism proper.[7] Many of the American poet-critics who were working towards their own versions of what came to be called New Criticism were affected by these essays: in 1935 Allen Tate called Blackmur's essays on Cummings and Stevens "the finest criticism of contemporary poetry in my generation"; Yvor Winters termed the Stevens essay "a masterpiece," and John Crowe Ransom would later call Blackmur "the best man there was—or was going to be" (Fraser, 55, 64). This group of essays was collected in Blackmur's first volume, *The Double Agent*, in 1935. Thirteen years later, in the heyday of New Critical influence, Tate graciously acknowledged this book's centrality, asserting that with its appearance Blackmur "probably invented what we call the New Criticism in the United States" (Fraser, 272).

To an extent, then, it is appropriate to see Blackmur's essays on Stevens and other modern poets published in *Hound and Horn* as helping to crystallize the orientation and direction of New Criticism; but Blackmur's early essays transcended the ideological strictures of conservative New Criticism, drawing praise across a wide spectrum of writers and readers of poetry, from the leftists Kenneth Patchen and Genevieve Taggard to the hard-headed old businessman Homer Pound (Fraser, 64, 99, 64). Despite its derivations from Eliot's criticism, and despite its importance for the development of explicative New Criticism, the essay on Stevens represented a break away from Eliot towards seeing Stevens as a central figure of modernist poetry. In particular, Blackmur's implication of the poet as a positive and active ethical force, rather than as alienated radical or agonistic Fisher-King, suggested his and Stevens's common divergence from the Pound-Eliot-Tate-Brooks tradition of high-modernist pessimism. The critic's use of Stevens in contrast to other prominent modernists reinforced this divergence by describing, as Walton's and Zabel's reviews had done less forcefully, the attractive nimbus of integrity given off by Stevens even in his sometimes alienating effort to be a totally original poet. If, as Blackmur suggested, a poet's originality derived from extreme "fidelity" to the heritage of the common language, then it followed that originality would be a quality of ethical virtue to the extent that it worked with and made accessible that cultural and linguistic potential to the reader.

Blackmur acknowledged that a number of responses were possible to the need for originality and precision felt by contemporary poets. Therefore the difficulty or obscurity that resulted from their efforts could take several distinct forms, by no means equally defensible ethically:

> In some notes on the language of E. E. Cummings I tried to show how that poet, by relying on his private feelings and using words as if their meanings were spontaneous with use, succeeded mainly in turning his words into empty shells. Mr. Stevens, by combining the insides of those words he found fit to his feelings, has turned his words into knowledge. Both Mr. Stevens and Cummings issue in ambiguity—as any good poet does; but the ambiguity of Cummings is the absence of known content, the ambiguity of a phantom which no words could give being. Mr. Stevens's ambiguity is that of a substance so dense with being, that it resists paraphrase and can be truly perceived only in the form of words in which it was given. . . . Reading Mr. Stevens you have only to know the meanings of the words and to then submit to the conditions of the poems. [53]

Cummings used a language with a private system of meaning, which claimed for itself a liberating spontaneity; but for Blackmur, the mysterious and imperfect nature of human language meant that the meanings of words were never spontaneous or unproblematic. To claim otherwise, as Cummings did, was to erect an edifice of superiority for the poet which allowed the reader no access to the common cultural heritage that should be available through the knowable words of poetry; the implied result, as many other readers of Cummings arrived at from a variety of paths, was an ethically unstable solipsism.

Blackmur left no doubt that, on this issue of the use of language in poetry, Stevens stood at the very head of his personal poetic canon by pitting him against the two most formidable reputations of avant-garde modernism: "the scope and reach of his verse are no less but different" from those of Eliot and Pound (67). In his discussion of "The Comedian as the Letter C," Blackmur went so far as to link Stevens with poetic giants of past and present: "The form he used is as much his own and as adequate, as the form of *Paradise Lost* is Milton's or the form of *The Waste Land* is Eliot's. And as Milton's form fitted the sensibility of one aspect of his age, Mr. Stevens's form fits part of the sensibility—a part which Eliot or Pound or Yeats do little to touch—of our own age" (79).

Blackmur's further distinctions showed that Stevens was quite possibly more significant than these other modernists because of his more genuinely ethical attempt to balance originality of expression with communicative effectiveness. Stevens's method of precise expression was for Blackmur implicitly superior to Eliot's and Pound's techniques of precision, which they realized through the use of highly personal cultural references: "it should be clear that whereas the obscurities of Pound and Eliot are intrinsic difficulties of the poems, to which the reader must come armed with specific knowledge and belief, the obscurities of Mr. Stevens clarify themselves to the intelligence alone" (71).

In a 1935 letter to Tate, Blackmur reiterated that Stevens's communicativeness—"his double adherence to words and experience as existing apart from his private sensibility"—was the basis of his own judgment of Stevens as the greatest success of American modernists and made Stevens, at least on this issue, worthy of comparison to Shakespeare (Blackmur quoted in Fraser, 93).

In contrasting Stevens's ethical difficulty with the more insurmountable obscurities of other poets, Blackmur revised another aspect of obscurity that had been damaging to Stevens's reputation: "nonsense." Blackmur saw two types of nonsense in Stevens, apparent and real, and incorporated both in his account of how Stevens demonstrated various ways of disclosing meaning to the reader. In poems such as "The Ordinary Women," the nonsense was only a surface beneath which a vein of satisfying meaning lay: "that the phrase is not nonsense, that on inspection it retrieves itself to sense, is its inner virtue" (56).

Even much of Stevens's nonsense, then, retained an associative fidelity to the heritage of verbal language.

Some nonsense, however, simply would not disclose itself as conventional meaning. Sometimes, as in "Disillusionment of Ten O'Clock," Stevens's poetry also disclosed another and more radical kind of nonsense-meaning:

> The statement about catching tigers in red weather coming after the white nightgowns and baboons and periwinkles, has a persuasive force out of all relation to the sense of the words. Literally, there is nothing alarming in the statement, and nothing ambiguous, but by so putting the statement that it appears as nonsense, infinite possibilities are made terrifying and plain. The shock and virtue of nonsense is this: it compels us to scrutinize the words in such a way that we see the enormous ambiguity in the substance of every phrase, every image, every word. . . . Half our sleeping knowledge is in nonsense; and when it is put in a poem it wakes. [57]

The key term in this remarkable formulation was *ambiguity*, following Empson, whose *Seven Types of Ambiguity*, appearing in America in 1930, was the newest critical rage when Blackmur wrote this essay. Indeed, in Russell Fraser's words, Blackmur wrote to Stevens in December 1931 that Empson's "was a book . . . he couldn't keep away from" (Fraser, 277). Empson's work has long been recognized as an important forerunner of American New Criticism, of course, and *Seven Types of Ambiguity* certainly addressed a number of the issues that concerned Blackmur in his *Hound and Horn* essays. Despite this, it would be a mistake to equate Blackmur's ambiguity with the term as it developed into one of the most ubiquitous New Critical shibboleths, tamed into the pleasant savoring of multiple, perhaps paradoxical, but knowable possibilities within a range of contemplative meaning. Blackmur's early use of the term here, in the very infancy of New Criticism, did not offer any comfortable resolution of opposites but flashed with an awareness of the dangerously unknowable nature of language—the "alarming," the "infinite," the "terrifying," the "shock," "the enormous ambiguity in the substance" of even the smallest unit of linguistic meaning. After such a rhetorical onslaught, one may wonder how substantial the "substance" of language could be. The very sensation of that rift in the texture of our waking knowledge, created through Stevens's nonsensical language, had for Blackmur an inexplicable but valuable "persuasive sense."

In this disposition towards an adventurous poetry of nonsense, Blackmur derived not only his sympathy for Stevens but a major part of his own early critical position from the "connoisseur of chaos" himself. In striking contrast to the typical New Critical view of literature as spatial stasis, Blackmur's conception of literature, like Stevens's, was based on a sense of the dynamism of language and a consequent mandate for the literary critic, as Edward W. Said has recently described: "Thus, if for Blackmur literature was about movement, if the place of literature was not restricted to a fixed spot (or *topos*), then it behooved the critic somehow to remain attuned to that fact, to describe literary experience as a zone, rather than an inert place" (38).

Blackmur's and Stevens's shared sense of language as a phenomenon of exhilarating dynamism was largely inimical to New Critical holism and shaped the prominent yet curiously marginal position held by both in the New Critical establishment of the decades to come. Although *The Double Agent* was historically central to the rise of New Criticism, it was Stevens, not Eliot, who was intellectually most central to *The Double Agent,* in being the subject of its most laudatory essay and in providing Blackmur with the book's principal thread of coherence. The logic of Blackmur's title derived from a dialectical balancing of opposing terms which came to him more immediately from his intimate knowledge of *Harmonium* than from the Coleridge he never studied in college.

Interpretations of critics' positions are shaped by intellectual hegemonies no less than are those of poets, however, and in 1948 Stanley Edgar Hyman was able to read the significance of Blackmur's title as being at the very center of mainstream New Critical thinking: "The double agent is in fact any pair of critical terms—form and content, structure and texture, writer and reader, static and dynamic, tradition and revolt, expression and communication—and out of their interaction arises a third thing, the poem, the essay, or in this case, Blackmur's book" (211). Far from being an uncritical apologist for New Criticism—in fact, his admiration for Kenneth Burke might have made him more sensitive to the idea of literature as dynamic process—Hyman was nonetheless writing at the height of New Critical dominance, in which the very terms and premises that this sort of formulation required would largely be shaped by those of New Criticism. His description of this fundamental imaginative process, with its emphasis on the product as object ("a third thing"), owed more to Brooksian reifications of the intervening years than Blackmur's own notion of doubling did.

As with Stevens's conception of such opposites, developed explicitly in *The*

Man With the Blue Guitar but present from his beginnings in such *Harmonium* poems as "Thirteen Ways of Looking at a Blackbird," Blackmur's dialectic did not unknot itself in the production of a synthetic object. Not only was neither term sufficient in itself, but the opposition could never be resolved completely; only in the very act of continually balancing them could one achieve a synthetic process (as opposed to a product) that led to understanding. This epistemology of poetry provided Stevens and Blackmur with an analogous commitment to creation and criticism: for Stevens, in the continual reexamination of the master relationship of consciousness to environment; for Blackmur, in what Said has called his "tense impatience with any attitude that does not see literature—no matter how well-wrought, how much 'itself,'—as poised uneasily between anarchy and form" (Said, 35).[8]

Blackmur's institutionally weak position, analogous to Stevens's own unwillingness to play games of self-promotion, meant that the development of New Critical intellectual positions through the next dozen years could largely evade or render safe the unserviceable or threatening side of Blackmur exemplified by his remarks on Stevens's "nonsense." The orientation away from unities and circumscriptions of linguistic meaning that made Blackmur's work problematic for New Criticism also helps to explain Stevens's slow growth within the literary culture even decades after Blackmur had showed the rich possibilities of reading him. Blackmur was to remain Stevens's only enthusiastic advocate among the major New Critical theorists. In contrast, six years after "Examples," Ransom would use Stevens's work as if Blackmur had never written, as a programmatic example of "pure poetry" which had "little or no moral importance" ("Poets Without Laurels," 60). Ransom would write substantially on Stevens again only after the poet's death, by which time his mild advocacy was less a shaping than a reflection of consensual perceptions of the poet ("The Planetary Poet"). After an enthusiastic beginning, Winters would eventually and famously come to condemn Stevens in *Anatomy of Nonsense* in 1943 as a "hedonist" of poetry, an evaluation, like Ransom's, which was ultimately derived from evaluative conditions of the 1920s. Robert Penn Warren and Cleanth Brooks would have even less to say about Stevens, mentioning him neither in Brooks and Warren's *Understanding Poetry* (1938) nor in Brooks's *Modern Poetry and the Tradition* (1939), and writing complimentary but only extremely brief statements for the 1940 *Harvard Advocate* issue on Stevens. Allen Tate never substantiated his high 1940 opinion of Stevens—"one of the best poets alive"—

with critical work of any particular breadth or authority.⁹ As he aged Blackmur himself would increasingly hanker after the sort of metaphysical totalities that Stevens's provisional and relativized poetics did not allow for; even the poet's major New Critical advocate thus became progressively less enthusiastic about his late work.¹⁰

Despite this lack of sustained advocacy of Stevens by central New Critics, enough converts were won in various ways through these decades to give him a very high literary standing by the time he died. Even so, it was only in the decade after his death, when the period of greatest New Critical dominance had passed, that the first real explosion of Stevens's academic reputation took place. Then Stevens would begin to play a central part in large-scale theories of literature, but more immediately, Blackmur's essay helped to shape the specific terms and directions of an idea whose time was coming, a new criticism of explicative sensitivity under which Stevens could be seen as a rich and interesting poet. Eventually Stevens would become the central modernist poet for much post–New Critical thinking. For that many readers are responsible, but none more than the early R. P. Blackmur, who demonstrated that Stevens was a poet of substance who was richer linguistically than Frost, more comprehensible than Pound, more sincerely communicative than Cummings, and more open to the potentials of imaginative expression than Eliot.

By 1935, despite Stevens's still limited output, it was possible for a young reader of modernist poetry to conceive of doing rewarding interpretive criticism on his work. The reevaluation of *Harmonium* in 1931 had shown that Stevens's position in contemporary poetic canons had begun to change. Even with basically the same body of poems to consider as in 1923, some younger writers, critics, and poets were coming to see Stevens no longer as a decadent hyperaesthete content to be a "minor" period poet but instead as a poet of formidable technical gifts who had the potential to address issues important to the modern cultural milieu. Consequently, despite the acknowledged prominence of Eliot, and to a lesser extent Pound, within the canons of avant-garde modernism, some critics were willing to place Stevens at or near the top of their personal canons of modernist poetry. This is not to say that there was any widespread embrace of Stevens by the critical mainstream in the second half of the 1930s. For the first time, however, Stevens did during these years become a sustained presence in the contemporary literary scene as he began publishing again at an astonishing rate.

The very fact of Stevens's surprising return to poetic activity had an important impact on readers' perceptions of him as a serious poet and deserves some attention as a prelude to examining the reception of the three books of the late 1930s. The question of Stevens's reemergence has been approached in a number of plausible ways: the poet had finally bought a large house for his family in 1932, giving him the privacy and quiet he needed to write and read at home; his daughter Holly had outgrown the stage of disrupting adult schedules; he was named vice-president at the Hartford Insurance Corporation in 1934, giving him a secure financial footing; and the economic and social disasters of the 1930s had challenged his identification with a life of high culture, spurring him to work through unexamined assumptions and beliefs. All of these factors and perhaps others may have entered into his return. Without intending to diminish the importance of any of them, the concerns of this study suggest an exploration of Stevens's return as an instance of the reciprocal interdependence of poet and readers in shaping and reshaping conceptions of literary value.

Certainly during the early 1930s, the poet experienced a marked increase in requests for poems, perhaps coming to feel that his poetry had been successful after all. Stevens gradually realized that his work was valued not only by a few peers of the early days of modernism but also by a new generation of readers of a new generation of little magazines, who took his abilities and concerns quite seriously—which argued for him to take them seriously as well. Along with *Hound and Horn* (founded in 1927), which had published Blackmur's essay, a group of little magazines begun by very young people between 1930 and 1934 were sites of new interest in Stevens's work, and such publications received most of his poetic output between 1930 and 1935. It is safe to say that in most cases, the editors of these fledgling magazines had written to Stevens requesting work, as editors had done since the late 1910s.[11] Rather than aiming for the larger markets of *The New Republic, The Saturday Review of Literature, Poetry*, or *The American Caravan*, all of which had editorial ears sympathetic to him, Stevens offered three-fourths of his magazine poems between 1930 and 1935 to such obscure and short-lived little magazines as *Harkness Hoot, Contempo, Smoke, New Act, Rocking Horse, Direction*, and *Alcestis*.[12] Only one of these seven survived 1935.

The particular prominence of this last venture, *Alcestis*, in encouraging his return to poetic activity should not be underestimated. J. Ronald Lane Latimer, its mercurial editor-publisher, elicited uncharacteristically friendly responses from Stevens, becoming his chief correspondent for several years and managing to procure permission from both Stevens and Knopf to publish *Ideas of Order* and *Owl's Clover* in lavish limited editions prior to Knopf's trade editions. Stevens was flattered enough by Latimer's admiration to overlook the unpleasant stories about the editor's character and publishing practices which he heard from his old friends Bynner and Williams (L, 270, 311). It is not unreasonable to suggest that Latimer's insistence upon publishing a book of Stevens poems opened the floodgates, which resulted in three books in three years.[13] The possibility or desirability of a second book first appeared in Stevens's correspondence late in November 1934, when he responded to Latimer's query, "about the book of poems, I cannot imagine anything that I should like more. The question is, however, whether I could gather together 50 pages satisfactory to me." But only two weeks later Stevens had resolved to try to write more poems, to adjust the tone of the group, and to fill out the pages necessary for a book. In the same week he was comfortable with and appreciative enough of Latimer to send him a private poem, something he had apparently done only for one other editor, Harriet Monroe, at the height of their friendship.[14]

It is important to note that Latimer's request for a book of poems from Stevens was not the first he had received. Given its willingness to reprint *Harmonium*, Knopf presumably would have been interested in publishing a second book at any time, and Conrad Aiken's efforts on Stevens's behalf had included the suggestion to J. M. Dent of an English reprinting of *Harmonium* in 1933 or 1934. Dent's response exceeded Aiken's expectations, as Dent asked Aiken to ask Stevens for a new book. To Aiken's request Stevens demurred, characteristically saying he had written nothing, but in 1936, upon their first meeting, Stevens politely told Aiken that it had been his request that started Stevens writing again (Aiken, *Selected Letters*, 305–6). Aiken's experience suggested that the numerous encouragements of the early 1930s, including his own, *had* genuinely impressed and flattered Stevens and had been instrumental in his return.

Stevens's correspondence with Latimer makes it obvious, however, that the poet felt more comfortable considering a return to work with admirers of later generations than with peers such as Kreymborg and Aiken. With Latimer, Stevens could play the role of authority figure with benevolent pleasure rather than with his customary evasions, advising the young Latimer on his publishing and personal ventures and fulfilling his request for a handwritten copy of a poem—the sort of gesture that could not be made among contemporaries without great embarrassment (L, 276). This befriending and patronage of much younger men was a pattern that would reenact itself over the last twenty years of Stevens's life, in both insurance and literary relationships—with James Powers and others in the former, and with Hi Simons, Delmore Schwartz, Richard Eberhart, José Rodríguez-Feo, Peter Lee, and Samuel French Morse in the latter.[15]

This pattern indicates that the entry of Stevens into an age of generational authority made it far more possible for him to see himself as a poet again by the mid-1930s. It might be going too far to assert that, if these admiring young readers had not appeared in the early 1930s, Stevens would never have begun to write again, but undeniably, in late middle age, in a decade when many of the more renowned poets of his generation—Frost, Millay, Jeffers, Pound, Fletcher, and Aiken, to name a few—lost creative energy or became more and more isolated, Stevens moved towards the center of American modernist culture, finally filling the prerequisite for poetic majority which he had so far neglected: the creation of a large, vitally developing body of work. That this entire process was bound up integrally with Stevens's sensitivity towards readers' response to his own work was suggested by his grateful letters to Morton Zabel, Ben Belitt, Julian Symons, and Hi Simons for their favorable reviews (L, 265, 314, 330, 345). The general importance of critical reaction to the poet would be confirmed unarguably by "Mr. Burnshaw and the Statue," his defensive verse response to Stanley Burnshaw's review of *Ideas of Order* in *The New Masses*.

Despite the Burnshaw contretemps, Stevens saw the decade as a thoroughly encouraging time for poetry. A questionnaire published in *Partisan Review* in 1939 showed how quick he was to give credit to readers and critics. In their overall magnanimity towards the literary and critical scene, his answers in this piece differed startlingly from nearly everyone else's. While most respondents said in characteristic avant-garde fashion that critics helped them very little, and several even commented on the clumsiness or uselessness of the questionnaire itself, Stevens remarked, "Much of the criticism one receives is a good deal keener than people . . . can know. Besides, critics are perhaps the most important part of one's audience."[16] Nearly alone among the respondents, he felt that "there is a place in the present economic system for literature as a profession" (even though, he admitted, he had never tried to attain it himself), and he deduced from his own encouraging experiences in the decade that "the audience for serious American poetry must have grown in the last ten years" ("The Situation in American Writing," 39–40).

The realization that there were people who considered his work enduringly valuable, brought home to Stevens by these readers who were much younger than himself, offered a strong inducement to reconsider his own identity as a poet and, on a broader level, encouraged him to try to articulate the role of the poet in modern society, a theme that would occupy much of his prose and poetry for the next two decades. For their part most readers perceived that *Ideas of Order, Owl's Clover*, and *The Man With the Blue Guitar* concerned themselves with the value of poetry far more conventionally and affirmatively than had the disturbingly avant-garde *Harmonium*. Their sense of Stevens's new accessibility and relevance allowed readers of the late 1930s to develop forceful ways of evaluating the poet favorably within more conventionally understood (and hence more easily canonical) frames of reference. Collectively the reviews of the three books of the late 1930s were both assertions and reflections of Stevens's increasing prominence in a cultural climate that held sensitivity and adaptability to a rapidly changing contemporary society among its paramount values. Stevens's shift in status from fastidious eremite to prolific participant forced nearly all readers and critics concerned with modernist poetry into a reevaluation of the dominant opinion of him as a dabbler rather than as a committed poet. Perceiving a sober but hopeful dialectic of change and continuity in Stevens's engagement with the contemporary world, many commentators concluded that he was one of the few modernist poets who was capable of doing important work in the future. The reception of these three books advanced Stevens's reputation so much that by 1940 he would possess a canonical potential equaled by few modernist poets.

Given the general awareness of Stevens's meager output, it is surprising that most reviewers of *Ideas of Order* took in stride the fact that they found a new Stevens book in front of them—and then found two more within two years. Almost no one expressed any strong surprise that Stevens's pen had not dried up permanently. Probably some knew that he was again sending pieces to magazines, although most of the recipients—*Alcestis* and its fellows—were hardly widely prominent. What this lack of surprise also suggests is that the younger critics who did much of the reviewing in the late 1930s had already come to see Stevens not as a purveyor of dated relics of aestheticism but as an immanent presence of contemporary poetry.[17] In the two years between 1935 and 1937, this impression was reinforced as major Stevens works emerged and reemerged in a bewildering publishing sequence that strongly encouraged reviewers to consider them as interdependent elements of an evolving oeuvre rather than as isolated volumes. *Ideas of Order*, published in limited edition by Alcestis Press in August 1935, garnered a few reviews on its own, and was then reissued by Knopf in October 1936, where it got a few more. Alcestis then issued *Owl's Clover* only a month later, before a number of periodicals had reviewed either edition of *Ideas of Order*; the result was several reviews that dealt with both works (and a few with *Owl's Clover* only). Then, Knopf's publication of *The Man With the Blue Guitar* in October 1937 included a revised version of *Owl's Clover*; again, a number of reviewers discussed both long works together. These books constituted a locus of ambitious work that definitively served notice that Stevens was back in the ranks of productive poets and almost completely dissipated the prevalent 1920s view of the poet as exasperatingly reticent miniaturist.

The timing of Stevens's comeback was especially fortuitous for his canonical potential. Had his prolific period begun ten years earlier, for example, in the mid-1920s, his second, third, and fourth works would have emerged in a far different critical climate, and evaluations of them and of his career would have followed a very different course over the next decades. Assimilated and perceived as works of the 1920s, these hypothetical poems, and Stevens's reputation, might well have met with far more resistance in the politically charged critical climate of the 1930s. As it was, *Harmonium* did come in for some castigation as "the kind of verse that people concerned with the murderous world collapse can hardly swallow today except in tiny doses" (Burnshaw, "Turmoil," 42). Had Stevens entered the 1930s with a significantly larger corpus on the order of *Harmonium,* by the end of the decade he might have been on his way to canonical oblivion as a frivolous aesthete marked so indelibly by the 1920s that his later efforts could not have reversed the process.[18] Emerging when they did, however, and bearing the mark of the poet's concerns with the times, yet refusing to give in to millenarian despair or utopian fantasy, Stevens's three works of the late 1930s achieved a balance of urgency and continued hopefulness which seemed to capture a large part of the critical mood.

Almost every reviewer saw these three volumes as coming from a poet in the midst of a major intellectual transition that had been brought about by contemporary social tumult. *Ideas of Order* was seen primarily as a negative movement, a rejection of an earlier poetic mode which cleared the decks for a new kind of poetry grounded in contemporary reality and positive statement. For Ben Belitt in *The Nation, Ideas of Order* was not fully realized poetry but "a volume almost wholly transitional," and John Holmes remarked that "recent moods of the real world have affected him, and they show in this book" (Belitt, "The Violent Mind," 709; Holmes, review, *Virginia Quarterly Review,* 294). *Owl's Clover* was seen predominantly as a not entirely satisfactory attempt at such definite statement, nonetheless to be commended to the poetry-reading public as an intermediate offering from a poet who was becoming increasingly important. Belitt described these two stages of Stevens's reconstructive project thus: "the edifice of a new technique begins to take shape amid the wreckage of the old" ("The Violent Mind," 710). Likewise, although Eda Lou Walton noted that *Owl's Clover* was "a little weighted with thought, a little less successful than the lyrics in *Ideas of Order,*" she ascribed the lack of success to the difficulty and importance of Stevens's attempt to achieve a broader poetry of direct and affirmative statement (review of *Ideas of Order,* 18).

By the time of *Owl's Clover,* reviewers had not yet assimilated the newly discursive and prolific Stevens; *The Man With the Blue Guitar* gave reviewers another, more accessible opportunity to extend the advocacy of Stevens many of them clearly wished to develop. Less than eleven months after their judgments of *Owl's Clover,* both Belitt and Walton reviewed *The Man With the Blue Guitar;* their enthusiasm suggested the tremendous advances in Stevens's ongoing explorations of what they now saw as consistent, recognizable, and relevant concerns—as Walton put it, "the relationship between the world of the imagination and the real world" (Walton, "Wallace Stevens's Two Worlds," 5; Belitt, " 'Lion in the Lute,' " 508). The immediate critical response to *Blue Guitar* was the most strongly favorable to any Stevens volume until *Collected Poems,* suggesting less about its intrinsic greatness than about the evaluative conditions at the time of its publication. *Blue Guitar* was the culmination and the beneficiary of the larger dual process Stevens underwent in this group of works: the recuperation from his earlier hyperaesthetic association and the authoritative assertion of his voice in the field of contemporary poetry.

Clearly reading conditions of the late 1930s differed dramatically from those of even the late 1920s. The near-universality of reviewers' perceptions of the changes that they felt characterized Stevens's new work suggests that, no less than the poet, critics were casting about for ways of making sense of the turbulence of the contemporary scene. Under these conditions, a poet's apparent ability and willingness to adapt to the times became an extremely important criterion by which he or she could be evaluated. Nearly all commentators on the trilogy saw the world of *Harmonium* as dead; those who persisted in denigrating Stevens felt that the poet had not succeeded in distancing himself enough from that world (Grigson, 18; Deutsch, review of *Ideas of Order*, 18; Schneider, 24; Roethke, review of *Ideas of Order*, 304; Van Ghent, 46). The majority of the evaluators, however, saw Stevens's intellectual journey as a movement of sensitivity and fortitude from an aestheticist complacency towards a more relevant and important position, both intellectually and within the ranks of modernist poetry. Even though *Ideas of Order* and *Owl's Clover* were not often seen as his finest work, many reviewers were willing to give this pilgrim Stevens the benefit of the doubt, finding adequate compensation for the relative disappointment they felt and expressing faith that he was on his way to doing major work in the future. The fullest expression of this sort of response to Stevens in the late 1930s was Walton's review of *Ideas of Order* in *The New York Times Book Review*, which placed his recent works in the context of his changing intellectual position in a changing world and perceived his unwillingness to rest within variously conceived "limitations":

> Since Wallace Stevens is undoubtedly one of our best poets, it is interesting to trace the changes in his artistic position. He has been the pure epicurean, sophisticated and intellectual. . . . Today he is certainly taking account of a world in which this philosophy is antiquated. He is trying to evaluate the position of the artist in a world of struggle, of action. If this means for a time, that his poetry is less surely perfect, it means also that his later poetry may be more significant than his earlier work. [Walton, review of *Ideas of Order*, 18]

Here one sees the identical valorization of "significance" over "perfection" that previous commentators had often used to denigrate Stevens, but now it was turned in Stevens's favor. Walton's acknowledgement and dismissal of potential faults in the poet suggested that evaluative stances toward Stevens had dramatically changed from those of 1923, when his virtues had been admitted and then ignored or devalued as he was relegated to poetic minority. Now even acknowledged shortcomings were placed within a favorable overall evaluation of his career and position within modernist poetry.

The widespread respect for Stevens seen in these evaluations of the late 1930s also began to manifest itself in an attribute that is perhaps central to the canonicity of any author or work: a chameleonic quality that enabled readers at many points along generational, political, and aesthetic spectra to view him as addressing important issues in ways congenial to them. Clearly his reputation no longer rested entirely on the support of a small avant-garde coterie of his own generation of readers. The veteran poets and critics of that generation who had supported Stevens's work for two decades—Monroe, Williams, Kreymborg, Moore, William Rose Benét—still expressed interest and sympathy with his development. On the other hand, several interested commentators—Schwartz, Burnshaw, Roethke, Fitzgerald, and Belitt—were still in their twenties, suggesting the emergence of a new generation of poets and critics in whose canons Stevens had already become a central figure, a generation whose devotion to and descent from Stevens would manifest itself in many ways over the next thirty years, culminating in Roethke's slightly rueful assertion to his fellows, "Brother, he's our father" ("A Rouse for Stevens," 117.) The strong feelings from which such declarations would come were only beginning to build in 1935, but they were there. Eileen Simpson's memoir of this generation of poets, *Poets in Their Youth,* notes in a revealing offhand way Stevens's role as a "master" whom the circle of young poets, including Schwartz, John Berryman, and Randall Jarrell, might evoke in praising one another's poetic achievements—as early as the late 1930s (32).

One of the evaluative patterns most often damaging to the reputation of aging poets might be seen as an oedipal phenomenon: the scorn or disinterest of a younger generation of poets and critics, who form their own creative identities at least partially through attacking their immediate predecessors as old-fashioned and worthless. Such impulses had already helped to erode the once-high poetic reputations of Lowell, Robinson, Masters, Millay, and Sandburg. This attack on the poetic parents was often accomplished by the portrayal of earlier historical and artistic trends such as popular modernism and

Imagism as dated or absurd. For Stevens, however, a younger commentator such as Schwartz was willing to go out of his way to connect Stevens's characteristic mannerisms sympathetically to the milieu of avant-garde modernism. Though he did not use the term avant-garde, Schwartz clearly understood the effect on Stevens of that characteristic mode of early modernism: "To be a poet at that time was to be peculiar; merely to be interested in the arts was to take upon oneself the burden of being superior, and an exile at home. It may be that as a result of some such feeling, Stevens called his wonderful discourse on love Le Monocle de Mon Oncle . . . thus mocking, as so often . . . the poem itself, as if the poet were extremely self-conscious about the fact of being a poet" ("New Verse," 49).

Beginning in such times and circles as Stevens did, Schwartz suggested, one would inevitably bear resemblances to certain other writers thought of as dandies—Van Vechten, Donald Evans, Santayana, Laforgue, Verlaine. This identification of a stylistic lineage was not, however, a condemnation to the datedness of most of these others: if the "resemblances" were "unmistakable," they were also "superficial," purely attributable to historical circumstance, and did not circumscribe Stevens's value (49).

This historicized view of Stevens's avant-gardism gave Schwartz and his readers the ability to see the poet as a product of his times, like everyone else, but also as a force with the potential to comprehend and make sense of changes in those times. For Schwartz, as for other interwar poet-critics who wished to distance themselves from early modernism, if the avant-garde was no longer a viable movement within contemporary poetry, it *had* had a recognized impact upon the larger cultural scene in having shaped, but not limited, its most powerful poets—which included Stevens.[19] For Belitt, another young poet with a kinship to Stevens, Ideas of Order showed signs of broadening the poet's range from the "fractional" Imagist aesthetic "toward a poetry of statement," which would complete the "full circle which returns both sound and image to experience and unites the fractional with the definitive insight" ("The Violent Mind," 709). For Belitt, Imagism was a stage that modern poetry had had to go through, but its great limitation of fragmentariness had become plain to those who came later. Stevens, however, had the potential to use Imagism's virtues without being stymied by its limitations, to build a poetics of definition and unity.

Even in the politically volatile literary climate of the mid-1930s, Stevens's work was received with respect and interest by writers from across the political spectrum. Though he came under mild scrutiny from the left, the most famous of these leftist "attacks"—Burnshaw's review of *Ideas of Order* in *The New Masses*, which was widely misunderstood by Stevens and by later critics—actually gave the poet a good deal of credit as an artist both of existing achievement and contemporary relevance. To Burnshaw, Stevens deserved to be placed among poets "whose artistic statures have long been recognized." If *Harmonium* was the sort of "verse that Stevens can no longer write," it was to Stevens's credit that he knew that and yet continued to attempt a different kind.[20] Rather than inhabiting "some escapist limbo," Stevens reflected the uncertainty and confusion of a writer grappling with belonging to a dying bourgeois class: "These writers [Stevens and Haniel Long] are in the throes of struggle for philosophic adjustment. And their words have intense value and meaning to the sectors within their class whose confusion they articulate. Their books have deep importance for us [Marxists] as well" ("Turmoil," 42).

Both a leftist critic and a longstanding admirer of Stevens's poetry, Burnshaw was a firm member of the interwar generation that saw Stevens as a figure of enduring achievement. As such, he was "frankly overwhelmed" when he heard that his review ("Wallace Stevens and the Statue") had spurred Stevens to the verse of "Mr. Burnshaw and the Statue."[21]

For Burnshaw, on the left, Stevens had undertaken the difficult struggle to "keep his balance" in the midst of drastic and inexorable changes in the ground of contemporary existence; for F. O. Matthiessen, nearer the political center, Stevens had managed to balance individual aesthetic integrity with acknowledged social responsibilities. In the *Yale Review,* Matthiessen distinguished Stevens from fellow modernists Frost and Jeffers, both for his attention to the character of contemporary existence and for the continued extension of his unique poetic voice and range; Stevens was "the one [poet at hand] whose lines yield both the sense of a strong individual life and a mature apprehension of actual society" ("Society and Solitude," 606). The valorization of continued development in middle-aged poets was apparent especially in Matthiessen's damning estimate of Jeffers, whose new book, *Solstice and Other Poems,* would "not heighten the estimate in which the work of Mr. Jeffers is held. His new volume reveals no new contours, but voices again his few basic assumptions" (605). In explicit contrast, Stevens's refusal to "rush to any easy extreme" of apocalyptic melodrama gave him a credibility that was both healing and sensible: "[Stevens] envisages life not merely as change but as continuity" (606). Stevens thus escaped the trap of moralizing from any side, while still vividly realizing in verse the sensation of living in the contemporary world; "his poems do not make statements about life; they create for the reader an illusion of sharing in a complete experience" (606).

For Marianne Moore, further to the right in her austere individualism, Stevens's work evoked the quality of "fortitude" (a concept that had also appeared in some of the 1931 reviews) in the midst of potentially disastrous situations. Moore felt that *Ideas of Order* soberly acknowledged the loss of what was best in the earlier world but did not constitute a requiem because of the vigorous integrity of Stevens's gaze upon the new world: "requiem is not the word when anyone hates lust for power and ignorance of power, as [Stevens] does. So long as we are ashamed of the ironic feast, and of our marble victories . . . there is hope for the world" ("Unanimity and Fortitude," 272). In her own way, then, Moore too acknowledged a substantial role for an artist such as Stevens: to decry not only the abuses of humanity by the appetites engendered in the realm of political power but also the tendency to ignore and thus allow the operation of such appetites.

The pervasive valorizations of change, adaptability, and adjustment in Stevens commentary suggest that in the middle 1930s an engagement with contemporary reality, an attempt to create poetry in and with sociocultural change, became a canonical criterion for ascribing literary value. Poetry's relation to the times could be conceived quite variably by readers and critics, but it had to have one. It is doubtful, however, that even the most doctrinaire Marxist critics believed that the advocacy or illustration of social change would in itself produce great poetry.[22] Stevens was valued not only because he had changed but because in changing he affirmed continuities with existing cultural values and images, most centrally with the value of poetry itself.

Critical perceptions of Stevens's new accessibility and relevance emphasized attributes in his discourse which suggested the poet's own newly felt (or at least newly expressed) connections to a cultural heritage held in common with his readers. *Ideas of Order* made it apparent that Stevens could no longer portray himself as the unflappable, absolutely independent aesthete to whom artistic and social convention meant little. Whereas the world portrayed in *Harmonium* had consisted mostly of exotic flora, fauna, and topography, creating a naturalistic landscape that seemed to have little direct connection to contemporary social existence, the landscape of *Ideas of Order*, according to many reviewers, brought with it "a new sombreness, a new gravity" in which "the colors are less exotic, the associations less strange" (Roethke, review of *Ideas of Order* 304).

Stevens's acknowledgement in "Mozart, 1935" that "the snow is falling / And the streets are full of cries" suggested that he had turned away from contemplating the cosmic winkings of fictive things to aver that he was indeed a part of the world of his readers—a humanizing and elevating concession to many. He no longer seemed interested in alienating readers by continually asserting his radical difference from—or indifference to—them; indeed, he appeared to have been shaken into commiseration, even empathy, with the problems of other humans. The most forceful expression of this change in Stevens's attitude towards his implied readers came from Burnshaw in *The New Masses*, who concluded that the "harmonious cosmos [of Stevens's early work] is suddenly screeching with confusion. *Ideas of Order* is the record of a man who, having lost his footing, now scrambles to stand up and keep his balance" ("Turmoil," 42). Such an analysis of Stevens's inner anxieties would have been almost inconceivable just after *Harmonium,* a volume that had been based around strategies for making itself and its creator invulnerable. Burnshaw's acute intrusion into Stevens's psyche was undoubtedly part of the reason his review hit such a nerve.

In contrast to the alienating avant-garde function of *Harmonium's* ebullient landscape of natural and linguistic exotica, the somber figurations on the surface of these new books performed an important function of admission, in two senses. Readers now felt admitted to, not alienated from, a world recognizable both in its physical topography and in its problematic social shape, with, for example, brooding old women and aimless young people so downtrodden as to be blind to the monuments to the human imagination around them. In allowing such changes into the world his poems depicted, Stevens could also be read as making an implicit admission that he had not yet considered the breadth of human experience and was now attempting to expand the scope of his poetry. By putting his formal authority behind the demand for an art that did indeed grapple with contemporary social themes, Stevens appeared to make a great concession to those who had had misgivings about the seriousness of his work.

Reviewers responded keenly to such admissions in the three books. In the passages they chose to quote, they concentrated heavily on the poet's numerous paradigmatic images of change. Figures of journeying, for example, in poems such as "Farewell to Florida" and "Sailing After Lunch," suggested to them Stevens's resolution "to withdraw from 'Floridian' self-indulgence and calm [and] to return to the violent mind," the mind of man in the poet's own natural home, the North (Belitt, "The Violent Mind," 710; also see Walton, review of *Ideas of Order*, 18). Where the headpiece to *Harmonium*, "Earthy Anecdote," had been avoided entirely by critics, "Farewell to Florida," heading the Knopf edition of *Ideas of Order*, was widely seen as a master demonstration of the current Stevens position. Gaudy rhetoric was explicitly subordinated to a forceful language of muted humility, as the speaker, professing uncertainly the conviction that things would soon be better, embarked on a fateful journey northward. Stevens similarly revised his tendency in *Harmonium* to use gestural patterns to depict pure motion rather than to communicate emotion. Established by the disordered flight of the bucks from the firecat in the first poem of *Harmonium*, "Earthy Anecdote," and reinforced in such poems as "The Jack-Rabbit," "Domination of Black," "Tea," and the final section of "Sunday Morning," the dominant gestural pattern of that volume had asserted the primacy of natural processes and forces over human concerns. In various poems in *Ideas of Order*—"Farewell to Florida," "Dance of the Macabre Mice," "Waving Adieu, Adieu, Adieu," and "Mozart, 1935"—this central gesture was revised and humanized into images of people in chaotic misery that could not be dismissed as complacently as the bucks could:

> Sudden clouds of faces and arms,
> An immense suppression, freed,
> These voices crying without knowing for what,
> Except to be happy, without knowing how.
> ["Sad Strains of a Gay Waltz," *CP*, 122]

Also noted prominently by early readers of these volumes were Stevens's figurations acknowledging the necessity, in a changing world, of reconceiving the conventions and functions of cultural forms such as music, dance, painting, sculpture, and poetry. Here again the poet appeared to revise drastically the individualistic avant-gardism of *Harmonium*, where he had promoted reader alienation by using hermetic poetic forms (anecdote and colloquy) and weird linguistic coinages (Hoon, Azcan, Don Joost). Evoking creators and forms from the mainstream of Western culture, *Ideas of Order* and its successors demonstrated for the first time to many readers that Stevens was a poet who had something important to say about the culture shared by poet and reader. In music, Stevens revealed a classicist preoccupation by prominently evoking Mozart ("Mozart, 1935") and Brahms ("Anglais Mort à Florence") as nostalgic remembrances of times of individualism and harmony. The musings of the "Botanist on Alp" used the idyllic landscapes of Claude to articulate the drastic changes that were remaking the culture Stevens had known. Remembering wistfully "how near one was" in Claude to a metaphysical center ("the central composition, / The essential theme"), Stevens's speaker ponders the present world of "Statues and stars, / Without a theme" but eventually concludes that the present "panorama of despair" cannot continue indefinitely in "this ecstatic air." As an empirical scientist, a taxonomist, an explorer of present existence, the botanist-poet will continue, despite his nostalgia, to monitor and derive knowledge from the landscape that actually exists rather than retreating into an idealized landscape of metaphysical yearning.

Often such references to art forms were mixed to create an expressive cultural package: music and dance in "Sad Strains of a Gay Waltz," dance and sculpture in "Dance of the Macabre Mice," the whole gamut in "Lions in Sweden." Stevens's usual pattern in such culturally allusive poems was, as Matthiessen put it, to note sadly "the emptiness that has crept into conventional forms of thought and feeling," to acknowledge "the stirring of the immense suppressed energies that are rising beyond those forms" ("Society and Solitude," 606), and then to suggest that if the old "sovereigns of the soul" were no longer useful in contemporary times, they needed replacement by new "modes of desire": "The truth is that there comes a time / When we can mourn no more over music / That is so much motionless sound" (*CP*, 121). This ambivalent evocation of changing cultural values was in explicit contrast to *Harmonium*, which had practically ignored the very existence of the cultural heritage that was now being transformed. Indeed, the two longest poems of Stevens's trilogy were both built on examinations of explicitly public images of artistic endeavor: the commemorative statue of *Owl's Clover* (and other poems) and the guitarist playing to an audience. Both of these central figures portrayed art as having a communal rather than a private significance and demonstrated Stevens's new concern for what Michael North has called "the relationship between poetry and politics, between the poet and his readers, and between the poetic and its material."²³

In perhaps the most crucial divergence from the avant-garde stance of *Harmonium*, Stevens now explicitly acknowledged the importance, even the urgency, of taking seriously his own poetry, the poetry of others, and poetry as a metaphor for living in the world. *Harmonium* had casually played with and undermined the poet and poetic activity in works as small as "Negation" and "Explanation" and as large as "The Comedian as the Letter C." In *The Man With the Blue Guitar*, however, Stevens was willing to figure the poet as producing "a substitute for all the gods" (*CP*, 176). It was clear to Schwartz from this poem that the new Stevens "justifies poetry, he defines its place, its role, its priceless value" ("New Verse," 51). Similarly, Blackmur noted what he saw as the increasingly sacral undertones of the Stevensian conception and method of poetry. In his remarks on *Owl's Clover*, Blackmur linked the developing concerns of Stevens's work to the poet's fundamental reconception of the role of poetry in the sustenance of a culture: "the conscious emphasis upon the imagination as itself a primary theme is something of an anomaly in the history of the arts. . . . [I]t is another sign, I suppose, that the artist has himself to do the work formerly done for him by Church and State and the operative morale of society: he has to establish in the very process of his work what a mature society took for granted . . . the nature and value of the imaginative act" ("The Composition in Nine Poets," 573–74). For several reviewers of 1937, Stevens succeeded in this double duty as few other modernist poets had done—he simultaneously argued theoretically and demonstrated technically the value of the imaginative act.

Aided by the poems' references to commonly significant cultural forms, reviewers perceived that Stevens's work not only meant to chronicle the tribulations of an isolated artist (as *Harmonium* had often been seen in the individualistic 1920s) but also sought ambitiously to make sense of a cultural totality. The very impersonality that had once made Stevens seem emotionless now offered tools for the enlargement of the social scope of the poet and poetic utterance. Readers such as Belitt applauded Stevens's increased ambition and scope: "Though the poetry of Wallace Stevens has not lacked themes of commanding contemporary stature, these have not, until recently, constituted his major concern" ("The Violent Mind," 709). Stevens's willingness to deal with themes of such magnitude meant that the experience of reading his poetry now produced a sense of striking authority and newly central relevance: "One ... is a little surprised by, the eminence of the poems. Not their excellence, for that is customary in Stevens, but a passionate sharpness of authority which I do not remember having felt before" (Fitzgerald, 153).

A significant part of this enlarged "authority" exuded by Stevens's poetry was its power to determine its own conditions and criteria of evaluation. In *Partisan Review*, for example, Schwartz suggested that the poems in *Blue Guitar* "constitute a special kind of museum, of a very familiar strangeness, located, because of the extent of the poet's awareness, in the middle of everything which concerns us." The oxymoronic quality of the poems' impact on Schwartz, and the basis of his evaluation, derived from the charge given to the player of the blue guitar. Like Schwartz's strange yet familiar "museum," Stevens's guitarist, and hence his book, aimed to preserve and evoke the remote peaks of human achievement ("But play, you must, / A tune beyond us") yet simultaneously to remain situated in the middle of the quotidian world, firmly grounded in the "real": ("yet ourselves, / A tune . . . of things exactly as they are") (Schwartz, "New Verse," 52; *The Man With the Blue Guitar* (CP, 165). Schwartz' conjunctions of the utterance of the individual artist with a public and social context for art clearly owed much to Stevens's own developing ideas about art in a world of political change and cultural upheaval.

It is not surprising that such perceptions of Stevens's "authority" and "passion" brought forth responses that portrayed the poet as a sort of hero of the imagination. Whereas for years Stevens had appeared to readers to have an "instrument," a "hand," or a "palette," finely wrought technical capabilities on which he made "music" or "painted" a relatively ephemeral product, now his capacious poetic abilities were often translated by reviewers into figures of "mind," an organically integrated force of the imagination which both exised inside each poem and transcended any given poem. Fitzgerald contrasted Stevens's "fantastic mind" of multiple, flexible facets, which demonstrated an "intellectual coherence," with the "exertions in sterility" of Yvor Winters's verse, "where 'thought' means a few highly wrought commonplaces in inanimate form, the life and play of the mind reduced to drill" (Fitzgerald, 154). Concepts such as "thought" and "mind" were as far as can be imagined from the frivolous intellectual noodling seen by early commentators; instead they were the basis of a moral significance for art. Schwartz, like Blackmur, experienced Stevens's precise, difficult formalism as an ultimate "justice"; upon perceiving it, the reader was "confronted with" the magnificence of "a mind of the utmost seriousness, aware and involved in the most important things in our lives," "a mind in love not only with the beautiful, but also with the just" (Schwartz, "New Verse," 50, 51).

Valorizations of Stevens's strength and flexibility in the face of both social change and continuity were often accompanied by the valorization of the sophistication and difficulty of his technique and by a concomitant reconception of poetic obscurity that was strongly beneficial to his reputation. For many reasons—not the least of which were Eliot's poetic and critical prominence, the proliferation of explicative performances like Blackmur's essays, and a greater overall familiarity with the techniques of modern poetry—readers of the mid-1930s were less taken aback by the rhetorical difficulty and tonal ambiguity of Stevens's poetry than those of 1923 had been. Reviewers of 1935 no longer felt it necessary to ascribe to Stevens the quality of terminal obscurity. Though no one claimed that he was an easy poet, there was none of the throwing up of hands over "the complete lack of any intelligible sense" seen after *Harmonium* ("Recent Books in Brief Review," 483). Indeed, Burnshaw explicitly undertook to revise the history of Stevens's unintelligibility, pointing out that in 1923 "nobody stopped to ask if [Stevens] had any ideas. It was tacitly assumed that one read him for pure sensation." Speaking for many younger readers and critics of the 1930s, Burnshaw rejected this sensationalist consensus, noting that "certain ideas weave through [*Harmonium*] consistently," giving it nodes of coherence ("Turmoil," 41). The assumption so damaging to Stevens's reputation in the 1920s—that suave sounds and profound substance in poetry were somehow inversely proportional—had by 1935 largely eroded.

John Holmes's brief notices of both editions of *Ideas of Order*, coming eight months apart, provided strong evidence of readers' growing confidence that they were understanding Stevens better. In April 1936, Holmes's characterization of Stevens evoked the well-known 1920s views of Louis Untermeyer and Llewellyn Powys, and his own evaluation of the poet was somewhat vague and old-fashioned: "[Stevens is] one of the most successful non-communicating poets of his day. But it is only ideas that he does not communicate. . . . Through the most fantastically logical world of imagery which these generations know, he does communicate feeling. . . . Meaning it has never had, in the ordinary superficial sense, because it has so little to do with the world of actuality. But this time some meaning has crept in" (Holmes, review of *Ideas of Order*, in *Virginia Quarterly Review*, 294).

The enthusiasm that was still confused in April had blossomed into confident understanding by December, and these earlier opinions had become obsolete for Holmes, who now felt that from his "earlier unintelligibility," Stevens "has suddenly become a poet whose meaning is at once reachable, while his unique skill with words, his ability to surprise the eye and mind, has grown more and more pronounced." Either Stevens had "become intelligible, or much reading [had] sharpened this reviewer's imagination" (*Boston Evening Transcript*, 2). Or both.

Many readers, then, no longer expected poetry to yield easy resolutions, obvious beauty, or ultimate truth, as genteel audiences had expected (and usually received). Thus the late 1930s were an especially fortuitous time for the methods of Stevens's later work, which played with ideas rhetorically in an exploratory discourse in which little was resolved but much was satisfyingly entertained. Walton, Belitt, and Fitzgerald each approvingly noted that among the major connotations of the blue guitar as a central symbol was an aesthetic based upon improvisation, which they then connected to such ethical values as "truth" or "integrity." Fitzgerald called his review "Thoughts Revolved," following the poem of that name, asserting that Stevens's poetry was nearly unique among contemporary verse in "being a thought revolved, i.e. displayed by the fantastic mind in its true facets and circling to a point of rest" (Fitzgerald, 154; see also Walton, "Wallace Stevens's Two Worlds," 5). Belitt emphasized the impressive rhythmic effectiveness of the blue guitar sequence, connecting the equation of form and content that Blackmur had developed to Stevens's new method of virtuosic improvisation: "it must be noted again that the logic and the music of the poem are indistinguishable—that the former is, indeed, simply a theme for instrumentation, and is not so much developed as *strummed*" (Belitt, " 'Lion in the Lute,' " 508; emphasis in text). Not resolution, then, but a kind of revolution—self-assertive, resistant to reduction through a perpetual multiplicity of perspectives, and productive of the temporary but refreshing satisfactions implicit in "rest"—was now seen as central to the Stevensian aesthetic.

Smilarly, Ruth Lechlitner linked Stevens's authoritative thematic breadth in *The Man With the Blue Guitar* to his aesthetic of eclecticism, which she found appropriate to both contemporary times and universal art: "The distinguished place which Wallace Stevens now holds among our active contemporary poets has been achieved because—apart from his technical accomplishments—he has chosen as a working basis a theme of sufficient magnitude to admit infinite variation" ("Wallace Stevens' Poetry," 2). Obviously, infinite variations were not simply the infinite repetitions of the same few themes for which critics such as Matthiessen and Zabel were condemning the work of Jeffers and Frost. For Lechlitner, Stevens's new work combined an impressive thematic scope with both an overwhelming technical versatility and a tonal flexibility that meant he could capture nearly any human mood or cultural reference: "he can combine harmoniously a metaphysical image having a seventeenth-century aura with a jazz-note hot from the modern ether." As such a virtuoso of technique, tone, and theme, Stevens was not a narrow aestheticist but a central exemplar of modern poetry: "As a master of form Wallace Stevens, who may be considered by some primarily a 'poet's poet,' should be studied by all aspirants to the art" (2).

Reviewers had apparently forgotten how much of *Harmonium* had been, or seemed to its first readers, casually and formlessly tossed off. Indeed, the improvisatory method of *Blue Guitar* was not at all incompatible with the casual informality of *Harmonium* poems such as "Nuances of a Theme By Williams," "Metaphors of a Magnifico," "Six Significant Landscapes," "Explanation," and even "Peter Quince at the Clavier," in which the figure of poet as improvisatory musician had begun for Stevens. Except for the last of these, such poems had always been marginal within Stevens's criticism in favor of more highly wrought poems such as "Sunday Morning" and "To the One of Fictive Music," but such qualities ignored or criticized as slight or trivial in *Harmonium* were now seen as constituting a usefully flexible method of thematic development for *Blue Guitar*. In employing an improvisatory method in *Blue Guitar*, Stevens was seen to be productively examining the question of the relationship of his poetry to central cultural concerns, as he had promised to do since *Ideas of Order*.

For Fitzgerald, Schwartz, Walton, Belitt, and Lechlitner, Stevens had appropriately addressed—if not quieted—his recent questionings by demonstrating that there were no final answers. This nonconclusion was not, however, to cede the poet's responsibility for engagement with social questions. If it was necessary to acknowledge that poetry, as part of a complex and difficult social world, would yield no easy or complete solutions, it did not mean that poetry was not potentially one of the strongest articulations of that world. Indeed, Lechlitner conceived of the blue guitar "in the hands of the poet . . . [as] a torch against dictators" since it continually affirmed the puissance of the individual imagination not in isolation from but in interaction with people and things as they were in 1937 ("Wallace Stevens' Poetry," 2). Insofar as they could be read as poems of "public significance and earnestness" (Fitzgerald, 153–54), Stevens had begun to fill the demand for verse that could help to make sense of the times, whatever the times might be.

If Stevens no longer seemed to be working in obscure forms of his own, his new accessibility and relevance in taking on these momentous cultural issues had cost him very little in what had always been his strongest point, an outstanding formal authority. For Marianne Moore the new poems were "marvels of finish" (review of *Ideas of Order*, 308); Lechlitner noted Stevens's "superb mastery of form," which had now been extended to an ambitious attempt to make blank verse into "a flexible instrument for modern prosody" (Imagination as Reality," 40). Matthiessen felt that Stevens had gained much scope while losing none of his prowess: "There is no longer the *dandyisme* of 'Le Monocle de Mon Oncle,' or the slightly affected traces as in the elaborate language of 'The Comedian. . . .' But there has been no waning in the lusty joy of his senses, or in the acute perception . . . or in what has always been his outstanding gift, the subtle resilient modulations of rhythm" ("Society and Solitude," 606).

For the readers who had wanted him to, Stevens had renounced the droning beaches of Florida for a "cooler, graver, 'northward' moving voice" (Lechlitner, Imagination as Reality," 40). On the other hand, for those (older) readers more interested in his formal elegance—Benét, Monroe, Moore—he remained "a beautiful and scrupulous artist" (Benét, 18). Such shifts in readers' perceptions of his seriousness meant that the formal authority Stevens had always possessed was gradually being unleashed from being a limited virtue, as in Untermeyer and Wilson, to become his most formidable claim to canonical importance.

To a number of his most favorable readers and critics, Stevens was now fully canonical: his work was permanently valuable and was central in determining the very direction of contemporary poetry. One of those readers was Moore, who had predicted in her review of *Harmonium* that Stevens would be a prominent figure in the process of making the poetic mind tougher and more flexible. Moore was now happy to pursue the canonical consequences of this result. In reviews of *Ideas of Order* in *The Criterion* and *Poetry*, she gave Stevens the highest possible evaluation by comparing him to "the universal parent, Shakespeare," to whom Stevens "not infrequently" pointed ("Unanimity and Fortitude," 269). This rather startling comparison placed Stevens at the center of the main line of lyric poetry in English, about as far from avant-garde solipsism as can be conceived.[24] Moore continued her canonizing efforts on Stevens's behalf by systematically drawing an equivalence of seriousness, influence, and ultimate importance between Stevens and the poet at the very top of the avant-garde modernist canon, T. S. Eliot: "as if it were Antipholus of Ephesus and Antipholus of Syracuse, each has an almost too acute concept of 'the revenge of music': a realization that the seducer is the seduced. . . . Each is engaged in a similar though differently expressed search for that which will endure" ("Unanimity and Fortitude," 270).

Blackmur's summary opinion of Stevens' poetry, even of one of the poet's lesser works, concurred with Moore's formulation: "with Mr. Stevens and Mr. Eliot . . . it is in that direction that the fate of poetry may be looked for" ("Composition," 575). Of course few enough readers and critics in the literary culture as a whole judged Stevens as highly as this, but the very willingness of influential critics to make such sweeping superlative claims for Stevens—as opposed to acknowledging that he was a much better poet than Alfred Kreymborg, as reviews of 1923 tended to do—suggested the rapid consolidation of the poet's reputation in the second half of the 1930s.

Stevens's leap into the upper ranks of modernist reputations was clearly indicated by two strongly evaluative texts of the turn of the decade: Morton Zabel's extensive survey "Two Years of Poetry: 1937–1939," published in *The Southern Review* in late 1939, and the *Wallace Stevens Number* of the *Harvard Advocate* in December 1940. Zabel's piece considered the canonical potential of many of the older American modernist poets from the end of a momentous decade and gave Stevens the highest marks of any of them; the *Advocate* issue indicated Stevens's institutional connectedness and his importance in the thinking of a forceful group of younger poets and critics.

Zabel's piece in the *Southern Review* was the last of a series of sweeping surveys of the poetic scene by leading critics which appeared in that journal in the late 1930s and were crucial in shaping the poetic canons of the next quarter-century. Zabel began by noting the continuing dominance of the poetic scene by "twentieth-century ancestors," early modernists with established reputations, at the expense of the generation of younger poets that "has met some abrupt halt," perhaps because of "an excess of critical intelligence [that] has lamed [its] creative confidence" ("Two Years of Poetry, 1937–1939," 569). Despite acknowledging the admirable hardiness of the early modernists, the essay was tinged with an evaluative stringency (characteristic both of Zabel and of the *Southern Review*) that professed little ongoing interest in most living modernists and their new work. Only to Stevens and, to a lesser extent, William Carlos Williams did Zabel's evaluative scales tip strongly in a poet's favor.

Zabel's remarks on most early modernist poets, often quite harsh, suggested that they could be easily pigeonholed in one of two ways, both of which strongly suggested that a poet's ability to change was a central evaluative criterion. For Zabel, older modernists had either, like Robinson Jeffers and Genevieve Taggard, accreted into an iron-willed redundancy; or, like Millay, Frost, and Cummings, gradually lost most or all of their intellectual and aesthetic fortitude, falling in their recent work into repetitive, self-caricaturing mannerisms of shrillness, complacency, or adolescent triviality (respectively). These two types of decline might seem to be opposed, since one suggested rigidity and the other an atrophying looseness; but equally underlying both indictments was an inability to sustain a challenging and flexible engagement with changing times. Jeffers was "rigid," representing "an extremely narrow state of mind," producing "the most exhausting variations on [a] single theme," a poetry of "obsession" in which "singleness of motive amounts to monomania," all of which led Zabel to deduce "a central triviality in his character" (583–85). Zabel let Taggard off a little more easily, remarking that her course into radical politics had led to a depressing aesthetic "conformity" in which the poet's individual stance had "fallen into the most blankly trademarked of sentiments and expressions" (586).

On the other hand, Zabel demonstrated very similar evaluative preconceptions in prefiguring the coming critical backlash against the more-or-less canonical figures of Frost, Millay, and Cummings. Spoiled by success, "occupying a rank of almost official national esteem," Frost had gradually fallen into a pattern of provincial smugness, in which "an alarming degree of high-handed complacency has been deftly concealed by humility of manner" (578). Zabel posited an integral connection between Frost's enormous reputation and his loss of creative integrity: "Reputation in his case has been fortified not only by the safe-playing taciturnity of his Americanism but by the fact that his convictions and language have stayed fixed" (577).

If, as times changed, Frost's inflexible manner was concealing less of his unattractive character than it had before, Millay's more and more extreme poetic gestures were for Zabel increasingly revealing the lack of substance underneath. He devastatingly anatomized her volume *Huntsman, What Quarry?* as consisting of a series of overfamiliar, falsely vivacious gestures: "a good many tart and girlish survivals of Greenwich Village impertinence," "several dashes into Park Avenue French," "a number of samples of last-minute indignation on Czechoslovakia and Spain," "rewritings of standard favorites," and "the inevitable batch of sonnets" (570). Though his virtues were still evident to Zabel, Cummings was unfortunately possessed simultaneously by both symptoms of decline, in which "obsessive manias" and "self-indulgence" have "come near to depleting his reserves and reducing his great gifts to triviality," a failing less and less redeemed by ingenious formal structures, since "much of his syntactical and verbal oddity has worn thin" (595–96).

In contrast to these and other grim stories of decline, disintegration, and ossification, Zabel described a smaller group of poets who still represented a continuing quest for aesthetic development, for the remaking of their poetic selves, which was prerequisite to a continued relevance to the contemporary reader. The youngest generation of poets had before them "the example of several poets of critical and intellectual fortitude who faced their problems in a decade even less encouraging to poetic salvation than the present one" (602). Inasmuch as the only British and American poets Zabel thoroughly discussed in this way—Eliot, Williams, Stevens, and Yeats—are four of the strongest figures of current modernist poetic canons, it seems reasonable to assume that Zabel's convictions of the importance of continued development were broadly operative throughout the culture through the next decades. Of these four, Zabel considered Eliot and Williams quickly and less centrally. Eliot's major work of these two years, *The Family Reunion,* indicating his apparent drift away from lyric poetry towards the drama, made him somewhat marginal within Zabel's canon. Nonetheless, Zabel recognized the difficulty and the integrity of Eliot's move towards drama and was not willing to rule out the possibility that he would produce more important work (590). The (pre-*Paterson*) Williams, on the other hand, had not changed significantly but had stayed fresh, both a "pioneer" and a "modern classic" of experimental lyric poetry. For Zabel, Williams remained "a poet of unquestionable freshness, sensitiveness, and integrity—one of the few American survivors of the pre-War awakening" (594–95).

Such a self-consciously historicizing and canonizing remark as this last one betokened both the scope and the selectivity of Zabel's survey. Stevens was the single one of these "few survivors" whom Zabel considered at length and in a wholly favorable light in the essay. Zabel's view of Stevens emphasized exactly the two qualities he had found lacking in so many of his contemporaries: the ability to change and an increasing sense of responsibility to work for a poetic mode that would stand up to the times. As with many of Stevens's reviewers of the late 1930s, the poet's ability to adapt successfully to altered circumstances was in itself much more important to Zabel than the perfect aesthetic realization he had not yet achieved: "Wallace Stevens's book shows another talent developing toward moral and aesthetic criticism, and shows it in an especially arresting way because Stevens's art once achieved so complete a style and so reduced an expression of its ideas, that the sudden extension of powers takes on a dramatic force" (603).

But Stevens's rise was not simply a demonstration of the ability to change; indeed, *The Man With the Blue Guitar* and its fellow works represented

> a remarkable growth of talent. Several years ago his strongest admirers thought his career had ended. It seemed unlikely that [he] would find something to say to a generation inflamed by social explosion or riddled by every kind of intellectual doubt. Yet the integrity and richness of his original gift have served him well, and he now touches the moral and human problem of the poet at its most sensitive point. He brings into focus the idea of poetry and the world of practical values, and plays his lens on the severest duty that confronts the artist today. [605]

Stevens's sober yet still hopeful premise was central to Zabel's view of what poetry might do in the world of 1939: "Facing the decade's disasters in society and politics, [Stevens] believes we may be 'entering a period in which poetry may be of first importance to the spirit'" (604). Such a view of the engaged, useful, and relevant poet was in direct contrast to Zabel's reading of Frost, whose complacency damned him doubly in the face of the alternative of integrity offered by Stevens: "[Frost] has implicitly reproved, throughout his career, the distractions and unrest of his contemporaries. His book [*Collected Poems*] has the didactic effect of holding in contempt not only the radicalism of art and ideas that has disturbed his times, but also the unguarded susceptibilities among which he sees his fellow-men and fellow-poets floundering" (577).

Under such evaluative conditions as these, in which a poet such as Stevens was valorized for having both the integrity to admit to "floundering" along with his readers—and also the fortitude and the creative resources to continue the quest for a viable cultural role—it is little wonder that *Ideas of Order, Owl's Clover,* and *The Man With the Blue Guitar,* flawed as all of them were seen to be, were able to raise Stevens's stature dramatically in less than five years. Directly from his discussion of Stevens, Zabel began his conclusion with the remark that "we come thus to Yeats and Rilke" (605), two cosmopolitan "masters" whose passing demanded a final canonical apotheosis. If he was yet unable to place Stevens on such a level as this, Zabel obviously saw it a logical and fairly direct step to move from Stevens to a delineation of the absolute heights of his own canon. One difference was that Stevens was still vigorously writing and had the opportunity to produce his best work still ahead of him.

Despite his present obscurity, it would be a mistake to underestimate Zabel's influence in the literary milieu of mid-century America. In 1939 he had been institutionally central for nearly fifteen years, first within the little magazine culture as an associate editor of *Poetry* and the immediate successor to Harriet Monroe, then within the increasingly important realm of the critical quarterly, writing numerous major articles for the leading quarterlies, especially the *Southern Review.* In 1937 he had edited the influential compilation-anthology of critical evaluations called *Literary Opinion in America,* whose major emphasis through twenty-five years and three editions (in 1937, 1951, 1962) would be on intelligent criticism of modernist writing, especially poetry, by most of the consensually important critics of the day.[25] This collection, including still useful reference apparatus such as bibliographical and biographical material on American critics, was a canonical standard of the New Critical heyday; since its main audience would have been graduate students and young scholars, it no doubt had a strong influence on the institution of literary studies in this country.[26]

Zabel was also prominent enough as a critic to be invited to write one of the five major articles in the *Harvard Advocate* number on Stevens in December 1940. Though it could not pretend to be a widely read magazine, the *Advocate*'s sponsorship of Stevens is important in indicating his centrality among up-and-coming critics and among a generation of poetry-reading undergraduates at a major institutional site of contemporary literary-critical activity. Coming only two years after a similar issue on Eliot, the *Advocate* asserted Stevens's near-parity with the figurehead of the Harvard intellectual elite and of the avant-garde modernist canon. In keeping with the inevitably celebratory nature of such a project, praise for Stevens ran freely in these pages. What was said was perhaps no more important than the composition of the people doing the remarks, who fell into four categories: poets contemporary to Stevens; young critics on the Harvard faculty; critics who had already written pieces on Stevens; and finally, a small group of young New Critics whose remarks automatically lent prestige to such an undertaking. Moore and Williams, two of Stevens's oldest, most faithful contemporaries, responded favorably as usual. Delmore Schwartz, Theodore Spencer, Harry Levin, and F. O. Matthiessen, leading young critical lights, were all teaching at Harvard at this point, and all wrote statements or articles for the issue. Schwartz and Matthiessen had already considered the poet in important review articles, thereby overlapping into the third (and perhaps a fourth) category of evaluators. The third category of "Stevens critics" included Howard Baker, Hi Simons, and Zabel—who overlapped somewhat with the New Critical establishment consisting of Tate, Brooks, and Warren. Collectively this lineup included a significant proportion of the important American critics of mid-century—excluding the radical left.

The fact that all these important young critics were willing to praise Stevens strongly was in itself significant. This issue of the *Advocate* brought together and culminated evaluative patterns prevalent in views of the poet during the 1930s and presented strong and multiple arguments for the poet's place within the ranks of "important" early modernist poetry. In doing so, many commentators were aware that they were arguing an unproven case and proceeded in an explicitly revisionary critical mode. John Finch's essay "North and South in Stevens' America" began with the defensively conceived sentence, "Wallace Stevens is not an exotic," and Harry Levin's first sentence echoed Blackmur's evaluative revision toward formal grounds: "The things which make the poetry of Wallace Stevens interesting are the very things which make the poetry of so many of his contemporaries uninteresting—diction and metaphor" (Finch, 23; Levin, *Wallace Stevens Number*, 30). Theodore Spencer undertook to revise "the orthodox view of Stevens' poetry"—Van Wyck Brooks's evaluation of Stevens as a purveyor of disintegrated fragments—as "inaccurate" (26).

Another group of discussions, more confident of the ethical force of Stevens's formalism, and less possessed by the need to revise conventional views, pushed ahead with the major strand of discussion of Stevens in the late 1930s, in which he was seen as a poet of communal "integrity," courageously admitting his trepidation and concerns while adhering to his distinctive formal gifts. Matthiessen reiterated his opinion that Stevens's "many-sided awareness of disruption and breakdown" had "called out new resources, and his imagination has projected . . . what integrity and coherence can mean," resulting in the superlative conclusion that Stevens's work was "more impressive in scope than that of any other poet now writing in America" (*Wallace Stevens Number*, 31). Cleanth Brooks's statement was also built around the concept of integrity, an "integrity to his craft . . . even at the risk of a great deal of misunderstanding and deprecation" (*Wallace Stevens Number*, 29). Zabel's essay on "Stevens and the Image of Man" continued to develop Stevens as a poet who had set himself a crucial, even redemptive task for the poet in the modern world: "to make of man himself the instrument of knowledge and the medium of universal values" (22–23), and Schwartz's piece reinforced earlier comparisons of Stevens's verbal and rhythmic richness to Shakespeare, concluding with the assertion of the poet's "inexhaustible richness of significance and connection" ("The Ultimate Plato," 16).

The remainder of the substantial discussions of Stevens in the *Advocate* functioned as a substitute for Stevens's exclusion from Brooks's *Modern Poetry and the Tradition*. All at once, relations between Stevens and various "traditions" could be defined, to the benefit of his reputation. Howard Baker's essay gave Stevens a prosodic heritage, evoking Spenser, Milton, and Shakespeare, and asserting, like Winters, that Stevens, "a forceful champion of metrical regularity," was the only modernist poet to hold successfully to the great metrical tradition of English poetry: "almost alone among his celebrated contemporaries, has not relaxed in his later work, has not let himself write loose parodies on his early style" (17–18). Schwartz continued his campaign to place Stevens in the philosophical mainstream of modernism in a self-consciously canonizing section he called "Hints for Historians." Here Schwartz asserted that much sense could be made of Stevens's work by placing it "in the context of the intellectual history of the last fifty or seventy-five years" and by making detailed comparisons among the most important poems (by Arnold, Valéry, Yeats, and Eliot) that had emerged from this period. In stature and import, major poems by these four writers more closely resembled a poem such as "Sunday Morning" than the superficial resemblances that could be inevitably derived from Stevens's beginnings in the atmosphere of the early-modernist avant-garde. In defending Stevens from being pigeonholed as a dated Village aesthete, Schwartz portrayed history as a (rather ahistorical) pantheon—a canonizing strategy that would become more and more common in modernist criticism over the next two decades.

Despite Schwartz's aims, perhaps, the *Advocate* issue on Stevens was also effective in sharpening the sense of Stevens's historical connection to the burgeoning milieu of early modernism. So long seen as a sort of poetic hermit in modernist circles, Stevens could now be seen as a quietly but significantly shaping part of that very cultural matrix. The group of poems heading the issue, which paired the brand new "Three Poems of 1940" with "Thirteen Poems (1899–1901)" from Stevens's undergraduate tenure at the *Advocate*, extended the poet what he had never appeared to have (and had perhaps never really wanted)—a point of aesthetic genesis and a creative continuity over forty years. Robert Penn Warren's brief statement recuperated *Harmonium* into a central position within the history of modernism as "one of the relatively small number of books of poetry of the 20's which have grown in stature with the passage of time" (32). This account of a book's emergence through the test of passing time was a canonically laden formulation, as was Warren's conclusion that the "concentration, intensity, precision, wit, and artistic conscience in that volume make it more important to us now than ever before" (32).

Hi Simons's long article "Vicissitudes of Reputation, 1914–1940," which began and ended the issue, was the fullest attempt until well after Stevens's death at integrating him into a central historical as well as aesthetic position within the development of modernism. Simons conglomerated various research sources into a description of Stevens's career that included the fullest biographical detail of the poet to that point, a sometimes acute historical sketch of Stevens criticism, an account of Stevens's influence on younger poets, a description of the rocky rise of Stevens's English reputation, and an affirmation of recent critical treatments of Stevens's work "as a reflection of the objective reality of his time," not excluding the negative aspects of that reflection in such accounts as Burnshaw's and Dorothy Van Ghent's. Confident that the poet's value was sufficient to withstand such attacks and—like so many other critics of the 1930s—convinced of the importance of making poetry relevant to contemporary existence, Simons believed that "Stevens's renown has suffered less from the criticism of the Marxists than from supposed services rendered to it by some of his earlier admirers" who would have preserved him as a poet of " 'pure formalism' " (*Wallace Stevens Number*, 44). Simons concluded his survey with another self-consciously canonizing assertion: "It is now taken for granted that no serious study of American literature of the past quarter-century is complete without thorough consideration of his work" (44).

Although this claim was certainly wishful thinking in terms of Stevens's canonicity through the entire literary culture, Simons's work, and the *Advocate* issue as a whole, served as a major summation and extension of a period of substantial consolidation of the poet's reputation as a major modernist poet.

As the 1930s ended and the era of New Critical dominance of the American literary-critical scene began, Stevens was certainly not as broadly canonical as Eliot and Frost, and probably Robinson and Pound, and would not be for at least another twenty years. It is clear, however, from the favorable evaluations of Stevens in the late 1930s that what is called here the poet's canonical potential was very high, perhaps higher than that of any other early modernist in at least one important sense: the probability that he would continue his impressive development in the future.

Many of the hardy first modernist generation were still producing work and occupying central generational and institutional positions. Yet for many poets' reputations an evaluative inertia had set in by 1940. Young critics and readers had come to possess an often subconscious but quite definite sense of the level of accomplishment of most of their precursors; these evaluative bases were both illustrated and reinforced by pieces such as Zabel's survey. Certain qualities prominent in past evaluations of various poets (Amy Lowell's preciosity, Stevens's dandyism, Frost's rustic simplicity) became more and more ingrained in the very texture of reading that poet. Such evaluative baggage could be argued against, sometimes successfully, as Blackmur and others had done with Stevens's dandyism; but more often it became part of a poet's work as integral to the reading experience as the imagery that characterized his or her work.[27] Most of Stevens's contemporaries never succeeded in breaking these dominant perceptions of their poetic attributes. Their new work would be treated with the sort of weary disinterest seen in Matthiessen's and Zabel's evaluations of Jeffers—incapable of change or development, Jeffers simply continued to spin out his few ideas in ever more melodramatic narrative structures. Many poets with relatively high reputations—Aiken, Millay, Frost—adopted new, often quite ambitious modes of writing poetry or turned to fiction or poetic drama, but they failed substantially to alter the dominant perceptions of them as poets which had been set up in the first two decades of their careers.

In contrast, those few poets who in middle or even old age did summon up the force to break this evaluative inertia generated much attention. Yeats's late lyrics, Eliot's plays and *Four Quartets,* Pound's *Pisan Cantos,* and Williams's *Paterson* all significantly altered prevailing evaluative patterns of those poets, suggesting that they were capable of continued creative development even as they approached — without meekly settling into — old age. Stevens was perhaps the strongest pattern-breaker of this entire early-modernist group, by returning so vigorously and surprisingly to publication in his late fifties. Stevens's work after 1935 positioned him as the poet most capable of a continuous and intelligent creative development unhampered by personal crises, external circumstances, or creeping cultural despair. Both the needs and the expectations of poetry's potential to serve as a central expression of human experience had increased since 1929. The new Stevens was seen to be attempting to meet contemporary needs that were perceived by readers as well as by the poet. Reviewers of those works — and, one may assume, readers at large — were increasingly able to fit Stevens's work into their understanding of those cultural needs. While younger readers were finding fewer and fewer ways of valuing most of his contemporaries, they were finding more and more satisfying ways to read and use Stevens.

FIVE

Life Anywhere But on a Battleship

The Poet's Wartime and Postwar Reception, 1941–1953

> His most persistent subject is the opposition between bare reality
> and what the imagination can make of it, a subject which he
> shares in part with Williams. But Stevens had thought more
> deeply upon the nature of art and celebrated
> > The magnificent cause of being,
> > The imagination, the one reality
> > In this imagined world.
> > —Spiller et al., eds., *Literary History of the
> > United States*, 1948

> He had to choose. But it was not a choice
> Between excluding things. It was not a choice
> Between, but of. He chose to include the things
> That in each other are included, the whole,
> The complicate, the amassing harmony.
> > —Stevens,
> > *Notes Toward a Supreme Fiction*, 1942

The late 1930s were perhaps the last years of the American literary culture in which middle-ground critical values had included both an interest in formal experimentation and a direct concern with progressive social ideas. In the early decades of modernism critics such as Untermeyer had professed a populist interest in the social and moral efficacy of poetry but had largely been blocked from producing articulate criticism by their anti-intellectual and sometimes xenophobic distrust of formal innovation (and analytical criticism) as decadent, effete, or antidemocratic. During the early 1930s this antiformalism had been reformulated by the literary left according to ideologies of social realism and had set the tone for much American critical discourse during the decade.[1] Both varieties of antiformalism held in common the artificially separated inverse relationship between form and content which helped to retard Stevens's reputation for the first two decades of his career. In the second half of the 1930s a relative and temporary equilibrium was reached, as the adoption of Popular Front cultural policies somewhat eased opposition to formal experimentation and originality, and the widespread concern for social relevance remained among many poets and critics. These characteristics of late-1930s poetic value manifested themselves in commentary on Stevens by offering the possibility of thinking about the poet both as "the foremost living master of his art in America" (Simons, "The Humanism of Wallace Stevens," 452) and as a serious analyst of the potential social role that creative activity such as poetry might play in America. Stevens's fulfillment of both conditions helped to vault him into the upper ranks of contemporary poetic reputations. Although his appeal in the 1930s was by no means limited only to politically or aesthetically centrist audiences, for the first time he filled a cultural role he had never before seemed suited to: spokesman for the concerns and hopes of a middle-ground bourgeois intelligentsia. Given the chance to develop, these critical premises of the late 1930s might eventually have become the basis for a historically and socially responsive portrayal of Stevens and of modern poetry in the succeeding decades.

Certainly, in the 1940s, the actions of the poet himself tended in the direction of further social and cultural engagement. As depression turned into world war and then to cold war, the multiple processes of admission Stevens had initiated in the mid-1930s—admitting readers into his province rather than erecting strategies for excluding them, admitting the incompleteness of his earlier position, admitting the crucial importance to human society of cultural forms such as poetry—continued and, indeed, formed the defining labor of the poet's later career. More and more central to Stevens's work was an interest in theorizing the relationships of social structures to creative activity, in exploring the many forms and functions that such a concept as "creative activity" might need to, and be able to, encompass in difficult times. Many short poems of the

1940s and long poems—"Examination of the Hero in a Time of War," *Notes Toward a Supreme Fiction*, and *Esthétique du Mal*—dealt with the perils and necessities of the present and future world and the place of artistic creation in that world.

In 1946 he put his concerns into succinct prose in response to the question of "the greatest problem facing the young writer in America": "If people are to become dependent on poetry for any of the fundamental satisfactions, poetry must have an increasingly intellectual scope and power. This is a time for the highest poetry. We never understood the world less than we do now, nor, as we understand, liked it less. We never wanted to understand it more nor needed to like it more. These are the intense compulsions that challenge the poet as the appreciatory creator of values and beliefs" (L, 526). Far from being a withdrawn figure intent upon his or her own apprehensions and satisfactions, Stevens's poet must strive to be an intellectual participant in the contemporary scene, developing ways to appreciate and affirm that world rather than rejecting it.

During these years Stevens also became an increasingly active presence within the institutional operations of the American literary culture.[2] While he had long been a strong but distant aesthetic and intellectual influence on a younger generation of poets, he now drew personally closer to various younger members of the literary culture. Although much has recently been made of Stevens's apparent insecurities about money, and his relish of the financial comfort he finally did feel, he can hardly be called miserly with his resources. In word and deed he maintained a longstanding support of little magazines put out by unknown editors and writers. Brazeau's interviews with those who hosted him at his university readings make clear that he consistently specified that his honoraria be donated to younger, needier writers (Brazeau, 167, 172, 218). His generosity of time and scholarly materials with such younger creators as the poets Delmore Schwartz, Samuel French Morse, and José Rodríguez-Feo, the scholars Hi Simons and Bernard Heringman, and the composer John Gruen suggests a hospitality that is quite at odds with the image of the remote and intimidating snob some have made him seem.[3] Stevens's generosity was undoubtedly selective, yet perhaps no more so than anyone of public eminence and reticent temperament with much to do and relatively little time left.

In discussions and correspondence with his friend Henry Church between 1940 and 1943, Stevens made efforts to institutionalize his efforts to theorize the cultural uses of poetry by helping Church to endow a chair at Harvard or Princeton. As "the essential thing in life," poetry deserved the sort of "study in the high academic sense" that it had never had in America (*L*, 358, 378). Stevens was not a born salesman, however; the diffident lawyer's tone of his memoranda to Church on the subject obscured (as they may have done to Church) how much the idea meant to him (*L*, 358, 376–78, 382–83). His error in this venture was to place too much faith in Church's resolution as a source of intellectual and institutional support and not to have acted more directly. The legacy of this project was not, of course, a permanent chair of the theory of poetry but several of Stevens's prose essays and a major text of modernist poetry, *Notes Toward a Supreme Fiction*.[4]

Also during these years Stevens began to give public readings of prose essays on the nature and character of poetry, beginning with "The Noble Rider" in 1941 and averaging nearly one per year through the 1940s. Stevens's turn to prose public addresses, against his deeply private and reticent personality, to elaborate the role of individual creation within a social matrix is a particularly revealing instance of his desire to achieve greater accessibility and more direct influence for his ideas during these years. Though his essays were not collected until 1951, and though readers did not receive them with uniform enthusiasm or understanding, Stevens's prose gradually took on an important role in conveying his intellectual and moral seriousness and his centrality to modernist poetry. To Hayden Carruth in 1952, for example, the volume of essays exerted a powerful corrective with which Stevens "saved himself" from "the devilishly uninformed and the deep blue connoisseurs" who constituted Stevens criticism ("Stevens as Essayist," 584).[5] For some other writers Stevens's prose validated his credentials as a poetico-philosophic sage, "the master of a remarkably precise and clear-sighted doctrine which over the years his poetry has been actualizing," who had created "a moral and philosophical center through which reality may be repossessed and recreated with each new poetic act" (Wagner, 144). With his prose work Stevens thus authoritatively demonstrated to such would-be canonizers his ability to communicate a philosophical or moral position in a format outside the opaque medium of poetry—as did nearly all the other poets of American modernism who have come to be considered "major."

Befitting his increasingly central position within modernist poetry, Stevens worked persistently during the 1940s in the spheres of his own expertise and influence to articulate a sociocultural agenda based on an inclusive pluralism of multiple perceptions, potentialities, and states of mind. The poet who had become legendary for shunning editors, critics, and most other poets alike, who two decades earlier had written his creative autobiography in the form of the apparently impenetrable and flippant antiodyssey called "The Comedian as the Letter C," and who for seven years had carried out his threat to give up poetry as not worth the effort, had come a long way towards affirming the value of such cultural forms as poetry and the importance of his own poetry to his identity. Next to the reactionary royalism, Republican complacency, and disastrous fanaticism of some of his most eminent modernist contemporaries, Stevens's efforts at institutional engagement, tentative as they were, hold up rather well.

Stevens's endeavors to connect the individual's creation of poetry to the sociocultural matrices of the mid-twentieth century might also have provided a useful basis for postwar evaluations of his place in American modernist poetry. During the years of World War II the direction of the relationship between literature and politics was still highly contested, but after the war, as the nation lurched into the ideologically volatile era of the cold war, American poetry criticism underwent a drastic shift in values, coming to distrust any explicit or emotionally intense concern with social or political issues and to embrace an almost exclusive focus on formal achievement that, it was assumed and asserted, transcended the tentacles of ideology. With each major occasion for comment on Stevens's work—*Parts of a World* and *Notes Toward a Supreme Fiction* (both published 1942), *Esthétique du Mal* (1945), *Transport to Summer* and a reissue of *Harmonium* (both 1947), *The Auroras of Autumn* (1950), and *The Necessary Angel* (1951), the potential portrayal of Stevens as a strong-minded, courageous advocate of human values and potentials was more and more submerged by a will to formalism that, by the time of the *Collected Poems* (1954), almost totally dominated American criticism.

It must be understood that this shift in values cannot be wholly equated with the intellectual and institutional development of New Criticism. The postwar reaction against the predominant 1930s conjunction of cultural and political was by no means limited to the mostly academic arenas in which New Criticism was taking hold; indeed, the influence of New Criticism can be viewed as much as a symptom as a cause of the turn away from political activism in American literary culture. The systematic neglect or denial of Stevens's sociopolitical resonance and, more generally, the denigration of the political in modern poetry can be seen with equal clarity in the wartime and postwar writing of three fairly distinct groups: the loosely affiliated group of academic "New Critics"; longtime commentators on modernist poetry such as Horace Gregory and Ruth Lechlitner; and an emerging generation of young poets who represented a third generation of modernism. By the later 1940s the brief critical equilibrium between formal and social had largely disappeared, as Stevens critics from across political, critical, and generational lines began to value most highly the same qualities that had hurt the poet's earlier reputation — formal virtuosity, ironic detachment, and apparent concentration upon the inner experiences of an individual consciousness. All of these attributes could be found in their purest form in *Harmonium*. By the time it was reissued in 1947, *Harmonium* had already became the object of intense critical nostalgia, which helped to submerge the intelligent assimilation of Stevens's later books.

Broadly speaking, Stevens criticism of the postwar era came to conceive of poetry not as intellectual, political, or moral substance but as the highly formalized expression of an absolutely individual consciousness that "created" and inhabited an aesthetic "world" separate from, and superior to, the sociopolitical world. In the cold-war years, deeply affected by such troubling political influences as atomic anxiety and anti-communist paranoia, American poetry criticism paradoxically attempted to shield itself by completely denying the political, largely refusing to admit that outside forces impinged upon poetry or upon itself or, in instances in which that impingement could not be ignored, characterizing the poetic results as aesthetically, or even morally, flawed, ingenuine, or inferior. The proclamation of an "end to ideology," which was characteristic of the 1950s, served as an ideologically laden strategy used by those desirous of establishing literature as a safe haven for the individual consciousness against the despoiling world. The integrated relationship between the individual's imagination and the broader world that had been posited during the 1930s, which Stevens was seeking to maintain, was polarized into a mythology of two mutually exclusive worlds, one containing transcendent and unfettered literary value, the other containing the pitfalls and degradations of political dogma.

The dominant postwar versions of poetic value were largely constructed around this need to repress the impact of the political or to insulate cultural activity from it. Those modernists who could not be read "apolitically" or antipolitically were read less and less by poetry critics, often coming to be dismissed as illustrating only the symptoms of the failure of aesthetic will.[6] While there were still poets publishing political verse during the decade—Langston Hughes, Thomas McGrath, John Beecher, Edwin Rolfe—such work was almost totally closed out of the academic and critical establishments. In the early 1950s even some well-established figures such as Pound, Williams, and Hughes became too hot for many critics to want to handle. In contrast, in this politically volatile time Stevens was an eminently safe poet. It cannot be denied that Stevens's work can be and has been read in ways congenial to the antipolitical critical positions that gained ascendancy after the war. Like the few other modernist poets whose reputations gained strength between 1945 and 1955, Stevens's work offered some convenient loophole for readers to whom his social concerns did not appeal; in his case, they were stated neither aggressively nor consistently enough to ensure that they would not be overlooked. While he clearly made an impression of general social relevance upon many readers, he did not threaten them with any hint of coercion or propaganda. Above all, they were sure that Stevens would never proselytize on behalf of any political agenda and thus would preserve his appealing artistic independence and integrity at a time when critics perceived those virtues under particular attack.

Importantly, however, neither logically nor practically does such an acknowledgement limit the possibilities of reading Stevens by those who *are* interested in articulating his sociopolitical resonance. That such a desire seems both emerging and plausible is abundantly demonstrated by the suggestive array of articles on "Stevens and Politics" in a special issue of the *Wallace Stevens Journal* in 1989; it is no accident that all but one of the eight articles in this compilation focus on Stevens's work and life between 1935 and 1950.[7]

From its inception, much contemporary commentary on Stevens's wartime poetry turned upon a curious double-edged process of vaguely acknowledging and then largely ignoring the seriousness of the poet's efforts towards social relevance. On the one hand, reflecting the still contested critical climate of the war years, several reviewers of *Parts of a World* did clearly see Stevens's engagement with social issues as an indication of the poet's continued development and connected this "growth" to his increasing stature in the canons of contemporary poetry. For Weldon Kees, for example, *Parts of a World* presented Stevens "extending and deepening the concern with society toward which [he had] been moving" since *Ideas of Order*; later in the article, Kees judged that

Stevens's "distinguished place in American poetry has never been more secure" (387, 388). Similarly, Frank Jones acknowledged a "steadily manifest" "growth" in Stevens, from the "enchanted country" of *Harmonium*, with its limited power and importance of the "individual yearning for a more perfect imagined universe," to the later volumes in which "the conflict of such longings with the increasingly cruel outer world is dramatized" and the focus is no longer upon the isolate individual but upon "all people." The result was that "the poet's power grows with his theme" (488). Theodore Weiss referred to Stevens's "always increasing clarity" as he had "moved from living in a world of words to living in a world of things," "an expanding world," which helped readers see that "Even as the reputations of others . . . have begun to shrivel, his importance to us has constantly improved" ("Three in One," 327, 326).

This consciousness of Stevens's continued development was clearly instrumental in securing his position in the critical canons of twentieth-century American poetry in the mid-century years, and yet strong undercurrents of dissatisfaction and discomfort with Stevens's current work lurked in reviews even as early as *Parts of a World*. This opening remark of Ruth Lechlitner, a longtime admirer of the poet, exemplified the curious ambivalence of urgency and escapism in the critical reception of that volume: "Once again Wallace Stevens, engaged during a time of total war with images "filling the imagination's need," has produced a book of cream out-of-this-world for poets" ("Creative Imagination," 26).

Lechlitner was by no means being ironic; evidently it was possible for a poet simultaneously to fill serious contemporary needs and to provide a way "out of this world." Dubbing Stevens the "famed poetical solipsist who wears the world in his hat," the reviewer for *Time* averred, "At first sight Stevens's mental world looks like a five-ring circus of private hallucinations" (review of *Parts of a World*, *Time*, 103). Surprisingly enough, however, the reviewer concluded from this survey of Stevens's exotic attributes that "he is, despite his snobbery, one of the most seriously purposive poets alive." Likewise, Horace Gregory ended his review by approvingly quoting (but not discussing) "Contrary Theses (I)" as a powerful war poem—but only after having judged Stevens exactly as he had done in 1931, as a hyper-individual comedian living in his own rarefield world, the "Whistler of American poetry": "I, for one, am happy to read Mr. Stevens as a poet of sensibility, and there is no one today writing poetry in English who can rival his high appreciation of the comedy which exists in a civilized milieu" ("Examination of Wallace Stevens in a Time of War," 59).[8]

Despite their sense of Stevens's continued growth, both Kees and Jones also saw much to trouble them in his recent work. For Kees, the enlarged scope and increased emotional intensity of Stevens's later work produced mostly "melancholy reflection" and "an increasing despair," and Jones failed to recognize the contradiction between his judgment that "the poet's power grows with his theme" and his dismissal of *Parts of a World*, whose "good doctrine" usually lacked "the light and music . . . that made his other world [*Harmonium*] so livable" (Kees, 388; Jones, 488). This curious evaluative ambivalence showed up most paradoxically of all in William York Tindall's review, in which he favorably estimated Stevens as "perhaps the best poet now writing in America" but nonetheless summed up this evaluation by reverting to the old cliché of the frivolous 1890s decadent: "No less conscious of the war than [Stephen] Spender, Wallace Stevens refines it by the Stevens process. . . . Though war drives us to fact, a poet must manage to return to what he wants fact to be. Having done so, Stevens stands alone, a dandy to the last, adjusting ruffle and cravat in a vacant lot" ("Literary Signposts," 120).

The recurrent tension of seriousness and escapism in these discussions suggests that during these years a fundamental disparity existed between the direction of Stevens's work and prevalent conditions of reading. The ambivalence of this canonization resulted from a disjunction between the changes occurring within Stevens—the growing desire to play an active social role—and the changes that a mostly younger generation of poets and critics were undergoing—increasingly disillusioned with the realm of the political, they looked inward for satisfaction and value. The same forces of social upheaval and war which Stevens called "the violence from without," which compelled him to respond with an imaginative "violence from within,"[9] were beginning to push his critics away from a serious exploration of his sociopolitical relevance. In their actual reading practices most critics were coming to prize the side of Stevens that offered escape from the violent "real" world to an "imagined" world of stunning aesthetic elegance.

One of the central critical manifestations of the widespread neglect and distortion of Stevens's concern with social questions appeared in the interpretation of the complicated relationship between the concepts of "imagination" and "reality" which underlay the poet's epistemological principles. By and large

Stevens saw "the imagination" not as an entity separated from the world outside itself but as the mechanism of human consciousness that made possible the very perception of the state of the world we call "reality." Just as the products of the imagination attain existence in the world of things, the imagination is not separate but is always already a part of reality.[10] Indeed, Stevens made clear in "The Noble Rider" that he did not oppose as much as "appose" them, put them near to one another (NA, 8).[11] In this essay as in the poems "Dezembrum" and "Man and Bottle," when Stevens wanted an opposing term for "the imagination," he used "the reason," preserving the unusual use of the definite article to cement the parallelism of these terms. Whatever the merits or defects of this Cartesian opposition, it does not engage in the solipsistic isolation in which Stevens critics indulged by opposing the imagination to reality.

Critics quickly seized upon this pair of terms for their own purposes. When Stevens referred to his central subject as "the relation between the imagination and reality" (NA, 7), critics tended to take him (and often still do) to be using the terms as parallel opposites (imagination vs. reality), which meant that they could posit unequivocally, as he did not, "imagination" not as a constitutive faculty but as a realm separate from the world of "reality." The usual critical strategy, of course, was then to denigrate "reality" and to portray "imagination" as an element of mastery over or escape from that reality. As Vivienne Koch put it, Stevens's concern was "the theme of the mind creating its own reality and by this process—art—asserting an autonomy of the will which gives meaning to the vulgar 'real.' "[12] The same pattern of thought has long assumed erroneously that by the "necessary angel" Stevens meant the imagination, when in fact he meant reality.[13]

Another important instance of the distance between the poet's formulations of these terms and critics' interpretations of them came in Stevens's note on poetry and war included in *Parts of a World*. Stating that "in the presence of the violent reality of war, consciousness takes the place of the imagination," the poet opposed the imagination not to reality (which he again portrayed as a universal state including the imagination) but to "consciousness," an alienated and passive awareness of the world in which the interactive potentiality of "reality" degraded into "fact."[14] Stevens went on to analogize the relation between fact and consciousness to the interdependence of reality and the imagination: "We leave fact and come back to it, come back to what we wanted fact to be, not to what it was, not to what it has too often remained." Critics have tended to quote and discuss this remark apart from the context of Stevens's next sentence, which posited an ongoing "fundamental and endless struggle with fact." Far from being a reactive flight from the pressure of reality by removing one's consciousness from it entirely, this "struggle" represented Stevens's conception of the imagination's proactive effort to engage with and transform the "facts" of the world. Clearly, accepting an "endless struggle" with something is exactly the opposite of escaping from it.[15]

In Ruth Lechlitner's review of *Parts of a World*, however, Stevens's careful distinctions were flattened out into a poetics of pure solipsism in which "imagination is the one reality"; in a world at war, "reality, the 'consciousness of fact,' is seen at war with poetry as the work of the imagination ("Creative Imagination," 26). For Stevens, poetry was a resource that could help the human mind neither retreat from nor vanquish "reality"—both ultimately impossible—but make it into more than mere "fact"; for Lechlitner, "poetry" and "the imagination" were simply "at war" with "reality," which was synonymous with fact.[16] Tindall's 1943 paraphrase of Stevens's formulation—"Though war drives us to fact, a poet must manage to return to what he wants fact to be" ("Literary Signposts," 120)—created a similar distortion, almost undetectable but fundamental, which was suggestive of the difficulty critics faced in accepting the poet's ideas. When Stevens asserted that "we leave fact and come back to it, come back to what we wanted fact to be," he suggested that our minds must always return to fact, no matter how unpleasant, but also that they were not without the potential of transforming it. Crucially, however, the possible transformation of fact into "what we want it to be" could only take place in the very act of coming back to fact. Tindall's paraphrase, on the other hand, implied the identification of "what we want fact to be" as a realm separate from the "fact" that most of us were trapped in; the poet's achievement, then, was the ability to escape the pressure of war by returning to that other realm away from fact.

For these critics the lines were clearly drawn up; like the Allied forces of 1942, the imagination needed effective defense against the invasions of reality. Unlike Stevens, who explicitly admitted no telos to this process, making clear towards the end of the statement that this struggle "goes on everywhere, even in the periods that we call peace," many of his critics leapt immediately from struggle to resolution, as if merely describing the struggle ended the necessity of engaging in it. Simons, for example, positioned *Parts of a World* rather inanely into the context of Stevens's recent work as exactly the sort of teleological resolution that Stevens rejected: "We left him, as the fabulists say, in [the books of the late 1930s] working his way out of the dilemma which the coexistence of things imagined and things-as-they-are posed to him. This new book shows how he finally did so" ("The Humanism of Wallace Stevens," 449).

In Lechlitner's review this distortion of the poet's emphasis upon the interdependent coexistence of the imagination and reality was connected to another prevalent critical strategy of the decade. After discussing Stevens's engagement with "events in the contemporary world: his concept of the 'reality' of war and its effect on the consciousness of humankind," Lechlitner closed with a strange reversion: "As for Wallace Stevens, as poet he is content to remain the 'capable man' who creates in his own mind 'the ultimate elegance: the imagined land'" ("Creative Imagination," 26). The lure of that final line from "Mrs. Alfred Uruguay," and the image of the young rider, was very strong. To be sure, this figure is one of Stevens's most vigorous, if most idealized, images of the powerful poet, but this final line of the poem has often been taken, as it was by Lechlitner, as an expression of Stevens's acceptance of a fundamental separation between the world of his imagination ("in his own mind") and any larger world.[17] Stevens's portrayals of Mrs. Uruguay and the young rider clearly militate against reading "the imagined land" as the solipsistic world of an isolated individual's imagination. It is Mrs. Uruguay who has ascended away from the village and the clocks, who has "said no / To everything, in order to get at [her]self," whose very intellectual purity has destroyed her ability to create or transform:

> And for her,
> To be . . . could never be more
> Than to be, she could never differently be,
> Her no and no made yes impossible. (*CP* 249)

In contrast, the young rider descends into the world of the village to accept the other ("the martyr's bones") rather than the self as material for creation. "The imagined land" that the rider eventually shapes is thus a rather utopian instance of the interdependence of the imagination with reality: not a land of a particular person's mind, but the common land as it might be imagined and reshaped. Such a process might produce "the ultimate elegance" exactly because it is not the haughty but easy elegance of the isolated lady intent upon her mountaintop but because it is an elegance achieved in the midst of a highly variegated and imperfect world. In this sense, it is profitable to see these characters as figures of different stages in the poet's thought and career: Mrs. Uruguay as an avatar in reduced circumstances of Hoon living in his "loneliest air"; the young rider, who reappears in the 1943 essay "The Figure of Youth as Virile Poet," as an expression of Stevens's hope that he himself had descended back into the world, and his belief that there were continued possibilities to be found there.[18]

Even in 1942 reviews, however, the poet's supposed opposition between reality and imagination was coming to function as a kind of critical shorthand, suggesting the extent to which it was becoming a central way of approaching him: "the book contains other . . . [poems] devoted to the reality-pole of the reality-imagination dichotomy" (Simons, "The Humanism of Wallace Stevens," 449). Regardless of the poet's apparent aims, this pair took on an ever more dichotomized life of its own, so that by 1947 Wilbert Snow's speech for Stevens's honorary doctorate from Wesleyan could flatly describe Stevens as "insisting upon the imagination as 'the only reality in this imagined world'" (394).[19] Snow's quotation did indeed come from Stevens's work, but tellingly it was from a poem written a quarter-century before, *Harmonium*'s "Another Weeping Woman" (*CP*, 25).[20]

Even writers who acknowledged that Stevens was attempting to achieve a synthetic balance could fall into a loose usage of the dichotomy: "The first . . . volume in prose by Wallace Stevens, seems at last to function on middle ground between the two careers of that distinguished poet-executive—or rather, following his terminology, between reality and imagination. Imagination, as might be expected and even desired, has the upper hand" (Levin, review of *The Necessary Angel*, 615). In spite of Stevens's discriminations, the unnoticed contradiction between "middle ground" and "upper hand" betrayed Levin's sense that what was needed was more imagination and less reality.

Not merely a way of describing Stevens's subject matter, the critical opposition between reality and the imagination became a way of evaluating Stevens's work as well. In his review of *Transport to Summer* in 1947, Peter Viereck could find Stevens guilty of not being faithful to the dichotomy that he had ostensibly established, chiding him that "reality and imagination must not become so completely mixed that they are interchangeable and their separate identities are lost" ("Stevens Revisited," 156).[21] For Viereck, this interchangeability had led to "incongruous juxtaposition: many a forced shotgun marriage of incompatibles" (156), which (for some reason left unspecified) vitiated the value of many of the poems in the volume.

The young poet Viereck was from a different critical universe from the modernist veteran Louis Untermeyer; but nonetheless Untermeyer's estimation of *Parts of a World* contained similar objections to Stevens's tolerance of "incongruity" in his poetry, which Untermeyer characterized as "a forced creation, an incongruity of serious wit and irresponsible whimsy" ("Departure from Dandyism," 11). Such criticisms suggested that Stevens's work refused sufficiently to follow dualistic categories of thought and perception (such as "imagination" and "reality") that critics were desirous of maintaining. The specific content of any particular dichotomy was perhaps less important than the will to dualism exhibited by many of these readers. In 1942, for example, discussing Stevens's use of "non-verbal expletives" such as "hurroo" and "da da doo," Gregory, strikingly like Viereck and Untermeyer, deplored Stevens's willingness to let "the Coleridgian distinctions between fancy and imagination become blurred beyond recognition and depart," with the consequence that "the various aesthetic values in the poem before our eyes become as incongruous in the relationship as the pairing of A. A. Milne's Winnie the Pooh with King Lear's Fool" ("Examination of Wallace Stevens," 60). The entertaining of "incongruous" aesthetic values added up to "the danger of whimsy," whose presence evidently ruled out first-rate art. Similarly, in *Intellectual America: Ideas on the March* (1941), Oscar Cargill objected to these same sorts of incongruities on a moral basis and noted, "Such a line as 'she scuds the glitters' [from "The Paltry Nude Starts on a Spring Voyage"] one would be more likely to attribute to the barker of an aquatic girlie show than to a leading poet" (256–57).

To be sure, Untermeyer's and Cargill's views represented old-fashioned positions within American criticism; but difficulties with Stevens's use of language also manifested themselves in such a trenchantly New Critical formal analysis as Donald Davie's 1954 discussion of "The Auroras of Autumn," in which "alliteration . . . and the play on the 'i' sound [in section four, lines 15–16 of the poem] . . . are obvious, rather vulgar effects," evidence of "the poet's touch fail[ing] him," which did "damage" to the poem's value (130). When Stevens's effects of language disturbed Davie, it was because their flamboyance violated the critic's sense of the level of diction appropriate to a poem of noble design and serious import; such techniques become not simply aesthetic failings but socially distasteful "vulgarity" (130, 135)—poetics that a vulgar person, not one of Stevens's refinement and social standing, might be expected to embrace.

The complaints of Stevens's "incongruities" by these five very different critics are all connected to Stevens's persistent refusal to keep the discourse of the exposition separate from the discourse of the midway, the nobly imaginative separate from the palpably real, the ideologically transcendent realm of "art" separate from the ideologically implicated realm of "popular entertainment." The disturbances caused by these antitotalizing tendencies in his work manifested themselves over an enormously wide critical range, from the stale moralism of Cargill to the sophisticated formalism of Davie. The strategies such readers developed for defusing Stevens's threatening side helped to shape the very notion of modernist canonicity in the postwar years.

The poet's impulses to include, unify, and integrate the elements of the world around him, and his critics' contrasting (and ultimately successful) desires to separate, dichotomize, and categorize them, can be seen nowhere more clearly than in the ramifications of the title of Stevens's 1942 volume, *Parts of a World*. Having also considered *The Man, That's All One Knows* (Brazeau, 86), Stevens eventually chose a title that captured his consistent affirmation of both the specific identity of concrete individual elements and their unification into an abstract collective whole. In contrast, the critical apprehension of this relationship was typified by Elizabeth Drew's use of two of Stevens's lines in her review of *Parts of a World*: " 'There is no such thing as life,' says Wallace Stevens in one of these poems; and in another, 'There is no such thing as truth.' Again, he sees no hope that the chaos of living will ever be ended, because the chaos of the nature of man will never be mended" (154).

With these quotations Drew constructed a version of the poet as an advocate of " 'being without description' and without doctrine; experience in itself" (154). Such a characterization of Stevens as pure phenomenologist became a standard stratagem in robbing his work of its sociopolitical resonance by portraying it as achieving a transcendent aesthetic realm beyond ideology, as being the work of a connoisseur of human chaos rather than a commentator upon it. Drew's first quotation, from "Parochial Theme," the poem that opened the volume, neglected to mention that Stevens, in a highly characteristic rhetorical maneuver, then went on to qualify his assertion drastically, thus establishing the irreducible multiplicity of interpretations of a protean concept such as "life":

> There is no such thing as life; or if there is,
>
> It is faster than the weather, faster than
> Any character. It is more than any scene:
>
> Of the guillotine or of any glamorous hanging. [CP 192]

Stevens's pluralism is not equivalent to Drew's life "without doctrine" but to a life that will exceed the scope of any *one* character, scene, or doctrine. This poem ends with a reference to the volume's title in the speaker's admonition to "piece the world together, boys, / But not with your hands." The multiple and by no means necessarily consensual addressees of this challenge will not succeed by merely using their hands, their physical "experience in itself" "without doctrine"; they must employ the multiple doctrines in their heads to construct a sort of intellectual and ideological patchwork, as heterogeneous, incomplete, and impure as its creators, but "the world pieced together" nonetheless.

This disjunction between dichotomizing and integrating the relations between individual and collective, specific and general, replicated itself in Drew's second reference, "There is no such thing as truth," from "On the Road Home." This time Drew's zeal to demonstrate Stevens's rejection of doctrine resulted in a revealing misquotation; Stevens's line reads "There is no such thing as the truth." The difference is crucial, meaning the difference between Stevens as a philosophical relativist-cum-solipsist who allows no social or ethical perspective outside of his own comfortable one, a sort of poetic Pontius Pilate, and Stevens as a pluralist who allows for the existence of infinitely many truths, all of which construe parts of our world but which do not add up to a single overarching truth of absolute or ultimate priority, as the poem clearly suggests a few lines later: "There are many truths, / But they are not parts of a truth" (CP, 203). That these multiple truths must be continually preserved and affirmed, that they cannot be reduced to any facile universal—even one such as "the supreme truth is that there are no ultimate truths"—is strongly conveyed by the structure of "On the Road Home." Stevens was careful not to construct the poem as a univocal assertion that might have belied his pluralist intentions but as a dialogic interchange between consciousnesses in temporary concord.

The poem presents not one but four formulations of this notion of irreducible plurality, each of which is potentially somewhat different in its implications and two of which emerge from the companion called "you." Also congruent with the contingent character of their realization is that the speakers possess no verification of the validity of their formulations but simply a shared perception of their refreshed and intensified connection to the world around them as a consequence of their meditations. In allowing that this could be merely a perception, and not an alteration in the fabric of reality itself, Stevens rejects the philosophical absolutism that a flatly doctrinaire expression of skepticism would come dangerously close to. Yet if there is no proof, no empirical or philosophical validation, there is equally no disproof that after their revelation "the night was roundest, / The fragrance of the autumn warmest, / Closest and strongest" (CP, 204). In any case, for speaker and companion the experience remains valid on a phenomenal and communal level.

"On the Road Home" asks the reader of Stevens's work to posit a relationship between individuals and wholes much as the title of the volume posits one between "parts" and the whole of "a world." Yet the import of Stevens's work is clearly not, as Theodore Weiss suggested in his 1943 review of the book, an attempt to "strip" man, to "spare him insulatory creeds," and to "let things in themselves be images enough ("Three in One," 327). Here Weiss exhibited the knee-jerk reaction against the "creeds" that supposedly threatened to apply unwarranted external pressure to the ideal purity of a poem. The immediate subject of Weiss's remarks was the poem "The Latest Freed Man" (which Stevens placed adjacent to "On the Road Home" in *Parts of a World*), another central text for exploring the ramifications of Stevens's sense of the relationship of "parts" to "world." Like the travelers home, the speaker of this poem is "tired of the old descriptions of the world" and undergoes a liberating perceptual experience that refreshes his relationship to his surroundings (CP, 204). Again, however, this experience, however momentous, does not constitute a permanent evasion of the necessity of "descriptions of the world." Having just awakened, in a temporary state between the perceptual limbo of sleep and the routinized dullness of everyday life, the speaker can perceive "the moment's rain and sea, / The moment's sun . . . / Overtaking the doctrine of this landscape." This is not to assert, untenably, that the doctrines, or descriptions, of this landscape do not still exist or will not still be necessary once this unusual moment has passed.

That Stevens makes "doctrine" and "description" synonymous in the poem suggests his understanding that all conceptual formulations, even ostensibly merely descriptive ones, are implicated in doctrinal—ideological, social, political—circumstances.[22] In a highly characteristic rhetorical paradox (which also occurs in such poems as "The Motive for Metaphor," written around 1943), Stevens cunningly portrays the perception of ideologically innocent "reality" not only as temporary and evanescent but in terms of multiple metaphorical figures ("the moment's sun" and "the strong man vaguely seen") that are anything but innocent. This male personification "bathes in the mist / *Like* a man without a doctrine" (emphasis added); the carefully chosen simile asserts and preserves a space of doubt, a resistance to the very male fantasies of the imaginer. That any notion of ungrounded reality must itself be imagined (and imaged), that the imaginer must be conscious that it is a fiction, is exactly the point, as Stevens has articulated elsewhere. Yet the perceptual level of the experience, temporary and fictional as it is, is equally important. It is the exhilarating apprehensions of "sudden rightnesses," those inklings of knowing belief in a fiction, which renew our interest in the "descriptions of the world" that must return as soon as we attempt to capture the experience in, for example, a poem. The distance between experience and descriptions of experience is often the unspoken focus of Stevens's work, as it is here, and such works as "The Latest Freed Man" can usefully be read as metacommentaries on the desires, needs, and capacities of the imaginative human existing in the world. Such poems, themselves "descriptions of the world" and therefore inevitably selective, reductive, and incomplete, are nonetheless the parts, which admittedly do not add up to a single truth but which are the only means of attempting to inhabit and make some sense of our world.

Following *Parts of a World*, in September of 1942, Stevens published his most ambitious work, *Notes Toward a Supreme Fiction*, which contained the fullest verse elaboration of his conception of the nature and function of human creativity. The *Notes* eventually came to be a central text for many of those who used the poet's work and poetics to elaborate post-New Critical conceptions of poetic value and modernist canonicity. Stevens elected to publish the poem initially in a limited edition by the Cummington Press rather than with Knopf; the poem did not appear in a mainstream publication until *Transport to Summer* in 1947. While in retrospect the Cummington's price tag of $3.00 seems quite a bargain, the relatively high cost and the limited distribution of the first edition meant that the poem's influence and early reputation were somewhat dissipated in the criticism of the war and immediate postwar era. The only substantial notice of the Cummington edition, by R. P. Blackmur in *Partisan Review,* offered a potentially valuable corrective to the critics' dualistic pigeonholing of Stevens's formulations. Blackmur once again indicated his congeniality to Stevens's own position by noting the general intellectual inadequacy of dualisms: "the doublet is never enough unless it breeds. War and peace need a third phase . . . as God the Father and God the Son need the Holy Ghost, and hell and heaven need purgatory, or act and place need time" ("An Abstraction Blooded," 298).

Blackmur perceived that Stevens's "habit of creative thought," and its expression in *Notes Toward a Supreme Fiction,* lay in the articulation of interdependences among multiple processes and states, in this case the triad of "three phases through which [the supreme fiction] must pass" (298). These three phases are not dialectical but simultaneously interactive since, as Blackmur accurately and importantly noted, "each phase is conceived as a version of the other two, that is, with a mutual and inextricable rather than with a successive relationship" (298).

Yet throughout the essay Blackmur demonstrated his inability to resist wholly the desire for the sort of teleological closure Stevens did not offer. Like many other critics of the period, Blackmur ultimately dualized Stevens's position by describing the poem as the result of a dialectical conflation of two of the poet's earlier formulations "into a third thing" (297). Although Blackmur attempted to capture Stevens's resistance to absolute assertion by noting that the third thing, "if never reached, is approached all round" (297–98), the very positing of this objectified entity implied a new cycle of antithetical opposition of terms and processes which was successive and never multiply simultaneous, as Stevens's triad would have it.

The widening gap between poet and critic also appeared in Blackmur's overall judgment of the poem, which he admired but which epitomized for him the contemporary poet's ultimate inability to achieve "great unity and heroic vision" rather than "only fragments, impressions, and merely associated individuations" (299). Despite his perceptive description of the logic of the poem's structure, Blackmur concluded that the *Notes* suffered from a certain arbitrariness in its conjunction of "formal circumscription" and fragmentary substance, as if the triadic form, arbitrarily imposed from without, were the only force containing and unifying the poem's otherwise chaotic content. Ultimately Stevens's failing was that "he lacks . . . the power of the 'received,' objective and authoritative imagination, whether of philosophy, religion, myth, or dramatic symbol, which is what he means by the imagination's Latin" (300).[23] This unmistakable reference to the post-conversion criticism of T. S. Eliot was reinforced at the end of this same paragraph when the critic invoked Eliot as the outstanding authority for determining "the proper domain of poetry" (300). Thus the force of the critical desire for the illusory wholeness of "tradition" gradually pushed even Stevens's most forceful and sympathetic advocate away from Stevens's tolerance of multiplicity and disorder and towards a conservative modernism of orthodoxy.

Ten years earlier, in "Examples of Wallace Stevens," there had been no such disjunction between Blackmur's views and Stevens's, as Blackmur had recognized and celebrated the tolerance of the disordered perception ("nonsense") in Stevens's work. Blackmur's turn away from Stevens's pluralist poetics is an illustration of the consolidating power of a New Critical orthodoxy which, despite the differences among its individual critics, shaped poetic evaluation more and more strongly as the 1940s continued. In the mainstream of New Critical thinking, Stevens had become seen as a poet whose formal virtues were enough in themselves to afford a measure of importance, but his relative ideological heterodoxy blocked him from being a central figure. Even more than other commentators of the 1940s, New Critics consistently focused on the Stevens work that most forcefully demonstrated his distinctive and spectacular aptitude with poetic form, at the expense of his later, more socially engaged work. This critical turn back to *Harmonium*, which could be clearly seen in the *Harvard Advocate* compendium of 1940, accelerated as the decade continued.

Blackmur's changing view of Stevens was not the only explicit illustration of this process among the New Critical elite during the war years. Yvor Winters's opinion of Stevens's work as an exemplary illustration of the "decadence" of modern poetry, expressed most forcefully in the long essay "Wallace Stevens, or the Hedonist's Progress" (in his 1943 volume *The Anatomy of Nonsense*), both reflected and influenced the critical absorption with *Harmonium* to the detriment of assimilating Stevens's recent work. Winters proclaimed loudly the "rapid and tragic decay of the poet's style" and, no less, of his intellectual and moral equipment after "Sunday Morning" (433). This ostensible degradation derived from Stevens's insufficiently rational sense of "moral judgment" which led him, like Poe, to embark on a self-destructive quest for "intense feeling" through the creation of novel effects in poetry rather than a search for "just feeling" (439). The result of such an empty aspiration was, for Winters, a sense of "ennui" that left only three equally undesirable options—the ever more obsessive, extreme, and futile struggle for novelty; meaningless self-parody; or a complete renunciation of one's art—all of which, he argued, were exhibited by Stevens's work at various points.

Winters has been characterized, with some justice, as a crank, but it would be a mistake to assume that his strongly expressed and sustained critique of Stevens's modernism was without influence on other views of the poet. While few critics shared the specifics of his philosophy of criticism or his account of Stevens's utter decline, Winters had, as Theodore Weiss noted in his exasperated 1944 attack "The Nonsense of Winters' Anatomy," "browbeaten not a few otherwise acute critics into humble acceptance" (212),[24] but it was not merely a question of Winters's forceful, even intimidating, manner of writing criticism that led to acquiescence by major New Critics. Winters's dismissal of any moral significance in Stevens's "hedonism" is closely connected to Ransom's treatment of the "pure poetry" of "Sea Surface Full of Clouds" a few years earlier and, more generally, dovetailed with the conservative moralistic hankerings after metaphysical and sociopolitical unity and order which operated covertly in the supposedly empirical formal emphasis of the New Criticism.[25]

Outside the New Critical elite itself, Winters also had a decided influence on views of Stevens. A 1948 review of *Transport to Summer* by Winters's associate, Alan Swallow, compactly recapitulated the basics of the "hedonistic" view of the poet: "Yvor Winters is surely correct in believing that Stevens was at his best in earlier poems. . . . In fact, Stevens has come to be something of the jester, the entertainer for those who care to be amused by his kind of entertainment; in him there is a kind of terrible smugness and self-satisfaction" (469).

Here the connection between the antihedonism of the Winters school and Cargill's moralistic objections to the poet's carnival barker persona became clear. "Those who care to be amused by his kind of entertainment" was a phrase worthy of a prim matron objecting to the floor show on the midway. Ostensible aesthetic standards thus became implements for legislating a particular (though certainly vague) system of hierarchical moralism in which a "jester" could only be allowed control over a somewhat disreputable side of poetry, but not over its central expressions.

Winters's premises about Stevens were shared by critics even as they felt it possible to differ from the extremity and dogmatism of his evaluative conclusions. In *Partisan Review* in 1946, for example, Wylie Sypher developed a critique and qualified appreciation of Stevens which was somewhat more balanced than Winters's position but which derived quite directly from it. Repeatedly evoking Winters, and occasionally echoing his tone, Sypher characterized Stevens as a "romantic" purveyor of "pseudo-reference" (Winters's term) "behind [whose] intellectualized phrasing is an imprecision of thought almost unparalleled in modern verse" (83). The Stanford critic's influence sometimes led Sypher to unfathomable readings of Stevens's works which transferred the critic's own intellectual quirks to the poet, as in this gloss of "Asides on the Oboe": Stevens's "dread of the glass man—the rational man— his contempt for the metaphysicians . . . means that he has set one human faculty—reason—over against another—sensibility—in a dichotomy that has deprived him of what the poet most needs, fictions themselves" (85).[26] The result of such a dichotomy was that Stevens was a "misologist"—a hater of ideas (85)—and therefore had no capacity to develop any intellectual position whatever. Most damning was Sypher's conclusion, also straight from Winters, that Stevens, cultivating emotions as goods in themselves, had "consumed his talents" in becoming a solipsistic "connoisseur of his own responses to the chaos about him" (87). Such a judgment was integrally related to a distrust of Stevens's philosophical and ideological tolerance of provisionality and difference (as in "On the Road Home"), which to absolutists such as Winters and Sypher seemed unacceptable relativist chaos: "Thus living in many sensuous worlds indicates a failure in imagination. The supreme fiction becomes fictitious indeed, a dizzy pluralism, a rage for order that cannot be spent" (90). The apprehension that Stevens actually meant what he said—that the supreme fiction should indeed be fictional, provisional, and plural and not a metaphor for a covert metaphysical authority—clearly perturbed such critics so that, despite their acknowledgement of his gifts, he was a rather menacing presence who had to be cut down to size to fit the narrow mold of the conservative New Critical conceptions of poetry.

Winters's characterization of Stevens as a solipsistic and anti-intellectual hedonist who had taken "emotion as a good in itself" ("Wallace Stevens," 432) also differed little in its premises from critics who would have had no truck with Winters himself. For example, Horace Gregory's laborious and persistent efforts to establish that Stevens was no philosopher but purely and simply "a poet of sensibility" differed from Winters's views mainly in evaluative conclusion: while Winters believed that such a characterization represented decline and wastage of talent, Gregory believed it to be a legitimate function for the poet ("Examination of Wallace Stevens," 58). Warren Carrier's 1953 article "Wallace Stevens' Pagan Vantage" approvingly summarized Stevens's viewpoint as "hedonism (. . . stop at feelings); aestheticism (Ah, bella!); and these within the framework of paganism," simply reversing the polarities of Winters's attack without calling into question the evaluative preconceptions behind them (168). Even Weiss, a strong Stevens advocate who poured substantial energy into his attempt to annihilate Winters's influence in "The Nonsense of Winters's Anatomy," attacked the critic's readings poem by poem rather than developing a sustained and affirmative exposition of Stevens's poetics, thus unwittingly allowing Winters's ideas to maintain control of the frame of reference for the debate.

One of the fundamental strategies of Winters's argument, which became widely used by other writers during the decade, was to beg the question of the decline of Stevens's later work by simply not discussing it.[27] Winters shared this strategy with Oscar Cargill in *Intellectual America*. The first step, familiar from 1920s commentators such as Untermeyer, was to disapprove vaguely of *Harmonium* as bizarre, unnatural, and frivolous: "poetry was for [Stevens] so definitely divorced from life—so much a pastime" as to stamp him as "the one American of whom it may accurately be said that he has written poetry primarily for amusement" (255). The second step, found only two pages later, came in Cargill's remark that "in a new seriousness the bravura of *Harmonium* is gone" (257), implying a nostalgia, not unlike Winters's for "Sunday Morning," for the spirit of the poet's early work and a concomitant lack of interest in his later, more serious output. Cargill cemented this judgment by concentrating almost exclusively on poems from *Harmonium*.

Such characteristic strategies were indicative of the stronger and stronger hold *Harmonium* had taken on the attentions of a variety of Stevens critics and readers even before its reissue in 1947. The increasing concentration on *Harmonium* was accompanied by the patterns of anthology selection and survey discussion of Stevens's work in the early 1940s. For example, *American Harvest*

(1942), edited by John Peale Bishop and Allen Tate, offered its readers only two Stevens poems, "The Emperor of Ice Cream" and "Sunday Morning," both famous from *Harmonium*. Though the choices themselves were unremarkable, the implicit rationale for selecting such already canonical works helps to reveal the evaluative tenor of the times. Among the editors' concerns in their introduction was to characterize the period between 1920 and 1940 as a turning point in the history of American culture, since it "represents what is, properly speaking, a literature" (9), in contrast to the imitative and provincial spirit of most nineteenth-century American writing. Such aspiration to canonize a whole period, also evident in the eponymous metaphor of harvesting, demanded an increased selectivity, a higher aesthetic standard, to ensure preservation and display of only those works with sufficient permanence to support the broader argument. Thus poetry such as Stevens's more recent work about which there was substantial difference of opinion, or which was simply so new that it had not been clearly assimilated by readers, tended to be ruled out.

Conrad Aiken's 1944 edition of his well-established Modern Library anthology, *Twentieth-Century American Poetry,* espoused a similar position on the poetry of the interwar period, arguing that the body of modern American poetry which "had seemed at best a very promising beginning" when the first edition was published in 1927 "was now secure and brilliant in accomplishment" (xix). As an important part of that accomplishment for Aiken, Stevens's work warranted a prominent place in the book; but despite the editor's expansion of the roster to include a generation of younger poets, he did no updating of his own Stevens canon, selecting eight poems, all from *Harmonium*. In their comprehensive 1946 *A History of American Poetry, 1900–1940* (dedicated to Untermeyer), Horace Gregory and Marya Zaturenska did no more than reiterate the familiar review opinions of the former by arguing that the character of Stevens's work and its place in American poetry, established by *Harmonium*, had remained in total stasis for two decades: "Since the publication of his first edition of *Harmonium* in 1923, Wallace Stevens has been the James McNeill Whistler of twentieth-century American poetry" (326). In probably the most canonically important anthology of the period, the 1951 edition of *The Oxford Book of American Verse*, F. O. Matthiessen did better, giving Stevens as much space as any twentieth-century poet, and reprinted fifteen poems written after 1930; even so, the inclusion of "The Comedian as the Letter C" still skewed the balance of pages drastically towards *Harmonium*.[28]

Stevens's long resistance to a collected edition of his work was a clear indication of the importance he placed on his recent development and his wish to keep it as prominently displayed as possible (L, 333, 510, 638, 693, 759). Knopf's decision to issue *Harmonium* for a third time in June 1947, just three months after *Transport to Summer,* however, provided a younger generation of poets and critics with renewed publicity for and access to the older book and served to intensify the devaluation of Stevens's recent work at the same time that it continued the consolidation of his canonical status overall.[29] The early reception of both *Transport to Summer* and *The Auroras of Autumn* (1950) was haunted by unflattering comparisons to *Harmonium.*

This evaluative pattern was especially prominent in the views of rising younger poets, who were nearly unanimous in casting their allegiance with *Harmonium* at the expense of Stevens's later, more socially resonant work. Peter Viereck's two reviews of *Transport* dwelt upon how *Harmonium,* one of the "most powerful catalysts of poetry" between the wars, "has outlived most of its contemporaries, including much of the later poetry of its own author," and that his current readers, "Transported to so hazy a summer . . . will welcome the equal opportunity . . . of being transported back again to his springtime" ("Stevens Revisited," 154, 157; see also "Some Notes on Wallace Stevens," 14–15). Rolfe Humphries yearned after the "good sensuousness along with music and idea" of the poet's first big success of thirty-five years earlier, "Peter Quince at the Clavier," remarking apologetically that "Mr. Stevens is probably heartily sick of hearing about" it (293). Robert Lowell concluded that "as one rereads, [*Transport*] too often appears muddled, thin, and repetitious. How willingly one would exchange much of it for the concrete, gaudy wit of *Harmonium*" (401).

Perhaps the most forceful and influential of the younger poet-critics writing on Stevens in the first postwar decade, Randall Jarrell, echoed and intensified this pattern. In his review of *The Auroras of Autumn,* Jarrell glossed over the serious issues in Stevens's later poetry, preferring the vivid sensory immediacy of *Harmonium*: "The best of *Harmonium* exists at a level that it is hard to rise above. . . . Often, nowadays, he seems disastrously set in his own ways, a fossil imprisoned in the rock of himself—the best marble but, still, marble" ("Reflections on Wallace Stevens," 142). Jarrell's formulation put Stevens in a double bind in which *Harmonium* established the foundations of his great achievement, "his own ways"; but these very ways then became the source of his recent failures when he could not wrench loose from them.

A similar trend could be seen developing in an emerging generation of academic critics and scholars. Louis Martz's deep admiration for Stevens's work, even the most recent, could not stop him from making the familiar invidious comparison: "It is true that, unlike [*Harmonium*], *Transport to Summer* is marred by a number of labored and muddy pieces" ("Recent Poetry," 339).[30] In the first critical monograph on the poet, published in 1950, William Van O'Connor dismissed *Parts of a World* with this remark in favor of Stevens's "pure poetry": "Often one feels willing to exchange many of these poems, with their heavy import, for a poem similar in artistry to 'Sea Surface Full of Clouds,' in which the associations are fused into a magnificent symbol" (*The Shaping Spirit*, 71).

Bravura, springlike, sensuous, musical, light—these were the virtues of *Harmonium* seized upon and celebrated by postwar critics. In comparison, *Transport to Summer*, a monumental volume that collected *Notes Toward a Supreme Fiction* and *Esthétique du Mal* with six other long poems and several dozen shorter ones, seemed to critics heavy, hazy, and abstract. Even Stevens's strongest advocates were unable to accept fully his later work; Samuel French Morse, writing in the tribute issue of *Trinity Review* in 1954, which he also edited, summed up this prevailing critical opinion by remarking, "The poems in *Harmonium* already seem indestructible," asserting doubtfully, "In time the later poems will be so, even though it sometimes seems that 'the damned thing doesn't come right' " ("Agenda," 34). Such readers as these chose to have Stevens both ways: they could admire him glancingly for being a poet engaged with serious contemporary issues, but they were not forced to engage themselves with that poetry because of the "cream out-of-this-world" of *Harmonium*. Their responses during and after the war set the tone for Stevens criticism until the mid-1960's and to an extent, even now: open admiration for the spectacular aestheticism of *Harmonium*, reluctant acknowledgement for the later work which, despite its greater seriousness, relevance, and scope, seemed to them a diminution of the pleasure offered by the distinctive "world" of Wallace Stevens.

Whatever one thinks of Stevens's later poetry, such postwar devaluations of it should be seen as neither intrinsically wrong nor right but as irreducibly contingent upon the historical (psychological, ideological, institutional) factors that largely determined the shape of the postwar literary academy. The most immediately circumstantial of these factors, and not the least important in the long term, was psychological in manifestation: the widespread expression of exhaustion and disillusionment with the effort to make literature conjoin with sociopolitical issues brought on by a broader revulsion against wartime (and indirectly Depression) traumas. Writing in 1946, Vivienne Koch summed up the overcompensation that followed the immediate release from the war's thrall: "It is becoming a kind of current drawing-room . . . mood to sniff at 'war poetry.' " Koch argued to the contrary, "It is frivolous to pretend that war, as the central fact of the time, has not affected the poets. The fact of the matter is that they *have* responded to it, whether some critics like it or not" ("Poetry in World War II," 10). Koch treated Stevens's *Esthétique du Mal* as one of the most substantial and valuable of these responses, but her acknowledgement of the efforts of poets to engage with the collective psychological trauma produced by the war was ultimately a dissenting voice lost in the postwar rush to universalize and depoliticize.

Involved in this psychological release of tension after the war were, of course, strong ideological factors influencing the shift away from the political. Part of the exhaustion with literary politics was a loss of faith in the specific institutions of leftist politics here and abroad. The disarray of the American left after the devastating curves thrown it by the Soviet Union in the late 1930s hardly needs rehearsing here. As Van Wyck Brooks put it, after the Hitler-Stalin pact, "the whole idea of progress through collective effort disappeared from the general mind of writers" (536). In the years following 1945, as suspended literary activities resumed inside and outside the academy, quickly reaching unprecedented levels, the reaction against the crudities and contradictions of criticism that espoused a political agenda accelerated. The conclusion widely drawn was that prewar political criticism was invariably naive, reductive, and without affirmative value. The virtual disappearance of the left from literary criticism meant that by the mid-1940s just about the only prominent criticism with an openly political bent still being published was the nationalist celebrations of Brooks himself, which came to many to function as bêtes noires of shoddy scholarship and Pollyannaish affirmation of American society.[31] Scholars with little overt interest in politics found themselves allied with both conservatives and anti-Stalinist former communists in rejecting Brooks's version of literary activism, which suddenly seemed to be the only one available.

The example of Brooks's dispossession illustrates that what happened during these years was not anything as simple as a right-wing takeover of the American literary culture, since some of those who objected to Brooks perceived him as being dangerously blind to the authoritarian drift of his patriotism. What was happening was that in the depth of their disillusionment with political manipulations, critics and writers were shifting their political models away from the relatively clear-cut ideological axis of 1933–39: left vs. right, socialism vs. fascism, with a middle ground between them. Certainly the Hitler-Stalin pact had thrown all convenient left-right oppositions into disarray; more ironically, the Allied-Soviet entente during the war continued to do so. The postwar political model that developed was based instead on a dynamic of freedom vs. authoritarianism.[32] The whole concept of ideology became seen, in contrast to the previous decade, not as a constitutive condition of an irreducibly political world but as a sign of a particular text's extrication in politics, then as a particular bias and limitation of interpretive scope, potentially and preferably to be transcended or avoided in one's own literary practice and criticized in that of others.[33]

Rather than any particular political orientation, it was politics itself that was seen to be a destructive intrusion into the realm of the literary. Though the development of a New Critical hegemony was symptom as much as cause of this rejection of the political, clearly the body of intellectual formulations known as the New Criticism was positioned advantageously to provide an apparently "nonpolitical" framework, not simply for methods of literary interpretation, but for the very conception of what literature and criticism were meant to be and do. Young reviewers, scholars, and teachers just back from the war did not need to like—or even be aware of—the politics of the New Critics to appreciate the pedagogical and scholarly usefulness of techniques of "close reading."[34] New Criticism appeared to be a methodology adaptable to texts of various orientations and to students of various social backgrounds, and it therefore seemed democratic, if not outside of politics altogether—an error not yet overcome.[35]

The operative evaluative effect of this "nonpolitical" hegemony, of course, was to invalidate any literary work that openly posited an engaged (rather than alienated) relationship to twentieth-century political developments. Since poetry written from more conservative positions, such as Eliot's, tended to affect an alienation from or transcendence of the political by couching its politics in terms of what Winters called "eternal verities," this turn against the topical particularly meant the exclusion of modernist work written from a progressive or leftist point of view. By 1950 even such an admirably activist critic as Matthiessen, rather than asserting the inextricable connection of literature with politics, could be found taking shelter in the safer waters of literary descent: "Any cataloguing of poetry in relation to political events is bound to be inadequate. How inadequate we may judge by realizing that such a catalogue would miss almost entirely the subject matter of, for example, Poe and Emily Dickinson, Frost, Eliot, and Stevens. A more inclusive apporach would bear in mind that, in the broadest terms, most of our later poets could be described as descendents of Whitman or as descendents of Poe" (*The Oxford Book of American Verse*, xxvii).

With this widespread revulsion against the political shaping much literary evaluation, William Van O'Connor's preference for *Harmonium* poems in *The Shaping Spirit* (1950) set the tone for the first academic study of Stevens, suggesting the extent to which the poet's later, "heavy" work would be devalued even as Stevens began to be elevated to canonicity in the burgeoning postwar literary academy.

The entrenchment of New Criticism as *the* approach for interpreting and evaluating modernist poetry was closely linked to this period of institutional expansion in the academy, especially with the emergence of a generation of critics and scholars, of which O'Connor was an older member. Many of this group of scholars had seen at least a bit of the war and the world, and many were more interested in the texts of American, modernist, and contemporary literature than in the cloistered philological tradition of English literature studies. Many were to become strong believers in Stevens's centrality to modernism. In the decade after the war they began to exhibit the first concerted academic attention to Stevens, resulting in O'Connor's book and then the first dissertations on the poet, by Morse and C. Roland Wagner (both 1952) and Bernard Heringman (1955). While these evidences of academic attention were minor compared to the avalanche in the decade after the poet's death, they already exhibited the strongly philosophical or phenomenological emphasis to criticism of Stevens's work; indeed, Wagner's work was done for Yale's philosophy department. In this same decade, articles on Stevens's work also began to make their way into learned journals, many of which were only then beginning to treat twentieth-century literature as a serious subject; between 1945 and 1955 pieces on Stevens appeared in such explicitly scholarly publications as *English Literary History, Modern Philology, The Journal of Philosophy, College English, PMLA, The Journal of Aesthetics and Art Criticism,* and *The Explicator*.[36] This new level of scholarly access to publication, in coming during a time of general "Stevens revival," as Sculley Bradley put it in 1951 (255), enabled his academic reputation to thrive during a period when those of most modernist poets were losing ground fast.

As interested as they were in modernist and contemporary texts, however, these postwar scholars were also very much beset by war exhaustion, a desire for a quiet normal life, and a deeply ingrained suspicion of the imposed systems of thought and authority which seemed to them to characterize mid-twentieth-century politics. Kermit Vanderbilt, who studied and worked with a group of them (including O'Connor) at Minnesota after the war, has portrayed these postwar graduate students and young professors as "war-weary veterans . . . with little taste for radical politics. Beneficiaries of capitalist largesse under the GI Bill, they quickly became the traditional professor's ideal student, the industrious bookworm, serious and mature and motivated, but the bookworm nevertheless. Very few, we suspect, had voted in 1948 for [Progressive party candidate for president] Henry Wallace" (Vanderbilt, 538).

In postwar academic criticism the industrious traditionalism of these younger scholars manifested itself in a prevalent mood of historical recapitulation and reevaluation. The drastic physical and psychological upheaval of the war drew up a convenient threshold that defined a literary-historical period — as Viereck put it, "poetry between the wars" ("Stevens Revisited," 154) — largely the same demarcation that formed the outlines of what later critics would call "modernism." This periodizing process was a major factor in the paradoxical canonization of Stevens through *Harmonium*, at the expense of his later work. The postwar critic was tempted by the nostalgic impulse to leave the miseries of the recent past and the excruciating anxieties of the present and to reenter what was coming to be seen as the golden age of American literature, with all of the ostensible innocence and freedom such a myth implied. The 1920s became (and is still) seen as the central time for "modernism" as it came to be defined after World War II. It was thus convenient for Stevens advocates to place *Harmonium* alongside a host of other key texts that defined the period of "high" modernism between World War I and the depression—*Hugh Selwyn Mauberley, The Waste Land, Ulysses, A Draft of XXX Cantos, The Bridge, Tulips and Chimneys,* and the like.

Reflecting this emphasis, Frederick Hoffman's landmark history of that decade, *The Twenties,* also became a standard account of American modernism as a whole. Hoffman's book was published in 1955, yet oddly its subtitle is *American Writing in the Postwar Decade,* as if everyone involved had neglected the existence of another major war that had ended exactly a decade before. Such an indication of the post–World War II critic's desire to return to the golden age before the last war, and the identification of the 1920s as that golden age, was also accompanied by a widespread denigration of the culture of the depression years. In Louise Bogan's 1951 account, for example, the 1920s were characterized by the cultural stewardship of *The Dial,* in which "political theory . . . bore no weight; the aesthetic impulse was allowed to function without ideological compulsion," while in the 1930s modern American poetry achieved consolidation "in spite of its entanglements with barren Marxian theory" (*Achievement in American Poetry,* 69, 78).

For Hoffman the major value of poetic experimenters such as Stevens, Williams, and Moore was that they "ask questions concerning the usefulness, the value, and the crucial functions of the imagination. Inevitably experiment in literature is both a process of 'making new' and one of cutting back to intrinsic meanings that have been overlaid by doctrinal and documentary irrelevancies" (217). The movement of these two sentences is highly characteristic of the post-World War II rejection of and paranoia about politics; beginning with a general critical notion of many possible implications ("a process of 'making new' "), Hoffman then erected linkages between literary works and politically or historically implicated concepts associated with the 1930s such as "doctrine" and "document," only to devalue or dismiss those connections by means of a rhetoric of "intrinsic" meaning and value.

The years after 1940 saw not only this sort of retrospective evaluation of American modernism among literary critics but also the vast expansion of American studies programs in the academy.[37] Clearly a war-influenced nationalism was partially behind this rapid disciplinary development. Even if it was not the sort of blindly affirmative mythology of American democracy that Van Wyck Brooks offered, the study of American culture did have a strongly educative and ideological purpose in the world of 1940, as the comprehensiveness and urgency of Robert Spiller's remark implied: "The study of American culture must become the center and the guiding principle of our entire scheme of liberal education from the earliest grades to the most abstruse levels of graduate research" (quoted in Vanderbilt, 461).

The nearly simultaneous rise of New Criticism and American literature study within the academy took a curious institutional turn, however, that has much bearing on the direction of Stevens criticism over the past forty years. Rather than conjoining their efforts to develop a historically and interpretively sensitive critical tradition of twentieth-century American poetry, adherents of the two fields effectively carved up the primary material: New Critics (and later, deconstructionists) adopted poetry, particularly that of the twentieth century, as their province of American literature, and Americanist literary historians largely abandoned the century, keeping as their own the pre-twentieth-century work with which they were already more familiar.[38] The concepts of literary form and literary history, relatively close together in the 1930s, were once again polarized by the end of the 1940s. This fundamental fissure in the study of American literature is only now beginning to be healed with the gradual and long overdue penetration of "New Historicism" into the study of modern American literature.

As it became more and more prevalent over the next fifteen years, the widespread neglect of Stevens's attempts at political relevance issued from stronger and deeper factors than the desires of readers tempted to escape their war weariness through the spectacular aestheticism of *Harmonium*. This neglect was highly symptomatic, and to some reciprocal degree causal, of the postwar cultural formation of "modernist poetry" and the canons associated with it. Whereas before the war "the new poetry" had consisted of numerous contesting attributes and lines of descent, many of them centrally concerned with the relations of sociopolitical issues to art, postwar criticism tended to identify all the modernism worth the name with the single strain of alienated avant-gardism associated most closely with Eliot and Pound. The reflexive devaluation of ideology itself came to function as a dogmatic ideology of American criticism. Most poets with aspirations to political engagement were largely dismissed or reduced to minority and still have not resurfaced, while Stevens and a few other fortunates were carried along for the ride in circumstances that greatly reduced their social resonance.[39]

Response to Stevens after the war embraced values of the nature and function of poetry which had been present in modernism since its beginnings (as in Pound's view of the artist at war with the world) and consolidated them into a version of poetic accomplishment as an alienated individualism based on a dualized conception of a "world of art" separate from, and implicitly superior to, the world of sociopolitical experience. This dichotomized view of the character of the poet and the function of poetry has permeated Stevens criticism for the past four decades.

This ideology of the poet's function had at its very center the premise that the world of poetry and the world of quotidian existence, in which was included all sociopolitical experience, were separate realms. This notion of a separate world of art can be found in Stevens criticism even in some of the reviews of *Harmonium*, where it functioned as a favorite metaphor of genteelly transcendent aestheticism (see, for example, Monroe, "A Cavalier of Beauty," and Seiffert). This dichotomous worldview had become problematic for both the poet and for many American critics in the 1930s. Stevens was never again comfortably able to turn back to the concept of a separate world of art; but critical discourse of the 1940s embraced the two-world paradigm, often using it as a measure of the consolation Stevens's gorgeously textured poetry offered in a bleak time.

O'Connor's preference for "Sea Surface Full of Clouds" over *Parts of a World* led directly into a characteristic expression of the trope: "The Stevens who wrote *Harmonium* was in possession of a world, the esthetic, but the Stevens of *Parts of a World* is in search of one" (*The Shaping Spirit*, 71). Such a judgment missed the import of the title and contents of *Parts of a World*: that a separate world of art, no matter how tempting, was no longer an idea that the poet could accept. Simons began his review of *Parts* in 1942 by explicitly connecting the ideology of two worlds to Stevens's high standing, making it a defining characteristic of modern poetic success: "Mr. Wallace Stevens is one of the few living poets who have constructed, each of them, a complete world for his imagination to inhabit" ("The Humanism of Wallace Stevens," 448). To the poet's longtime detractor Untermeyer, "Stevens seem to be less anxious to establish a relation between imagination and 'the' world than making 'a' world—another world of the intellect"; even in rejecting the validity of an autonomous world of poetry, Untermeyer accepted the dichotomy as a way of characterizing Stevens.[40]

Postwar instances of the paradigm of two worlds were often distinguished by a rather paranoid corollary: the notion that the quotidian, not simply an uninteresting or mundane realm, continually threatened to ooze in and despoil the purity of the world of art. In literary criticism this cultural Manichaeism manifested itself in the postulation of two distinct, absolutely hierarchized types of discourse: one of genuine creativity and one of didactic or moral purpose. Only the first was considered a valid aesthetic achievement. Thus when they could not be ignored, Stevens's explorations of the social responsibilities of the poet—of all humans—tended to become didactic utterances and therefore aesthetic failures: "But at times the ironic, smiling guitarist, who doesn't care whether or not he is overheard, seems momentarily replaced by an earnest business executive who is trying to clarify and expound his ideas in a staff meeting but finds that everything he says comes out as double-talk" (Dillon, 98).

Here George Dillon forced evaluations of poetry into a framework of two severely dualized discourses: when Stevens failed as a poet, his disclosure was not just unsuccessful poetry but the "double-talk" of the other world of business and other tiresome quotidian activities. Even Stevens's most discursive works sound nothing like the professional jargon of a businessman (a philosopher, perhaps); Dillon's characterization was undoubtedly shaped by his awareness of Stevens's career as an executive in a large corporation. Thus Stevens's failures represented destructive intrusions of his "other life" into his poetic world.

In Dillon's formulation a central element in the unfortunate transformation of Stevens from poet into businessman was a shift in tone from "ironic" to "earnest." According to the ideology of postwar criticism, in order to produce poetry of requisite purity, the poet could not be emotionally engaged with contemporary realities but had to attain an ironic state of Confucian disinterestedness. In the sort of spiritual contentment Stevens achieved, readers could find, according to Jeremy Ingalls, "a record of the ancient indignities and indignations," but in a tone that was "transmuted by a venerable serenity" (48).

In 1947 Eberhart suggested that for Stevens a sense of urgency must give way to serene contemplation of a realm of imagination which largely precluded an active social role: "the purity of his aesthetic argues a uselessness, a rarity, the pleasure of ideal contemplation" (252). Frank Jones went so far as to generalize "a severance from the actual" as a precondition to producing first-rate literature: "Colossal effort of will is needed to dwell for the needed time 'where,' as Henry James phrased it, 'in the dim underworld of fiction, the great glazed tank of art, strange silent subjects float.'. . . How is the artist to 'return,' to set his art right with the world, if to do so he must employ the only creative processes he knows, those which established his unique world, his true mythical self" (488). The lesson to be drawn from such remarks was that a poet's purity could be seen as directly proportional to his or her uselessness to a social discourse.

Within this limited cultural scope postwar criticism focused on two (often overlapping) functions for the poet—to entertain and to express his or her individual identity. Neither allowed the poet a central role in the society's intellectual and cultural life, as Stevens advocated. Certainly various poets have been content to play the roles of epigrammatist, performer, or singer; such roles do in fact serve a valid cultural purpose, but to limit the possibilities of poetry to those activities is a different question. Stevens had been explicitly aspiring to wed the two roles of performer and serious intellectual, to produce through his verse both sensory pleasure and substantial cultural commentary, at least since *The Man With the Blue Guitar*. Despite his own arguments for the necessity of a poetry of expanding social and intellectual scope, many readers refused to allow him—or any poet—this role. Gregory felt strongly enough about the question repeatedly to "insist that Mr. Stevens is not an intellectual and that the value of his poetry cannot be measured in intellectual terms ("Examination of Wallace Stevens," 57, 58). Gregory was not alone in dismissing Stevens's attempts at the intellectual exposition of ideas and issues in poetry. In Dillon's remarks above, Stevens's richly symbolic guitarist was transmuted into an earlier musician, the "ironic smiling" persona of *Harmonium* who "doesn't care whether or not he is overheard," or as Swallow put it more harshly, "the jester, the entertainer for those who care to be amused by his kind of entertainment" (461). Stevens's works could generate pleasure in the reader but also a certain contempt at their pretensions to intellectuality: "Sometimes his poems are no more than delightful fooling. Usually they seem to say more than they say" (Tindall, "Literary Signposts," 119).

A guitarist-poet of this sort was valuable mainly for the sensuous "music" that he offered his readership, rather than for any intellectual content—which meant the valorization of *Harmonium* over later work. For Mary Colum in 1942, for example, Stevens's recent poetry was sterilely "intellectual rather than . . . sensuous. We can have no great poetry without intellectual brooding, but when the speculative intellect is too dominating . . . the result, no matter what command he has over rhythms and words, is something other than poetry" (12).

For Gregory, Stevens was not intellectual; for Colum he was too much so. Despite this opposition, however, both readers held in common a rejection of the intellectual in favor of the sensuous in their definitions of poetry. Such a tactic illustrated the general narrowing of what poetry might be to a point where not only adherence to a specific doctrine but the act of intellectual speculation itself was seen as ruinous to aesthetic value. Only something such as "intellectual brooding"—a highly emotionalized form of thinking—could be admitted. Similarly, Jarrell remarked of *The Auroras of Autumn*, "The habit of philosophizing in poetry—or of seeming to philosophize, of using a philosophical tone, images, constructions . . . has been unfortunate for Stevens. Poetry is a bad medium for philosophy" ("Reflections on Wallace Stevens," 139).

Even more extremely, to Tindall in 1943, Stevens gave "the impression of systematic thinking. But . . . it is never altogether clear what the thinking is about. Concealing his thought, if any, in indirection, nonsense, and exquisite goofiness, Stevens conveys the sensation of thinking, which for most of us is all that thinking comes to anyway" ("Literary Signposts," 119). Whether Stevens was or was not thinking clearly and systematically in a given poem might always be a legitimate issue for debate, but a society in which that was virtually impossible, in which "most of us" including the poet were capable of no more than "the sensation of thinking," would have no poetry that contributed meaningfully to its cultural and political discourse.

In 1948 Viereck summed up the period's reaction against the conjunction of political and literary in a passage that also reveals how that broader reaction had a direct impact on the manner in which Stevens was being canonized and on the role he was coming to play in the postwar modernist poetry canon:

> Readers of the later books of Stevens have attached too much significance to what critics would call his "increasing concern with social problems." Never is Stevens deeper in dreamland and more detached from material realities

than when, as a would-be concession to "reality," he refers to economics. The result is an unintentional surrealism, more bizarre than any of his Novembers off Tehuantepec. If there is a "true" Stevens (Stevens as a Platonic Idea), then it is still the sentimental and unsocial one. ["Stevens Revisited," 154]

When Stevens tried to mix poetry and economics, the result could only be a "bizarre" hybrid, for reasons that were apparently too obvious to Viereck's readers to require elaboration. Better that Stevens remain "true" (which Viereck clearly meant despite the quotation marks) to his "Platonic" poetic self and forget social concerns. If the poet would not do so, Viereck offered critics and readers a mandate to ignore his treatment of them. The most insidiously ideological effect of this anti-intellectual campaign was that almost all participants have presented such evasion not merely as an interpretive choice by poet or critic—"Here, unlike elsewhere, Stevens in his poetic practice and/or I in my critical practice elect not to concentrate on political questions"—but as the poet's own intentional and exclusive focus, as his limitation (or "overreaching," to use John Enck's term [132]), as his essence, or even worse, as the essence of poetry itself.[41]

The second (and more highly valued) role for the poet in critical discourse of this period was that of self-expression. The goal of poetic expression, almost universally if vaguely conveyed, was self-fulfillment. Consequently in Stevens criticism the term "poet" has often been taken quite narrowly, not in Sidney's and Shelley's sense of a representative of articulate humanity, but as a hermetic, hyperindividual figure seeking only to express and fulfill himself. Stevens's continual use of the terms "poet" and "poetry" have been assumed to refer to a writer of lyric verse such as himself, rather than as only one of his large stock of figures for persons of imaginative aspirations engaged with their environment.[42] On the contrary, Stevens's "poet," far from a Poundian notion of the lofty figure contemptuous of the rabble of uncreative humanity, is largely a collective concept, that capacity in any and all of us to articulate by various means the pleasures of merely circulating or the agonies of those "buried in their blood." One might have hoped that Stevens's continual use of musicians and listeners, painters and observers, in this same role would have made it impossible to interpret the trope so narrowly. Instead, the presence of such myriad creative figures in Stevens's wartime poetry as the "floribund ascetic,"

Mrs. Alfred Uruguay, the young rider, The Latest Freed Man, The Man on the Dump, the Sleight-of-Hand Man, The Well-Dressed Man with a Beard, Jumbo, and Lady Lowzen were taken to mean not that "the poet" implied all creators but that all creators reduce to the poet, and particularly to the rather hermetic fellow who crafted baubles in the comfort of his Hartford home and insurance office.[43] The scope of Stevens's poetry has thus been consistently reinscribed into an isolated autobiographicality that largely swallowed up the possibilities of seeing poetry as a viable basis for social dialogue.

The rigid autobiographicality that such critics have posited in Stevens's work reflected a broadly emergent limitation of poetry in postwar American criticism to self-expression, self-presentation, rather than seeing it as the potentially powerful articulation of collective human experience. Such an autobiographical imperative, in which a poet's main task was to establish his or her own unique identity, personality, or voice, had political causes and consequences. In his review of *Esthétique du Mal*, Dillon approached a recognition of this relationship when he developed an explanation of the obscurity of modern poetry as a reaction against "the proliferation of what Hayakawa calls 'venal poetry,' i.e. advertising copy," which had led discerning readers to "value especially the original, gratuitous, or 'absolute' effects of language" (97). To the stultifying instrumentality of advertising one might add another form of social discourse influencing the critical valorization of uniqueness and formal elegance: political propaganda, whose nightmarish possibilities were, even as Stevens and Dillon wrote these texts, shifting into a mode of nuclear apologetics and cold-war hysteria. However understandable it might have been, the unfortunate consequence of the critical reaction against socially implicated discourse should be all too clear; if speech was of value only when it possessed rarity and nonreproducibility, the whole idea of collective articulation was discredited.

The postwar fetishization of poetry as self-expression was, then, at least partially a reaction against collective articulation and action, which were threatening to critics in its association with the mass movements of communism and fascism (and, less consciously, in connection with their personal experiences with the American military machine over the previous few years). In Stevens commentary, this manifested itself in the widespread evaluative rhetoric that each of the greatest poets of the time must construct "a complete world for his imagination to inhabit" (Simons, "The Humanism of Wallace Stevens," 448). Simons's phrase suggests the incommensurability of those poets' "worlds" with one another and the isolation of each in "his" individual identity. It followed that genuine poets had no interest in persuading readers of anything, could not produce articulations of collective humanity, indeed could not even be identified critically as part of a cultural polity without significant damage to the perceived value of their work: "One of the contributors to *Others* was Wallace Stevens, who, however, has never identified himself with any group and owes nothing to the puffery of any clique" (Cargill, 225).[44] To Gregory in 1944, the history of modernist poetry of which Stevens's career formed a significant part was defined entirely by individual rather than collective accomplishment. Stevens's association with an aging, durable generation of American poets was little more than an accident of birth, since that generation "has fortunately survived the events, the distractions, the superficial changes in poetic styles which had taken place in two world wars. Whatever 'moral' may be derived from this phenomenon, it is one that asserts the merits of individual distinction, and not of group influences" (review of *Notes Toward a Supreme Fiction*, 583–84).

"Group influences," presumably, were superfluous but still infectious intrusions of social and historical factors—of geography, personal acquaintance, political orientation, ethnic identification, emotional temperament, socioeconomic class—into the "world" of poetry. What truly mattered was the unique individual of inexplicable greatness whose fellows and all the history they shared were, incredibly, no more than "distractions."

This concern for identifying the characteristics and the individuals who qualified as poets of "individual distinction" indicates the impulse towards hierarchical and exclusive canonization which characterized the evaluative tenor of the postwar period. Instances of these star-making efforts on Stevens's behalf sometimes took amusingly self-conscious form, as in Gerard Previn Meyer's 1946 review "Wallace Stevens: Major Poet," which began sententiously, "There are major poets in our midst, and Wallace Stevens is one of them" (7). On the other hand, sometimes they took on a rather disturbing tone, as in Simons's remark, "Minor men, half-poets, write out of more or less temporary adjustment between their personalities and their environments. Stevens writes from a unique, whole vision of life" ("The Humanism of Wallace Stevens," 448–49). Here Simons brought together the ideology of the self-created world by the unique individual with a distorted version of Stevens's concept of "major man" to create a sinister Nietzschean hierarchy of humanity.

The pluralistic and skeptical resistance to reductive absolutes which characterized most of Stevens's poetry of the 1940s did not preclude critical attempts to graft it onto the ultimate, elusive goal of the ideology of two worlds, which was not only to withstand the intrusive pressure from the sociopolitical realm but to reverse it in a kind of aesthetic manifest destiny, producing moments in which the imagination dictated terms to the quotidian world. Postwar critics' use of the reality/imagination dichotomy as a first principle for reading Stevens often took on politically charged, conflictual formulations that reflected cold-war pressures, ironically displacing political anxieties onto what critics wished to preserve as a purely aesthetic or epistemological realm. To Louis Martz in 1947, Stevens's central vision was this: "in a world of 'calculated chaos,' the human imagination can create its own intense and ordered world from materials provided by the world of physical objects. The 'transport to summer' consists in seizing with the imagination some pleasurable physical object, and then, by metaphor, clarifying it and relating it to other objects, until one has formed an integrated composition of the 'ideal' and the 'real.' By such man-made credences we dominate and enjoy our environment" ("Recent Poetry," 340).

Martz's description of the "integration" of the ideal and real suggests that he nearly overcame the stubborn two-world dichotomy, but in the last sentence its persistence came clear in strongly territorial terms: to "enjoy" our environment we must first "dominate" it. Otherwise, Martz suggested, the "calculated chaos" of the "world of physical objects" not under the control of the imagination will dominate us.

Martz's choice of terminology evokes almost by necessity one of the few Stevens poems that became a staple of the New Critical canon, "Anecdote of the Jar," which also deals with the role of artistic creation in the relationship of imagination to environment. Undoubtedly the poem's tantalizing epigrammatic ambiguity was part of its appeal to mid-century readers, but just as prominent to its success was its presentation of an obviously and intriguingly "symbolic" object at a time when "symbolism" was becoming a central locus for theorists of American literature.[45] Indeed, in 1953 "Anecdote of the Jar" could be seen by Charles C. Walcutt as an exemplary text for developing a pedagogy based on symbolism. A student of Walcutt's—obviously a New Historicist ahead of his or her time—produced "in an advanced class in poetry analysis" a reading of the poem as "a Republican treatment of the TVA," whose

" 'dominion' is oppressive, unproductive, wasteful," stopping river commerce and refusing to "give of bird or bush" (447). In using this paper as a case study of misuse of the concept of the symbol, Walcutt advanced pedagogical objectives that established the goal of literary interpretation as the identification of an "abstract universal" out of "the tones and connotations found in the close literal reading of the poem" (448). Aside from the shaky positivist assumption that anyone can actually determine what meanings are and are not supported by the literal texture of a poem, Walcutt's deployment of the symbol erected a de facto prohibition on literary analysis that might use a text's particulars to derive a vital sociopolitical meaning from the experience of reading it.

In this case, the abstract universal that might legitimately be derived—according to Walcutt, that the jar is a symbol of the sterility of machine-age artifice—dovetailed with the nostalgic distrust of technology and politics seen everywhere in conservative New Criticism. Walcutt's conception of the abstracting supremacy of the symbol, highly characteristic of the era, thus served to eliminate anything topical from the realm of first-rate literature, reducing such material to the notorious New Critical ghetto of "allegory" (453–54). To exaggerate slightly, an implicit rejection of New Deal principles could be achieved in first-rate poetry through the use of symbolism, but explicitly expressed rejection of the New Deal itself was off limits (and advocacy even more so), to be relegated to second-class citizenship. The student's questions to his or her classroom interrogators—"why after all the jar was placed on a hill in Tennessee, of all states? And was not the TVA the most significant unnatural establishment there?" (449)—are of the sort that readers of 1992 might well find themselves asking or encouraging their students to ask, but Walcutt's symbol-based conception of literary meaning and value allowed such issues no purchase.[46]

No less appealing for readers within the two-world paradigm was the opportunity "Anecdote of the Jar" provided for choosing a side in an ostensibly dichotomous relationship between apparent abstractions (between, say, "nature" and "art") which actually housed a strongly political debate—the question of humankind's "dominion" over environment. In 1948 Viereck attempted to supersede the art/nature debate by noting the absurdity of various dualistic readings of the poem (Winters: "anti-artifice, pro-nature"; others "pro-art, anti-nature") and by arguing for a third, intermediate state of "ironic neutrality betweeen" the two. In spite of himself Viereck then undercut his synthesis with a remark that brought the two-world paradigm right back into dominance: "whatever lip service he may pay to nature in theory (even assuming he was pro-wilderness and anti-jar), in his own practice Stevens fortunately leaves all folksy primitivism to the ghost of Rousseau" ("Some Notes on Wallace Stevens," 15).

As mired in the old dichotomies as those whose readings he objected to, Viereck saw two worlds: nature as primitive, art as sophisticated; nature as chaotic, art as ordered; nature as threatening, art as "fortunately" reassuring. He easily gave up the briefly entertained "ironic neutrality" to choose art for Stevens. Stevens's own insistence on the necessity of "choosing" in such poems as "Asides on the Oboe" and *Notes Toward a Supreme Fiction* reflected quite a different level of decision, not which of two opposing options to place one's belief in, but in what way to believe in anything—in the case of the jar in Tennessee, whether or not the individual or collective will should allow the placing of one's jar to dominate a landscape.[47] For postwar criticism, however, such a question was largely invisible. Prevalent conditions of thought and reading led to an emphasis on themes of dualistic struggle in which domination of the environment was seen as unquestioned good.

That commentators of such widely divergent orientations and temperaments as Viereck, Winters, Gregory, and Weiss insisted on maintaining the outlines between the "worlds" of poetry and the polis reflected the influence on the literary culture of a series of broadly historical events between 1940 and 1955. Contrary to Gregory's wishful notion that the great generation of modernist poets was but little distracted by the disasters of recent history, after 1945 the involvement of poets in politics loomed alarmingly large in ways far different from the 1930s and helped to discredit or deflect interest from poetic attempts such as Stevens's to integrate poetry and social concerns. In particular, the arrest and committal of Pound made for highly unsavory associations between modernism and politics. The decision of the 1948 Bollingen Prize committee to honor *The Pisan Cantos* represented a broad-based effort to override the instability of the relationship between poets and politics by establishing a precedent for intrinsic aesthetic value. Though that tactic met with little immediate success, generating some furious debate, the consensus since has been that the defenders of the award fared best. Undeniably one result of the controversy was to make all sides wary of talking about Pound's explosive politics for nearly two decades—which paradoxically enabled his academic canonization during that period.[48] As the 1950s began, American writers and intellectuals were further chilled by witch-hunts from the federal government and various right-wing periodicals which were indiscriminate enough even to reach Stevens's old comrade, the plain-speaking humanitarian physician from Rutherford (Mariani, 651–66).

Advocacy of the reticent businessman from Hartford between 1945 and 1960, however, posed no risk of association with unwanted or even dangerous political labels on either left or right. The spate of major awards given to him during the era of McCarthy and Virginia Kent Cummins's *Lyric*—a Bollingen Prize, two National Book Awards, and a Pulitzer Prize—neatly indicate the poet's perceived "innocence" in a climate of extreme volatility between the literary culture and benighted civil authority. In particular, the Bollingen award to Stevens the year following the Pound debacle, as Meyer put it, "was received with almost universal acclaim," "in happy contrast to last year's Bollingen" ("Bollingen Winner," 19). This decision conveniently served both to give an overlooked poet a lifetime achievement award and to reestablish the damaged credibility of the Bollingen Prize itself ("now safely in charge of the Yale University Library," as *Saturday Review* editor Harrison Smith put it in "More Gold Medals," 23) with the general public and its self-appointed cultural watchdogs.[49] One such was *Time* magazine, whose review of *The Auroras of Autumn,* entitled "Prize Pies," portrayed Stevens as a leader among modern poets, who were figured as "patty-cakers" forming unintelligible mud pies "into shape for the admiration of themselves and their playmates" (106, 108). In its inimitable style of facetious scorn for anything even remotely avant-garde, *Time* made much of Stevens's "double life": "By definition (he is a business executive, therefore he is normal), Wallace Stevens cannot comfortably be classified as just a mud-dauber" (108). Such compliments, left-handed as they were, nevertheless contrasted favorably with Stevens's prize-winning predecessor, who, *Time* did not fail to remind its readers, was "now (as then) a mental patient in St. Elizabeth's Hospital" (108).

In such a hostile climate, in which middlebrow America characterized poets either as dangerously unstable snakes in the grass or as harmless cutups, most of the literary culture opted to embrace the latter. In Brazeau's oral history, Léonie Adams, one of the four voting members of the 1949 Bollingen jury, reminisced candidly about the discussions preceding the award. According to Adams, the jury felt that to honor the obvious choice, yet another collected edition of Frost's poems, would be too blatant an attempt "to say [that] after all, we're good Americans even though we did vote for Pound" (quoted in Brazeau, 177). The choice of an ultrapopular figure such as Frost would have represented too great a capitulation to the external political pressures, but the selection of Stevens, someone whose reputation and readership were housed almost entirely within the professional literary culture, reasserted the right of specialists to choose for and from themselves without being swayed by the know-nothings outside.

However much Stevens might have deserved these honors, the fact remains that he was an ideal compromise figure for the literary climate of the early 1950s: no flag-waver, but respectable, buttoned-down, tangible evidence of the potential creativity of corporate America. In having had a long and distinguished career that was nonetheless almost totally unsullied by evidence of involvement with the sordid or disturbing political realities of the previous twenty years, Stevens epitomized the politically innocent side of twentieth-century American literary culture, as Pound and leftist poets then epitomized the dark side. Stevens's late and collected volumes were thus in exactly the right place at the right time to be accepted enthusiastically as the work of a major poet, but the sociopolitical commentary of his work was in exactly the wrong place and time. Based after all on the cardinal rejection of absolutism and dogmatism, it commanded or coerced no one to listen, obey, or decry; and it was largely skipped over. Since poetic texts do not exist independently of the ways in which they have been read and written about, when modernist poetry is read today, the reader to an extent reproduces this postwar critical mistrust of politically engaged poetry. In examining the politics of canonicity, it would be a mistake to identify a poet's potential social resonance with decades of writing by a generation of critics trying to shore up the ruins of elite culture or seeking to make manifest their intellectual or professional destinies.

SIX

A Shaping Spirit

Stevens and the Canons of Modernism, 1954–1966

> Now, at seventy-five, as I look back at the little that I have done and as I turn the pages of my own poems gathered together in a single volume, I have no choice but to paraphrase the old verse that says that it is not what I am, but what I aspired to be that comforts me. It is not what I have written but what I should like to have written that constitutes my true poems, the uncollected poems which I have not had the strength to realize.
>   Humble as my actual contribution to poetry may be and however modest my experience of poetry has been, I have learned through that contribution and by the aid of that experience of the greatness that lay beyond, the power over the mind that lies in the mind itself, the incalculable expanse of the imagination as it reflects itself in us and about us. This is the precious scope which every poet seeks to achieve as best he can.
> —Stevens,
> receiving the National Book Award, 1955

> [W]e have in this book poems which are beautiful, impeccable, and famous, poems which are so intimate a part of our time and scene that we are almost persuaded to say, appropriatively, "This is what we have been able to do; by these works we are willing to be known."
> —Hayden Carruth
> on *Collected Poems*, 1955

To a significant number of younger poets, readers, and critics, Stevens was fully canonical by mid-century. Soon thereafter, three events within three years—

publication of his monumental *Collected Poems* on the poet's seventy-fifth birthday in October 1954, his death ten months later, and then the appearance of *Opus Posthumous* in 1957—provided occasions for retrospective evaluation from this faithful generation of poets and critics who had acknowledged him as one of their poetic masters for nearly two decades. Clearly evident among even the least enthusiastic of the responses to these events was an acknowledgment of the poet's almost overwhelming authority. It was now thoroughly possible to assert—and for many, impossible not to admit—that Stevens was central to twentieth-century American poetry. Collectively the discussions of Stevens in this decade reveal a fundamental shift in the primary role played by his reputation in American literary discourse: from a potential canonicity to a full level of canonicity in which his work was implicated in the very process of constituting conceptions of American poetic value, a level that among American modernist poets has been reached only by Eliot and perhaps Frost and Pound.

The analysis of the reception of Stevens's work and its cultural significance will now shift as well, to concentrate not on articulating the critical preconceptions and objectives that determined whether or not readers chose to evaluate Stevens favorably but on answering two lines of inquiry related to his established status: how was the increasingly unavoidable belief in Stevens's centrality used, its character shaped and reshaped, to confirm the preconceptions and further the objectives of various readers? How did it help to constitute those assumptions and goals themselves? Earlier pages have already touched on the first of these processes as it manifested itself in the criticism of the later 1940s and early 1950s, which opted to concentrate almost exclusively on the "aesthetic" side of Stevens, thus enlisting his reputation in the broader campaign to lead American poetry and criticism away from any explicit engagement with politics. In the later 1950s more varied meanings and uses of his work began to proliferate, and the narrow critical focus on *Harmonium* and Stevens's "pure poetry" began gradually to broaden. By many Stevens came to be perceived as a standard-bearer in the reassertion of a Romantic aesthetic against the prevalent anti-Romanticism of high modernism and New Criticism; others saw him as an arch-rationalist, enacting in his work the pathos of a worldview without the possibility of transcendence; still others found that this ability to participate in and celebrate the everyday rather than the transcendent was exactly his distinction and value; by still others this relationship was seen as a frankly possessive mastery of "reality" with desperate or apocalyptic overtones. Clearly the chameleonic quality to this catalog is itself an indication of the more and more broadly canonical status Stevens was attaining in American literary discourse.

For an indication of Stevens's canonicity among many younger poetry practitioners which existed even before *Collected Poems*, one can glance at John Ciardi's selective anthology *Mid-Century American Poets* (1950), which offered both prose manifestoes and verse from fifteen poets who were, according to the editor, "all part of what will be recognized as a poetic 'generation' . . . that arrived within the last ten to fifteen years" (xxvi). Among these fifteen poets were at least ten (Wilbur, Viereck, Roethke, Shapiro, Lowell, Jarrell, Holmes, Eberhart, Ciardi, and Schwartz) who had paid or would pay explicit homage to Stevens, and another (Elizabeth Bishop) whose kinship to him has long been understood. Furthermore, in his introduction Ciardi noted the "first arrivals of [yet a] newer generation" whose work, if anything, was heading even more in Stevens's direction: "more decorative and less inclined to statement," "markedly more traditional in form, and . . . more verbally excited within the stricter outline" (xxvi). For this proto-generation "Wallace Stevens and Dylan Thomas" were the "most admired masters" (xxvi).[1]

This growing canonicity consolidated further after the publication of *Collected Poems*. The timing of *Collected Poems* with a milestone birthday—complete with a gala luncheon and a limited, individually numbered first edition courtesy of Knopf—contributed to a strong impulse to treat the event as an "occasion" for "celebration" (Schwartz, "In the Orchards," 16) and commemoration, which softened the attitude of even a stringent critic such as Jarrell, who remarked, "I have before this written about both his best poems and his worst, but on occasion (and a book like this is truly an occasion) a critic can behave like posterity" (review of *Collected Poems*, 100). During the same year this sense of moment also produced a festschrift for Stevens in the *Trinity* (Hartford) *Review*, a journal then edited by Samuel French Morse, and a special issue of critical discussion of Stevens's work in the journal *Perspective*.[2] The convergence of attention to *Collected Poems* from the institutions of criticism, publishing, and prize-giving bodies might be compared in scope and effect to the hullaballoo surrounding the publication of *The Waste Land* in 1922, and this had a significant impact on Stevens's reputation in both the short and the long term.

One reason that Stevens's collection was poised to receive intensive attention and adulation was because it was no ordinary "collected poems." Most other poets of Stevens's generation had, for commercial or other reasons, already published incomplete collections well before the end of their lives. For a sense of the relative finality and comprehensiveness of Stevens's entry, note in contrast the various recyclings of Frost's work: three editions of *Selected Poems* since 1923, two editions of *Collected Poems* since 1930, a Modern Library *Poems of Robert Frost* in 1946, and then a massive *Complete Poems* in 1949. Each of these compilations was different, and because Frost was still alive and writing in 1955, none was truly complete. Stevens had long felt that collecting his work would have an effect of closure on his sense of himself as a working poet; hence his resistance to its appearance. But such finality, harbinger of creative cessation that it was, also gave the book a quality of weight and importance to audience as well as author. Stevens's postponement of *Collected Poems* until so late in his life and career delayed the intensive retrospective attention that was needed to make him fully canonical, but it undoubtedly intensified the response to his poetic summation once it finally came.

To have waited as long as he did also helped Stevens's success in the accumulation of official laurels. Though Stevens had won some important awards in the previous five years, there still existed the perception that he had been unjustly neglected for many years and that to honor him not only commented upon the book at hand but upon his work as a whole. Now here was his work as a whole; how could one not honor it? The pressure to honor Stevens was intensified by such reviewers as Ciardi, who engaged in a kind of literary extortion by remarking, "Despite the fact that he has published five of the best books of poetry ever written by an American—the first one as far back as 1923—he has never attracted the notice of the Pulitzer Prize Committee in Poetry. By this time I don't see that the committee has any choice: if Stevens doesn't win the Pulitzer for '54 the committee might as well turn the prize into a blue ribbon and award it at the National Horse Show, for any relevance it will have to poetry" ("Wallace Stevens's Absolute Music," 346).

Evidently the juries agreed; *Collected Poems* swept the two major poetry awards, the Pulitzer and the National Book Award. These validations by the official guardians of poetry prizes also helped to give Stevens a belated notoriety beyond the realm of the literary specialist into the realm of cultural "news." His collected volumes penetrated much further into the capillary channels of American literary culture than any of his previous volumes of poetry. Various mass-circulation newspapers around the country ran reviews, undoubtedly exposing more people than ever before to Stevens's work.[3]

As *Harmonium* had made possible a critical synthesis of Stevens's work which his scattered magazine publications before 1923 had not, so the *Collected Poems* and *Opus Posthumous* made possible, even demanded, criticism and evaluation of Stevens of a greater scope than ever before. The relatively minor discriminations within an accepted frame of reference that critics had gotten used to making (did the poems in *Transport to Summer* or *The Auroras of Autumn* represent a falling off from the standard set by previous books?) gave way to attempts at commentary and evaluation to match the comprehensiveness and coherence of the collections. Critics were drawn to address such questions as: What was the meaning of the poet's whole career? What was the extent of his permanent value to American poetry? The archival character of *Opus Posthumous* generated predictions of intensive critical activity around Stevens's work in the near and distant future, as in Rosemary Deen's remark that it "ought to signal the beginning of the comprehensive studies of his work," since interested readers, scholarly and nonscholarly alike, "now have available to them an almost complete canon of Stevens's writings" (620). The canonical stakes were thus raised, and as Jarrell suggested, the question of "posterity," once easily enough evaded in commentary on Stevens, now became unavoidably primary.

An immediate effect of this enlarged frame of evaluative reference was to encourage widespread and vigorous claims for the permanence of Stevens's poetry. In not recycling old material, Stevens had enabled a collected poems much of which would have been unfamiliar (or at least not overfamiliar) to many readers. Opening with the *Harmonium* poems, which many had been rereading intensively in previous years, the book then offered nearly four hundred pages of less-known material, including two dozen new poems ("The Rock"), which almost everyone agreed were superb. Far from the wearily respectful receptions that late or collected works tend to generate after their authors have outlived the era in which they made their reputation, Stevens's collected works seemed to readers vital forces that "have acquired the verisimilitude of life" and continued to "grow in the mind" (Morse, review of *Col-*

lected Poems, 3; Schwartz, quoting Blackmur's 1932 essay, "In the Orchards," 17). Schwartz developed this perception further by remarking, "The growing continues, astonishing and inexhaustible. . . . And as his poetry grows in one's mind, the greater the abundance of comment which it seems to require. Clearly the primary comment must be the conviction that Stevens is a great poet" (Schwartz, "In the Orchards," 17).[4]

Schwartz's language suggests that to evaluate *Collected Poems* in 1954 was to experience a strong sense of authority emanating from the work, which drew or even forced readers to "comment" on Stevens more and more; and the first thing they had to profess was their conviction of the poet's "greatness." The poet's "inexhaustibility" had evaluative ramifications not only for the present moment but for the indefinite future as well. Schwartz's mixed feelings of delight and awe at the authority of Stevens's work were amplified by Jarrell's extravagant (but not implausible) claim that "some of these cool, clear, airy poems, which tower above us in the dazzling elegance, the 'minute brilliance' of yachts or clouds, ought to be sailing over other heads many centuries from now" (review of *Collected Poems*, 100).

The authority exerted by Stevens's collections resulted in assertions by many readers that his work had become a constitutive part of various aspects of existence: of literary modernity, of the American scene, of reality, of language, or (somewhat comically) of the very earth itself ("Setting out on Stevens for the first time would be like setting out to be an explorer of the Earth," Jarrell, "The Collected Poems of Wallace Stevens," 180). These widespread perceptions that Stevens had become part of the fabric of "things as they are" was a hugely important step in the process of naturalizing his textual authority so that it gradually became no longer a struggle or a surprise to acknowledge Stevens's greatness but the most natural and undeniable thing in the world — the final precondition for an author's full canonicity.

Stevens's close connections to the modernism of the early part of the century had long been assumed, of course; but the collections triggered a fundamental reorientation of this relationship in which Stevens's work was no longer seen as merely a part of the rise of modernism but as a model containing that phenomenon within itself, as a gallery contains the whole history or tradition of art in microcosm. For Robert Pack, Stevens was "the perfect example of the contemporary western sophisticate" (xiv), and Irving Howe argued that Stevens's work represented "a profoundly serious effort to grapple with the distinctively 'modern' in modern experience," which was possible because he had remained profoundly aware of "the defeats and losses of the century" which "loom" in the background of his work (16, 19). Hayden Carruth figured his perception of the cosmic inclusiveness of *Collected Poems* as "an incredible, incomparable gallery" of modernity in whose elements "the many influences on the art of our time can be seen clearly: French, pastoral, metaphysical, Homeric, etc.; and the many aims: to originate, to shock, to re-examine, to analyze, and above all to deal uncompromisingly with the realities of the contemporary world" ("Without the Inventions of Sorrow," 289). For Carruth, Stevens's texts thus presented to readers "the whole movement of this century in art" (288).

More surprisingly, perhaps, several critics described Stevens's work as offering an exemplary representation of the essential texture of the American landscape. Schwartz argued that an overlooked but significant part of Stevens's value was as a "New England poet" whose poems were "at times comparable to the precious and strange objects which Yankee skippers acquired in the China trade," not without connection to exotic alien places, but no less—perhaps more—a part of America for that connection ("In the Orchards," 17).[5] Carruth pointed out that the conventional portrayal of Stevens as a purveyor of tropical exotica was superficial and that after *Harmonium* the poet's "characteristic scene is not tropical but northern," as likely to be a celebration of "drab and wintry occasions as of summer"—thus indicating Stevens's willingness to engage with the actual climate of his and most of America's reality ("Without the Inventions of Sorrow," 291).

Bogan gave this argument even broader significance by arguing that Stevens had "extracted the essence of American climate and atmosphere" from Florida to New England. As "the first modern American . . . to deal with the American scene in imaginative rather than purely topical or regional terms," Stevens had thus deepened our ability to express "the American spirit of place" (review of *Collected Poems*, 201–2). Stevens thus became seen as an integral builder of an authentic poetry in and of American culture, "one of the chief of those 'who brought the Muse to this country' " (Bogan, "*Harmonium* and the American Scene," 20). These poet-critics' sympathetic portrayals of Stevens as a quintessentially American poet would soon be matched by more ideologically regressive counterparts in the academy, especially in the influential version of American poetic history constructed by Roy Harvey Pearce.

Schwartz summed up the various processes of identifying Stevens as constituting essential and multiple parts of existence in a breathless catalog of the poet's various roles: "Then there is Stevens's assimilation and mastery of the lessons of modern painting, *vers libre* and imagism, or the traditional norms of the blank verse style in Shakespeare and Milton, his inventive and original use of place names, of foreign and archaic words, and his witty coinages, his relationship to Whitman and Baudelaire (two poets who almost never are a combined influence upon any modern poet")" ("In the Orchards," 17).

To begin to see Stevens as such an authoritative exemplar (assimilator, master, synthesizer) of so many apparently irreconcilable aspects of his times was to make possible a thoroughgoing alignment, even identification, of readers' own consciousnesses with the poet and what he stood for. Carruth's expression of this sense of identification was typical: "We have in this book poems which are beautiful, impeccable, and famous, poems which are so intimate a part of our time and scene that we are almost persuaded to say, appropriatively, 'This is what we have been able to do; by these works we are willing to be known.' "[6]

The process of "appropriation" to which Carruth referred intensified after the poet's death, with the passing of the power of preservation and exclusion from Stevens to others (such as Morse, as editor of *Opus Posthumous*): "As for those who believe the writer himself should have the final say as to what should or should not be preserved, the answer might be, yes, supposing the writer were able to be present after his death, with the benefit of some metaphysical insight which neither he had nor we have, in life. As matters stand, it is surely *our* business to know what of his is valuable to us to keep" (Gibbs, 54).

Such writers were implying a kind of mutual surrender of poet and reader to one another: if readers yielded themselves to the portrayals of reality conveyed by the poems, this allowed readers to identify, both emotionally and perceptually, Stevens's achievements as their own. Readers were becoming more Stevens's all the time; but paradoxically he was also becoming more theirs.

Gerard Previn Meyer noted that Stevens's aspirations to forge this kind of enormously ambitious connection between poet and reader could be found clearly expressed in his own work; *Collected Poems* revealed the greatness of Stevens's accomplishment in actualizing "what he conceived the poet's function to be, the poet's duty or service to his readers (for though coteries have done somewhat to isolate him for their own, it is clear Stevens has not been writing all these years for the coteries). It 'is to make their imagination theirs and . . . he fulfills himself only as he sees his imagination become the light in the minds of others' " ("Actuary Among the Spondees," 27).

For Meyer, as for most readers, Stevens's value had permanently transcended the limitations of cliques or coteries to command multiparty allegiance throughout the culture. Thus, according to Schwartz, although the poet might never be famous in a conventional sense, his immortality was assured: "millions who sit upon furniture which is what it is because of Picasso have never heard of Cubism. So too the poetry of Stevens will modify the speech and consciousness of many generations indirectly. His inventions, his discoveries, his long labor in the orchards of the imagination will directly affect other poets more and more in the future, giving a new unintended and triumphant meaning to a pronouncement in his first book . . . 'I am a man of fortune greeting heirs' " ("In the Orchards," 18).

Schwartz's adaptation of Stevens's own articulation of the potential sociocultural power of language, not least of poetry, was an apt example of the critical acceptance of the worldview purveyed by the poet's work. Both directly and indirectly, to all his descendants, both the poets and the "millions," Stevens was becoming a universal parent and benefactor.

Ultimately the most significant critical deployment of Stevens's reputation during the middle and late 1950s was to contest the ideological traditionalism and the strongly hierarchical canon embodied in the poetic and critical reputation of T. S. Eliot. Critical comparisons or contrasts between Stevens and Eliot had of course appeared occasionally for thirty years, as when Edmund Wilson had evoked Eliot's tragic scope to demonstrate the relative triviality of *Harmonium* in 1924, or on the other hand, when in 1931 Eda Lou Walton had contrasted the "fortitude" of Stevens's contemporary engagement with Eliot's "retreat" into royalism and Anglicanism (Wilson, "Wallace Stevens and E. E. Cummings," 102; Walton, "Beyond the Wasteland" 263). Undoubtedly Wilson's framing of the comparison had been the predominant one as Eliot had become ever more central to American poetry criticism through the end of the 1940s, by which time his influence was felt in virtually every corner of American literary culture. The impressive bulk and scope of Stevens's *Collected Poems* now offered commentators a new opportunity to measure his relative importance against this reigning king of the canon. Though Stevens's reputation would gradually equal and in many ways surpass Eliot's canonical supremacy over the next quarter-century, in 1954 when head-to-head comparisons were made, Eliot's authority was usually strong enough to withstand the immediate challenge. Commentators repeatedly called upon the tactic of describing Stevens as "the best poet writing in America," thus conveniently evading the necessity of explicit comparison; but since this tactic was clearly invented for the purpose of doing so, it represented an implicit deferral to Eliot's authority.[7] In other cases, an exact or near equivalence was openly posited, as in Schwartz's assertion that "Stevens is a great poet, [whose] work as a whole is as important as that of Frost and Eliot" ("In the Orchards" 17), or in Louis Simpson's vacillating remark that Stevens's "prestige stands on a par with T. S. Eliot's, or a mere step below" (240).

Even during the years of the New Critical heyday which followed the war, however, reactions against the authority of Eliot were beginning to appear, and, sometimes in indirect or implicit ways, the reputation of Stevens served an important function in such rebellions. As early as 1938 Stevens himself had hinted at a desire to resist the authority of Eliot in favor of a less exclusive and more flexible conceptualization of literary evaluation itself. His remarks for the Eliot issue of the *Harvard Advocate* began quite flatly with an expression of disapproval of the position that Eliot had come to occupy: "I don't know what there is (any longer) to say about Eliot. His prodigious reputation is a great difficulty" (41). Such "[m]ore or less complete acceptance" of the centrality of any figure helped "to create the poetry of any poet," but that very dominance "also help[ed] to destroy it" (41). Eliot's work was apparently of value to Stevens only when read "out of the pew, so to speak," "eliminating from [one's] mind all thought of his standing" (41). Stevens then indulged in a bit of buffoonery that attempted to cut this "prodigious" reputation down to size by comparing the experience of reading Eliot's poems to encountering "a Giotto in what is called a breakfast nook" (41)—implying the absurd, even grotesque disproportion and more than a hint of pretension that was involved in the maintenance of such a level of reputation. A dozen years later Stevens would reiterate this distaste for the role Eliot played in a letter to O'Connor: "After all, Eliot and I are dead opposites and I have been doing everything that he would not be likely to do" (*L*, 677).[8]

In 1949 Schwartz expressed the frustration felt by many at Eliot's canonical dominance in an essay notably entitled "The Literary Dictatorship of T. S. Eliot." Although Schwartz claimed, "A literary dictatorship . . . is quite unlike a political one because you cannot force people to like poets or poetry, although you can persuade them" (573), this denial was disingenuous: to use such a term to describe anyone in 1949, especially in the pages of the quintessential antifascist, anti-Stalinist periodical, could not be an act free from political connotation. At some level, perhaps beneath the scope of conscious argument, Schwartz meant to suggest exactly those "unfortunate political associations" he purported to deny (573). The impossibility of completely defusing the explosiveness of Schwartz's terminology gave a raw political edge to what was for the most part an admiring discussion of Eliot's success in persuasively articulating judgments about a great many poets and in estimating their contemporary value—as well as his ability to stay on his dictatorial podium even as he drastically revised his own previous evaluations.

Near the end of the essay Schwartz brought Eliot's self-revisionism to bear on the whole issue of exclusive canons and their pernicious consequences, asking, "Is it necessary, in order to praise poets A, B, and C, to condemn poets D, E, F, G, H, and the rest of the alphabet?" (586). He further asserted that the evidence of the wholesale changes in judgment "which prevail throughout literary history," and the occasional stupidity and injustice that could be seen within the work of "even the greatest critics" (such as Eliot), might be used to argue for the establishment of a less hierarchical, less exclusive way of conceiving of the history of poetry than Eliot's reign had allowed (586). Such a scrutiny of Eliot's critical career, then, might ultimately enable one to "see how it might be desirable to have no literary dictators" (587). Schwartz did not explicitly refer to Stevens in this essay; but his great regard for the older poet was amply expressed in numerous other contexts, suggesting that to argue against the dominance of Eliot and to advocate Stevens's importance was an eminently feasible conjunction. The metaphor of resistance to dictatorial control of thought and evaluation upon which Schwartz based his argument was not widely employed by others; but over the next dozen years various poets and critics found a number of ways to use Stevens to achieve such resistance to the formal, ideological, and institutional authority of Eliot—thus furthering the constitutive importance of Stevens within the mid-century poetry canons.

One of the main angles from which critics approached this Stevens vs. Eliot contest concerned the question of influence on younger poets. Stevens's importance to younger poets had been noted for thirty years but had not generally been considered as being in the same league as that of Eliot. As Meyer put it in a review of O'Connor's book in 1950, "many . . . have noted that the new generation of poets in our land are hitching their wagons to Stevens's star, rather than — as was formerly customary — to T. S. Eliot's" ("Bollingen Winner," 19).

Julian Symons, one of Stevens's reluctant English admirers (in 1954 there was still hardly any other kind), admitted that, on the question of influence, "if a young poet were looking for a model . . . he might gain much more, and with much less chance of harm, from Stevens than from Eliot or Pound" (45). Though Symons did not specify why this was so, his suggestion was borne out by a middle-aged American who remembered exactly such a search for poetic models, a poet who now had sufficient distance to cast a retrospective glance over the careers of himself and his peers. Kenneth Rexroth found that it was the early work of Stevens which "hit my generation with an unforgettable impact. *The Waste Land* may have made more noise, but when it was over, it left only a pose. *Harmonium* left wisdom" ("Art of Compromise," 269). Though, like so many others, Rexroth was less enthusiastic about Stevens's later work, he still felt comfortable ranking him with his greatest hero, Williams, as "poets of world importance" ("The Influence of French Poetry on American," 159).

In other instances these sorts of comparisons were not explicitly aimed at diminishing Eliot's importance as such, but nonetheless they worked against the exclusivity of his influence by placing Stevens in positions of equivalence with it. For example, in her philological study of the grammatical, syntactic, and linguistic elements of poetry of the 1940s, Josephine Miles (yet another noted poet from the interwar generation) featured Stevens as a main focus of her results. In her examination of the proportions of parts in speech in contemporary poetry, Miles discovered that Stevens's employment of adjectives, nouns, and verbs (9 to 18 to 9 per 10 lines) hit a "central balance," exactly the same proportion as the average of the twenty-one poets she examined (Eliot differed from this average only slightly at 9-19-8) (391). Elsewhere, Miles valorized "the balance of prediction and qualification" that she found in Stevens's and Eliot's vocabulary: "The statements are rich with color and substance and at the same time active and mobile. The language of state of mind has both the stability of time and shape and the vivacity of emotional consideration" (393).

As opposed to the "extremes" of Cummings and the Sitwells, she called this balanced pattern of usage "the normal selection of material, as Stevens or Eliot represents it" (393). For some time Eliot had indeed functioned as a sort of poetic norm; to assign Stevens such a role was a new development. Miles's revision of the conventional view of Stevens's status was clearly a conscious act, as she went on to acknowledge: "That the poems of Wallace Stevens should provide exemplification of the characteristic poetic interest may surprise readers who treat him affectionately as a rarity. Yet we have seen that the proportioning of his recent work is that of the decade's poetry as a whole, and that even the individual terms of his choice are the terms of his time" (393–403).

Miles then demonstrated this assertion by reading "God Is Good: It Is a Beautiful Night" and "To So-and-So Reclining on Her Couch" as exemplary texts in which the reader may find "much of the sound and sense of modern poetry" (405). This identification of Stevens's work with the central concerns and formal elements of "his time," as *The Waste Land* and Eliot's criticism had long been seen to exemplify the concerns of their time, was an important step towards seeing Stevens as well as—or even instead of—Eliot as central to the poetry of the postwar period.

Critics of the mid-1950s often based their judgments that Stevens's importance was equal or near to Eliot's upon two ways of articulating the distinction of Stevens's work: as a totally coherent unity and as a celebration of life's possibilities. Both of these tropes not only acknowledged Stevens as a poet of the first rank but also established him as a viable instrument for contesting the poetic tradition and the ideology of high modernism which Eliot represented. The perception of formal, intellectual, and emotional coherence was opposed to the poetics of fragmentation upon which Eliot's early poetry had been based and for which critical enthusiasm had waned. Even more, the notion that life on this physical earth was cause for celebration flew in the face of the wasteland models of modern culture which both Eliot's poetry and social criticism, and indeed much New Criticism as well, had purveyed.

Stevens's unfulfilled wishes to entitle his collected works *The Whole of Harmonium*, a mirror of his desire in 1923 to call his first book *The Grand Poem: Preliminary Minutiae*, expressed his sense of the unity and concentration of his poetry which readers came to share after the assembly of nearly all of it in *Collected Poems* and *Opus Posthumous* (*L,* 237, 831, 834). Many readers newly recognized a quality of total coherence to Stevens's poetry and career which linked everything he did, every single piece of work, in a web of self-reinforcing logic and meaning. This assumption of coherence to Stevens's work was a major critical revision; indeed, one of the arguments against Stevens's majority had long been his inability to synthesize meaningfully the various pleasurable but still fragmented observations within his poems.[9]

O'Connor had prefigured this turn in his 1950 book by remarking on the poet's "singleness of purpose and subject matter"; the "certain amount of repetitiousness" that had resulted was "small enough payment for the depth, firmness and complexity" it had enabled (*The Shaping Spirit*, viii–ix). In his review of *Collected Poems*, Meyer emphasized Stevens's assertion, expressed many years before in a "now-famous" letter to Williams, of "the extreme necessity" of "a fixed point of view"—"realistic, imagistic, or what you will"—from which to "stick to" one's attempt to observe and understand one's world.[10] Commentators took up various ramifications of this portrayal of Stevens as a tenacious and largely successful seeker after a single goal. Meyer himself concluded that "it is one of his singular triumphs that he has been able consistently from the very first to produce 'infinite incantations' on very nearly a single theme" ("Actuary Among the Spondees," 26).

Through such a concentrated effort Stevens had "added to his, and our, ways of knowledge . . . by developing in himself . . . the kind of virtuoso skill that the musician develops through years of playing variations" (26). Morse echoed both Meyer and Stevens's letter, arguing, "What gives his best work its astonishing power and vitality is the way in which a fixed point of view, maturing naturally, eventually takes in more than a constantly shifting point of view could get at" (Morse, review of *Collected Poems*, 4).

This revision resulted in the view that in its depth of concentration Stevens's oeuvre attained an almost metaphysical coherence that extended into every aspect of his writing and thought. In his introduction to *Opus Posthumous*, Morse characterized Stevens (with the poet's own words) as " 'an extremist in an exercise,' " able to maintain a consistency of focus that "creeps into even the briefest of the prose pieces, including the purely occasional bits" he delivered as acceptance speeches for awards (xiv, xvi). This emphasis was evidently influential among reviewers such as Barbara Gibbs, who quoted from Morse's introduction and who herself found, "There is nothing in this book that is not related formally and thematically to everything else in it" (54), a remarkable quality for a compilation of odd pieces written over a lifetime.

William Carlos Williams's review of *Opus Posthumous* was entitled "Poet of a

Steadfast Pattern," and it noted that Stevens's "genius as a poet" came from the fact that he had successfully "followed with amazing fidelity this steadfast pattern" he had "fixed in his mind" (6). Such coherence could be found not only in Stevens's verses but in everything he wrote; "In one sense Stevens wrote nothing but poems—the prose pieces are structured like poems and written like poems, line by line with the utmost immediacy, image set against image . . . huge clarities rather than reasoned arguments" (Gibbs, 54). Concentration, consistency of focus, practice, patience, mastery, "single-minded intensity" (Pearce, 405)—these were the virtues critics of the late 1950s most strongly emphasized in Stevens. For these readers, to argue that everything about Stevens could be seen "to add something to the 'construction' " (Gibbs, 55) was not to reduce his work to the expression of one idea but to express their sense that he was a poet with a well-defined goal who had succeeded all the more fully for remaining undiverted by side issues. As Daniel Fuchs put it in 1963, even the changes in Stevens's work were "different ways of exploring the same themes, themes which are sufficiently complex to justify a lifetime's meditation" (vii).

These qualities of coherence and commitment exerted authority even on those readers who found the particular character of Stevens's focus limiting and reductive. In *Opus Posthumous*, Anthony Hecht perceived the "pathos" in Stevens's awareness of "those qualities of experience [which were] beyond or apart from his literary sensibilities" in having placed such a "steadfast confidence in and reliance upon the constructs of the mind" (608). Similarly, the arch-Romantic Karl Shapiro responded with "sorrow" to the rejected and neglected pieces that made up *Opus Posthumous*, finding a similar pathos in picturing Stevens "moving back and forth through the cosmic dreariness of Hartford, . . . between the smokeless factory of the insurance company and the poet's writing table" (246). Yet if there was pathos and limitation for these readers, they had to admit that Stevens's "relentless" concentration on a single objective had lifted him out of the bloodless realm of the aesthetic into a state of passionate intensity which could not but be admired (Carruth, "Without the Inventions of Sorrow," 289). For Hecht, if there was an obsessive concern with a single objective in Stevens, there was also a "dedication so steady and determined and patient" as to constitute "a sort of heroism" (607). This "heroic loneliness" (608) was echoed by Shapiro's conclusion that, although Stevens was caught in the trap of rationalism, "suffer[ing] from the congenital and evil dualism . . . [that] separates Art and Life, Reality and Imagination," his "dogged handling of the Problem" would itself mean we would "always read him" (247). Williams typified this response in summing Stevens up as "a sad but triumphant figure, showing in the end above his frustrations a modern poet, whose final note is a cock cry" ("Poet of a Steadfast Pattern," 6).

The eventual goal of this intensely maintained activity of acute observation of the world was often portrayed as the construction—or reconstruction—of a coherent version of that world: "These words . . . like almost everything else he has written, assert . . . that taking the world apart is for Wallace Stevens only preliminary to seeing the world whole" (Morse, review of *Collected Poems*, 3). According to Williams, Stevens had laid out his constructivist objective in an early poem entitled "Architecture," which cemented its resolution to "design a chastel de chasteté" by aspiring to "Pass the whole of life hearing the clink of the / Chisels of the stone-cutters cutting the stones" ("Poet of a Steadfast Pattern," 6). For Howe as well, a figure of spatial construction was primary in describing "the theme of discovery, the desire to transform and renew" which had "given shape to all of Stevens's work" (19). In 1958 Martz noted that this portrayal of the poet as an advocate for "the power of *thinking,* for the constructive power of deliberate choice," represented a significant alteration of "the sort of values that were being attributed to Stevens fifteen or twenty years ago"—a poetics of sensibility, hedonism, and fragment ("Wallace Stevens," 214).

The impulse to view Stevens's work as a model of the constructing and ordering imagination took a variety of directions. One of the most important was the use of it to argue a view of American poetry and society against the prevailing high-modernist aesthetic that poetry was little more than a shoring up of fragments against the ruins of a degenerate civilization whose decline could be made poignant only through nostalgic evocations of a better past. Stevens's *Collected Poems* made it possible to contest that view with another well-developed, coherent, consistent version of modernism. Numerous commentators on the collected volumes emphasized that in the poetics of Stevens, life in twentieth-century America was depicted as cause not only for lament but for appreciation and even celebration through "attentive thinking about concrete things with the aim of developing an affectionate understanding of how good it is to be alive" (Martz, "Wallace Stevens," 227). To find a modernist poet engaged not in rehearsing what had gone wrong but in discovering what was still possible, while also appearing to see the state of things as they were without utopian illusion, was an extremely appealing prospect for such critics.

One of the strategies used to give a canonical significance to this celebratory dimension in Stevens was to link his work to a comic tradition that had generally been neglected by the Eliotic and New Critical versions of modernism. Morse asserted that one of Stevens's distinctions among twentieth-century poets was to place comedy in a primary position within a serious aesthetic framework: "The Comedian as the Letter C" was "the only major poem . . . of our age which is deeply rooted in the tradition of intellectual comedy" (review of *Collected Poems*, 3). Similarly, Robert Pack entitled the first chapter of his 1958 book "The Comic Spirit" and argued that Stevens's vision was primarily comic in being concerned with "finding the amusement and delight in daily life, of finding the extraordinary hidden within the ordinary," a process that might bring to readers a fundamental reorientation of human priority in enabling them to "measure wealth by all the landscapes to be seen, and measure human dignity by the pleasure music may bring to the ear" (3, 4). In 1963 this view of Stevens was further developed in a critical study called *The Comic Spirit of Wallace Stevens*, in which Daniel Fuchs argued that Stevens's comic sense was "central" not only to the poet but "essential" and "typically modern," again portraying Stevens as an exemplar of modernity (viii).

For these critics, there was more in a poetics of comedy and celebration than simply a way of laughing off the evils of the world. The celebratory impulse in Stevens could be seen as a secular sacrament of the value of life itself. In an evaluative context long dominated by the dour tragedy of Eliot's view of the modern world, an aesthetic of celebration and delight might itself form an ethic of freedom and possibility. Jarrell asserted that Stevens's finest work, while often expressing the sorrows of "what it is to be human," constituted "a kind of celebration of our being" ("The Collected Poems of Wallace Stevens," 182). Stevens had "learned to write at will, for pleasure," which had been "impossible for many living poets—Eliot, for instance" (186). For Schwartz, even more broadly, Stevens offered convincing reasons to continue the difficult road of human aspiration itself: "Here is a modern poet who has celebrated the fact that it is good to be alive and that the goodness is magnified by that powerful way of being alive which is the writing of poems. For example, one of his poems begins 'What more is there to love than I have loved?' How many human beings, how many poets are capable of this sovereign affirmation?" ("In the Orchards," 16-17).

Further developing this view of the poet as affirmer, Meyer used the recurrent image of the candle—a secular source of light in Stevens, but one that evoked, and replaced, a religious one—to describe the poet's aims and his ultimate success ("Actuary Among the Spondees," 26-27). In "Valley Candle," early on in the poet's career, the candle had "burned alone in an immense valley," a tiny light persisting against the "beams of the huge night"; that the candle and its creator had survived and flourished was illustrated for Meyer by Stevens's late and precise comment on his own achievement in "A Quiet Normal Life" that "There was no fury in transcendent forms. / But his actual candle blazed with artifice." Meyer concluded with his own use of the image to summarize Stevens's living legacy of affirmation and celebration by noting, "The candle, you see, burns brighter than ever," a coherent, reliable source of illumination.

Commentators also emphasized that Stevens's affirmations of life—rather than only criticisms of it—had an ethical dimension in being eminently communicable and adaptable as sanctions for readers' existences. For Carruth, Stevens's celebratory poetry of "opulence" and "plenty," manifested through the poet's "delight in language," was "infectious," its generation of "pleasure" "endless" and "transmissable because we too, in reading his poems, share that mastery" ("Without the Inventions of Sorrow," 289). Similarly, Babette Deutsch emphasized Stevens's affirmations of the potential goodness of the things of everyday life ("particulars peculiar to a certain occasion in Florida, in Hartford"); "Speaking of these, delighting in their suggestiveness, communicating his own quiet exhilaration," Stevens allowed the reader to "enjoy the liberating experience of a traveler" ("Poet's Harvest," 3). Irving Howe described Stevens's final poems in *Opus Posthumous* as "the last quiet efforts to realize life through connecting with whatever is not human" (19). Finally setting to rest the charges of frivolity against Stevens, this potential for both "liberation" and "connection" in his celebratory poetics drew out of the personal and experiential aspects of his poetry broader theoretical and social significance.

Another indication that Stevens's aesthetic of comedy and affirmation was coming to be sensed as an ethics and a politics came in readers' emphasis on Stevens's empathy for the everyday and the alien alike—a combination that high-modernist models of the contemporary world distinctly lacked. Gibbs felt that from Stevens in old age came a "sense of power together with an extreme humility and gentleness" (57). Stevens was thus not only a stylistic model of how to employ language effectively in poetry but a kind of sage, commanding great power but demonstrating how it could be used for gentle and humble purposes. For Carruth, Stevens's "delight in language" was not merely a pleasurable by-product of technical expertise but itself formed the "larger content" of the work, "concomitant to his entire vision, his argument," which was of a magnitude to occupy "scholars and critics for many, many years." Eventually the attention of these scholars would move views of Stevens even further in an ethical direction by showing "more and more clearly how *humane* is the desire which has given us, in these poems, a delight that is interpretative of our world" ("Without the Inventions of Sorrow," 289). These perceptions of the poet's unique value to contemporary readers were summed up by Geoffrey Moore who, in a 1958 lecture, admired Stevens as "a hero of our time" because "seriously, consistently, and with great courage he tackled what he saw to be the central problem of the age"; if Stevens had been "relatively ignored" while Eliot had been "assiduously followed," Moore concluded, it was largely because "From the choppy water of the 'Hippopotamus' Eliot turned into the harbor of the *Four Quartets*. It was safe there. Outside [where Stevens remained] all is unknown. But outside, perhaps, is where things are going on" (269–70).

Stevens's willingness to voyage outside the safe harbor, to discover where things were going on, gave him a quality of courage not found in Eliot. As Schwartz put it, "Stevens's career," mediated and compromised as it was by the necessity of his business activities, nevertheless offered "a parable of what is possible" for Americans in American culture ("In the Orchards," 16).

To be able through the work of a modernist poet to "interpret" "our world" with a measure of delight and humanely to offer that delight to readers—hardly possible since the heady early days of modernism—was indeed a liberating experience for readers, critics, and scholars of the middle and late 1950s. Stevens's poetic methods were thus linked to a pluralistic ethic of open-mindedness, geniality, and tolerance towards all potential experiences: "Anything can be looked at, felt about, meditated upon, so Stevens *can* write about anything" (Jarrell, "The Collected Poems of Wallace Stevens," 186). The specific subject of the writing was less important than the creative process itself. Indeed, as it would soon be for poststructuralist theorists who saw Stevens as the central poet of modernism, the action of "interpretation" was viewed as a crucial element of Stevens's reconstruction and affirmation of the world. Schwartz argued this point most fully:

> Interpretation is the key—and the glory—of Stevens's poetry; the power and richness of interpretation is made infinite by the poetic imagination. Uniting interpretation with imagination, Stevens arrives at a system of perspectives which makes or can make anything and everything poetic; everything which exists can be a rich instance of the poetic, once it is seen from the right bias, angle, or attitude of interpretation. If Molière's bourgeois gentleman had lived to read Stevens's poems, he might have been delighted to discover at last that he had been speaking poetry, not prose, all his life without knowing it. ["In the Orchards," 18]

The democratic implications of the act of consciousness that Schwartz called interpretation—constructing a provisional description of one's phenomenal experience of the world which could be shared with, rather than imposed upon, others—were far from the totalizing and elitist projects of high modernism, such as Pound's attempt to write a poem containing history, or the excruciating lengths to which poets like Eliot and Pound went to differentiate not only their own poetry, but Poetry itself, from the base language of bourgeois gentlemen.

In 1958 Howe most fully developed this line of thinking about Stevens's ethic of affirmation and celebration, again using the poet as an instrument of explicit resistance against the ideological formation of Eliotic high modernism. Howe rejected the narrow emphases of most previous portrayals of Stevens—"gaudy mystifier," "aficionado of strange hats," "enemy of the days' routine," and "even the gamesman of epistemology" (16)—to describe him as a searcher after the most basic and central issues about life in modern America. Since Stevens's "main concern is with discovering, and through his poetry, *enacting the possibilities for self-renewal in an impersonal and recalcitrant age*" (18; emphasis in text), he offered a healthy corrective to the tendency of much modern literature to wallow in the loss of former anchors of belief and certainty. At the same time, Stevens maintained credibility through his always present cognizance of the recalcitrance of the age; at "the base of Stevens's work" "lies a pressing awareness of human disorder in our time—but an awareness radically different from that of most writers" (16). In explicit contrast "to Eliot and the later Auden, it becomes clear that Stevens is relatively free from religious and ideological nostalgia" (17); instead of futile nostalgic yearning "there is instead a recognition . . . of where we happen to be" (17). "He knows and feels" the twentieth-century "crisis of belief" and disorder but had not been blocked by it and had even "begun to move beyond it" (17). Given such premises, Stevens was able to integrate goal and process, the dualism of "conception" and "creation," which *The Hollow Men* depicted as being hopelessly sundered in modern existence: "Each nuance of perspective noted in a Stevens poem matters not merely in its own right, but as a comic prod to animation, a nudge to the man whose eye is almost dead" (18). Readers' perceptions of Stevens's ability to come to grips with "where we happen to be," coupled with his focus on the possibilities and methods of self-renewal, produced the belief that his work made a viable argument that there was indeed a "beyond" to be sought not merely in the next world, as Eliot asserted, but in this world. To a literary world sated on the transcendent anti-utopianism of Eliotic high modernism, Stevens's combination of utopian and quotidian emphases offered a great deal.

Critical appropriations of the reputation and character of Stevens's poetry in the late 1950s made valuable contributions to the erosion of the high-modernist hegemony in American poetry. At the same time, there were also potentially disturbing elements in some of these uses of Stevens's work. Stevens's work and position were sometimes employed, for example, as strategies for associating poetry with an agonistic, unabashedly elitist view of literature. The belatedness of Stevens's recognition was made to seem evidence of a universal truth about the relationship of contemporary poetry to American society: that one measure of a poet's value was the extent of his or her neglect by contemporary audiences. Ciardi began his review of *Collected Poems* with such an assertion: "No poet of real talent will find an audience ready for him in our time. To the extent that he has achieved his own way of seeing and of saying he will be entering areas for which few but the most devoted readers will be ready" ("Wallace Stevens's Absolute Music," 346).

That such a process has at times been noted is a plausible historical observation; to claim that it must happen is an ideologically regressive distortion. One of the founding mottoes of modernism, *Poetry*'s admonitory but hopeful epigraph from Whitman, "To have great poets there must be great audiences too," was here inverted into a very un-Whitmanesque cynicism that assumed the taste of the contemporary audience to be worthless, turning the agony of neglect into exaltation by constructing an evaluative hierarchy around it.

The logical extension of this antibourgeois antagonism—that poets who do find audiences ready for them cannot be writers of real talent—was embraced by other commentators on Stevens during the period. Joseph Bennett's admiring review of *The Auroras of Autumn* in 1951, for example, clearly illustrated the elitist tendencies of postwar formalist criticism. While Bennett's discussion of Stevens was devoted to a close focus on the title poem's prosodic structures and its affective significance, it was prefaced by his disparaging "review" of Sandburg's *Complete Poems*, in which he sarcastically termed that book "a handy, and certainly an authoritative compendium of the dominant institutionalized attitudes toward the art of poetry in America" (133). In contrast, Bennett argued, Stevens could "show us what the American poet *is*, what a lifetime of patient devotion to the highest standards can accomplish" (134). Both in this sentence and in the title of his piece ("Five Books, Four Poets"), Bennett denied that Sandburg was a poet at all (something that, notably, Stevens himself was unwilling to do).[11] That "the dominant institutionalized attitudes towards the art of poetry" should be portrayed as having nothing to do with real poetry suggests the avant-garde antagonism that was motivating some youngish poets and critics in the 1950s. The strongly antipopulist poetry criticism of *Hudson Review* cofounders, Joseph Bennett and Frederick Morgan, is a useful illustration that an avant-garde antagonism was prominent not only in fugitive little magazines but in relatively institutionalized arenas of literary discourse as well—making it all the more paradoxical as a cultural position. Such valorizations of Stevens's obscurity (in two senses), translated into such notions as "patient devotion to the highest standards," were by the mid-1950s central strategies in enshrining this elitist critical orientation within mainstream literary culture.

The result of employing Stevens's reputation in this way was often to portray him, at least at the level of thumbnail literary history, as the exemplary poet of American elitist modernism, through such ham-fisted distortions of his career and thought as this:

> Stevens, caught in the depression, was aware of the hovels of the poor, the inordinate demands of workers, the picket lines around the auto works, the swarming of Polacks in Jersey City, and, above all, the menace of commu-

nism, bad business for businessmen. Regarding those aspects of a "leaden time" without sympathy or hope, he devoted "Owl's Clover" (an unfortunate, long thing, wisely excluded from *The Collected Poems*) to his fears for order and art.... [T]he mass of men constitute "the pressure of reality" that poets must resist or evade. Without social, moral, or political obligation, the true poet refuses to confuse the values of life and art. [*Wallace Stevens*, 8]

These remarks come from William York Tindall's 1961 University of Minnesota pamphlet on Stevens, undoubtedly one of the most widely read introductory texts on the poet for a number of years. In this passage Tindall managed to warp the "pressure of reality," a phrase that had expressed the poet's hope that the extremity of the times would call up new resources of strength in poets, into an explicitly misanthropic elitism. He also achieved a culmination of sorts in the campaign to choke off the social potential of poetry by severing utterly "the values of art" from "the values of life." In jauntily appearing to approve of the sentiments they imputed to Stevens, such remarks represented the postwar ideology of two worlds at its most politically reprehensible. Like it or not, some form of this critical elitism informed the version of Stevens first taught to most postwar readers.

While the history of Stevens's reputation was sometimes employed in the service of elitist ideologies of art, a broader and more disturbing use of it came in yoking Stevens's explorations of the creative imagination to themes of the self's possession and mastery of the nonself. One manifestation of this critical belligerence was in the evident masculinism of many of these descriptions of the poet's imaginative "heroism." The emphasis upon "Architecture"—a poem almost forgotten before *Opus Posthumous* but after 1957 taken more than once as emblematic of Stevens's whole project—and its construction (with phallic chisels) of a "chastel de chasteté" revealed once again the prevalence of the male-critical fantasy of poetry as a sort of grail-quest (transformed in Pearce's account below into a dangerous mission behind enemy lines). This was not the chastity of the Victorian woman, but the virile purity of the knight in imaginative armor who, in order to achieve transcendence, had to remain free of the social entanglements represented by the female of the species. The tendency to this sort of intellectual phallogocentrism, remarkably widespread in much American criticism between 1945 and 1965, functioned as a devious psychological compensation for criticism's cession of an activism in the world in favor of a heroism of the word.

During the cold-war years some critics did come to see that there were broad sociopolitical issues at stake in various competing versions of modernism, and they adopted Stevens as a potential ideological counterforce to Eliot's old-world traditionalism. As Sculley Bradley noted in 1951, Stevens's "naturalistic-relativist" worldview formed the crux of "the differences between Stevens and Eliot, for the latter ascetically rejects society as hopeless save in hands appointed and patrician, while Stevens is seen to be the hedonistic and robust believer in life . . . willing to entrust the history of man to the continuous conflict between intelligent individualism and the law of necessity" (255).

Although the uses of the ideological ramifications of Stevens's poetry were probably more democratic than Eliot's could ever be, these formulations sometimes used the recreative potentials of poetry to shape an imaginative imperialism of startlingly nationalistic and aggressive proportions. Bradley's view that the relation between the individual and the collective system ("the law," in his dichotomy) was one of "continuous conflict" (rather than one of "interaction," "interdependence," or "alliance") was one sign of the aggressiveness and paranoia of much of this critical thinking. The notion of an imaginative manifest destiny—of poetic subject as master of the chaotic "other" world—was often present in the use of the ubiquitous jar to describe the ordering power of the human consciousness in terms that emphasized the imaginative domination of the environment rather than the poet's own sense of the more balanced interaction of the two elements: "the jar is certainly a symbol of a fixed point of view from which 'Ideas of Order' . . . radiate, to assemble disorderly 'Parts of a World' . . . into a new and eminently more satisfactory pattern than 'the world in flux' " (Meyer, "Actuary Among the Spondees," 27).

Likewise, Louis Simpson argued that "Anecdote of the Jar" "stated the poet's fierce belief in the supremacy of the created, artificial world over the natural" (240), ignoring the complicated debate over the significance of the jar which had been going on for years, instead blithely opting to portray Stevens as an imaginative land-developer with little interest in environmental preservation.

Even Howe's sophisticated and amiable valorization of Stevens partook of the characteristic postwar desire to see the literary realm transcend the inevitably tainting realm of the ideological. More than any other modernist poet, according to Howe, Stevens had made substantial "progress" towards "learning to write as if in his poetic person he were a forerunner of post-crisis, post-ideological man" (17). Thus the affirming freedom from the paralyzing high-modernist nostalgia for lost belief which Stevens had achieved could be seen as a rejection of any implication of culture and politics. For Howe, the moral and social value of Stevens's work was most convincing exactly because it was not put into the overtly religious, historical, or political terms that to postwar critics (especially for a New York intellectual) would have verged dangerously on demagoguery: "Stevens is too much of a realist, too aware . . . of the sheer inertia of human existence, to suppose that the crisis of belief can be quickly overcome either by private decision or by public commitment" (18). Using experience and observation rather than doctrine or dogma, Stevens qualified as the only acceptable sort of literary moralist, "a moralist of seeing" (19).

In the same year, expressing a view of the cold-war world far less sanguine than Howe's, Robert Pack also saw Stevens's portrayal of the imagination as the strongest—but still inadequate—lifeline of hope for a potentially better world. Stevens was especially valuable in having "the same love for mankind, the delight in energy and in life" that Whitman had had (xv). Given Pack's conviction, "There can be no doubt but that we are living in the apocalyptic hour" (xv), Stevens's "cosmic optimism" was necessarily muted, "less exuberant, less boyish, less adventurous" (xv). Asking "what wisdom is most precious?" in such times, Pack concluded, in another rejection of Eliot, that it was not "the prophetic voice reminding us of what we cannot bear to know" (xvi). Instead, the implications of the Stevensian assertion that "Death is the mother of beauty"—what would we lose with the death of our world?—formed Pack's concluding affirmation of Stevens's value: "This paradise, rich with the transformation the imagination makes of ordinary experience, is what Wallace Stevens envisions and evolves, it is the treasure most accessible to our modest lives, and for many it would define the sum of human loss were it to be relinquished" (xvi).

In the face of our "incredulity" and "helplessness" at the apparent "imminence of self-destruction," to be able to summon up the sense of potential loss, hardly possible if one already viewed the world as a wasteland, thus became the most significant political affirmation possible. For readers already overwhelmed by cold-war helplessness, however, Pack's argument was an enervating diminution of poetry's capacity to move from the level of personal and experiential alienation to a broader sociopolitical level of discourse that might more fully articulate the precarious position in which the human race had put itself.

One response to these sorts of cold-war dangers and fears, perhaps more vigorous but less humane, was to counterattack by embracing the rejection of political or worldly concerns as a prerequisite to aesthetic superiority. In the decade after the poet's death his work would be used as a sort of invisible guiding deity to two influential academic accounts of the course and character of American literature which embodied that rejection. Both Marius Bewley's *The Eccentric Design* (1959) and Richard Poirier's *A World Elsewhere* (1966) used Stevens most explicitly in their epigraphs (and in Bewley's case, in the title drawn from those lines). These books' uses of Stevens were especially notable for demonstrating the possibility of reorienting canons of pre-twentieth-century American literature around readings of American modernism, of which Stevens was a central element. Bewley's analysis of "Form in the Classic American Novel" (the book's subtitle) was a subject that would seem to have little enough to do with a modernist poet such as Stevens (14). Bewley saw earlier American writers as struggling unhappily against the same symbolist closed circuit that Stevens was destined to articulate and enact most convincingly and affirmatively. Confronted with a society "in which the abstract idea and the concrete fact could find little common ground for creative interaction" (18), "there was really only one subject available" to the nineteenth-century American novelist—"his own unhappy plight," the "essence" of which was "his isolation" (15).

In themselves these ideas were not necessarily linked specifically to Stevens and to the critical role he had often played since the 1940s; but given the poet's prominence in entitling and opening the book, his work must be seen as integral to Bewley's thinking. Bewley drew his first epigraph from "Connoisseur of Chaos," which referred to "a law of essential opposites, / Of essential unity," which, once imagined, would be for the imaginer "As pleasant as the brushstrokes of a bough, / An upper, particular bough, in, say, Marchand." Here Bewley presented one side of Stevens—the aesthetic connoisseur—as the poet's essence, while limiting the scope of his own argument to the aesthetic rather than the more vigorously social. The precious hyper-aesthetic quality of these lines was by no means arbitrary, expressing Bewley's sense of these novelists' desire, as the old saw has it, to "recreate their own worlds" aesthetically rather than socially. The second epigraph, from "Like Decorations in a Nigger Cemetery," further extended this disdain for actual social landscape and made it the basis of writers' creative individuality:

> It was when the trees were leafless first in November
> And their blackness became apparent, that one first
> Knew the eccentric to be the base of design.

Here Bewley's excerpt implied that the form of any such recreation must be insistently original, even "eccentric," standing in an oppositional relationship to the bleak and distasteful social landscape the novelists (and the critic?) found America to be. It was the combination of a self-defining oppositionalism with an escapist aestheticism which captured the ideological core of Bewley's rejection of the constrictions of society. The distinction of Bewley's American novelists was their ability through the eccentricity of their own creative identities to ascend from the trash-littered social landscape of the cemetery into the "upper bough" of the imagination as the only place to achieve the desired "unity of opposites." Stevens was evidently seen as the ideal author for articulating such a process.

The use of Stevens to comment on the dream of escaping to a separate, more orderly, and more satisfying realm of the imagination, of language, of style, was even more central to Poirier's *A World Elsewhere: The Place of Style in American Literature*. Poirier's evocation of Stevens came in an epigraph to his preface, in which he seized upon the constructivist emphasis of many Stevens commentators of the previous decade. Drawn from "Architecture," the epigraph posed two questions: "What manner of building shall we build?" and further, "In this house, what manner of utterance shall there be?" Poirier immediately reduced these open-ended lines to a single formalist interpretation, making clear that the sort of "building" that interested him in "Emerson and his successors, including Stevens," was the sort that "refers less to structures in the world . . . than to structures of the mind and to analogous structures of language" (vii). The second epigraph, arranged so as to answer the queries of Stevens's lines, was Thoreau's characterization of "the best works of art" as "the expression of man's struggle to free himself" from the "family mansion" and "family tomb" he had built for himself in America. In *The Unusable Past*, Russell Reising has amply demonstrated Poirier's tendency to fetishize "style" as a full-scale escape route away from history, tradition, and politics to a world elsewhere (187–99). Here it is enough to note that Poirier's use of Stevens as an exemplary expression of this defining American desire to reject the entangling and corrosive touch of concrete social relationships was a particular one-sided interpretation of both these specific lines of Stevens's poetry and his overall meaning to American literature.

The potent political consequences of the adoption of Stevens as a social exemplar which these two texts only hinted at were shaped by Roy Harvey Pearce into the quintessential cold-war version of American literary history. In what was probably the most influential account of American verse published between1950 and 1970, *The Continuity of American Poetry* (1961), Pearce used Stevens as an explicit and exemplary "Adamic" counterforce against Eliot's "mythic" traditionalism. More systematically but not unlike several of the reviewers of Stevens's collections, Pearce portrayed Stevens as an appealing yeasayer against Eliot's morose nay-saying. As the source of the "profoundest yes" of modernist American poets, Stevens functioned for Pearce as a culminating illustration of "the continuity of the most deeply-rooted tradition of American poetry," its "Adamic phase" (376). For Pearce, as for numerous other critics, the core of Stevens's poetic transformation lay in intense observation of and engagement with the world, as opposed to Eliot's renunciation of it: "for Stevens the world is alive because man is. This is to be observed; if the observation is accurate enough, the observer will discover that he has participated in what he has observed—that he has in fact observed, and so in a way made, himself. Against this: ardour and selflessness and self-surrender, and only for the saint" (428).

Pearce's use of Stevens, though effective in shaping an influential view of American poetry not dominated by the ideological and canonical pathologies of Eliot and the New Criticism, was itself thoroughly and damagingly shaped by cold-war ideology. It began by reproducing the paranoid framework of conflict which marked so much American thought in the 1950s and ended by promulgating a cure that was quite possibly more dangerous than the malady. Pearce used the distinction between Stevens and Eliot to construct a version of the American character and American poetry as consisting of a series of irreconcilable binary oppositions: "the egocentric as against the theocentric, man without history as against history without man, the antinomian as against the orthodox, personality as against culture" (423). While the American character was constituted by both sides of these oppositions, the Adamic Stevens and the mythic Eliot, Pearce made clear, "There is, between these two utterly real worlds to which the poets would commit us, no compromise" (428).

Despite the impasse this formulation logically implied, Pearce clearly preferred the values represented by Stevens, placing the poet at the very top of his canonical arsenal in the book's long final chapter, which bore the high-stakes title "Wallace Stevens and the Ultimate Poem." With Stevens the Adamic phase of American poetry, in Pearce's characteristically extreme terminology, "reaches the point of no return" (376). Stevens had been able to realize this Adamic element only through his drastic and uncompromising commitment to the "discovery, made as the result of a desperate need to save himself alive, that the poet's sole ground of being is itself" (377). This radical "egocentrism" was at the heart of yet another binary model of the world, "characterized above all by an extreme version . . . of that radical opposition which has obsessed so many American poets . . . between the poetic and anti-poetic—between the self and a reality which is not part of that self" (381). Pearce's development of this familiar enough relationship of self and world came to be an aggressively nationalistic poetics. Recasting Stevens's anti-authoritarian abstraction of the "glass man" from "Asides on the Oboe," Pearce constructed a sort of ugly glass American who reflected the participation of the literary culture in a cold-war ideology of imperialist democracy:

> How may we know what we believe? How may we know it even as we believe it? How may that impossible man be made possible? asking such questions in his later work, Stevens brought to its point of culmination, its point of no return, a major tradition of American poetry. For asking such questions, Stevens, like Emerson and Whitman before him, dared search for the ground on which the modern American self might base its sense of its own identity and so carry out its historical mission—to project itself into the future and into the world at large. The American was fated to be the Everyman of the modern world. [392]

Such a mission was not for the half-hearted or skeptical. Pearce's portrayal of Stevens as the apotheosis of this nationalistic critical ideology extended into his interpretation of the supreme fiction and the issue of the character of belief in Stevens. Far from offering a sufficing vision of provisional belief, Stevens's central ideas demanded an inevitable, absolute conviction that approximated uncomfortably the global ideological tensions that loomed in the years he wrote his book. In explicit contrast to the work of Eliot, Stevens's poems "are not such as to bid us only to entertain their ideas seriously; they demand of us rather than we absolutely believe or disbelieve in them" (423). Stevens's supposedly total commitment to this battle was enacted in his quest for what Pearce called the "ultimate poem," which was the only means "directly [to] confront . . . the rock in which is grounded the possibility at once of ourselves and our world, imagination and reality" (410). Successful late poems such as "The Rock" represented "one man going to the brink of the ultimate poem, and taking us with him" (410). The paradoxical but absolute value of such a process was the triumph over the fundamental oppositions of self and other through the obliteration of the very ground on which the separation existed: "This is the necessary beginning, a re-beginning of our necessary end. The poem would annihilate all that's made, so to evoke the condition, the substance, and the act of making" (410). In its apocalyptic purity and abstraction, "the ultimate poem" would seem to function much like the line of military thought that destroys a target, a city, a world, in order to save it.

This hawkish critical rhetoric was reinforced by the widespread use of quasi-military tropes of confrontation with a threatening alien force: "containment" (382), "apogee" (382), "brink" (410), "jettison" (416), "triumph" (416), "annihilate" (420), "violence" (424), "defend" (431), and "the ultimate poem," (evoking the then-common phrase "the ultimate weapon"). These prevalent figurations suggested that this poetic "mission," to be carried out by the American Everyman, had incalculably high stakes and was worth any level of effort or sacrifice: "The tragedy is that to say yes, Stevens had in the end to say no to so much—to jettison the creative for the decreative, the actual for the possible, men for man, the world for the Rock. Yet he did so to save himself and those who would read and listen to him: to save himself and them for the creative, the actual, the men, and the world to which, once they know themselves as and when they were, they might triumphantly return" (416).

In the book's final pages, Pearce sought once again to emphasize that Stevens functioned as a kind of spearhead in a broader project (or "continuity" or "mission") of American poetry as a whole: "to defend man," particularly "the idea of man as maker." The foe in this combat was a version of the quintessential high-modernist anxiety about communal activity: "all those forces of modern rationalized, technified, bureaucratized society which would have man made (or processed), not making" (431). This description was highly reminiscent of contemporary caricatures of communists' aims for maliciously depersonalizing and mechanizing the world they sought to dominate.

In an astonishing summary passage from the book's conclusion, in the midst of his effort to establish a meaningful relationship between American culture and its poetry, Pearce instead replaced the anxieties of living in a world of cold war with a chilling view of American poetry and society, as an apocalyptic conflict between two mutually exclusive worlds, which was dominated by absolutist and dualistic thinking:

> Certainly the situation of American poetry has been the sort which we now know always and everywhere to have been characteristic of American life: a situation of extreme alternatives, each seemingly ruling out the possibility of the other. The basic styles of the poetry which was meant to comprehend this situation came to be as extreme. They manifested, as only poetic styles can, the two radically opposed ways of life open to modern man in the world he had made for himself. The poet, searching among the actualities of his culture for a means to authorize his very existence as poet, could not compromise. Either the world was his, or he was the world's. [421–22]

Pearce here assembled and intensified several of the interrelated strands of Stevens criticism of the previous two decades: the alienated dualisms of reality and imagination, business and culture, politics and poetry; the (ostensibly) divided nature of American life and American poetry's relationship to it; the valorization of single-mindedness and purity; the implications of seeing belief as inflexible certitude rather than self-conscious provisionality; the issue of the domination of human consciousness over its environment; the perils of compromise with the forces of the other; and the do-or-die nature of the conflict between self and other, or individual and group. Pearce's nationalistic synthesis of these themes at least had the virtue of making plain the strongly political implications that were so often left concealed or unacknowledged in commentary on the poet and on modernist poetry. Pearce's Stevens is not, however, the poet who can help us live our lives more sanely and humanely.

Collected Poems and *Opus Posthumous* collectively functioned as a summation of a career that was increasingly seen as "co-extensive with the development of modern art," as Carruth put it ("Without the Inventions of Sorrow," 289). This sense among readers that Stevens's life's work somehow encapsulated in microcosm the broader history of modernism, and therefore offered a key to understanding it, strongly encouraged institutional steps towards his long-term academic canonization among a generation of scholars and historians who were turning their attentions towards articulating the significance of American poetry in the twentieth century. Possessing not only all of Stevens's significant work to date but the knowledge that he would be producing no more, American scholars finally began to make Stevens a major focus of their attention. Within only a decade after the poet's collected publication and his death, various disciplinary tools important for the continuing study of Stevens were generated: a preliminary bibliography in 1954 (expanded in 1963), a concordance in 1963, the compilation of the poet's fugitive publications, and the collection of his letters, books, and manuscripts in libraries. A measure of Stevens's rising academic status, and especially the increased sense of his importance as a subject of scholarship, came from a 1962 Modern Language Association conference on official scholarly editions of American writers, whose members were in general agreement that fourteen authors were worthy of "full and fine editions"—including among the modernist poets only Eliot, Frost, and Stevens (Hubbell, *Who Are The Major American Writers?* 279). This concerted collection of scholarly resources in the decade after his death both asserted Stevens's centrality to American poetry scholarship and enabled the continual replenishment of scholarly interest in his work which still thrives today.

The increased scholarly access to Stevens's work began to pay handsome dividends almost immediately, generating in the decade after his death an explosion of articles, doctoral dissertations, and critical monographs which was unmatched in the history of twentieth-century American literature scholarship. It is true that the timing of Stevens's collections and his death coincided fairly neatly with the period of greatest institutional expansion in the American academy and that the overall level of scholarly publication increased noticeably in these years, but the jump in attention to Stevens was by far the most dramatic of that of any American modernist poet.

The pattern of periodical articles listed in various reference sources is one indication of the intensifying interest in Stevens in the academy after 1950. Leary's *Articles on American Literature, 1950–1967* listed 192 articles on Stevens in the eighteen years it covered. Eliot, Pound, and Frost were the only American modernist poets to outnumber him. Edelstein's 1973 bibliography of Stevens also revealed the steady increase in the number of total items on Stevens published in periodicals between 1931 and 1970.[12]

1931–35	8	1951–55	78[b]
1936–40	24[a]	1956–60	56
1941–45	13	1961–65	87
1946–50	36	1966–70	83

a. includes 12 mostly short items from the 1940 *Harvard Advocate* issue
b. includes 22 mostly short items from the 1954 *Trinity Review* issue

Averaging fewer than four per year before 1945, the number of Stevens articles quadrupled to an average of seventeen articles per year throughout the 1960s. This rate of increase in attention to Stevens between the early 1940s and the early 1960s easily outstripped Eliot's increases during the same period.[13]

The magnitude of Stevens's sudden prominence in academic contexts in the decade after his death is borne out even more clearly by the pattern of dissertations which were completed in that decade on a group of 26 modernist American poets born between 1868 and 1900.[14] The 51 such dissertations in the 1957–61 period did not represent a substantial increase (only 9 percent) over the 1952–56 total of 47; Stevens's own increase from 2 to 5 was substantial in percentage but modest in number. In 1957–61 and 1962–66, however, it appears that there was a large jump overall, from 51 to 82 (an increase of 61 percent), but if the Stevens figures are removed from both periods, the increase shrinks to only 26 percent (from 46 to 58). The nearly fivefold leap in attention to Stevens, from 5 dissertations in the 1957–61 period to 24 in 1962–66, dwarfed that of any other modernist poet. Dissertations on Eliot went from 8 to 15 in the same interval; leaving out both poets, there was surprisingly very little increase in such topics in the early 1960s (from 38 to 43, 13 percent). Clearly, through the mid-1960s Eliot and Stevens were the only significant canonical beneficiaries of the expansion of modernism into American doctoral programs. The expansion of scholarly interest in these two poets meant no wider acceptance of modernist poets in general; if anything, these dissertations strongly bear out the argument that the postwar expansion of the academic literary field contributed to a narrowed modernist canon, at least through the 1960s.

Patterns of completed dissertations are among the most solid measures of the level of academic interest in an author over a given period; such projects suggest a level of commitment and intensity over a period of years which figures on articles cannot approach. A cluster of dissertations on an author also presupposes a certain amount of preexisting academic canonicity, since most graduate professors would not agree to direct topics dealing with authors they considered insignificant. The fairly small number of dissertations written on Stevens between 1945 and 1960, despite numerous other indications that his academic reputation was growing significantly, suggests that a previous group of scholars, many of whom were interested in Stevens, had been unable to take him as a subject for their own dissertations but later encouraged their students to do so. Altogether, between 1960 and 1966 there were 27 dissertations completed on Stevens at 21 American universities, by far the largest number on an American modernist poet during those years. In contrast, Eliot was the main subject of 15 dissertations completed during the same years; Pound 11; Aiken and Williams 5 each; Robinson, MacLeish, Jeffers, and Crane 4 each; Frost only 1; and Moore none.[15]

The doctoral interest in Stevens in these years represented an unprecedented density of scholarly study of an American modernist author. From such a rash of dissertations on a given author, it would have been easy to predict a continued level of scholarly activity over at least the next two or three decades as the individuals involved gradually begin to teach classes, serve on curriculum committees, and direct graduate students of their own. Dissertations will also generate articles and, either directly or indirectly, monographs. The 27 scholars who wrote dissertations mainly on Stevens between 1960 and 1966 would publish 34 articles on the poet through 1975; 10—Burney, Buttel, Fuchs, Lensing, Lentricchia, Nassar, Peterson, Riddel, Stern, and Sukenick—have published books on the poet.[16] With the publication in England of Frank Kermode's *Wallace Stevens* in 1960, a small avalanche of books on Stevens began. Altogether 14 volumes—7 critical studies, 3 collections of essays, 2 pamphlet-sized introductions, a concordance, and a bibliography—appeared between 1960 and 1966 alone (with 5 more to come between 1967 and 1969). Many of these early critical studies are doubtless little read today, representing the relatively pedestrian "introductory" level that the criticism of an author's work seemingly must undergo, which also had been delayed by Stevens's resistance to compiling his work. Yet collectively these books and articles were extremely significant in helping to catapult Stevens's reputation into the top reaches of American academic canons.

Within a decade, Stevens had become no longer a subject of an isolated article or monograph but an author with a substantial body of criticism and scholarly apparatus, which had certainly not exhausted all there was to say about him and had invested him with substantial academic legitimacy. One new publication that was a function of an expanding academic field during the 1960s was the American Literature Association's annual *American Literary Scholarship*; beginning in the first volume in 1963, the authors of the bibliographic essays on modernist poetry remarked on Stevens as a critical phenomenon year after year. In 1963 Oliver Evans noted, "Interest in this poet . . . is mounting steadily," and six years later A. Kingsley Weatherhead noted without surprise that "Wallace Stevens once again leads all the rest" in his essay's area. (Evans, 189; Weatherhead, 279). That the editors of this series had rather curiously chosen to put Stevens, along with Williams, in the "Poetry: 1930 to the Present" category, rather than the earlier 1900–1930 period, meant that these observations were not made in comparison to scholarship on Eliot and Pound; the fact remains, however, that Stevens was clearly seen as a phenomenon in the academy of the 1960s. Writing around 1972, Jay B. Hubbell summed up this canonical shift by noting that, while in 1955 American academics "would hardly have ranked either Fitzgerald or Stevens as a major American writer," by the end of the 1960s both were viewed as such (*Who Are the Major American Writers?* 260). For Hubbell, evidence of this turn towards Stevens was abundant; in Jackson Bryer's 1968 poll of 138 academic critics asking which twentieth-century writers should be the subjects of the new reference volume *Fifteen Modern American Authors*, Stevens, with 87 votes, ranked a comfortable fifth overall, trailing only Frost (108) among the ranks of the poets (282–83).[17]

Scholarly and critical interest in a recently deceased author is quite a familiar phenomenon and does not in itself fully explain the explosion of attention to Stevens in the decade after his death. Even in its unprecedented swiftness and density, Stevens's scholarly rise was integrally related to broader changes taking place in the academy after 1955. One of the most significant institutional trends of this period was the gradual erosion of the New Critical hegemony in Anglo-American critical practice, aided by such theoretical critiques of New Critical poetics as Murray Krieger's *The New Apologists for Poetry*, which was published in the year between Stevens's death and the publication of *Opus Posthumous*. Writing retrospectively for a paperback edition in 1962, Krieger suggested that, even at the time he finished writing the book, New Criticism was barely any longer a "living movement": "Time was running out of its vitality, and its little life was soon to be rounded with a sleep," which the intervening years had made even clearer (vii). This judgment was hardly the whole truth; certainly it could be argued that New Criticism, if asleep, has haunted many of our own dreams during the past three decades, but Krieger's assessment of the eclipse of the New Critical star during these years largely held true for the elite circles of the academy.[18]

A concomitant development was even more important for the course of literary studies in America: the initiation of a full-scale disciplinary change from "literary criticism" to "critical theory" as the site of the intellectual cutting edge within academic literary discourse. Just as a number of poets and nonacademic critics had embraced Stevens as an alternative to Eliot's position as the central poet of the modernist period, up-and-coming critical theorists such as Pearce, Northrop Frye, Frank Kermode, J. Hillis Miller, Harold Bloom, Joseph Riddel, and Frank Lentricchia all used Stevens to attack the prevalent assumptions and practices of New Criticism. Possibly the already existing close connection between modernist poetry—especially Eliot's—and the poetics and the methods of the New Criticism made it a natural step for younger critics to adopt another, apparently opposing modernist poet as a canonical focus for their aspirations to supersede New Criticism.

In the decade after Stevens's death, his centrality to various canonical configurations—American, romantic, modernist—was connected again and again to attempts to map out a new field of "systematic aesthetics" and to tap into the "revelatory powers" that such a new approach appeared to offer in the confident early days of American critical theory (Krieger, *The New Apologists*, xi). Despite the many differences among these writers' evolving positions, all of them employed Stevens's reputation as an integral part of their constructions of literary and critical value. Through their work the poet was firmly established, not merely as an individual author valued by a small or large number of readers, but as a constitutive element of the emergent theoretical principles of literature's production and function and thus of prominent conceptualizations of poetic value in America. It would hardly be an exaggeration to assert that intellectually and institutionally no single author was more important to the rise of American critical theory than Stevens. At any rate it is indisputable that he was *the* modernist poet to emerge as central to the development of this ambitious and influential discipline between 1957 and 1966. By that latter date he was on his way to becoming the most solidly canonical figure of American modernism.

How does one explain the adoption of Stevens rather than someone else as the particular modernist of choice for the post–New Critical era? There was no single quality of Stevens and his work which attracted all of these critical theorists to him: Frye admired Stevens's ability to synthesize fleeting individual perceptions into a coherent system of understanding; Kermode and Lentricchia valued Stevens's notion of "fictions" as flexible and pragmatic heuristics for existence; Bloom valorized Stevens's kinship with the English Romantic tradition; Miller and Riddel saw Stevens as a poetic exemplar of their interests in concepts of phenomenological reality and linguistic undecidability. One element common to the thought of all of these theorists (as well as Pearce and Krieger), despite their varied treatment and evaluation of the terminology and traditions of Romanticism, was a turn away from the autotelic product-text of New Criticism, towards seeing literature as a process of generating meaning, a process grounded in updated versions—humanistic, existential, mythical, agonistic, phenomenological—of the Romantic poetic subject. Unlike the New Critics, who had never been completely comfortable with Stevens's explorations of those acts of the mind, and so had remained fixated on a solid symbol like the jar (and even that damned thing wouldn't come right, as the endless debate over its meaning suggested), these younger writers all found Stevens's vivid and intricate articulations of the continuously fluctuating interactions of consciousness and environment highly congenial to their own theoretical projects.

Stevens's aptness in the turn back to the primacy of the speaking subject over the reified notion of the individual text could be found not only in these academic theorists but in the remarks of more casual reviewers as well. Writing in *Poetry*, Barbara Gibbs, for example, was "fascinated by [*Opus Posthumous*] as a demonstration of process . . . the poetical processes of one poet" and argued that the "object" of the "construction" constituted by Stevens's work was the definition of "an individual human consciousness" (52, 55). Pack took issue with the "illusion" of the conventional characterization of "impersonality" in Stevens's work, arguing that "Stevens's imagination is his most personal possession, and he presents its activity to us with vivid directness; we come to know the adroitness of his mind, touch what he touches, see what he sees" (6–7). Prefiguring Bloom's approach to Stevens, Rosemary Deen argued that the poet represented "the tradition of the great English romantic poets of the early nineteenth century, the 'other' poetic tradition from that represented by Mr. Eliot. This has long been an unpopular tradition, and it is good to have Mr. Stevens holding the most deep-dyed romantic theories and making use of them, as inspiration or material, for many of the best and greatest poems of our time" (620).

Deen made clear that her positioning of Stevens as the standard-bearer against an anti-Romantic poetic tradition meant a thoroughgoing reorientation of the source of literary meaning towards the individual poetic subject. For her the "key idea" among the "romantic theories" exemplified by Stevens was that "among the causes of a work of art—the artist, the audience, the substance of the work, the form—the most important is the artist." The "central question about art" was therefore "the problem of perception or imagination—how the artist sees things" (620). The return of the subject thus became one more method of liberating poetry from the formal authority of the autotelic New Critical text and from the high-modernist anti-Romantic authority of Eliot.

It was in the developing field of academic critical theory, however, that the return of the poetic subject had its greatest impact both on Stevens's canonical status and on the American literary culture as a whole. The first of these influential theoretical uses of Stevens came in the year of *Opus Posthumous*. More than any other book, Northrop Frye's *Anatomy of Criticism* (1957) initiated the development of the intellectual field of critical theory in North America. The most momentous element of the *Anatomy*'s argument was the advocacy of a fundamental alteration of the discipline of criticism from its position as a naively empirical handmaiden to literature, which often limited itself to a microscopic and fragmenting focus upon the individual text, towards reformulation as a systematic and synoptic "theory of criticism whose principles [would] apply to the whole of literature and account for every valid type of critical procedure" (14). Surprisingly, *Anatomy of Criticism* barely mentioned Stevens. In the same year this magnum opus appeared, however, Frye published a long article on Stevens, written near the time of the book's completion, in which Frye made the argument that Stevens was "one of our small handful of essential poets" ("Realistic Oriole," 370). Frye's sense that Stevens's work constituted a coherent unity of many elements, rather than a collection of discrete fragments, was an important source of the poet's usefulness for the disciplinary reformation to which Frye aspired.

A crucial step in Frye's effort to create a field of critical theory in the *Anatomy* was to clear the existing critical ground. Frye characterized current criticism as "a mystery-religion without a gospel" populated by "initiates who can communicate, or quarrel, only with one another" (14); the portrayal of the current state of criticism as a closed religious society was no accident, representing yet another gesture of rebellion against high-modern New Criticism. Frye sought to reject the arbitrary evaluations of texts, according to the often unfathomable whims of these individual initiates, in favor of a relatively eclectic inclusion of any work that seemed valuable to a particular critical project. Ironically, in doing so he helped to mystify the processes and bases of literary evaluation even further than before by forcing them into hiding (from which we are still trying to drag them), but at the time the liberation from critical debates based on rigidly hierarchical and obviously subjective patterns of evaluation (such as Eliot's and Winters's) was a powerfully attractive quality of Frye's argument for theory.

Such rejection of New Critical evaluative practices was, however, not aimed at restoring neglected or obscured relationships between literature and other fields of study or endeavor such as history, theology, anthropology, or politics. Frye largely accepted the New Critical desire to assert the unique identity of criticism as analogous to a branch of the sciences, which would possess its own set of self-contained assumptions, terms, and institutional structures.[19] This meant that a linchpin of Frye's argument was the absolute independence of criticism from all other disciplines; he rejected all reductive and extrinsic "determinisms," "whether Marxist, Thomist, liberal-humanist, neo-Classical, Freudian, Jungian, or existentialist," the presence of which invariably meant the "substituting of a critical attitude for criticism" (*Anatomy*, 6). The theory of criticism should instead be based upon "an examination of literature in terms of a conceptual framework from an inductive survey of the literary field" (7). Frye took this campaign against extrinsic forms of literary criticism and evaluation so far as to generalize, "There are no definite positions to be taken in chemistry or philology, and if there are any to be taken in criticism, criticism is not a field of genuine learning" (19). To assert, as Frye did, "One's 'definite position' is one's weakness, the source of one's liability to error and prejudice" (19) was to erect as a primary principle of American critical theory the rejection of literature's engagement with sociopolitical concerns and to extend even higher the walls that were supposedly preserving the unique identity of the literary realm but, more to the point, were also shutting literature off from all that was going on outside.

It was not that Frye's explicit interdiction against the "definite position" blocked a desire to establish the activity of criticism as an ethical force. The ethical force he sought for literature was the cultivation and distillation of a general attitude towards one's surroundings (including texts) from the specific cases encountered (not unlike Howe's "moralist of seeing" who sees all but does little). Frye's rejection of the New Critical emphasis on the individual case extended to this ethical dimension. The everyday and particular—empirical, so to speak—ethical act was in itself no more than a "mechanical reflex of habit" (*Anatomy*, 348). The only way to make the ethical impulse meaningful and communicable lay in the process of abstracting or theorizing: "to get any principle of freedom in it[,] we need some kind of theory of action, theory in the sense of *theoria*, a withdrawn or detached vision of the means and end of an action which does not paralyze action, but makes it purposeful by enlightening its aims" (348).

Thus any desire to link literature with ethical values wound up being yet another mandate, this one moral, for Frye's vision of a universalized theory of criticism: "the moment we go from the individual work of art to the sense of the total form of the art, the art becomes no longer an object of aesthetic contemplation but an ethical instrument, participating in the work of civilization" (349).

Frye's sense of the necessity for abstraction from immediate and particular situations had, however, another ramification that militated against the ethical force that he envisioned for the *Anatomy* and for the field of critical theory: "The goal of ethical criticism is transvaluation, the ability to look at contemporary social values with the detachment of one who is able to compare them in some degree with the infinite vision of possibilities presented by culture" (348).

This transvaluation was necessarily to be achieved through a "detachment" from "contemporary social values." If that goal meant the attainment of a quality of "historical perspective," coupled with an activist utopian desire for the "possibilities" of human culture, then criticism might have possibilities beyond its own sheltered bower. Ultimately, however, Frye suggested the critic should have little connection with the state of actual society; the effects of this transvaluation appeared to stop at the level of conferring upon its individual practitioner "a state of intellectual freedom" (348), not a recognition of involvement and contingency but an Archimedean reference point, an end in itself not far away from the New York intellectuals' sometimes repressive fetishization of "freedom."

In order to undertake the vigorous disciplinary and ethical development Frye advocated, criticism needed a constructivist emphasis, "a coordinating principle, a central hypothesis which . . . will see the phenomena it deals with as parts of a whole" (*Anatomy*, 16). The "assumption of total coherence" (16), which such an embryonic discipline would need to make, can certainly be linked to Eliot's seminal argument in "Tradition and the Individual Talent": that the existing monuments of literature "form an ideal order among themselves," constituting the living tradition of that culture (50). In terms of the actual texts of modernist poetry, the poetry of Eliot—at first expressing fragmentation and disorder, then having recourse to an extrinsic system (the church) around which he built its coherence—was far from exemplary of the potential for literary criticism to develop its own conceptual and theoretical universe. One canonical consequence of Frye's redefinition of the relationship between literature and criticism in the direction of theory, therefore, was to valorize texts that presented themselves neither as prayers necessarily and absolutely dependent upon an extrinsic religious system, nor as fragments shored against the ruins of elite culture, nor as objects isolated and impenetrable like Mauberley's medallion, but as elements of systematic thought which valorized and embodied the virtues of intrinsic coherence and thus validated Frye's argument for the need for theory. Stevens's later works, those self-conscious, mutually referential examinations of the processes and potentials of human consciousness, whose theoretical bases and practical results were seamlessly integrated, would fulfill these criteria admirably for Frye.

The first sentence of Frye's article on Stevens, "The Realistic Oriole," revealed the importance of Stevens to Frye not just as a fine poet but as a uniquely valuable precursor of the same impulses towards abstraction and theory that Frye exhibited: "Wallace Stevens was a poet for whom the theory and the practice of poetry were inseparable" (353). Stevens's holistic poetics were thus in direct "contrast to the dualistic approach of Eliot, who so often speaks of poetry as though it were an emotional and sensational soul looking for a 'correlative' skeleton of thought to be provided by a philosopher" (353). Poetry, then, was by no means purely emotional or perceptual but intellectual as well;

however, the structure of its ideas had to be intrinsic to its field of observation. Contrary to Eliot's "dualistic fallacy," Frye argued, "No poet of any status . . . has ever 'taken over' someone else's structure of thought" (353). The integrated relationship of theory and practice in Steven's work made him "of particular interest and value for the critical theorist, because he sees so clearly that the only ideas that the poet can deal with are those directly involved with, and implied by, his own writing: that, in short, 'Poetry is the subject of the poem'" (353).

Here Stevens is linked explicitly and integrally with the development of the disciplinary term "critical theory." Stevens's inductive survey of the world around him and his acute awareness of "the processes of poetic thought at work" (354), which could apprehend that world, made him a poetic version of Frye's will to theory. Not coincidentally, however, in portraying Stevens as the pure example of the theoretical poet, Frye's argument resealed the closed circuit of poetry's subject matter—that it must be itself and itself only—which had helped to disable the broader cultural resonances of Stevens's work.

Frye also adapted Stevens's own notions of "the pressure of reality," the imagination's capacity to resist such extrinsic pressures upon the consciousness, for his larger argument in the *Anatomy* that all proper approaches to criticism must arise intrinsically from within a conceptual framework derived from the study of literature itself. Echoing Stevens's terminology (but drawing a rather different conclusion from it), Frye noted that "historical periods differ greatly in the amount of pressure put on free consciousness by the compulsions of ordinary life." Frye characterized "our own day" as a time in which "the pressure has reached an almost intolerable degree that threatens to destroy freedom altogether and reduce human life to a level of totally preoccupied compulsion, like the life of an animal. One symptom of this is the popular demand that the artist should express in his work a sense of social obligation" ("Realistic Oriole," 354).

To ask that artists express a sense of social obligation was to abet the reduction of human life to the level of an animal! That a relatively moderate critic such as Frye felt it necessary in 1957 to trundle out the heaviest artillery he could command against this rather mild demand for "expressing a sense of social obligation" suggests the extent to which the whole realm of politics was still perceived as a dire threat to the survival of the "free consciousness." The reputation and characterization of Stevens once again played a major role in a defense of literature and criticism against the bogey of the political.

Throughout his essay Frye reinforced the portrayal of Stevens as the quintessential theoretical poet. Stevens's impulse towards achieving a secular version of the synoptic goals of religious adherents was illustrated by his continual use of "the symbol of the alphabet or syllable, the imaginative key to reality" ("Realistic Oriole," 356). Much as Frye's theory of criticism would postulate the "total coherence" of its field, the "theoretical postulate of Stevens's poetry" was "a world of total metaphor, where the poet's vision may be identified with anything it visualizes" (367). Such a world, "where subject and object, reality and mental organization of reality, are one," was, Frye asserted, not peculiar to Stevens but in fact constituted "the formal cause of poetry" itself (364). The utopian references to "a world of total metaphor" evoked a passage at the very end of the *Anatomy* in which Frye expressed his glowing hopes for the potential of the systematic theorizing of criticism he had outlined: "reforging the broken links between creation and knowledge, art and science, myth and concept, is what I envisage for criticism" (*Anatomy*, 354). Once again a critic was finding Stevens uniquely useful for moving beyond the paralyzing binary oppositions of high modernism, and Stevens was being appropriated in the service of an antipolitical ideology of criticism that obscured his own resonance (and the potential resonance of poetry itself) in that area.

As for Pearce, for Frye the stakes and the rewards of Stevens's enormously ambitious attempt at imaginative synthesis were so high as to embody a quasi-religious transcendence: "For such poetry [as Stevens's] the most accurate word is apocalyptic, a poetry of 'revelation' " ("Realistic Oriole," 367). Frye argued that this sort of striving after transcendence was not peculiar to Stevens but was, again, the primary function and value of poetry, "the normal language of the poetic imagination itself" (368). As an exemplar of this preeminent impulse towards imaginative transcendence and revelation, Stevens, whose poetry was "centrally in the Romantic tradition" (355), deserved a central place in Frye's own Romantic pantheon.[20]

Frye also fell into alignment with the nonacademic critics who had described and admired the "fixed point" from which Stevens had patiently constructed his own success and value as a poet. Much as the theoretical field of criticism needed a "central hypothesis" (*Anatomy*, 16) from which to proceed inductively, Stevens functioned as "a central poet," "working outward from a beginning instead of onwards toward an end" ("Realistic Oriole," 357). Such "persistence" as one found in Stevens's constructive combination of "rhetorical skill" with "novelty and freshness of approach" added up to "a quality of courage" (370). Indeed, given the strength of the ethical imperative to construct theory which Frye had expressed in the *Anatomy*, it is not surprising that for him this most theoretical of poets was also "one of the most courageous poets of our time" ("Realistic Oriole" 370). As would usually be the case in the critical theorists' use of Stevens, Frye's praise of Stevens was to an important degree an act of reinforcement of the critic's own position. Most importantly for our purposes, Frye's appropriation of Stevens for the nascent field of critical theory was an act of evaluative power that had substantial effect on the academic canons of American modernist poetry. In the next decade Frye's demonstration of how Stevens's work could be appropriated and exploited by American critical theory would be adapted and extended by other writers, consolidating the poet's centrally canonical status within the post-New Critical academy.

Despite Frye's enormous prominence after the publication of the *Anatomy*, American critical theory from the early 1960s came to be characterized by a strongly European bent, in contrast to (and partially in reaction against) the very high-Anglican emphasis of New Criticism. Much as the young Stevens had done in his search for poetic models, young theorists often looked to France for their models, strategies, and mannerisms, and forged links between new developments in European intellectual life and American critical discourse. This turn in American critical theory and Stevens criticism towards European existentialism and phenomenology was closely connected to the desire to reestablish the subject-consciousness as the focus of critical attention. Howe, for example, had articulated the objective of Stevens's aesthetic as an experiential rather than an intellectual one, "not any conclusion in the realm of thought but a revelation in the realm of experience" (18). Though he was not exactly a phenomenologist himself, Frye had argued in his essay on Stevens that "the imaginative act breaks down the separation between subject and object" ("Realistic Oriole," 367), the dichotomy that had characterized high-modernist New Criticism. To younger theorist-critics the new philosophies from France appeared to offer ways of overcoming that potentially paralyzing impasse of subject and object—and so did Stevens, who was quite capable of describing reality in terms very dear to a phenomenologist's heart.[21]

As early as 1957 the poet Howard Nemerov had posited a strong congruence between the orientation of existentialist-phenomenologist thinking and Stevens's poetry. Next to the exhilarating (if daunting) challenge Stevens offered to the reader, Nemerov treated the familiar interpretive paradigm of New Criticism as little more than a quaint object of vague nostalgia: "we . . . wish a little wistfully for a moment requiring esoteric knowledge, as with Eliot" (3), but these safer waters of interpretation were inadequate for dealing with Stevens, whose work was "essentially different from almost everything else in English" (1). To gloss Stevens's poetics Nemerov resorted to Camus's description of Husserl's phenomenological worldview, which "declines to explain the world, [but] wants to be merely a description of actual experience" (7). Stevens's poetics, based on a fundamental reorientation of human existence as an interaction among an infinite succession of minute phenomenal events, succeeded in recording and articulating the central processes of consciousness: "that subtle drama of inductions of which we lose or throw away a thousand examples daily, so that we have formed the prudent habit of calling it trivial, just as though all that we regard as decisive in the world did not depend precisely on this triviality: 'the poem of the act of the mind' " (3).

The emergence of this phenomenal episteme led to several consequences that have been critical to much American critical theory, and to Stevens criticism, for the past thirty years. The epistemological and social relativism that Stevens had been expressing for twenty-five years was finally beginning to be noticed and taken seriously by critics who had gathered from books of modern philosophy, as well as from such poems as "On the Road Home," that "there is no truth, but merely truths" (Camus, *The Myth of Sisyphus* [1955], quoted in Nemerov, 7; "On the Road Home," *CP*, 203). The fundamental reorientation of text from product to process was primary in Nemerov's reading of "Anecdote of the Jar"; "it is not the establishment of such an image, in Platonic domination, that is the theme, it is, rather, the act of establishing," which is "never final and must always be repeated" (10). Thus Stevens asserted that life was an open-ended process of "meditation" on the flux of the world, whose only possible closure was "death (an end but no solution)" (9).[22] For Nemerov, despite, or perhaps because of, the difficulty and unfamiliarity of the position Stevens had arrived at, his achievement represented "the difficult art of a man who, so far as thought is concerned, may prove to have been the only truly *modern* poet of his time" (13).

To be the only "truly modern poet" by means of having assimilating contemporary "thought" meant, as Frye had also perceived, that there were potentially powerful ethical and social consequences in Stevens's theory of the constructive capacity of the imagination and its relationship to "reality." In "The Realistic Oriole," Frye had sketched the consequences of what he called "false" or "perverted myths," through which Stevens had accounted for wars as "a 'gigantomachia' of competing aggressive myths" (365). Frye's heavily mythographic perspective, however, locked him into the view that there could be nothing but a cycle of various "competing" myths, allowing for no clear priority either in ethics or methodology for one myth over another; "The war-myth or hero of death is the great enemy of the imagination: he cannot be directly fought except by another war-myth" (366).

Beginning in his 1960 study of Stevens, and especially in his influential analysis of myths of apocalypse, *The Sense of an Ending* (1966), Frank Kermode found an ingenious way out of the mythic impasse Frye had left Stevens in. Kermode, like Frye, and like many intellectuals who had lived through the Moscow trials and the rise of nazism, possessed—was possessed by—an excruciating awareness of the destructive power of myth. It was no accident that the canonical modernist poet most closely associated with myths of apocalypse came in for strong criticism in Kermode's argument (*Sense*, 111–12).[23] Designed to counter this apocalyptic tendency in high modernism was Kermode's most important theoretical insight, which derived directly from the pragmatic aspect of Stevens's concept of the "supreme fiction." Reversing Pearce's unfathomable argument for the necessity of absolute belief in Stevens's views, Kermode posited a fundamental distinction between myths and fictions, which delineated two ways of believing in imaginative structures: "Myth operates within the diagrams of ritual, which presupposes total and adequate explanations of things as they are and were; it is a sequence of radically unchangeable gestures. Fictions are for finding things out, and they change as the needs of sense-making change. Myths are the agents of stability, fictions the agents of change. Myths call for absolute, fictions for conditional assent" (*Sense*, 39).

Kermode's use of Stevens did not deny or ignore the inevitable operation of "versions of the world" (which one might call ideologies), as Frye, Howe, and other postwar critics had aspired to do, thus allowing them the unbridled if covert authority of myths. Instead Kermode's formulation advocated a continual critical examination of such positions from a skeptical perspective that treated them as nonontological fictions.

Kermode's distinction was also part of the turn away from the authority of the impenetrable New Critical text towards the power of the individual speaking (and interpreting) subject. For Kermode, to believe in a myth—religious, political, social—required an absolute submission of the will of the individual (writer and reader) to the worldview contained by that myth and to the rituals of behavior prescribed by it. It was the very absolutism of this level of belief, representing the subject's total self-abnegation to received "texts" of ritual behavior, which made possible unimaginably horrible (yet all too real) consequences. On the other hand, to believe in a fiction, which one knew and acknowledged to be fictional, was to make "an experimental assent," which, "if we make it well"—Kermode never explained this value system—would produce the "gain" of "never quite resum[ing] the posture of life and death that we formerly held" (*Sense*, 41), resulting in some degree of change in the world. Kermode's valorization of change over stasis can be linked to Stevens's position that the supreme fiction "must change" as well as to the phenomenological reconception of the world as a flux of forces inevitably and constantly in change, which must be recognized and accommodated. Despite its problems and exaggerations, amply outlined by Lentricchia (*After the New Criticism*, 35–39), Kermode's quasi-existentialist use of Stevens's concept of the fiction as a sufficing, provisional construction of discourse in which one could place one's experimental assent—and around which one could orient one's behavior—provided a basis for seeing Stevens's work as a potential ethical agent rather than merely as an object of aesthetic pleasure.[24]

While Frye and Kermode (and their versions of Stevens) leaned towards mythographic and existentialist paradigms, respectively, a number of slightly younger American theorist-critics took views of the poet more explicitly in the direction of phenomenology.[25] The extent to which these appropriations of Stevens were pitted against the New Critical Symbolist influence upon literary and critical thinking was suggested by Geoffrey Hartman in a 1965 essay on Frye. In attempting to articulate the significance of Frye's influence, Hartman argued, "When we recall the rejection of myths of depth in contemporary literature and phenomenology, and when we think of how Wallace Stevens tries to return to a fundamental insight of the Romantics obscured even in him by traces of Symbolist cultism, we easily perceive Frye's link to the modern movement which insists on demystification. The 'virile man standing in the sun' [Frye's phrase] begins to merge with Stevens's virile poet and central man who declares he has outlived the esoteric muses" (117–18). Here Hartman brought together several of the strands of theoretical discourse since the *Anatomy* which were making integral use of Stevens: Frye's desire to reject the literary and social mystifications of symbolism (and its cult of New Criticism) for an unmysterious system of archetypes; the mounting critical interest in phenomenology and the revival of Romanticism; and the belief in the importance of Stevens as the poetic exemplar of these impulses.

The goal of all these revisionists of the symbolist tradition—Frye, Stevens, phenomenologists, the unnamed members of the "modern movement," and presumably Hartman himself—was a "demystification" of literature (and criticism) which had a democratic and humanistic import: "Thus art contributes to a supreme fiction, an archetypal or total form, which is the forerunner of a new, demystified theory of participation" (116). Into this burgeoning aspiration of "modern literary theory," Hartman also included "the Marxist concept of types, the Western historians' concept of topoi, the renewal of interest in Biblical typology," and "the varieties of myth-criticism," all of which were "implicated in transcending the view that art is a private or elitist enterprise" (116). Both by way of the shared image of the poet as virile human figure, and by the rhetorical identification of Stevens's "supreme fiction" with Frye's "total form," Hartman equated Frye's authoritative critical achievement and Stevens's poetic authority. Stevens was thus figured both as having predicted the direction of contemporary critical theory and as having exemplified that direction in his poetry better than any other modernist writer.[26]

Of the many theoretical appropriations of Stevens between 1957 and 1966, the portrayals of the poet in the early work of Harold Bloom and J. Hillis Miller developed the fullest and most influential arguments for seeing Stevens as a central poet of the Romantic tradition and of philosophical modernity, respectively. Beginning in *The Visionary Company* (1961), Bloom advanced forceful arguments for seeing Stevens as one of a very few worthy inheritors of the mantle of the great Romantic poets. In the concluding two chapters of his 1965 book, *Poets of Reality*, Miller contended that Stevens and Williams were virtually the only American modernists to have forged a fundamentally new relationship between human consciousness and reality. These were remarkably inclusive canonical claims for a poet who a mere dozen years before had been of no special academic interest. As culminations of sorts in the use of Stevens to construct a body of post–New Critical theory, the work of these two critics through 1966 will serve to bring this analysis of Stevens's canonization, if not to a tidy close, at least to a resting place.

Like many other important works of the period, Bloom's ambitious early "reading of English Romantic poetry," *The Visionary Company,* deployed his sense of Stevens's importance not frontally but diffusely, sprinkling brief, suggestive, and value-laden remarks about Stevens throughout his discussions of Blake, Wordsworth, and Keats. Most often "Stevens" functioned as a rhetorical shorthand for the impulses, goals, and assumptions of the great Romantics as they descended into twentieth-century poetry: "All of them knew increasingly well what Stevens seems to have known best among the poets of our time, that the theory of poetry is the theory of life" (3). Here Bloom used a phrase from Stevens to describe retrospectively one of the fundamental insights of the members of his Romantic canon, much as Bewley and Poirier had reread earlier American authors in light of their reading of Stevens. For Bloom, Stevens was the most important bearer, almost the sole modern bearer, of the Romantics' "enormous desire and eloquent hope" (2) to use poetry to establish the creative imagination as an indomitable force that defined humanity and made it meaningful: "In the accents of our own voice Wallace Stevens, the legitimate heir of these aspirations, says of poetry that it is 'a present perfecting, a satisfaction in the irremediable poverty of life' " (1).

Yet, importantly, in *The Visionary Company,* the accent was not on the temporary perfections to be achieved but on the irremediability of life's poverty. To be sure, Bloom exhibited the return to the subject seen among most of the younger theorists who wrote on Stevens, but more than Frye and Kermode, Bloom conveyed such individualism as having a disturbingly solipsistic tendency that gave even his early work an edge of agonistic desperation: "we say of Blake and Wordsworth that they are the greatest of the Romantic poets, and indeed the first poets fully to enter into the abyss of their own selves, and we mean that they perform for us the work of the ideal metaphysician, which is the role our need has assigned to the modern poet" (7).

The overriding "need" of modernity—to establish a space of transcendence in the absence of gods—had taken its ideal form when poets created an individualist metaphysics by plunging ever deeper into the yawning emptiness of the self. This formulation commented upon an epigraph from Stevens's "The Figure of the Youth as Virile Poet," which discussed the notions of God, heaven, and hell as "merely poetry not so called." Stevens's remark in that essay that no matter how glorious the creation, no matter what it had accomplished, the poet would still have been "a man who needed what he had created," had a commonsensical therapeutic cast very different from Bloom's characterization of the self as an "abyss" that could be escaped from or conquered only by fully losing oneself inside it, effectively obliterating any world outside the self.

The paranoid rejection of extrinsic systems of values prominent in both Frye's delineation of the field of criticism and in Pearce's rejection of the "mythic" for the "Adamic" aspect of American poetry emerged even more extremely in Bloom, for whom the great Romantics distinguished themselves exactly by resisting (and offering a model of resistance to the critic) all such extrinsic demands on their identity: "As they would not yield [the theory of poetry] to historical convention, so they could not surrender [the theory of life] to religion or philosophy or the tired resignations of society. They failed of their temporal prophecy, but they failed as the Titans did, massive in ruin and more human than their successors" (*Visionary Company,* 3).

Once again a freedom from religion, philosophy, society—forces seen as identical in their soul-destroying extrinsicality—was the ultimate goal and victory for the poet. From Bloom's point of view this imputation of "failure" in the temporal realm was crucial. If the failure was merely "temporal," it could be denied that it was a real failure altogether. Indeed, within Bloom's agonistic paradigm, temporal failure was itself a sort of triumph (making the writers "more human"), if the "ruin" took a "massive" enough form. In the febrile intensity of its yearning, Bloom's agonistic use of Stevens (who has also been seen as among the least agonistic of poets) is close to Pearce's apocalyptic portrayal of Stevens as achieving the "ultimate poem" of America, the instrument of decreation designed to bring on massive temporal failure in order to enable the creation of a higher extratemporal realm.

The glancing references to Stevens throughout Bloom's argument were often designed to attack high modernist and New Critical doctrines, such as the notion of the poetic image as correlative object to a nugget of meaning in a poem. Bludgeoning the arch-imagist and anti-Romanticist T. E. Hulme as "an inadequate theorist, a man who did not know enough, least of all poetry," Bloom utterly rejected the centrality of the image, which, "far from being the primary pigment of all poetry . . . is irrelevant to much of the highest poetry" (*Visionary Company,* 172). When Bloom described Stevens as (like Wordsworth) "forsaking the image" (172), a reader might be forgiven for feeling that Bloom's version of Stevens was a narrow characterization created for the critic's own purposes, especially since the particular quotation from Stevens which Bloom chose to demonstrate his anti-Imagist argument, which began "The greatest poverty is not to live / In a physical world," actually appeared to affirm the physicality and corporeality of this world—a habit of Stevens's which Bloom acknowledged at other points in the book. Did that acknowledgement then exclude images of the things of this physical world? Were images of no preexisting object but of human invention—as in a painting, engraving, or poem—despite their participation in the life of the imagination, not part of this physical world as well?

In general, very few references to Stevens in *The Visionary Company* allowed for any contrast, or even difference, among Stevens and Blake, Wordsworth, Keats, or the other poets he discussed; most references to Stevens fit a rigid pattern of identity such as "or, as Wallace Stevens says in our own day." Often important concepts and images from Stevens's poetry seemed to have no distinct identity of their own but were totally subsumed into the thought of the earlier Romantics: "Wordsworth's Imagination is like Stevens's 'Angel Surrounded by Paysans'" (127); Shelley's Promethean man "finds its modern analogue in the 'major man' or 'central man' of Wallace Stevens" (317); the rock of Prometheus's captivity "is the stony world of Urizen, 'the gray particular of man's life,' as Wallace Stevens called it" (306); Keats's "idea of poetry is best expressed outside of his own work by the latest embodiment of the figure of the youth as virile poet, the rider" who passes Mrs. Alfred Uruguay "as she slowly approaches her reductive real" (368); "For Wordsworth, as for Stevens, the earth is enough" (127); Keats's "To Autumn" "finds its companion" in "Sunday Morning" in such expressions as that "the earth is enough" (405). Thus Wordsworth equaled Keats equaled Stevens. Bloom used Stevens, then, as a sort of infinite reservoir of remarks and illustrations which could be brought in whenever the critic wanted to demonstrate the existence of a "Romantic tradition" extending past the middle of the nineteenth century.

Such "misreadings" of Stevens as a warrior in the campaign against high Modernism, repeated throughout the critic's career, created a highly influential portrayal of the poet as little more than a version of the individualist-cum-solipsist Romantic Self (of which Bloom constructed himself into a critical avatar). Bloom's deployment of Stevens thus captured in microcosm the ambiguous process of canonization which the poet's work had undergone over the previous two decades. In adopting Stevens as the major modernist repository of the insights of Romanticism, by often rereading and explicating the Romantics through the illuminating (if anachronistic) glass of his poetry, Bloom paid Stevens an enormous tribute, forcefully demonstrating the poet's constitutive canonicity within one of the two main lines of English-language poetry. On the other hand, by so completely emphasizing the Romantic, nonintellectual, antipolitical, self-absorbed side of Stevens—worse, by implying that there was no other—Bloom's career served to decontextualize Stevens even further, to prevent his work from assuming a meaningful place in another kind of literary and cultural history, a kind that Bloom would not even admit as genuine.

Bloom made clearer his urgent commitment to Stevens and Stevens's centrality to his own ultra-Romanticist position in a 1966 article, "The Central Man: Emerson, Whitman, Wallace Stevens," which again employed Stevens's own concepts and phraseology to articulate the descent of Romanticism into America and the twentieth century. Bloom's inclusion of Emerson and Whitman in his Romantic continuity meant that Stevens was no longer the sole American purveyor of Romanticism who only began writing a century after its heyday, at best an anomaly, at worst an anachronism. He was now portrayed as the contemporary culmination of a major strain of American poetry as well: "The heir to these bards [Emerson and Whitman] . . . is Wallace Stevens, whom it is no longer eccentric to regard as the ironically yet passionately balanced fulfillment of the American Romantic tradition in poetry" ("The Central Man," 25). This relative contextualization of Stevens within American Romanticism had the distinct virtue of giving Stevens nearer antecedents within an existing historical framework than *The Visionary Company* had allowed for, suggesting that Bloom's position did not come out of his own fantasies but had a cogent line of historical descent.

Not surprisingly, in extending his argument to these three American poets, Bloom again took up the question that had been seen as crucial to many Stevens critics—humanist, Romanticist, existentialist, or phenomenologist—over the previous quarter-century: "struggles between the Romantic Imagination . . . and the hard 'given' of natural experience, the inescapable necessity of confronting the Not-Me" ("The Central Man," 26). These American Romantics, including Stevens, "came to realize that the imagination had to separate from nature if it was to go beyond nature" (26); Bloom did not argue so much as assume that the confrontation with the Not-Me was identical to going "beyond nature." Bloom frankly preferred the orphic Emerson who asserted the "autonomy of the imagination," who spoke prophetically, but all too seldom, of "the kingdom of man over nature . . . —a dominion such as now is beyond his dream of god" (31), and whose ultimate "lesson," quoting Stephen Whicher, was "not virtue, but freedom and mastery" (31–32). As realized in Emerson's "strongest" poems, this "mastery" was "clearly not that of nature, no matter how idealistically viewed, but of possession, and the possessing force is that of the central man, or man at the center of men, the human globe" (32–33). No fusion of humanity and nature was possible or desirable; what was wanted instead was an ecstatic "possession," a remaking of the very globe into the image of man.

Despite the recreative and mastering potential sometimes evoked by American Romanticism, for Bloom the descent of Romanticism from Wordsworth through Emerson and Whitman to Stevens was characterized by smaller and smaller claims for the efficacy of the relationship between nature and human beings, culminating in a point of crisis and ecstatic destruction in Whitman and "re-asserted" with massive qualifications by Stevens. Bloom made plain that the aspect of "the central man" which he valued most highly was this inevitable and total triumph-through-ruination; the central man of American Romanticism was "most authentic when he ebbs, and merges himself, wrecked, as part of the sands and drift, man absolute, but man on the dump, a savior who could not save himself" (24).

The extent to which Bloom was selecting elements of these poets' thought, neglecting all but two visions of the central man among many possible ones, to construct his own idiosyncratic version of Romantic agonism was suggested by a passage on the central man which conjoined passages from "As I Ebb'd With the Ocean of Life" and "Asides on the Oboe." Bloom argued from these passages, "Between two visions of the central man, we have an approximation of the central man himself" (24). The curiously tautological quality of this remark masked Bloom's self-portrayal as the synthesizer and completer of the actual being ("the central man himself") from the incomplete and half-understood insights of these poets; in other words, this was a story of the critic as "the central man himself." A similar defense of his massive and selective reshaping of the character of his poets came later in the essay, with Bloom's assertion, reminiscent of Pearce's apocalyptic terminology, that "As I Ebb'd" was "Whitman's absolute poem." Despite acknowledging that his choice of these specific poems as touchstones was "of course an individual and arbitrary matter," in the next breath Bloom claimed with considerable exaggeration that the mandate for his emphasis on these poems was to be seen as an absolute natural or historical axiom: "there is a universal and inevitable tendency among us these days to turn most readily to Emerson at his most apocalyptic and to Whitman at his most despairing. The Orphic, primary Emerson and the tragic, antithetical Whitman are what we want and need" (34). Other versions of the poets "we are done with, and in good time" (34). Of course this principle of manhandling poets by "strong" critics applied equally to Bloom's portrayal of Stevens.

Once one has registered these important objections to Bloom's frenetically apocalyptic portrayal of Romanticism (and of contemporary criticism) in which Stevens occupied a central position, it is still possible to find his view of Stevens in this essay congenial, as it is possible to value his 1977 critical study *Wallace Stevens: The Poems of Our Climate* much more highly than his later theoretical books. For Bloom, Stevens provided a synthesis of the antithetical impulses, mastering and self-immolating, which formed the characteristic achievements of Emerson and Whitman, respectively. In being "the asserter, or re-asserter, however self-qualified, of the imaginative fable of the Central Man" ("The Central Man," 36), Stevens thus enabled a viable modern reactivation of the Romantic dialectic. Despite Stevens's myriad ironies and ambiguities of diction, syntax, imagery, and personae, he nonetheless persisted in making once again possible the "qualified assertion" that was more than "an asserted qualification" (37). Although "The Central Man Stevens celebrates" was but "a 'prodigious shadow'" (37), he was, as Stevens said, "not man yet . . . was nothing else" (38). At the essay's end Bloom could even be found affirming Stevens's rejection of the sort of apocalyptic stalemate Emerson and Whitman had embodied, by returning to a state of relative innocence and trust in nature which appealed to the Romantic innocent in the critic as well: "the Northern lights [in "The Auroras of Autumn"] are seen finally as signifying the desperate necessity for an assertion of the autonomy of the human imagination, and even for its freedom from every worn conception of existence. The aurora terrifies, because imaginative freedom terrifies, but the poet's courage is to insist that the aurora *is* benevolent and innocent" (40).

A bit later Bloom continued this constructive affirmation of both terms of the central self/nonself relationship, rather than his more usual rejection of nature in favor of a desperate imaginative autonomy, by remarking that "out of this innocence of the earth emerges finally, however tenuously, the figure of the rabbi, the humanist teaching his congregation the doctrine of the hallowing of the commonplace," from whose teaching might eventually emerge once again the "vision of the possible impossible, the central man" (41). Here at least, Bloom acknowledged the importance of what he has so often denied, Stevens's lifelong, humane, and decidedly nonapocalyptic emphasis upon the ongoing processes of imagination, rather than upon their annihilation in a moment of ostensible transcendence.

The use of Stevens to outline a moment of sufficing equilibrium and relative affirmation which Bloom achieved at the end of this 1966 essay was unfortunately not the primary direction of his later work. The extremity of Bloom's belated Romantic agonism and the quirkiness of his interpretive methods may inhibit the long-term survival of his theoretical influence. In the shorter run, the forceful ingenuity of his arguments and his distinctive use of Stevens undeniably had a major impact on the shape of post-New Critical canons of modernist poetry, which in the last three decades have exhibited turns towards not only Stevens but also such Bloom favorites as Hart Crane, Ashbery, Ammons, and Merrill.

The names of Bloom and J. Hillis Miller have long been linked in critical discourse because of their close association as institutional colleagues, as "Yale critics." As is usually the case with such pigeonholing, their similarities have been emphasized at the expense of a sensible understanding of their differences. Especially at this early stage in their careers, Bloom and Miller had relatively little in common in their theoretical uses of Stevens, outside of a shared interest in returning to the poetic subject and, following Frye, a fascination with the possibilities of synoptic critical method. Miller's distinctive account of Stevens offered a vigorous and healthy corrective to the tendency to social despair and paranoia seen in Frye and Kermode and to the thirst for apocalyptic mastery and closure seen in Pearce and Bloom.

Miller's first account of Stevens came in *Poets of Reality* (1965), a book that extended to the twentieth century Miller's analysis of Victorian authors' responses to the breakup of the Christian hegemony begun in *The Disappearance of God* (1963). For Miller, the nineteenth-century phenomenon of the disappearance of God was characterized by the onset of the same "dichotomy of subject and object" (2) which he shared with Bloom and nearly all of those employing Stevens in their theoretical positions during these years. Unlike most of them, Miller developed this dichotomy along lines of a phenomenologist ethic that was far from Frye's mythological cyclism or Bloom's Romantic agonism. Miller argued that the later nineteenth century after the Romantics was characterized by the perception that God had disappeared not only from the human heart (the subject) but from nature (the object) as well. One response to this psychic event was to see God "not as invisible but as nonexistent" (2), an insight that had tended towards solipsism ("When everything exists only as reflected in the ego, then man has drunk up the sea" [3]) and "nihilism," "the nothingness of consciousness when consciousness has become the foundation of everything" (3). This nihilism had meant the abnegation of any basis for ethical force and value: "Nothing now has any worth except the arbitrary value" that the subject chose to set on things (3).

Unlike Bloom and Pearce, however, Miller saw the potential total domination of the subject of consciousness not as the site of an apocalyptic triumph but as a vacuum of humane values which threatened apocalyptic defeat. He drew provocative links between "romanticism and technology," noting that in the "objectified world," which was the logical conclusion of Romantic subjectivism, "the triumph of technology" was equivalent to "the forgetting of the death of God" (5). Into this vacuum of values and guidelines for behavior could rush (had rushed) only the "will to power" (4), "man's limitless hunger for conquest," which had become "the chief determinant of man's sensibility in many parts of the world today" (5). Despite the presence of the somewhat disabling assumption, highly characteristic of these cold-war decades, that it was inevitably "technology" itself rather than particular ideologies controlling it, which was the symptom and instrument of this inhumane nihilism, the use of Stevens that Miller went on to make possessed an ethical component more genuine than Bloom's, more sensitive to the dangers of imaginative imperialism than Pearce's, and more able to preserve the multiplicity of forces and processes of consciousness than Frye had been.

The foremost goal of *Poets of Reality* was to delineate an alternative tradition of modern writers ("a countercurrent moving against the direction of history"

[5]), who had "exposed" the subject-object dilemma as the nihilism that it was (5), who had with various degrees of success groped their way beyond paralysis towards affirming the immanent "union of inner and outer, natural and supernatural, in the transience and nearness of the real" (11). Far from accepting the resignation and isolation of post-Christian subjective consciousness, Miller posited the possibility of finding "an escape through the darkness" to a rediscovery of "a spiritual power external to [one]self," which, though it appeared as "an inexpressibly threatening horror, still . . . is something beyond the self" (7). The extremity of the modern situation demanded a response of equally extreme expression, which Miller called "the most dangerous of choices, a leap into the abyss," a surrender of one's "most cherished certainties," "abandoning the independence of the ego," stepping, "as Wallace Stevens puts it, 'barefoot into reality' " (7). Yet despite the extremity of rhetoric in his introductory essay, Miller and his "poets of reality" were no lovers of apocalypse. These writers were saved from this fate by their understanding of the implications of viewing existence as a nonteleological flux of forces. Miller's healing leap into the abyss of the self, unlike Bloom's, meant giving up the all-encompassing sense of the self which was both the most cherished and the most paralyzing of these post-Christian certainties.

Like the various nonacademic portrayals of Stevens as the congenial affirmer of the ordinary, the reinterpreter of the familiar rather than the transcendent Tiresian prophet of doom, Miller's Stevens was a thoroughgoing phenomenologist, seeing reality as "a universal fluctuation" of "things . . . curving through space, vibrat[ing] or oscillat[ing]" (226). The perception that "each moment is 'abulge' with multiplicity," "a swarming plenitude of things moving together," changing "from moment to moment," "full of an enormous amount of activities born of the interchange of imagination and reality" (273), meant the necessity of a fundamental reorientation of the relationship between imagination and reality.

This central phenomenological insight applied to Stevens allowed Miller to reformulate typical truisms of Stevens criticism in atypically sophisticated and humane terms. For example, Miller described the relationship between imagination and reality not as the demonic struggle for the individual's soul seen in Bloom and Frye, nor as Pearce's global battlefield, but as "like two charged poles which repel one another as they approach and can never touch, though the relation between them creates a vibrant field of forces" (233). The choice of the analogy with the forces of physics was itself characteristic of the phenomenological, process-based description of Stevens which Miller was developing. Miller perceived that in Stevens these two fundamental polar terms were not reified entities or opposing sides but invisible valences that meant nothing without one another. It was exactly the "vibrant field of forces" produced by their constant interaction which was the dynamic space of consciousness. Under such a definition of reality, "poetry is the search for those fortuitous conjunctions between self and world which show that they are not irreconcilable opposites, but two sides of the same coin, 'equal and inseparable' " (224). In one of his few full-scale readings of an individual poem, Miller demonstrated the fruitful ambiguity of the experience of reading a text such as "Sea Surface Full of Clouds," pointing out the equal plausibility but ultimate incompleteness of readings which emphasized either the dominance of the imagination over reality or vice versa. The very ambiguity of the poem's meaning was its lesson, a demonstration of the power of poetry to articulate the complicated and multivalent texture of existence and to provide a continuous sanction for perpetuating that existence rather than desiring its annihilation: "Every novel conjunction [of the scene and the imagination] may be crystallized in a poem, but in order to keep up with the fluctuations of reality the poet must make poem after poem" (240).

Miller also demonstrated his formal sensitivity to the poetic methods Stevens had gradually developed to keep himself attuned to this "concern with the phenomenological sensation" (228). Stevens's central technical problem was to create strategies that would enable these conjunctions while remaining true to the ineluctable "mobility of the moment" (270). The result was "a poetry of fleeting movement, a poetry in which each phrase has beginning and ending at once" (270). Stevens's poetry was based on "juxtaposition of images," a formal acknowledgement and reinforcement of the insights that "nothing exists in isolation" but only in "an interaction of two or more things" and that "the being of each thing depends on these interchanges" (229). The logic of Stevens's characteristic syntax of appositives was that "The rapid substitution of one phrase for another keeps up with the motion of time and shares its strength" (272). The poet's "lavish use of color words" (228) and, especially in the later poetry, his concentration on medium colors, "things which are neither quite one thing nor quite another, but are poised halfway in an unlikely equilibrium" (272), were attempts "to find words which will be true to these intermediate realities" (272). His habits of working with continuously self-qualifying rhetorical nuances, and with multiple visual perspectives like a cubist painter, were also consequences and approximations of the principle that "reality is never visible in its totality at any one time or from any one viewpoint. It 'is not what it is. It consists of the many realities which it can be made into' " (236).

Stevens's employment of nonsymbolic images that "entirely contain their own reality" (228) indicated a particularly important desire, simultaneously anti-Romantic and anti-Symbolist, to invest the creations of the imagination once again with an immanent reality, as actual pieces of the physical world: "As in the paintings of abstract expressionism, there is no 'beyond' to which the images refer, and they do not appear to exist against a background which exceeds them and goes backward into invisible distances" (227), an insight that was congruent with "Stevens's rejection of any transcendent beyond" (259). Though Stevens always remained conscious that "even the most straightforward poem" was still "at one remove from reality" (251), the very impossibility of ever fully or permanently seizing or transcending the constantly changing nature of reality was, in his later work, not cause for despair but the basis for continued effort in a never-resting attempt to express the evanescence of time in motion: "change is no longer seen as something to be resisted. Now the poet knows that the poem shares in reality only if it keeps up with the dizzy speed of time" (271).

Miller extended this phenomenologically sensitive version of the relationship between imagination and reality into an ethical dimension, attacking the tendency toward imaginative imperialism which had often emerged in critical formulations of Stevens's sense of the recreative power of the interchange of imagination and reality. To Miller, Stevens's occasional "accounts of those ecstatic moments when he sees that reality is contained in the mind" (256) did not represent the poet's essence but only "a momentary hallucination, the outcome of a frantic need to put a stop to an endless conflict" (257). For many other critics, those moments were Stevens's strength and achievement; for Miller, they were moments of weakness in which Stevens showed himself to be not as closely integrated with reality as was Williams, in whose work such lapses were largely absent. At his most resolute, however, Stevens's aspirations to conjoin imagination and reality, far from being "the easy reshaping of a passive reality by a sovereign imagination," required "elaborate stratagems of self-effacement."

Such self-effacement as a positive goal meant that Miller was reversing Bloom's apocalyptic conception of the self for a vision of a continuous immanent present in which "the romantic dialectic of movement through stages to attain a goal disappears. In place of advance in steps toward an end there is the continuous present of a poetry which matches in its speed the constant flight of time" (9).

The human rage for order, if it gave life meaning, had nonetheless to be resisted as a seductive agent of reductive totalization and falsification: "Nothing, the poet has discovered, is more mistaken than to seek for unchanging stability"; instead, only by working to "keep up with" the "ever-never-changing same" of continual fluctuation from moment to moment can man, "like a cork bobbing on the waves," "stay alive" (265). Not unlike the text it echoed, Crane's "The Open Boat," Miller's image of the fragility of human life constituted an imperative for communal behavior which encouraged a respect for and sensitivity to the independent existence of the myriad reality "which exceeds it and which it has not made" (8). In contrast to Bloom's agonism and Pearce's radical "egocentrism," the very impossibility of capturing the movement of reality like a beast in a cage was not a justification for a frustrated lashing out at the nonself, but a mandate for patience, tolerance of difference, and above all, "humility, for 'the humble are they that move about the world with the love of the real in their hearts' " (235). Miller evoked the anti-imperialist pluralism of Stevens's poetics most clearly when he remarked that "Stevens's poetry contains in its inner development an implicit rejection" of a civilization that "has been built both theoretically and literally on the idea that it is possible to understand and control reality by doing something to it, whether this takes the form of trying to possess things by turning them into images, perspectives, metaphors, 'world views,' or whether it is the literal making of machines out of the earth" (267).

This sort of antiteleological and nonpossessive conjunctioning of consciousness and reality was most prominent in the later poetry, beginning with *The Man With the Blue Guitar*, a poem that had for Miller "a special place in Stevens's work" in marking "his turning to the new style" (260). Miller echoed some of the earliest commentary on *Blue Guitar* by describing it as a text of "open-ended improvisation, created from moment to moment by the poet's breath" (260). As a few commentators of the 1930s had done, Miller went on to affirm the implications of that aesthetic of improvisation: with no defined start or end, the poem (like reality) "could be endless," the man with the guitar remaining as "a permanent presence, someone always there in the mind's eye watching the poet and reminding him of his obligation to a faithful thinking of life as it is" (261). If this "life as it is" had neither start nor finish, then a poem "must be a constant flowing of images which come as they come and are not distorted by the logical mind in its eagerness for order" (261). Miller's turn back to *Blue Guitar* as a crucial text in Stevens's work after two decades of critical neglect illustrated his commitment to developing a version of Stevens fundamentally different from the imperialist and apocalyptic uses to which the poet's account of the imagination had been put in much criticism of the 1940s and 1950s.

Already moving towards a poststructuralist emphasis upon textual free play, Miller saw in Stevens (and Williams) poetic versions of a world of discourse which had moved beyond the paralyzing Romantic-modernist dilemma of "a world riven in two, split irreparably into subject and object, imagination and reality" (274). In a powerful summary passage, Miller demolished the two-world dualism that had bedeviled Stevens criticism for a quarter-century: Stevens's greatest achievement was the lifelong and difficult process of teaching himself

> that there is after all only one realm, always and everywhere the realm of some new conjunction of imagination and reality. The later Stevens is beyond metaphysical dualism, and beyond representational thinking. It is no longer a question of some reality which exists already in the world, and of which the poet then makes an image. The image is inextricably part of the thing. . . . There is only one mode of existence: consciousness of some reality. Imagination never exists separately. Reality never exists separately. All that ever exists, anywhere, for man, is imagination-reality. [274–75]

The creations of the imagination, springing from interaction with reality, themselves became immanent and affective parts of a reality that was therefore altered. The result, since nothing could be apprehended outside of the processes of consciousness, was that everything participated in a universal principle of textuality: "Words are tangled inextricably in the event they describe. 'The poem is the cry of its occasion, / Part of the res itself and not about it' " (276).[27] Thus Miller reversed the view of Stevens as naive philosophical realist wistfully hoping for "Not Ideas About the Thing But the Thing Itself," making him instead into the harbinger of poststructuralist sophistication in which "things" are themselves texts and vice versa.

The consequences of Miller's phenomenological reorientation of the concept of "reality" in Stevens and Williams had notable consequences for critical theory and methodology. If for these poets the world was, as Miller often reiterated, a "universal turning or flowing" (227), then a poet's texts might as well be seen as a group of things in constant fluctuation as a critic or reader apprehended them; indeed, if what the critic apprehended was exactly this oscillating motion of texts, then it could be assumed that each of them possessed no unitary or unchanging identity but simply formed part of the universal flux. A critical method congruent with such insights as these was to have an important influence on academic criticism. The preservation of the particularity and the temporal movement of individual poems was thrown over by Miller in favor of a discourse of almost total intertextuality in which innumerable textual fragments appeared to exist simultaneously in a state of continuous presence in poet's, critic's, and reader's consciousnesses.[28]

Nevertheless, Miller's critical technique of continuous intertextual reference, while often impressively illuminating, meant an increased reliance on the titanism of the poetic subject at the expense of various other methods and goals that one might call "historical." In effect, the poet became a huge undifferentiated "text" for reading and arranging in whatever fashion the critic deemed best. The chronology of composition, the ongoing development of an aesthetic or intellectual position, the personal or historical circumstances under which particular phrases or ideas were created, all were overwhelmed by the monumental subjectivity of the poet, whose body of work became a version of the "total form" that Frye had described all of literature as being. Miller could thus explicitly brush off Stevens's periodic impulses to write openly about the impact of historical events in causing and enforcing the characteristic nihilism of modernity: "But the real answer to the question [of nihilism's causes] is simpler than [Stevens's account], and more disquieting. It takes no French or Copernican revolution, no catastrophic world wars, no industrializing of the world to overturn everything" (220–21).

One may admit with Miller that these revolutions and catastrophic wars need not have happened while still feeling it inappropriate to dismiss their importance in understanding and ameliorating this overturned world. Miller's intertextual method thus created a certain contradiction, or tension at least, between his argument that the foremost achievement of these poets was, in varying degrees, to reintegrate their own isolated subjectivity into the forces and processes of "reality," and his own critical focus that remained resolutely and atemporally upon the free-floating consciousness of the poetic subject.

The struggles of Miller's poets for "effacement" of the ego before reality, remarkably lucid and appealing when posited in his introduction, also turned out to be excruciatingly difficult to achieve and to have a curious and troubling hierarchical canon. Of the six writers Miller dealt with in *Poets of Reality*, only five were poets, only three were born as Americans, only two died as Americans, and only those same two achieved substantial progress in getting beyond nihilism back to reality, the other (Eliot) having opted for the consolation prize of "a new version of Christian immanence" instead (358). Each writer Miller turned to represented a slightly further stage in the evolutionary process of reality-seeking that he described and advocated, culminating in an intense and influential celebration of Williams's work.

Even if one were to accept the book's structure of evolutionary hierarchy and its methodology of intensive intertextuality, the very smallness of the canon Miller admitted into his account of literary modernity might well remain cause for concern. Although Miller acknowledged that such attempts to recover immanence in reality could also be seen in the work of a few creators in other artforms, still it appeared that these few figures were the only ones to buck the entire "direction of history," to forge new phenomenological linkages with reality. Unless they were not unique but representative of broader historical tendencies, one could hardly have much faith that these few voices would mean much against the crushingly enormous forces arrayed against them. One effect of including only six twentieth-century writers in such a monumentally ambitious project was, then, in spite of its admirable intentions, to erode its operational effectiveness for any level of "reality" outside the relation between that particular poet and his or her immediate environment (his, as it turned out in Miller's canon).

Such a paradox was an apt metonymic illustration of the tendency of most post–New Critical writers on modernist poetry to adopt, and indeed even to exacerbate, the New Critical tendency towards valorizing only a few writers of any given period. These shrinking canons were an unfortunate by-product of the return to the poetic subject, which, in Bloom and Miller—though less so in Frye and Kermode—meant a reliance upon a few poets as titanic, all-inclusive figures. As the influence of intertextual and deconstructionist criticism increased through the next decade, the lesson offered to younger readers and scholars, say those who entered graduate programs in American universities through the early 1980s, was that these few were virtually the only modernist poets worth close attention. Such a restrictive and elitist canonical hierarchy could only run contrary to the democratizing and humanitarian aspirations for literature which many members of the profession, and some of these theorists themselves, possessed. So while it was not the choice of Stevens as the particular focus for conceptualizations of poetic value which retarded the social value of literary studies in this period, the very intensity and exclusivity of the theorists' canonical gaze on only a few writers did form (and remains) a great stumbling block to their hopes to actualize the enormous social and cultural potential—as Miller put it, "the radiant promise" (358)—latent in American modernist poetry.

SEVEN

Afterword

His Own Best Critic?

> How he ever became a Canon is the real problem.
> —Stevens (on Canon Aspirin of
> *Notes Toward a Supreme Fiction*), 1943

> It is possible to develop radically different notions of Stevens's aims as a poet, and for each of these it is easy to find apposite passages from the texts.
> —J. Hillis Miller, 1965

As a measure of Stevens's firmly consolidated canonical status during the past quarter-century, scholars and publishers have found value in issuing more and more of his private and occasional writing—journals, letters, notebooks, and even essays on insurance.[1] The precedent for such voluminous documentary publication on Stevens was set, of course, by the appearance of *Letters of Wallace Stevens* in 1966. *Letters* completed the poet's main body of texts, and its reception largely completed the processes of canonization of the writer whom "most readers of poetry would [now] grant . . . at least a place with Eliot and Frost and Pound" (Litz, "Wallace Stevens: Books and a Sonnet," 85); or more exclusively, the writer who was "becoming our central poet" (Riddel, *Review of Letters*, 421). Perceived as "a permanent contribution to the history of American poetry" (Stanford, 763) and "an event in American literary history" (Kunitz, 26), *Letters* was "bound to have an impact on our understanding of modern poetry" (Riddel, review of *Letters*, 421). While a full analysis of that impact since 1966 is beyond the scope of an afterword, a brief consideration of the reception of *Letters* will afford the opportunity of ruminating on the relationship between a twentieth-century poet's canonical authority and the changing practices of contemporary criticism which continue to reconstitute that authority.

A volume of letters can be deceptive in its effects on critical access to a writer's position in literary history. At first glance a lifetime's worth of letters would seem to offer a rich vein for tracing the mutual relations between an author and his or her network of interaction within a historical field, but the typical format for epistolary volumes, including Stevens's, offers only one side of the historical conversation. Reading Stevens's letters is to hear the sound only of his own voice, not those of his fellows, who remain shadowy and silent and who can be interpreted and understood only by the tenuous and difficult method of patching together the contexts in which Stevens spoke to them. These letters emerged in a period of intense critical fascination with Stevens and presented his literary authority in a new form equally as vivid and extensive as his poetry (as Corman put it, "Letters, essays, or poems, the voice is one and singular," 96). The energetic canonical authority generated by the presentation of this aspect of Stevens paradoxically served to promote the critical treatment of the poet as a titanic, all-inclusive figure decontextualized from twentieth-century American literary history.

Listening to the epistolary voice of Stevens for nine hundred pages can indeed be an overwhelming experience, or "compulsive reading," as Marie Borroff put it (446). The authority that had been steadily increasing throughout Stevens's poetic career, reaching an especially intense level in the *Collected Poems*, was, if anything, even more apparent to early readers of the *Letters*. Hilton Kramer began his review with the remark, "With the passage of time the poetry of Wallace Stevens tightens its hold on the mind" (18). For Cid Corman, *Letters* illustrated an important aspect of this authority, the impressive strength of Stevens's "inimitable and indomitable nature": "At no time in his life . . . does Stevens bow to any man's opinion at the loss of his own" (39). Richard Howard developed this perception of Stevens as a sort of natural force of overwhelming magnitude most fully and astutely, describing "The authority that rises like a mist . . . from the further hundreds of pages about poetry as a subject . . . [which] is so distinct from the substitutes for authority we are accustomed to put up with—crankiness, incantation, bad temper, self-promotion—that it is easy to resent Stevens and almost essential to resist him at his most overpowering" (40). Stevens's canonical centrality had become so strong that to these readers his authority seemed not part of some scheme or pantomime of literary self-puffery but a "peculiar presence" (Corman, 94), a part of the fabric of reality—and was thus, at least for Howard, somehow threatening, requiring a measure of "resistance."

The authority generated by Stevens's *Letters* manifested itself both in biographical and critical dimensions. In 1966 there was no substantial biographical publication on Stevens, and the many readers interested in the poet's work were eager for such knowledge. Litz remarked upon this fact by noting that *Letters* was the first work to begin "to provide us with a personality outside the poems" (85) to place alongside the Stevens of the poetry. That the *Letters* fed a biographical fascination unsatisfied elsewhere was also suggested by Kroll's remark that the volume "tunes the reader in to the very pulse and heartbeat of the most elusive of animals—the man who makes poetry" (114). Other readers held that the poet in *Letters* was not only "our best source of information about Stevens's life and work" but his own ideal and sufficient biographer: "Though the letters published and excerpted in this volume represent less than a third of Stevens's correspondence, they are all we will ever need" (Stanford, 757), forming "the most authoritative biography Wallace Stevens could have" (Borroff, 447), or "as close to a true biography as we are likely to get or need" (Pearson, 53). True, as autobiography, Stevens's letters are probably more reliable and accurate than many more traditional autobiographies (such as William Carlos Williams's) because they were not reshaped by the writer's hindsight at a particular time of life and because they provide windows to his thoughts throughout his life, but Stevens's letters cannot be a viable substitute for critical biography because they were produced by the poet himself and edited by his daughter. Magnificent as they are, they remain always dominated by the sound of that deep, carefully modulated voice, telling people what he wanted them to know with an almost hypnotic self-assurance.

Similarly, the Stevens of the *Letters* was seen by many readers as his own superlative critic. Astonished by the amount of time and effort Stevens had spent to help his correspondents explicate and understand his work, numerous reviewers resorted to superlatives: "Few poets in their letters have talked so freely about their art and their intentions and scruples. Even fewer have talked so well" (Pearson, 4). The letters formed "the most extensive commentary that any major poet has ever provided on his own work" (Kunitz, 26); "the most consistent meditation any poet in any language has ever put in writing on the sense of his own work" (Howard, 39). If such responsiveness to his readers was an admirable aspect of Stevens's sensitivity, it also made for certain problematic results. In his remark about Stevens's efforts, superficially like the others already quoted, Joseph Riddel intimated (without elaborating) that such extensive self-exegesis had an aspect that was unfortunate: "There is probably no fuller record anywhere of a poet's annotating his own work, for better or worse" (Riddel, review of *Letters*, 422). If a poet was seen as his own best critic, then what of possible advances and innovations in criticism? According to Helen McNeil, Stevens's overwhelming bulk of "lucid and graceful comments about his own work" "set a standard which critics will be hard put to equal" (635), and Howard agreed that Stevens's own commentary would exert a definitive corrective authority on critical perceptions of his goals and methods, remarking (optimistically) that "it is indeed impossible that the graduate-student part of ourselves should ever again make the mistakes that have so often been made" (39). Some readers even felt that the substantial body of self-exegesis that Stevens had provided made further criticism of the poet by others virtually unnecessary. Kunitz remarked that "perhaps nobody will have to write about [Stevens's poetics and main assumptions] since Stevens has already supplied whatever gloss is needed" (26), and Kramer found the volume "particularly valuable as a record of Stevens's intentions and strategies in a number of crucial poems. There is material here for an entire monograph on *The Man With the Blue Guitar*, though the nature of the material precludes the necessity for such a monograph. (Not that this will prevent it from being written)" (19).

Although its emphasis has changed, this notion that the letters formed a kind of ideal exegesis on Stevens's life and work has never disappeared. *Letters* has come, like "Adagia," to be employed as an infinite reservoir of poetic pronouncements virtually interchangeable with Stevens's poetic texts. But no matter how beautifully crafted, witty, or astute they are, Stevens's letters are neither poetic texts nor prose essays. Even more than his poems or essays, they are the cries of their occasions and must be contextualized within those occasions as fully as possible through the use of other historical sources. The more they have been treated as authoritative statements from Stevens's timeless poetic wisdom, the less historically useful they have become.[2]

The fate of the *Letters* is a symptom of the broader and longstanding tendency among American literary critics to attempt to efface their own inevitably affective positions from the texts they discuss. While the phenomenon I have been calling a poet's "authority" is undeniably felt by readers, it should not be seen as an immutable or irresistible force. It is simply a poet's job (and a lawyer's, for that matter) to persuade, convince, or dazzle readers; Stevens developed tonal and rhetorical skills that were especially effective in doing so. However, as Howard pointed out, it is part of the reader's and critic's job to resist being persuaded completely by the authority of any poet. The notion that any writer can be his or her own best critic is a myth of potentially pernicious consequences. When critics efface their inevitably primary role in continually recharacterizing the cultural functionings of even the most canonical of poets, they avoid their responsibility to make as plain as possible their evaluative preconceptions and their cultural goals. The force of Stevens's canonical authority, which peaked in the *Letters*, created the opportunity for critics to cloak themselves in the authority of their subject. The interpretive methods of intertextuality and deconstructionism which prevailed in elite American criticism from the late 1960s through the 1970s, while purporting to reject the notion of the parasitic "secondariness" of the critic's role, still invested heavily in the paradigm of the author as isolated individual largely transcending historical contingencies. Most Stevens criticism of those years, sophisticated and influential as it was, did little to help us understand Stevens's connections to the personal, social, or political conditions in which he lived and worked.

The lineage of the antipolitical and antihistorical ideology of postwar criticism which I described in the later chapters of this book continued to dominate Stevens criticism until just a few years ago. Clearly, however, this critical ideology did not operate exclusively upon readers and critics of Stevens, but helped to shape criteria of poetic importance throughout the literary culture since 1945. Its strictures, not appreciably eased by the shift of critical focus from Eliot towards Stevens after 1960, helped to maintain an exclusive academic canon of six or eight American modernist poets. Having long outstayed its welcome in my view, this narrow canon still serves to retard our understanding of the social and cultural potentials of American modernist poetry.[3]

While the most influential myths of postwar criticism—the radical dualism of the aesthetic and worldly realms, the poet as alienated and autobiographical lyricist, the inevitable inferiority of political poetry—no longer hold unchallenged dominance, all remain with us to some extent.

As even the casual reader cannot fail to have noticed, however, my criticism of these narrow modernist canons does not mean that one of my goals in this study has been to decanonize Stevens. Indeed, his work provides me with an apparently inexhaustible source of challenge and delight. Nor have I ever felt oppressed by the enormous canonical authority Stevens currently possesses, but undoubtedly there are some who have; for those readers Stevens does not fulfill the needs or desires they seek from poetry. Fortunately we are finding it easier to see that what Schwartz hoped in 1949 is possible: that it is not necessary to condemn poets D to Z in order to valorize poets A, B, and C. The selectivity that any reader, critic, or teacher must inevitably employ does not preclude an openness of attitude towards emergent writers, nor does it offer any justification for promulgating critical and theoretical positions such as Kenner's or Bloom's, which attempt to transport a few writers into a monolithic olympus of literary value, leaving all others out in the cold. Rather than calling into question Stevens's place in any canon, then, I would suggest continued scrutiny of the very idea of "the canon." We should attempt to discover what lies beyond the model of literature as a pantheon of "great works" of supposedly intrinsic value, a notion that, in an increasingly multi- and pop-cultural society, has become more a regressive fantasy of conservative nostalgia than a way of effectively interesting contemporary students and readers in literature.

The one conclusion that should be practically indisputable and broadly applicable as a result of this study is that the character and the value of Stevens's poetry has been highly dependent upon broader conceptions of poetic value as they formed and shifted through the decades of this century. If we take seriously the reception theorists' principle that the character of poetic texts is inseparable from the history of their readings, we must also acknowledge that, when the interests and values of critics change, those poets they opt to discuss will appear to change—in effect, will change. This process of continual reconstitution of Stevens persists, as many readers who value his work are now generating interpretations of his significance and value in light of their desire to reconceive modernist poetry as a discourse not isolated in an illusory realm of its own but vitally engaged with its society. Reviewers' accounts of the demise of useful Stevens criticism after the *Letters* were, fortunately, greatly exaggerated. The strength and magnitude of the "Stevens industry" in American academic circles continues to astonish (and occasionally dismay) those trying to keep abreast of it. Between 1980 and the end of 1990 there were at least 33 monographs, 5 books of essays, 62 doctoral dissertations, and over 300 journal articles which took Stevens as a primary subject.[4] In the realm of literary biography alone, we have gone from having almost no reliable biographical material in 1966 to being able to choose among at least eight substantial studies. These works approach Stevens from a great variety of methodological and evaluative perspectives, including Brazeau's fascinating oral transcriptions, Richardson's detailed psychoanalytic portrait, Lentricchia's challenging ideological meditation, and Filreis's indefatigable archival analysis. Such critical heteroglossia is surely a sign of the enrichment that his work offers to contemporary scholars and critics.

Yet, as so often, Stevens criticism is not simply a passive reflection of the trend towards new historicism and ideological criticism but a shaper of that trend. The most suggestive and challenging works on Stevens in recent years, Bates's *Wallace Stevens: A Mythology of Self*, Lentricchia's *Ariel and the Police*, and Filreis's *Wallace Stevens and the Actual World*, represent some of the most notable accomplishments to date in American modernist scholarship towards developing what we might call, to appropriate Fredric Jameson's term, a criticism of the political unconscious. To judge by such rich integrations of history and interpretation as these, the paradigm shift in American criticism from deconstruction to historicism over the past decade has meant no diminution of the value scholarly readers derive from their attention to Stevens.

Within the still developing context of American New Historicism, there is no reason that the discursive entity we know as "Stevens" cannot continue to serve effectively the progressive aspirations for literary criticism advocated and exemplified by the best of his contemporary historicist critics. As Miller has remarked, and as the disagreeing reviews to *Letters* and the various directions of Stevens criticism also suggest, the poet can be and has been portrayed as supporting many different positions.[5] By now, it is clear that Stevens's cultural, social, and political attitudes were enormously complex, often ambivalent, in continual flux, and of great importance to many people interested in twentieth-century American culture. Indeed, this complexity is part of Stevens's continued fascination for us and is a quality now so strongly invested within the institutions of the American academy that future criticism will likely maintain Stevens's position at least in the foreseeable future.[6]

To predict that Stevens will probably remain canonical indefinitely is not to claim that we must or should keep him so. Those of us who appropriate "Stevens" for our critical purposes must frankly admit the lack of a metaphysical authority for any particular interpretation or evaluation of his texts, settling happily enough for the hope that our uses of Stevens will prove useful or helpful to ourselves and others. My hope is that this study, in recovering the oscillating, often contradictory values and interests that elevated Stevens to canonicity, will aid the historicist project of recent years by undermining the long-dominant portrayal of the poet as an apolitical formalist and by suggesting that there have been and continue to be other more humane and inspiring directions for reading and valuing him. I trust that readers have been able to discern which influential conceptions of Stevens's value I have found congenial (the early Blackmur, Matthiessen, Kermode, Miller, Lentricchia) and which I have not (Untermeyer, Pearce, Tindall, Bloom, Perloff); and I hope that they will pursue further the possible uses of Stevens which they find valuable.

To place these aspirations in a somewhat broader context, I will close by noting that the ways in which present and future critics will reinterpret the work of authors such as Stevens will have an impact not only on our understanding of those particular texts but also on their position—and on the position of literature itself—within our culture. Is modern poetry in America to be seen as inhabiting a realm "safe" from the degradations of historical contingency, offering a small number of accomplished readers a reservoir of inherent aesthetic value? Or will it be seen as engaging in substantial dialogue with the social, cultural, and political elements of its times and ours? The answer to such questions does not lie anywhere in the poetry itself but in the ways readers opt to use it. As readers, poets, critics, and teachers, we do largely run the canonical show, whether or not we admit it to ourselves. Since there is no ontologically privileged discourse able to capture the "real" meaning or value of a Stevens or of modernism, all critical discourse is part of a praxis taking place, in Lentricchia's words, "where we always stand in the interpretive act: not on the realist's terra firma but in active ideological contest to shape our culture's sense of history" (*Ariel and the Police*, 21). If we value Stevens and other modernists, if we want them to survive as sources of cultural enrichment and health, we should work towards methods of reading them which will actualize the beneficent social, political, and cultural potentials of their work. We should do so not because the poets meant us to (or did not mean us to), not because that is the only really important function of poetry, but because if we do not succeed in the ongoing ideological contest for what "history," "modernism," and "poetry" mean in America, others will.

Notes

Chapter One

1. As Russell Reising has pointed out, Tompkins's "solutions don't do much more than reverse the roles without solving the underlying problems" (251).
2. One effect "of prohibiting or inhibiting explicit evaluation is to forestall the exhibition and obviate the possible acknowledgement of divergent systems of value and thus to ratify, by default, established evaluative authority" (Smith, "Contingencies," 5–7).
3. I have argued this position more systematically in "Canonical Ahistoricism vs. Histories of Canons."
4. As the ironic adverb "doubtless" suggests, whenever it appears, Bloom's praise for Kenner's critical achievement is yanked away in the next breath: "[Kenner's] Pound may be *the* Pound, even if his Joyce somehow seems less Dublin's Joyce than T. S. Eliot's Joyce" (1).
5. Perloff's binarism has also been usefully critiqued by Kronick, 139–40, and by Schaum, "Lyric Resistance," 191–92.
6. See also 504–5, where Perloff hierarchizes the two poets' employment of geography in their work, approving of Pound's "painstaking exactitude" and pointing out that, in contrast, a map will be of no use in reading Stevens's "An Ordinary Evening in New Haven," as if this told us something conclusive about the poem's ideological propriety. Similarly, in a later article, "Revolving in Crystal: The Impasse of Modernist Lyric," she indicts Stevens because his poems from World War II do not contain explicit references (dates, names) to the momentous world-historical events happening as he was writing them, neglecting the evident if not explicit impact of the war in many of his poems of the period (passim, especially 41–47). For a fuller response to Perloff's portrayal of Stevens during World War II, see Brogan, "Stevens in History," 168–90.
7. For a discussion of this phenomenon of the literary culture of the 1950s as it was enacted in the pages of a seminal little magazine of the period, see Golding, "Little Magazines and Alternative Canons," especially 711–15.
8. These remarks all come from reviews of *The Dance of the Intellect* by George Bornstein, Anthony Woodward, Neil Corcoran, and Vincent Sherry.

9. For a discussion of the premises and consequences of a model of human interaction as a linguistic marketplace, see B. H. Smith, *On the Margins of Discourse*, 79–106.

10. Gerald Graff makes a related point about the course of American literary studies by arguing that twentieth-century definitions of literature as autotelic have implicitly conceded far too much ground to those who dispute that it has any sociopolitical usefulness (28, 46, 141–49).

11. For example, see the remarks that conclude Paul Lauter's essay on "the American literary canon": "Certain other significant forces . . . remain to be examined in detail. But I have found nothing thus far that conflicts with the patterns I have sketched" (37). If it were the case that nothing conflicted with *any* particular pattern, then canonical change, which has obviously not disappeared since the 1920s, would be impossible.

Chapter Two

1. For an indication of how the poet himself felt about this "legend," see his response to O'Connor upon first seeing the book. He disapproved of the first chapter but applauded "the essential part of the book . . . and since that is the part that matters we shall just have to forget about the legend" (L, 677).

2. In chronological order: Peter Brazeau, *Parts of a World: Wallace Stevens Remembered*; Glen G. McLeod, *Wallace Stevens and Company: The Harmonium Years, 1913–1923*; Milton J. Bates, *Wallace Stevens: A Mythology of Self*; Joan Richardson, *Wallace Stevens: The Early Years, 1879–1923* and *Wallace Stevens: The Later Years, 1923–1955*; George S. Lensing, *Wallace Stevens: A Poet's Growth*; Frank Lentricchia, *Ariel and the Police*; Alan Filreis, *Wallace Stevens and the Actual World*.

3. Tracing something as protean as a literary "generation" will not be an exact process. In *The Generation of 1914*, Robert Wohl provides an invaluable critique of totalizations of generational thinking, while still establishing the usefulness of a historicized and relativized version of the concept of "generations" (203–37). I use the term in a far more modest way than the generational theorists discussed by Wohl, not to signify any overarching biological nature or cultural destiny, but to chart a body of formative personal and intellectual experiences which a wide variety of American writers underwent under roughly similar historical circumstances. In analyzing generational kinship and change in this study, I have used a combination of dates of birth and the points at which writers became part of the national literary scene. These generalizations can be made. I will use the term *early modernist* to describe writers who first emerged between around 1910 and 1918. Because of the unusual lack of opportunity encountered by poets who came to adulthood

in the 1890s and 1900s, this term includes a relatively large chronological span of writers born between about 1869 (Masters, Robinson) and 1892 (Millay). The second cluster of modernist writers, the so-called *lost generation,* born mostly between 1892 and about 1899, first came on the national literary scene in the five years or so after the Great War. Their war experiences were often crucial to their sensibilities and substantially divided them from the younger *interwar group,* which consisted of writers born mostly after 1900 and before about 1920, who came on the scene between around 1925 and the late 1930s. Members of this third group were young enough to have passed their adolescent rebellions reading the work of Eliot and Pound, or Frost and Sandburg, rather than Tennyson and Whitman, and can thus be viewed as the first American writers weaned in a cultural environment of modernism.

4. For perhaps the most prominent articulation of the generational structure of literary modernism, see Malcolm Cowley, " 'And Jesse Begat . . .' " (3).

5. Cowley's description is typical of high-modernist hindsight in simply leaving out important figures such as Sandburg and Lindsay, almost exact contemporaries of Stevens, because they have not remained generally canonical, thus skewing the patterns of birthdates toward the 1880s.

6. For helpful accounts of the cultural and professional difficulties faced by some of these writers, see Ziff and C. P. Wilson.

7. C. P. Wilson, 43. Ziff traces the somewhat comical but prevalent distinction genteel editors and publishers made "between great literature and a publishable work," which signified the subservience of innovation to the marketplace even in the established arenas of culture (127–29). For the reaction of genteel editors like Richard Watson Gilder of *The Century* to the cultural democratization of the mass magazines, see John, 237–38.

8. For a provocative analysis of the ideology of the genteel publishing oligopoly which had practically eliminated aesthetic changes in American poetry in the years before 1910, see Lentricchia, "Lyric in the Culture of Late Capitalism" 67–75.

9. For helpful discussions of Stevens's poetic efforts during this decade, see *Souvenirs and Prophecies: The Young Wallace Stevens,* Holly Stevens, ed., and Buttel, *Wallace Stevens: The Making of Harmonium.*

10. C. P. Wilson 48, 195. Ziff discusses the short-lived 1890s precursors of the modernist little magazines (132–45).

11. Figures compiled from Hoffman, Allen, and Ulrich.

12. For an account of this conflict see Ellen Williams, 26–27.

13. McLeod notes that the "Patagonians"—Allen Norton, Donald Evans, and Carl Van Vechten—had met while working at *The New York Times* in 1913 and had schemed to use their newspaper connections to manipulate middlebrow attitudes

in publicizing their avant-garde projects, something done with great success by the organizers of the New York Armory Show and later by the New York Dadaists (4–7). In 1914 Evans started his own short-lived but provocative publishing house, Claire Marie Press, while Norton began the little magazine *Rogue* the following year. Also, Stevens and his Harvard friends, Walter Arensberg, Pitts Sanborn, and Witter Bynner, spent some time as journalists (McLeod, 21).

14. For discussions of the impact of the Armory Show on Stevens and his New York friends, see McLeod, 6–7, 19–22.

15. All figures on publishing totals compiled from Tebbel (2:675–710; 3:680–83). Books of poetry and drama are discussed together because they were measured together in the year-by-year *Publishers' Weekly* totals; Tebbel notes that these figures cannot be taken as exact but that they reflect broad trends fairly accurately.

16. For an account of these new publishers, see Tebbel, 3:113–17, 128–46; Gorham Munson provides a more anecdotal account in *The Awakening Twenties*, 125–48.

17. As a number of commentators have pointed out, much of Stevens's early work, even from 1909, is tinged with the attributes of Imagism. See, for example, Lensing, *Wallace Stevens*, 87–88.

18. Stevens's own comment on this question, made many years later, is pertinent: "[After college] I wrote occasionally [but] it was not until ten or fifteen years later when some friends of mine came down from Cambridge that I became interested again" (quoted in Hatfield, 30).

19. Richardson, 1:424; Kreymborg, *Troubador* 199–200, 219–21. While class origin is by no means an unimportant factor in the development of modernist literature, it does not explain everything; the working-class editor Kreymborg presided over a magazine that professed little interest in political and social issues, while the patrician Harriet Monroe championed such populist writers as Masters, Sandburg, and Lindsay.

20. "We have assumed to be the organ of a great art, the exhibition-place for its best current products" (Monroe, "These Five Years," 33).

21. "Gathering together the things for my book has been so depressing that I wonder at Poetry's [sic] friendliness" (L, 231).

22. "Have you seen this month's *Little Review* with the quotation from the Chinese? Miss Anderson!"; "Signor Alfredo's [Kreymborg's] *Broom* was not such a much"; "Isn't *The Measure* about the worst ever?" (L, 215, 223, 222).

23. In 1922 Stevens told Monroe that he sent her "what I like most" (L, 230).

24. A recent discussion that strongly emphasizes Monroe's relationship with Stevens at the expense of *Others* is in Lensing, *Wallace Stevens*, 245–67.

25. In this autobiography Kreymborg writes of himself in the third person.

26. In 1916, for example, William Carlos Williams could speak of the "triumph" the magazine's inner circle had felt at having been noticed in these widely circulated periodicals ("The Great Opportunity," 137).

27. Both words were used by Kerfoot, 568, and by an anonymous writer (perhaps Kerfoot again) in *Review of Reviews*, 761.

28. "Sunday Morning" eventually appeared with only five of its eight sections in the November 1915 issue of *Poetry*. For further discussion of this episode see chapter 2.

29. One judge dissented adamantly enough to demand a note to that effect ("Prize Announcement," 160).

30. Adding insult to injury, Henderson's attributions to the *Others* work she quoted gave two names incorrectly and reduced others to diminutives ("Rob Carlton Brown," "Skip Cannell"). This parody provoked a good bit of ill-feeling from *Others* poets; Kreymborg responded with a puckish poem, and Alice Groff haughtily called Henderson's piece "amusing but childish" (Poetry 8 (1916): 158). In the following issue of *Poetry*, when Monroe undertook to smooth out these ruffles by making more genial reference to *Others*, she still portrayed herself as the older sister tolerant of her rather manic younger siblings: "*Others* for April . . . arrives rather tardily. We always look for *Others*, no matter who or what is waiting" (*Poetry* 8 (1916): 212). The "gay defiance of wind and weather" by which Monroe repeatedly characterized *Others* implied the frivolity of the latter's avant-gardism (212). To weaken further the peace offering in that same issue, Max Michelson's overdue review of *Others for 1916* was no more than a formulaic catalog of contents, and his review of *Idols*, the new volume by *Others* co-founder Walter Arensberg, nowhere mentioned the magazine ("The Radicals," 151–55; "Arensberg and the New Reality," 208–11).

31. See four separate essays in Aiken's influential 1919 collection of essays *Scepticisms*, 62, 161, 238, 241.

32. For an account of Lowell's feud with *Others*, see Mariani, 134–36; but also see Lowell's favorable response to *Harmonium* in Damon, 656.

33. The pattern of specific Stevens poems mentioned by commentators through 1935 suggests the continuing prominence of *Others* poems. Mentioned or quoted at least once through 1935 were 13 of the 20 poems originally published in *Others*, and 26 of 40 in *Poetry*—exactly the same percentage. But the 13 *Others* poems were mentioned 73 times in all, and the 26 poems from *Poetry* were mentioned little more than half as often, 77 times in all. Of the four magazine poems that could be called Stevens's canonical works during this period—"Peter Quince" (mentioned by 22 commentators); "Le Monocle de Mon Oncle" (17); "Sunday Morning" (16); and "Thirteen Ways of Looking at a Blackbird" (13)—three ap-

peared first in *Others*. Though it is unlikely that issues of *Others* were actually more familiar to these commentators than those of *Poetry*, clearly the poems they found most significant had more often first been published in *Others*.

34. "Current Poetry," 1300–1303; Braithwaite's selections were mentioned in two other important cultural journals: the *Dial* (59 (1915), 477), and *The New Republic* (Soule 223).

35. *Reviews of Reviews* 761; Monroe and Henderson, *The New Poetry* (New York: Macmillan, 1917, 1923).

36. Monroe, "Others Again" 160; Fletcher, "Some Contemporary American Poets" 29; and reviews of *Harmonium* by Marianne Moore, *Dial* 56 (1924), 89; by Raymond Holden, *Measure* 4 (March 1924), 17; by Untermeyer, "Among the New Books" 160; by J. C. Squire, *London Mercury* 12 (1925), 657; and by the reviewer for the Boston *Transcript*, December 29, 1923, pt. 6, p. 5.

37. Information compiled from *Granger's Index to Poetry and Recitations*, 3rd ed. (1940).

38. *Others* anthologies were mentioned by *Poetry*, *The Nation*, the *New York Times*, and smaller periodicals.

39. The percentage of *Others* contributors who were still actively publishing poetry in the 1920s and who appeared in *The Dial* was significantly higher, since this list of thirty-seven includes several figures such as Man Ray and William Zorach, who were visual artists and not primarily poets by all.

40. The fifth was not an *Others* rival but *The Dial* discovery E. E. Cummings, who belonged to a later generation.

41. Figures compiled from *The Borzoi, 1920*.

42. Kreymborg, *Mushrooms* (1916); Johns, *Asphalt and Other Poems* (1917); John McClure, *Airs and Ballads* (1918); Pound, *Lustra* (1918); Bynner, *Beloved Stranger* (1919) and *A Canticle of Pan* (1920); Eliot, *Poems* (1920); Bodenheim, *Advice* (1920); Aiken, *Punch: The Immortal Liar* (1921) and *The Pilgrimage of Festus* (1923): Adelaide Crapsey, *Poems* (1922); Stevens, *Harmonium* 1923.

43. Bodenheim placed 42 items in *Others*, 22 in *Poetry*; Hoyt 13 and 41; Kreymborg 43 and 14; Pound 7 and 81; Sandburg 13 and 63; Stevens 20 and 42; Williams 28 and 40. Figures compiled from Sader, *Comprehensive Index to Little Magazines*.

44. Zukofsky, 29; for an informative discussion of the strong kinship Zukofsky felt with Stevens, and of the implications of that kinship for the dualistic conception of modernist poetry set forth by Marjorie Perloff in "Pound/Stevens: Whose Era," see Golding, "The 'Community of Elements,' " 121–40.

45. "The Free Verse Movement in America"; "Wallace Stevens," 39–45; *A Poet's*

Life, passim. Also see Lensing, *Wallace Stevens*, 262–64, for futher discussion of Monroe's later advocacy of Stevens.

46. For a typical example of the major/minor duality as applied to Stevens, see Edmund Wilson, "Wallace Stevens and E. E. Cummings" 102–3.

47. I use the term *canonical potential* in a way that should be distinguished from Alastair Fowler's term *potential canon,* which he uses to refer to any work preserved anywhere for possible readership. My term is meant to describe specifically the changing status of a reputation over the decades in which attributes of implicit permanence and centrality begin to develop around writing from that author's own generation, and is thus closer to Fowler's term *accessible canon.* See Fowler, 230–33.

48. Monroe, "A Cavalier of Beauty," 327; Josephson, 236: "his production . . . has influenced many of his younger contemporaries, and in them, at least, it leads to pretense, and murkiness."

Chapter Three

1. Aiken referred readers to Monroe and Henderson's *The New Poetry* for Stevens's work.

2. Munson also noted that the essay containing this observation, written in 1925, had trouble finding magazine space exactly because Crane had not published a book. It first appeared in 1928 in Munson's book of critical essays.

3. This omnibus format was itself a point of contention in the scramble for critical recognition. As he often would, Aiken spoke out on Stevens's behalf, objecting to *Freeman* reviewer John Gould Fletcher: "Stevens and I have both reached the point that we deserve something better than a few lines in a group review" (*Selected Letters*, 83).

4. Letter to Williams quoted in the Preface to *Kora in Hell*, reprinted in Williams, *Selected Essays* 13.

5. Monroe, " 'Others' Again" 156; *A Poet's Life* 342. In the issue of *Poetry* which contained "Phases" Monroe suggested her mystification by remarking in the biographical notes that "Mr. Wallace Stevens is as yet unknown to the editor" ("Notes on Contributors" 97).

6. Josephson referred to Stevens, Williams, Moore, and Cummings as having "cultured hands"; see also Untermeyer, who called Stevens's instrument of language "a color-palette" ("Among the New Books," 159).

7. This very apt phrase is Joseph Riddel's, from "The Contours of Stevens Criticism," 110.

8. To see how Gorham Munson's *Secession,* for example, treated Monroe less

than reverently, see no. 2 (1922), in which Secessionist Matthew Josephson is facetiously described as having been "recently wounded in a duel [that] arose, it is rumored, from a quarrel concerning a certain lady editor and poetess of Cass Street, Chicago" (1). I suspect it is no coincidence that Munson and Josephson both exhibited a strong early interest in Stevens which never flowered into effective advocacy.

9. Glen McLeod has made connections between such Stevens poems as "Anecdote of the Jar" and Marcel Duchamp's salutary critiques of the conventional mechanisms and standards of value in the visual arts (34–39). Whatever the level of congruence between their theoretical intentions, Stevens's acquaintance with Duchamp and his work is unquestionable.

10. "The very titles of his poems accentuate this disregard of perspective and mass not only by their charming incongruity with the lines which follow them but in their equally arbitrary selection for mere color values" (Untermeyer, *American Poetry Since 1900*, 324); Fletcher spoke similarly of "the deliberate use of misleading titles" ("The Revival of Aestheticism," 356).

11. The habit of naming poems with a particular form is found in other avant-garde modernists, but usually with very different functions. Pound often updated old forms like the villanelle and the ballad, but with a straightforward respect for their conventional attributes. Eliot most often used the reader's knowledge of the form and the discrepancy between its normal tenor and his use of it, to make ironic comments about his world. Prufrock's love song was sung to no one who loved him, and to no one he loved, but in this disparity the formal term "love song" still signified a recognizable form within a cultural tradition.

12. "The authentic poet walks in his own world, is native of his own country, and speaks a language not wholly intelligible to any other" (Seiffert, 154).

13. For a discussion of the widely held "Paterian" view of the poem, which Monroe's stanzaic arrangement would have made all the more accessible to early readers, see Bates, *Wallace Stevens*, 111–12.

14. The poem's remarkably casual attitude towards life was confirmed by Stevens in a 1928 letter, in which he paraphrased the last two lines as, "Life is meaningless as dew" (L, 250).

15. Ficke's note to Harriet Monroe is quoted in Monroe, *A Poet's Life*, 390.

16. As, for example, the stringency of William Carlos Williams's work was eased by his public persona, who, despite having plenty of avant-garde antagonism, obviously and passionately believed in the value of writing poetry.

17. This account sounds as though Stevens would not lift a finger to help Van Vechten and Knopf put the project together, which was not strictly true.

18. For a survey of Stevens's remarkably sluggish reputation in England, see Lensing's "Wallace Stevens in England," 130–48.

19. He continued with a civil attack on non-Stevens views of the poem: "A mind that examines such a poem for its prose contents gets absolutely nothing from it" (L, 251).

20. See, for example, Munson, "The *Others* Parade" 228–34.

21. In "Interstice Between Scylla and Charybdis," 30, Munson explicitly identified "the American literary milieu of the past decade" as the target of *Secession*'s campaign of "resignation from a milieu whose objects are other than ours."

Chapter Four

1. "Dear Mr. Knopf, You wrote to me in the spring about reprinting Harmonium . . . ," Stevens's reply of October 16, 1930 (L, 259).

2. Hutchison's terminological confection of "ideas," "life," and "emotion" is rendered even more confused by the final point about doctrine, since Stevens's only doctrine, according to the reviewer, has been that of "pure poetry."

3. These phrases are from the following reviews: *Boston Evening Transcript*, September 2, 1931, pt. 4:3; Shepard, 207; Hutchison, 4.

4. The essay was also reprinted in Blackmur's volumes *The Double Agent* (1935), *Language as Gesture* (1952), and *Form and Value in Modern Poetry* (1957).

5. See, for example, Stevens's 1928 comments on "Domination of Black" (L, 251).

6. In *Stevens and Simile*, Brogan provides an extensive and useful discussion of the importance of the poet's employment of *as if* as conjoining "the unitive and disjunctive processes of language in a precarious threshold of impossible possibility" (133).

7. For example, the soon-to-be-ubiquitous doctrine of the "objective correlative" from Eliot's essay on *Hamlet* lurked behind this remark, which set up a familiar isolationist distinction between rhetorical (literary) language and merely communicative language: "rhetorical language, dealing . . . with inflections, employed with . . . seriousness, creates a surface equivalent to an emotion by its approximately complete escape from the purely communicative function of language" (73).

8. In considering the descent of Stevens into contemporary poetry, Michael Davidson relies upon a somewhat similar distinction between the poetics of orthodox New Criticism and those of Stevens.

9. For the statements by Brooks, Warren, and Tate, see *Wallace Stevens Number, Harvard Advocate*, 29–32.

10. Melita Schaum has analyzed the sequence of Blackmur's eventual movement away from Stevens (*Wallace Stevens and the Critical Schools*, 68–76).

11. Stevens in March of 1933: "For some reason I have had a good many requests for poems recently" (*L*, 265).

12. This count represents 23 of 31 poems published between 1930 and 1935. Included are 3 poems sent to the *Westminster Magazine*, which had been around since 1911 but in 1935 had been recently reconstituted by young editors. Of the other 8 poems, 5 went to *The New Republic*, 2 to *Poetry*, and 1 to the *Southern Review*. Figures compiled from Edelstein.

13. For further discussion of Latimer's role in Stevens's return, see Lensing, *Wallace Stevens*, 122–23.

14. *L*, 271, 273, 274; for the Monroe letter, see *L*, 218.

15. For accounts of many of Stevens's professional and literary friendships, see Brazeau, 69–93. Brazeau quotes Eberhart on Stevens's generational authority: "He was a very distinguished-looking man. I was twenty-five years younger, so I think he was a sort of father figure. You had a certain respect for him due to his age, not only his position in letters" (147–48).

16. For contrast, see the responses of Allen Tate (28–30), Kenneth Fearing (33), Gertrude Stein (40–41), and William Carlos Williams (42–43), particularly to question 3 on the value of criticism to a writer.

17. There is some evidence that recent readers of *Harmonium* had been struck by the qualities of Stevens's work that seemed new or current rather than what seemed familiar or dated. The patterns of *Harmonium* poems mentioned by reviewers in 1931 suggest that they were drawn for the first time toward Stevens's more austere "philosophical" poems such as "The Emperor of Ice-Cream," "The Doctor of Geneva," "The Man Whose Pharynx Was Bad," and "The Death of a Soldier," at the expense of some of the formally spectacular poems prominently praised and abused in the 1923 reviews ("Bantams in Pine-Woods," "Peter Quince," "Last Looks at the Lilacs," "The Paltry Nude Starts on a Spring Voyage.")

18. Such declines of earlier modernist reputations in the 1930s were numerous. Amy Lowell fell perhaps the greatest distance, though the comparison with Stevens is perhaps unfair since she had no opportunity to face the depression years. The fates of Mina Loy, Conrad Aiken, John Gould Fletcher, and Alfred Kreymborg are also relevant here. Loy, like Stevens, published a single overdue volume of spectacular avant-garde verse (*Lunar Baedeker*, 1924) but then made no strong comeback in middle age, and her reputation virtually disappeared until the 1960s. Aiken, Fletcher, and Kreymborg, all several years younger than Stevens, published prolifically through the 1910s and 1920s, gaining reputations as polished and interesting, perhaps "minor," poets, as Stevens was also seen, but their reputations de-

clined sharply in the 1930s, partially because they had been too clearly typed as aesthetes of those earlier decades. Despite the ambition of some of their later work, these poets were never reclaimed by later readers from appearing dated.

19. Over the next two decades Schwartz would further develop this historical account, with an ever-increasing belief in Stevens's majority, in "The Ultimate Plato With Picasso's Guitar" "Instructed of Much Mortality: A Note on the Poetry of John Crowe Ransom," and "Wallace Stevens: An Appreciation." For further discussion of the important kinship between Stevens and Schwartz see Bauer 206–225.

20. George Lensing takes Burnshaw's evaluation of Stevens out of context, misreading Burnshaw as flatly saying that " 'Stevens can no longer write' " (*Wallace Stevens*, 126), suggesting that the critic believed that Stevens's ability had been utterly destroyed by the times and thus trivializing Burnshaw's analysis of Stevens's concerns into mere "cant" (127). This misunderstanding is highly symptomatic of a tendency among later commentators on Stevens to distort, devalue, or dismiss the poet's engagement with contemporary political conditions. On the contrary, I believe Burnshaw was quite correct in seeing widespread "turmoil" in writers of "the middle ground" in 1935—including Stevens.

21. For an example of how the Burnshaw review is seen by the author himself and by contemporary commentators, see Filreis and Teres, 109–21, and Burnshaw, "Reflections on Wallace Stevens" 122–26.

22. Actually, more often such rigid responses came from the right wing, from critics like Yvor Winters, Howard Baker, and Morton Zabel, whose evaluations suggested that urgent engagement with contemporary social problems made first-rate poetry impossible.

23. North, 189. For his helpful analysis of Stevens's use of the imagery of public monuments, see 186–89, 207–27.

24. Interestingly, Moore's comparison was echoed by an interwar poet-critic, Robert Fitzgerald: "after the reader has admired certain lines because Shakespeare might have written them, he begins to admire them because only Stevens could" (154).

25. Zabel's volumes aspired to span the gamut of mainstream American critical positions, from leftists such as Cowley, Wilson, Newton Arvin, and Philip Rahv to the New Critical conservatives Winters, Brooks, Warren, Ransom, and Joseph Wood Krutch.

26. It undoubtedly also had a strong influence on its canons of poets. Zabel's editorial influence was by no means anonymous, asserting itself by including, for example, Yvor Winters's devastating essays "Robert Frost: or, the Spiritual Drifter as Poet" and "Robinson Jeffers," both of which were in evident concord with Zabel's views of these poets in the *Southern Review* essay.

27. Such a process, taking place largely at nonconscious evaluative levels, illustrates the extent to which canons have strong links to the workings of ideology, most effective as they become so perfectly a part of the perceptual and evaluative apparatus that they seem to disappear altogether. A major part of contemporary critics' aspirations to broaden literary canons, then, is a dual effort: first, to identify and anatomize the negative characterizations of previous readers as characterizations rather than as the structure of reality itself; and then to break through these evaluative encrustations to a position in which writers and their work can be reread and reevaluated with relatively open minds. In modernist studies this kind of strategy has so far been practiced most successfully by feminist critics who have begun to free a number of important female poets from the highly sexist preconceptions of much New Criticism.

Chapter Five

1. See, for example, the review of *Ideas of Order* in *The New Masses* by Isidor Schneider, who sounded at times much like Untermeyer fifteen years before: "But [Stevens] pays the usual price for over-concern with craftsmanship. With the delighting sound there is rarely comparably delighting sense, and only too often the sound is won at the cost of sense" (24).

2. Brazeau, for example, describes the seventy-one-year-old Stevens's busy schedule of New York appearances in 1951 (189).

3. On Stevens's relationships with Heringman, see Brazeau 199–205; with Gruen, see Brazeau, 205–9. Stevens's friendship with Simons is reflected especially in L, 496–97. There is also an entire volume of Stevens's correspondence with Rodríguez-Feo, *Secretaries of the Moon*, Coyle and Filreis, eds.

4. For more information on these efforts, see Brazeau, 182–83. Also worth noting is Bauer's suggestive description of Steven's conception of a chair of poetry as an institutional "positive force in a matrix of forces" which make up culture and his concomitant rejection of autotelic New Critical notions of the poem divorced from history and culture (210–11). As Bauer points out, Stevens indicated his particular admiration for Schwartz by strongly recommending him as a participant in this project (211).

5. See also the review by John Unterecker, who posited that *The Necessary Angel* "may well become a basic text of modern criticism" (25).

6. For an example of this process, see Frederick Morgan's 1953 characterization of Archibald MacLeish's later career: "the liberal-pamphleteering poems that date from the New Deal era—and very dated they are—are probably the worst; but this kind of basic uncertainty of purpose seems to have dogged MacLeish throughout

his career, largely vitiating . . . his poetic accomplishment." MacLeish had all too often been tempted from his true calling as a lyricist by "some nervous compulsion to retreat from the hard task of making verse, and to seek refuge in a more reassuring external reality" (132). Thus Morgan put himself in the dubious position of implying that in 1953 it was somehow an artistic and moral evasion to have dealt with the "more reassuring" realities of depression, world war, and McCarthyism, instead of making the superhuman effort to write a really good poem (131–34).

7. Particularly valuable in this collection is Jacqueline Vaught Brogan's article "Stevens in History and Not in History: The Poet and the Second World War," which offers the fullest account of a Stevens who was "deeply responsive to the politics and reality of his times" (168). For other sympathetic attempts to read Stevens works politically, see Frank Lentricchia, *Ariel and the Police* (3–28, 135–244); Melita Schaum, "Lyric Resistance: Views of the Political in the Poetics of Wallace Stevens and H. D."; and my article "Life Anywhere But on a Battleship: Stevens's Wartime Poetry and the Apolitics of Postwar Criticism."

8. For Gregory's earlier opinion of Stevens see his review of *Harmonium*, 28.

9. "The Noble Rider and the Sound of Words" (written 1941), in *NA*, 36.

10. "A poem is like a natural object" (*OP* 1989, 205); "the imagination does not add to reality" (*OP* 1989, 203).

11. As Helen Vendler has argued, the grammatical appositive was one of Stevens's prevalent strategies for creating poetic forms that captured the provisionality and relativity of his themes (*On Extended Wings*, 14–17). It might be added, however, that Vendler's emphasis tends to be on Stevens's "credence . . . that these things are all genuinely parts of the truth" (16), portraying him as a diminished latter-day romantic unhappily unable to make such affirmations straightforwardly; my emphasis is to see the very equivocality and doubtfulness of these affirmations as positive forces, as a skeptical balancing of resistances, equally opposed to nihilistic despair and to the ideological blandishments of the status quo.

12. "The Necessary Angels of Earth," 665. To be fair to Koch, at other points she acknowledged that this "opposition" was less dichotomous and more interactive; for example, in her title and in the essay, she quoted the revealing phrase "the necessary angel of earth" from "Angel Surrounded by Paysans" (see note 14).

13. In 1954 Stevens flatly stated as much (*L*, 852) in commenting on "Angel Surrounded by Paysans," the poem which ended *The Auroras of Autumn*, and which refers to "the angel of reality" and "the necessary angel of earth" (*CP*, 496–97). See also *L*, 661, where he says he was "definitely trying to think of an earthly figure, not a heavenly figure."

14. It is reasonable to say that in this formulation "reality" is to "fact" as "the imagination" is to "consciousness." Also, this state of mere "consciousness" is

closely connected to Stevens's reference to "the pressure of reality" in "The Noble Rider" as "the pressure of an external event or events on the consciousness to the exclusion of any power of contemplation" (*NA*, 20).

15. The poet argued this point more explicitly in his first prose address, "The Irrational Element in Poetry," in 1936: "Resistance is the opposite of escape. . . . Resistance to the pressure of the ominous and destructive circumstance consists of its conversion, so far as possible, into a different, an explicable, an amenable circumstance" (*OP*, 225). Also see Schaum's discussion of Stevens's conception of "resistance" in "Lyric Resistance" (201–2); and Litz's useful delineation of Stevens's use of the terms "pure poetry," "escapism," and "the pressure of reality" ("Wallace Stevens's Defense of Poetry," 111–32).

16. Similarly, Louise Bogan reshaped Stevens's distinction between imagination and fact into a cutting insinuation of the poet's snobbishness and insularity: "of late . . . Stevens has begun to write poems obliquely directed against the blundering obtuseness of 'politic man.' . . . He now seems obsessed by his defense of the imagination against 'the world of fact' " (review of *Parts of a World*, 72).

17. See, for example, the final sentence of a 1947 essay by Fred Laros: "Finally, it is one of the peculiarities of the present development of poetry that Stevens's esthetic ideas should have placed him in a position of isolation as the poet of 'the ultimate elegance, the imagined land' " (15).

18. In his review of *Parts of a World*, F. Cudworth Flint also saw this line functioning to affirm the interdependence of the terms "the imagination" and "reality." Flint asserted that Stevens's poetic "pluralism" was clearly rooted in material reality ("knowledge is attained not by denying objects or explaining them away, but by dwelling on them, by clinging to them intently with our minds") but also that "imagination" and "reality" were unified by the "elegance of his imagery, his diction, and his rhythms so that the total body of his poems moves toward 'The ultimate elegance: the imagined land' " (134). For his part Stevens remarked in 1940, "I don't agree with the people who say that I live in a world of my own; I think that I am perfectly normal, but I see that there is a center. For instance, a photograph of a lot of fat men and women in the woods, drinking beer and singing Hi-li-lo convinces me that there is a normal that I ought to try to achieve" (*L*, 352).

19. In his autobiography Snow openly acknowledged his refusal to accept fully anything Stevens wrote after *Harmonium*—a judgment that Stevens himself knew and disapproved of (395).

20. Published the year after Snow's speech, *Literary History of the United States*, that monumental compendium of the preconceptions and biases of the mid-century literary culture, also referred to Stevens's main concern as "the opposition between bare reality and what the imagination can make of it," evoking the same

phrase from "Another Weeping Woman" as well as the "ultimate elegance: the imagined land," the widely quoted phrase from "Mrs. Alfred Uruguay," (Spiller, 1355).

21. Contrast remarks such as Viereck's with Stevens's own insistence, in his delineation of the character of "the possible poet" in the modern world, on the necessity of *not* making this exclusive choice: it will be "imperative for [the possible poet] to make a choice, to come to a decision regarding the imagination and reality; and he will find that it is not a choice of one over the other and not a decision that divides them, but something subtler, a recognition that here, too . . . the universal interdependence exists, and hence his choice and his decision must be that they are equal and inseparable" ("The Noble Rider," NA, 24).

22. Discussing "Description Without Place," Brogan suggests the importance of Stevens's use of the word "description" in demonstrating his depth of awareness of the power and ubiquity of politically implicated discourse: "Given how powerful 'descriptions' had proven to be—in reality—given that they can determine a place, and by dissent or consent, start or end an atrocious war, it seems to me that Stevens is ethically correct (rather than escapist) when he says that he finds it impossible to believe that he is living in the 'Atomic Age'. . . . Accepting the description of our world as 'Atomic'—or now 'Nuclear'—is suicidal" ("Stevens in History," 184).

23. Here Blackmur suggested that Stevens acknowledged his own failing through the use of the phrase "the imagination's Latin," but this is clearly a debatable interpretation, arguably a substantial distortion, of the eighth section of "It Must Change," in which the poet's task is to "compound" "the imagination's Latin" with "the lingua franca et jocundissima" in order to "speak / The peculiar potency of the general" (CP, 396). Blackmur's isolation of the former phrase from its context was yet another instance of the critical tendency to abstract one element from a pair (or more) of interdependent terms, an action that undermined the validity of the entire formulation. In this case, what was lost was Stevens's sense that, whatever its cultural heritage or past value, if "the imagination's Latin" was not put into play with the lingua franca, then the poet's "peculiar speech" became as dead a language as Latin.

24. Weiss mentioned Cleanth Brooks and Ransom by name ("The Nonsense of Winters' 'Anatomy," 212).

25. See "Poets Without Laurels," in the seminal New Critical text, *The World's Body*, where Ransom's comparison between the poetry of Stevens and Tate, ostensibly descriptive of two "distinct styles of modernity" (58), was laden with judgments that devalued Stevens's work as "pure poetry" with "no moral, political, religious, or sociological values" (59), "trifling" subject matter (59), and "little or no moral importance" (60).

26. The antirationalist "dread" Sypher speaks of in Stevens is surely not borne out by "Asides on the Oboe," in which the "glass man" is portrayed as "the impossible possible philosophers' man" who "in a million diamonds sums us up," who chants "for those buried in their blood," and in whose "poems we find peace" (*CP*, 250–51).

27. In his entire long essay, the only post-*Harmonium* work Winters quoted from was taken out of context. "The Mechanical Optimist," the first part of the 1936 poem "A Thought Revolved," is in its title and positioning a relatively explicit description of an inadequate or incomplete mode of thinking that would be questioned and modified by the other three parts of the poem as they were revolved by the persona; Winters treated it as if it were a complete, representative poem.

28. Stevens was given 47 pages, as was Frost; Robinson occupied 46, Pound and Eliot 36 each, and Hart Crane 35.

29. As evidence of this process, these years saw a dramatic increase in the salability of Stevens's books. From *Ideas of Order* through *Parts of a World*, Knopf's first editions had consisted of about 1,000 copies. In 1947 *Transport to Summer*'s first printing was for 1,750 copies (with another printing of 1,500 in 1951). Just three years later Knopf could feel confident issuing both *The Auroras of Autumn* and *The Necessary Angel* in first printings of 3,000 copies. Despite not being new work, *Harmonium* 1947 sold quite as vigorously as any of these new books, going through printings of between 1,000 and 1,500 copies every three years, being reprinted in August 1950 and December 1953 (data compiled from Edelstein).

30. For a similar assessment, see also Daiches, 355–56.

31. For an account of Brooks's postwar reputation, see Vanderbilt, 466–68.

32. Bender offers a brief but useful discussion of the fetishization of "freedom" through the whole postwar New York art scene as it contributed to "the making of the U.S. interpretation of the Cold War" (339–40).

33. Wald has ably chronicled this seductive postwar notion of an end to or freedom from ideology in *The New York Intellectuals* (226–49). Wald's work is especially valuable in placing the growth of this position into the context of the powerful group of depression-era-leftists-turned-postwar-anticommunists named in his title. More than the perpetually right-wing New Critics, the New York intellectuals exemplified the trajectory away from politics in American literary criticism between 1935 and 1960.

34. Vanderbilt offers a helpful account of the enthusiasm with which young professors greeted the principles espoused in Brooks and Warren's *Understanding Poetry* during these years (485–88).

35. For an excellent analysis of the persistence of New Critical assumptions in the literary academy, see Cain, 85–121.

36. Before 1945 the only pieces on Stevens in such journals had been one article in *Romanic Review* in 1934 and one item in the *Explicator* in 1944; figures compiled from Leary and Edelstein.

37. For accounts of the startlingly quick rise of American studies, see Vanderbilt, 488–90, and Gleason, 343–58.

38. The dynamics of this split, and particularly the historians' abandonment of twentieth-century literature to "critics," can be seen as far back as 1929, with the founding at Duke of the first journal in the field, *American Literature*, whose stated policy for years was to publish only articles on dead authors. As editor Jay B. Hubbell presented the journal's policy in the first issue, "For those who wish to discuss the work of living authors, there are many periodicals available" ("Foreword," n.p). Such periodicals were not found in the academy in 1929, and very few existed even twenty years later.

39. For further discussion of the changes in critical conceptions of modernist poetry beginning around 1940, and their effects on the reputations of prominent poets, see my article "Archibald MacLeish and the Poetics of Public Speech: A Critique of High Modernism."

40. Untermeyer, "Departure from Dandyism," 11; for another example of a critic's imputation of his own two-world dichotomy onto Stevens, see Winters's careless dualized reading of "Stars at Tallapoosa": "As far as I can penetrate this poem, I judge that it postulates an absolute severance of the intellectual and the emotional" ("Wallace Stevens," 434).

41. This slighting anti-intellectual and antipolitical view of Stevens and of the function of poetry runs in a direct line through the past five decades of criticism, manifesting itself most prominently of all in Harold Bloom's undercutting of Stevens's intellectual seriousness in order to buttress his own theories of poetry as influence anxiety. B. J. Leggett has recently analyzed Bloom's strategies in his *Wallace Stevens and Poetic Theory* (60–71).

42. Note, for example, "the janitor's poems / Of every day" in "The Man on the Dump"; also see L, 340. On the other hand, note Martz's emphasis on the insularity of "the poet" in his description of that most communicative of Stevens's later poems, "Of Modern Poetry": "And as this actor speaks his meditated words, they find a growing response on a certain invisible audience, which is not simply us, the readers or listeners, but is first of all the larger, total mind of the poet himself, controlling the actor, who is some projected aspect of himself" ("The World as Meditation," 224). For a more balanced description of the place of communication in Stevens's work, see Jarrell's remark on "The World as Meditation": "When Stevens writes . . . of Penelope waiting for Ulysses, it is not Penelope and Ulysses but

Stevens and the sun, the reader and the world—two in a deep-founded sheltering, friend and dear friend" ("The Collected Poems," 182).

43. As recently as 1984, Helen Vendler quoted Stevens's informal valediction to our profession, which he inscribed in the copy of *Collected Poems* owned by his daughter's English professor in 1955. There Stevens cautioned the professor to remember that "when I speak of the poem, I mean not merely a literary form, but the brightest and most harmonious concept, or order, of life" (*Wallace Stevens*, 5). Not "my life"; simply "life." Yet just a few pages later, Vendler's first principle for the "neophyte deciphering Stevens" is this remarkably reductive advice: "substitute 'I' whenever Stevens says 'he' or 'she': for 'Divinity must live within herself,' read 'Divinity must live within myself,' and so on" (44). Vendler's example is especially inapt; there is nothing in "Sunday Morning" which dictates substituting "I" rather than "we"; indeed, the second half of the poem abounds with collective formulations, climaxing in a crucial opposition of singular and plural pronouns, between the obsolete stones of Jesus' grave ("where he lay") and the vital human world of the present ("we live in an old chaos of the sun").

44. Six years later Fred Laros echoed Cargill almost exactly (15). The obsession with remaining free of "cliques" and "schools," which was one of the most central features of early modernist rhetoric and which lessened during the 1930s, made a strong comeback afer the war to become a major tenet of the "major author" fetish that substantially narrowed the canons of modernist literature by the 1960s.

45. The most extensive critical use of "symbolism" in these years was, of course, Charles Feidelson's *Symbolism and American Literature* (1953). Feidelson briefly used Stevens's "The Idea of Order at Key West" as an illustration of the principle that the symbolist's "characteristic subject is its own equivocal method," in which "poetic speech is its own best theme," once again emphasizing the enfeebling closed circuit of poetic subject matter and meaning in which Stevens critics have tended to place the poet's work (73).

46. Remarkably enough, Walcutt's article never once mentioned a much more obvious reason for rejecting the student's reading than its faulty use of symbolism: the fact that the poem was written in 1919. That this anachronism was apparently of no concern to Walcutt suggests that the student's error might well have been a result of the New Critical habit of teaching texts without supplying dates of composition (or sometimes even without authors' names). To let the text 'speak for itself' by so radically decontextualizing it from the circumstances of its production was thus to discourage or even make impossible historically sensitive reading practices.

47. My thinking here is indebted to Frank Lentricchia's juxtaposition of "Anecdote of the Jar" with William James's protests against American imperialism in the

Philippines and with Michael Herr's *Dispatches*, to form "three voices from a tradition of American anti-imperialist writing" (*Ariel and the Police*, 21).

48. So much so that, despite the rise of a great industry of Pound criticism after 1955, it was not until the late 1970s that anyone translated excerpts and briefly discussed the suppressed Cantos 72 and 73, in which the worst of the Poundian conjunction of literature and politics came clear (see Eastman and Bucigalupo). Only in very recent years has the critique of Pound's politics attained weight sufficient to produce a full-scale canonical debate, thanks largely to Robert Casillo's *A Genealogy of Demons*.

49. Smith's magazine had been the sponsor of the most vociferous attacks in the campaign against the Bollingen award to Pound the previous year. Alan Filreis advances a similar theory of Stevens's appropriateness during these years in *Wallace Stevens and the Actual World* (245–46).

Chapter Six

1. In the same year Louise Bogan seconded this estimate of Stevens by noting, "Now that he is so widely imitated, it is important to remember that his method is a special one; that modern poetry has developed transparent, overflowing, and spontaneous qualities that Stevens ignores" (review of *The Auroras of Autumn*, 130). Here Bogan felt the need of explicitly distinguishing between "Stevens" and "modern poetry," as if his actual or potential influence were so great as to subsume the whole notion of what modern poetry was—a process that had largely happened with Eliot some years before.

2. *Trinity Review* 8 (May 1954); *Perspective* 7 (Autumn 1954).

3. There were apparently no reviews of *The Auroras of Autumn* in mass-circulation newspapers outside New York. *Collected Poems*, on the other hand, was discussed by dailies in Pasadena, Chicago, San Francisco, Baltimore, Hartford, Louisville, Dallas, and Providence; probably as a result of the success of the 1954 volume, *Opus Posthumous* was noticed even more widely, by dailies in Bridgeport, Los Angeles (2), Nashville, Buffalo, Indianapolis, Dallas, Richmond (2), Madison, San Francisco, Fort Wayne, Chicago, Cleveland, Houston, Hartford, and Louisville. Information compiled from Edelstein.

4. In 1958 Barbara Gibbs echoed this theme of inexhaustibility by describing Stevens's last poems in *Opus Posthumous* as "poems that can be read and re-read, becoming more marvelous each time" (56).

5. Perhaps such a remark can be used to evoke (one last time) the importance to Stevens's canonicity of that network of values and assumptions centered around Harvard, the quintessential institution for maintaining the myth of New England as

the center of American civilization. This Harvard network had, in various ways, strongly supported Stevens throughout his career, from his undergraduate literary experiences, to his first entry into the literary culture in the mid-1910s, through the 1940 issue of the *Advocate,* and in the continuing evaluations of such Harvard-associated critics as Schwartz and Matthiessen.

6. Also see the review of *Collected Poems* by Morse, who asserted that the most prominent Stevens texts "have become part not only of the way we look at things, but also of what we see. They are part of the reality of our century" (3).

7. "The Poetry of Wallace Stevens" *(Times Literary Supplement)* 46; another favorite tactic, still evasive but impressive enough in itself, was to call him "one of the greatest of living poets" (Jarrell, review of *Collected Poems,* 100).

8. This remark came, interestingly enough, in the context of Stevens's initial response to the first critical book on himself. Likening the experience of reading the biographical chapter of *The Shaping Spirit* to "looking over a batch of negatives from a photographer," Stevens acknowledged that this was a "universal" response and that he would "limit [him]self to one thing" to object to. This one thing was his objection to O'Connor's statement that Stevens knew Eliot even slightly. It seems as if Stevens found bothersome the experience of seeing Eliot's name associated with himself in his own book and wanted to state unambiguously that they had never met.

9. See, for example, Van Wyck Brooks's remark, "Reading [Stevens's] poems one felt as if a window of Chartres had been shattered, and the lovely bits of color lay on the grass, and one forgot the picture, which one could scarcely reconstruct, in the pleasure of letting these fragments fall through one's fingers" (quoted in Spencer, 26).

10. "Actuary Among the Spondees," 26: the first of the quoted phrases in this sentence came from Meyer, the rest come from Stevens's letter.

11. See Stevens's bemused but affectionate 1954 comment on Sandburg's massive popularity (L, 765–66).

12. The figures I refer to here are listed under Edelstein's category "Articles in Periodicals." Book reviews are nominally not covered in this section, but the bibliographer has included some reviews that were presumably judged to contain more substantial content than a sheerly ephemeral notice would have.

13. The following information on Eliot is compiled from Martin. These figures included many ephemeral items and fluctuated rather drastically with the review fortunes of Eliot's plays. While they are not ideally comparable to the Stevens results, if we examine the respective percentages of change between the 1940s and the 1960s, they do prove illustrative:

NOTES TO PAGES 204–206   265

1931–35   392 items
1936–40   301   1951–55   350
1941–45   186   1956–60   274
1946–50   546   1961–65   542

The yearly average between 1956 and 1965 was 81.6 items, less than twice the average of 48.7 in 1936–45, and slightly less than the 89.6 items per year between 1946 and 1955. Thus we can postulate that overall critical attention (though not necessarily scholarly attention) to Eliot peaked around 1950 and declined somewhat after 1955. (The 1961–65 figure is clearly skewed by the large number of obituaries in 1965, which produced a total of 96 entries, the largest yearly number since 1954.)

14. The figures on dissertations are compiled from Woodress. A note on procedure: unless specified otherwise, I counted titles that mention either one or two modernist poets, but not more than two. Both foreign dissertations and those still in progress when Woodress's volume was printed were excluded. The poets covered were Stevens, Eliot, Aiken, Stephen Vincent Benét, John Peale Bishop, Bodenheim, Hart Crane, Cummings, H.D., Fletcher, Frost, Jeffers, Kreymborg, Lindsay, MacLeish, Masters, Millay, Moody, Marianne Moore, Pound, Ransom, Robinson, Sandburg, Tate, William Carlos Williams, and Wylie. Each of these was a subject of at least one dissertation before 1966.

15. Of the 27 dissertations on Stevens during these years, 26 dealt only with him; the other dealt also with Yeats. A 28th dealt with Stevens and two other authors. Eliot was a partial subject—to the extent of being included in the title along with two or more other authors—in 8 more studies. He had also been the subject of 19 dissertations before 1956, and Stevens had been the subject of only 2. Overall these figures illustrate Eliot's longstanding integration into the scholarly tradition of English and American literature, but even more strongly they reflect a striking shift towards Stevens as a subject for intensive scholarship after 1960.

16. In contrast, only 4 of 15 of the dissertation writers on Eliot between 1960 and 1966 have generated books on the poet to date (Rees, Knust, Lu, and Carol Smith); these 15 scholars published only 12 articles on Eliot through 1975. It is fair to say that the doctoral candidates who worked on Stevens in the early 1960s were significantly more likely to extend their interest to further scholarly writing. These figures were compiled from Edelstein's bibliography and from the volumes of the MLA bibliography from 1960 to 1975.

17. The fact that Eliot was included only in the English section of the MLA bibliography undoubtedly kept his vote totals down (to 29). Leaving him aside, the poll's results illustrate that Frost, Stevens, and Pound were the only clearly canon-

ical American modernist poets in the academy at the end of the 1960s. After Pound's 76 votes there was an enormous drop to Robinson with only 46 votes, creating a two-tiered structure to that canon: 8 strongly canonical modernists, 3 of them poets, followed by a larger number who could be called marginally canonical at best.

18. Krieger's own connection to Stevens also became more explicit over the next two decades; in his most ambitious book, *Theory of Criticism* (1976), Krieger called Stevens "the ultimate modernist" (205). Frank Lentricchia has argued that Stevens is in fact the "guiding genius" of *Theory of Criticism* (*After the New Criticism*, 247).

19. Indeed, Frye's effort to argue a discipline into existence at the expense of the existing institutional hegemony had a notable New Critical precursor in Ransom's 1938 essay "Criticism, Inc." Sometimes Ransom's and Frye's arguments formed curious mirror images of one another, as when Ransom complained about existing methods of treatment of literature which "see a lot of wood and no trees" (328) and called for a discipline freed from the shackles of historical scholarship and primarily geared around "studies in the technique of art" (346) — exactly the microformalist emphasis Frye would later castigate. Yet perhaps more often, Frye and Ransom sounded notably similar in their desires to see the institutional establishment of criticism as a science or something like it — as long as it retained its independence from all other "sciences": "criticism must become more scientific, or precise and systematic" (329); "In [economics, chemistry, sociology, theology, and architecture], it is taken for granted that criticism of the performance is the prerogative of men who have had formal training in its theory and technique" (337). These scientific analogies of Ransom's could as easily have come from the introduction to the *Anatomy*.

20. For a discussion of Frye's marked proclivity towards Romanticism, see Denham, 159–60.

21. See, for example, "A Collect of Philosophy" (1951), in which Stevens quoted a passage from Whitehead which insisted upon the "abandonment of the notion that simple location is the primary way in which things are involved in space-time" in favor of an awareness that "everything is everywhere at all times, for every location involves an aspect of itself in every other location." That Stevens found such recastings of the nature of reality to have intense ramifications for the poetic imagination was suggested by his gloss on the passage: "These words are pretty obviously words from a level where everything is poetic, as if the statement that every location involves an aspect of itself in every other location produced in the imagination a universal iridescence, a dithering of processes, and, say, a complex of differences" (*NA*, 192). See also the poet's glosses on similar passages from Bergson and Joad in "The Noble Rider" (*NA*, 24–25).

22. Ultimately Nemerov found that the "illumination" of Stevens's poetry was "the epiphany not of what is real, but of the self poetizing. This is our reality, that . . . 'Life consists / Of propositions about life' " (9). This remark indicates the connection between the return to the poetic subject of the early 1960s and the assertion of existence as total textual freeplay which became prominent after such projects as Derrida's and Foucault's disrupted the status of the "self."

23. See also Kermode's discussion of Eliot's fellow high-modernists Yeats, Pound, and Lewis (104–10).

24. Kermode argued that his theory of fictions suggested a "duty" for critics: "to abandon ways of speaking which on the one hand obscure the true nature of our fictions—by confusing them with myths . . . —and on the other obscure our sense of reality by suggesting that fictions represent some kind of surrender or false consolation" (*Sense*, 124).

25. Lentricchia has provided an account of the sudden influence of philosophers in the phenomenological tradition—especially Poulet, Heidegger, and Husserl—in certain elite circles of the American academy in the early 1960s (*After the New Criticism*, 63–74).

26. Hartman's investment in Stevens's theoretical value was further reinforced by the essay's title, "Ghostlier Demarcations," a phrase drawn from the end of "The Idea of Order at Key West," in which Stevens described the capacity of the human creative capacity to develop a greater understanding "of ourselves and of our origins" / In ghostlier demarcations, keener sounds" (*CP*, 130).

27. The importance of this phrase from Stevens's "An Ordinary Evening in New Haven" (*CP*, 473) to Miller's position was indicated by his decision to repeat it in his concluding pages as the achievement of all of his "poets of reality" (358).

28. Just as the integrity of the individual text could be collapsed into the intertextual whole of a poet's work, after Derrida's decentering of the subject the demarcation of the texts of an individual unitary creative mind would come to be seen as similarly artificial and insupportable. With no more romantic or humanist glue to keep it together, the concept of the "author" could simply disintegrate, leaving a description of the world as a conglomeration of textual forces in free play.

Chapter Seven

1. This list includes previously unpublished poetry and prose in Robert Buttel's *Wallace Stevens: The Making of Harmonium* (1967) and in the collections *The Palm at the End of the Mind* (1971) and *Souvenirs and Prophecies* (1977) edited by Holly Stevens; an updated and expanded edition of *Opus Posthumous* edited by Milton J. Bates (1989), which includes the essays "Insurance and Social Change" and "Surety

and Fidelity Claims"; a specialized collection of letters (many of which had already been published in the 1966 volume) called *Secretaries of the Moon: The Letters of Wallace Stevens and José Rodríguez-Feo* (1986) edited by Beverly Coyle and Alan Filreis; two of Stevens's poetic notebooks, *Sur Plusieurs Beaux Sujets*, edited by Bates (1989), and "From Pieces of Paper," published in Lensing's *Wallace Stevens: A Poet's Growth* (1986); and the steady stream of miscellaneous scholarly data published in *Wallace Stevens Journal* since 1970.

2. A commendable corrective to this tendency appears in Filreis's *Wallace Stevens and the Actual World*. Filreis has done much to fill in the gaps in the historical conversations represented one-sidedly by Stevens's published correspondence. While the thoroughness and density of his historical method sometimes makes his book excruciatingly slow going, that method does produce a forceful and exhilarating sense of reading a narrative of actual people interacting meaningfully in an "actual world," and thus it offers the subtlest and most convincing account of Stevens's complex and shifting relationship with the society and politics of his times.

3. Finally beginning to appear are some outstanding studies based upon aspirations to enlarge these narrow canons, particularly Alicia Suskin Ostriker's *Stealing the Language: The Emergence of Women's Poetry in America*, and Cary Nelson's *Repression and Recovery: Modern American Poetry and the Politics of Cultural Memory, 1910–1945*. Notably, the titles of both of these works indicate the explicitly revisionist stance that one must still adopt in trying to broaden canons of American poetry within the mainstream of the academy.

4. Information compiled from issues of the MLA bibliography since 1980.

5. For example, Kunitz felt that *Letters* revealed that Stevens's politics were "reprehensible" (24) and that he was "not great-hearted" (26); Stanford argued that they demonstrated that "Stevens was not so far right politically as has been commonly thought" but had "considerable sympathy for the workers, and for all of the poor, for he was basically a kind and gentle man" (762). See also Corman, who noted that the "kindness and gentleness" in the *Letters* were "moving testimony to a 'good man' " (106). In a nine-hundred-page book covering nearly sixty turbulent years, it should hardly be surprising that both views could be supported.

6. There are also indications that an awareness of Stevens as a major American poet is finally filtering into certain arenas of contemporary popular culture, where he has never before been a strong presence. In the past year or two, I have encountered Stevens (and his wife) as the subject of a *Peanuts* comic strip (reproduced on the cover of the *Wallace Stevens Journal* for spring 1991); as the source of an epigraph for a rock and roll album, *World War Two Point Five*, by the Swimming Pool

Q's; and as a shorthand reference for the businessman-creator on an episode of the television series *thirtysomething* (where a character is called "the Wallace Stevens of advertising"). Undoubtedly these chance encounters of mine might be augmented by the experiences of other readers.

Works Cited

Abbreviations in the Text of Wallace Stevens Titles

CP   Collected Poems. New York: Knopf, 1954.
L   Letters of Wallace Stevens. Edited by Holly Stevens. New York: Knopf, 1966.
NA   The Necessary Angel. New York: Knopf, 1951.
OP   Opus Posthumous. 1st ed. Edited by Samuel French Morse. New York: Knopf, 1957.
OP 1989   Opus Posthumous. 2nd ed. Edited by Milton J. Bates. New York: Knopf, 1989.

NOTE: Books reviewed are by Wallace Stevens unless otherwise noted.

Aiken, Conrad. "The Ivory Tower I." *New Republic* 19 (1919): 58–61.
– – –. *Scepticisms: Notes on Contemporary Poetry*. New York: Knopf, 1919.
– – –. *Selected Letters of Conrad Aiken*. Edited by Joseph Killorin. New Haven: Yale University Press, 1978.
– – –. "A Tribute." *Trinity Review* 8 (May 1954): 16.
– – –, ed. *Twentieth-Century American Poetry*. New York: Modern Library, 1944.
Alfred A. Knopf, 1915–1940. New York: Elmer Adler, 1940.
Arac, Jonathan. "F. O. Matthiessen: Authorizing an American Renaissance." In *The American Renaissance Reconsidered*, edited by Walter Benn Michaels and Donald Pease, 90–112. Baltimore: Johns Hopkins University Press, 1985.
Baker, Howard. "Add This to Rhetoric." *Wallace Stevens Number, Harvard Advocate* 127, no. 3 (December 1940): 16–18.
Bates, Milton J. "Stevens' Books at the Huntington: An Annotated Checklist." *Wallace Stevens Journal* 2.3–4 (1978): 45–61; 3.1 (1979): 15–33.
– – –. *Wallace Stevens: A Mythology of Self*. Berkeley: University of California Press, 1985.
Bauer, Paul. "The Politics of Reality, 1948: Wallace Stevens, Delmore Schwartz, and the New Criticism." *Wallace Stevens Journal* 13 (1989): 206–25.
Belitt, Ben. " 'Lion in the Lute.' " Rev. of *The Man With the Blue Guitar*. *Nation* 145 (1937): 508.
– – –. "The Violent Mind." Rev. of *Ideas of Order*. *Nation* 143 (1936): 708.
Bender, Thomas. *New York Intellect*. New York: Knopf, 1987.

Benét, William Rose. "The Phoenix Nest." Rev. of *Owl's Clover*. *Saturday Review of Literature*, January 16, 1937, 18.
Bennett, Joseph. "Five Books, Four Poets." Rev. of *The Auroras of Autumn*. *Hudson Review* 4 (1951): 133–37.
Bewley, Marius. *The Eccentric Design: Form in the Classic American Novel*. New York: Columbia University Press, 1959.
Bishop, John Peale, and Allen Tate, eds. *American Harvest*. New York: L. B. Fischer, 1942.
Blackmur, R. P. "An Abstraction Blooded." Rev. of *Notes Toward a Supreme Fiction*. *Partisan Review* 10 (1943): 297–301.
———. "The Composition in Nine Poets." Rev. of *Ideas of Order*. *Southern Review* 2 (1937): 572–76.
———. *The Double Agent*. New York: Arrow, 1935.
———. "Examples of Wallace Stevens." *Hound and Horn* 5 (1932): 223–55. Reprint. In *The Achievement of Wallace Stevens*, edited by Ashley Brown and Robert S. Haller, 52–81. Philadelphia: Lippincott, 1962.
———. *Form and Value in Modern Poetry*. New York: Doubleday, 1957.
———. *Language as Gesture*. 1952. Reprint. London: Allen and Unwin, 1961.
Bloom, Harold. "The Central Man: Emerson, Whitman, Wallace Stevens." *Massachusetts Review* 7 (1966): 23–42.
———. *The Visionary Company: A Reading of English Romantic Poetry*. 1961. Reprint. Ithaca: Cornell University Press, 1971.
———. *Wallace Stevens: The Poems of Our Climate*. Ithaca: Cornell University Press, 1977.
———, ed. *Ezra Pound*. New York: Chelsea House, 1987.
Bogan, Louise. *Achievement in American Poetry*. Chicago: Regnery, 1951.
———. "*Harmonium* and the American Scene." *Trinity Review* 8 (May 1954): 18–20.
———. Rev. of *The Auroras of Autumn*. *The New Yorker*, October 28, 1950, 129–30.
———. Rev. of *Collected Poems*. *New Yorker*, December 11, 1954, 201–2.
———. Rev. of *Parts of a World*. *New Yorker*, October 10, 1942, 72.
———. Rev. of *Transport to Summer*. *New Yorker*, May 3, 1947, 116.
Bornstein, George. Rev. of *The Dance of the Intellect*, by Marjorie Perloff. *English Language Notes* 24 (1987): 80–82.
Borroff, Marie. "Stevens: His Letters and Poetry." Rev. of *Letters of Wallace Stevens*. *Yale Review* n.s. 56 (1967): 446–48.
The Borzoi, 1920. New York: Knopf, 1920.
Bradley, Sculley. Rev. of *The Shaping Spirit*, by William Van O'Connor. *American Literature* 22 (1951): 255–57.
Braithwaite, William Stanley, ed. *Anthology of Magazine Verse for 1916*. New York: Gomme and Marshall, 1916.
Brazeau, Peter. *Parts of a World: Wallace Stevens Remembered*. New York: Random House, 1983.

Brogan, Jacqueline Vaught. *Stevens and Simile*. Princeton: Princeton University Press, 1986.
———. "Stevens in History and Not in History: The Poet and the Second World War." *Wallace Stevens Journal* 13 (1989): 168–90.
Brooks, Cleanth. *Modern Poetry and the Tradition*. 1939. Reprint. New York: Oxford University Press, 1965.
———, and Robert Penn Warren. *Understanding Poetry*. New York: Holt, 1938.
———. Untitled statement. *Wallace Stevens Number, Harvard Advocate* 127, no. 3 (December 1940): 29–30.
Brooks, Van Wyck. *Autobiography*. New York: Dutton, 1965.
Brown, Ashley, and Robert S. Haller, eds. *The Achievement of Wallace Stevens*. Philadelphia: Lippincott, 1962.
Bucigalupo, Massimo. "The Poet at War: Ezra Pound's Suppressed Italian Cantos." *South Atlantic Quarterly* 83 (1984): 69–79.
Burnshaw, Stanley. "Reflections on Wallace Stevens." *Wallace Stevens Journal* 13 (1989): 122–26.
———. "Turmoil in the Middle Ground." *New Masses*, October 1, 1935, 41–42.
———. "Wallace Stevens and the Statue." *Sewanee Review* 69 (1961): 355–66.
Buttel, Robert. *Wallace Stevens: The Making of Harmonium*. Princeton: Princeton University Press, 1967.
C. T. C. Rev. of *Harmonium*. *Boston Evening Transcript*, December 29, 1923, sec. 6: 5.
Cain, William. *The Crisis in Criticism*. Baltimore: Johns Hopkins University Press, 1984.
Cargill, Oscar. *Intellectual America: Ideas on the March*. New York: Macmillan, 1941.
Carrier, Warren. "Wallace Stevens' Pagan Vantage." *Accent* 13 (1953): 165–68.
Carruth, Hayden. "Ideality and Metaphor." Rev. of *Three Academic Pieces*. *Poetry* 72 (1948): 270–73.
———. "Stevens as Essayist." Rev. of *The Necessary Angel*. *Nation* 174 (1952): 584–85.
———. "Without the Inventions of Sorrow." Rev. of *Collected Poems*. *Poetry* 85 (1955): 288–93.
Casillo, Robert. *The Genealogy of Demons: Anti-Semitism, Fascism, and the Myths of Ezra Pound*. Chicago: Northwestern University Press, 1988.
Chase, Stanley P. "Dionysus in Dismay." In *Humanism and America*, edited by Norman Foerster, 205–30. New York: Farrar Rinehart, 1930.
Ciardi, John, ed. *Mid-Century American Poets*. New York: Twayne, 1950.
———. "Wallace Stevens's Absolute Music." Rev. of *Collected Poems*. *Nation* 179 (1954): 346–47.
Clymer, W. B. Shubrick, and Charles R. Green. *Robert Frost: A Bibliography*. Amherst, Mass.: Jones Library, 1937.
Colum, Mary. Rev. of *Parts of a World*. *New York Times Book Review*, November 29, 1942, 12.
Cook, Howard Willard. *Our Poets of Today*. New York: Moffatt Yard, 1918.
Corcoran, Neil. Rev. of *The Dance of the Intellect*, by Marjorie Perloff. *Modern Language Review* 83 (1988): 988–89.

Corman, Cid. "The Angel of Necessity." Review of *Letters of Wallace Stevens*. In *At Their Word: Essays on the Arts of Language*, 91–115. Santa Barbara: Black Sparrow, 1978.
Cowley, Malcolm. " 'And Jesse Begat . . .': A Note on Literary Generations." In *. . . And I Worked at the Writer's Trade: Chapters of Literary History, 1918–1978*, 1–20. New York: Viking Press, 1978.
"Current Poetry." *Literary Digest* 51 (1915): 1300–1303.
Daiches, David. "Some Recent Poetry." Rev. of *The Auroras of Autumn*. *Yale Review* n.s. 40 (1950): 352–57.
Damon, S. Foster. *Amy Lowell: A Chronicle*. Boston: Houghton Mifflin, 1935.
Davidson, Michael. "Notes Beyond the *Notes*: Wallace Stevens and Contemporary Poetics." In *Wallace Stevens: The Poetics of Modernism*, edited by Albert Gelpi, 140–60. Cambridge: Cambridge University Press, 1985.
Davie, Donald. "The Auroras of Autumn." *Perspective* 7 (1954): 125–36.
Deen, Rosemary. "Wonder and Mystery of Art." Rev. of *Opus Posthumous*. *Commonweal* 66 (1957): 620–21.
Denham, Robert. *Northrop Frye and Critical Method*. University Park: Pennsylvania State University Press, 1978.
Deutsch, Babette. "Poet's Harvest: Seventy-Five Years of 'Piecing the World Together.' " Rev. of *Collected Poems*. *New York Herald Tribune Book Review*, October 3, 1954, 3.
―――. Rev. of *Ideas of Order*. *New York Herald Tribune Books*, December 15, 1935, 18.
Dial 59 (1915): 477.
Dillon, George, "A Blue Phenomenon." Rev. of *Esthétique du Mal*. *Poetry* 68 (1946): 97–100.
Drew, Elizabeth. Rev. of *Parts of a World*. *Atlantic Monthly* 170 (1942): 154.
Earle, Ferdinand. *The Lyric Year*. New York: Mitchell Kennerly, 1912.
Eastman, Barbara C. "The Gap in *The Cantos*: 72 and 73." *Paideuma* 8 (1979): 415–27.
Eberhart, Richard. Rev. of *Transport to Summer*. *Accent* 7 (1947): 251–53.
Edelstein, J. M. *Wallace Stevens: A Descriptive Bibliography*. Pittsburgh: University of Pittsburgh Press, 1973.
Eliot, T. S. "Tradition and the Individual Talent." In *The Sacred Wood*, 47–59. 1920. Reprint. London: Methuen, 1960.
Enck, John. *Wallace Stevens: Images and Judgments*. Carbondale: Southern Illinois University Press, 1964.
Evans, Oliver. "Poetry: 1930 to the Present." In *American Literary Scholarship 1963*, edited by James Woodress, 184–97. Durham: Duke University Press, 1965.
Feidelson, Charles Jr. *Symbolism and American Literature*. Chicago: University of Chicago Press, 1953.
Filreis, Alan. *Wallace Stevens and the Actual World*. Princeton: Princeton University Press, 1991.
―――, and Harvey Teres. "An Interview with Stanley Burnshaw." *Wallace Stevens Journal* 13 (1989): 109–21.

Finch, John. "North and South in Stevens's America." *Wallace Stevens Number, Harvard Advocate* 127, no. 3 (December 1940): 23–26.
Fitzgerald, Robert. "Thoughts Revolved." Rev. of *The Man With the Blue Guitar*. *Poetry* 51 (1937): 153–57.
Fletcher, John Gould. "The Revival of Aestheticism." Rev. of *Harmonium*. *Freeman* 8 (1923): 355–56.
―――. "Some Contemporary American Poets." *Chapbook* no. 2 (May 1920): 1–31.
Flint, F. Cudworth. "Images of Secret Life." Rev. of *Parts of a World*. *Virginia Quarterly Review* 19 (1943): 133–35.
Fowler, Alastair. *Kinds of Literature*. Cambridge: Harvard University Press, 1982.
Frankenberg, Lloyd. "Secretions of Insight." Rev. of *The Auroras of Autumn*. *New York Times Book Review*, September 10, 1950, 20.
Fraser, Russell. *A Mingled Yarn: The Life of R. P. Blackmur*. New York: Harcourt Brace Jovanovich, 1981.
Frye, Northrop. *Anatomy of Criticism*. Princeton: Princeton University Press, 1957.
―――. "The Realistic Oriole: A Study of Wallace Stevens." *Hudson Review* 10 (1957): 353–70.
Fuchs, Daniel. *The Comic Spirit of Wallace Stevens*. Durham: Duke University Press, 1963.
Gibbs, Barbara. "A Spirit Without a Foyer." Rev. of *Opus Posthumous*. *Poetry* 92 (1958): 52–57.
Gioia, Dana. "The Emperor of Hartford." Rev. of *Wallace Stevens: A Mythology of Self*, by Milton J. Bates. *New York Times Book Review*, October 27, 1985, 13.
Gleason, Philip. "World War II and the Development of American Studies." *American Quarterly* 36 (1984): 343–58.
―――. "The 'Community of Elements' in Wallace Stevens and Louis Zukofsky." In *Wallace Stevens: The Poetics of Modernism*, edited by Albert Gelpi, 121–40. Cambridge: Cambridge University Press, 1985.
Golding, Alan C. "A History of American Poetry Anthologies." In *Canons*, edited by Robert von Hallberg, 279–307. Chicago: University of Chicago Press, 1984.
―――. "Little Magazines and Alternative Canons: The Example of *Origin*." *American Literary History* 2 (1990): 691–725.
Graff, Gerald. *Literature Against Itself*. Chicago: University of Chicago Press, 1979.
Granger's Index to Poetry and Recitations. 3rd ed. Chicago: McClurg, 1940.
Gregory, Horace. "Examination of Wallace Stevens in a Time of War." Rev. of *Parts of a World*. *Accent* 3 (1942): 57–61.
―――. Rev. of *Harmonium*. *New York Herald Tribune Books*, September 27, 1931, 28.
―――. Rev. of *Notes Toward a Supreme Fiction*. *Sewanee Review* 52 (1943): 584.
―――, and Marya Zaturenska, *A History of American Poetry, 1900–1940*. New York: Harcourt Brace,1946.
Grigson, Geoffrey. "The Stuffed Goldfinch." *New Verse* no. 19 (February–March 1936): 18.

Guillory, John. "The Ideology of Canon Formation: T. S. Eliot and Cleanth Brooks." In *Canons*, edited by Robert von Hallberg, 337–59. Chicago: University of Chicago Press, 1984.
Hartman, Geoffrey. "Ghostlier Demarcations." In *Northrop Frye in Modern Criticism*, edited by Murray Krieger, 109–32. New York: Columbia University Press, 1966.
Hatfield, Jerald E. "More About Legend." *Trinity Review* 8 (May 1954): 30.
Hecht, Anthony. "Poets and Peasants." Rev. of *Opus Posthumous*. *Hudson Review* 10 (1958): 606–8.
Henderson, Alice Corbin. "A New School of Poetry." *Poetry* 8 (1916): 103–5.
Hoffman, Frederick. *The Twenties*. New York: Viking, 1955.
— — —, Charles Allen, and Carolyn Ulrich. *The Little Magazine: A History and a Bibliography*. Princeton: Princeton University Press, 1946.
Hogan, Charles B. *A Bibliography of Edwin Arlington Robinson*. New Haven: Yale University Press, 1936.
Holden, Raymond. "The Word of Music." Rev. of *Harmonium*. *Measure* 4 (March 1924): 17–18.
Holmes, John. Rev. of *Ideas of Order*. *Virginia Quarterly Review* 12 (1936): 294.
— — —. Rev. of *Ideas of Order*. *Boston Evening Transcript*, December 19, 1936, sec. 6: 2.
Howard, Richard. Rev. of *Letters of Wallace Stevens*. *Poetry* 111 (1967): 39–40.
Howe, Irving. "Another Way of Looking at the Blackbird." Rev. of *Opus Posthumous*. *New Republic* 137 (1957): 16, 19.
Hoyt, Helen. "Anthologies and Translations." *Poetry* 10 (1917): 277–78.
Hubbell, Jay B. "Foreword." *American Literature* 1 (1929): n.p.
— — —. *Who Are the Major American Writers?* Durham, Duke University Press, 1972.
Humphries, Rolfe. Rev. of *The Auroras of Autumn*. *Nation* 171 (1950): 293.
Hutchison, Percy. "Pure Poetry and Mr. Wallace Stevens." Rev. of *Harmonium*. *New York Times Book Review*, August 9, 1931, 4.
Hyman, Stanley Edgar. *The Armed Vision*. 1948. Reprint. New York: Vintage, 1955.
Ingalls, Jeremy. "Man's Mind Grown Venerable." Rev. of *Transport to Summer*. *Saturday Review of Literature*, April 12, 1947, 48.
Jarrell, Randall. "The Collected Poems of Wallace Stevens." *Yale Review* n.s. 44 (1955): 340–53. Reprint. In *The Achievement of Wallace Stevens*, edited by Ashley Brown and Robert S. Haller, 179–92. Philadelphia: Lippincott, 1982.
— — —. "Reflections on Wallace Stevens." *Partisan Review* 17 (1951): 335–44. Reprint. In *Poetry and the Age*, 133–48. New York: Farrar Straus Giroux, 1953, 1972.
— — —. Rev. of *Collected Poems*. *Harpers* 209 (1954): 100.
Jauss, Hans Robert. "Literary History as a Challenge to Literary Theory." *New Literary History* 2 (1970): 7–37.
John, Arthur. *The Best Years of the Century*. Urbana: University of Illinois Press, 1981.
Jones, Frank. "The Sorcerer as Elegist." Rev. of *Parts of a World*. *Nation* 155 (1942): 488.
Joost, Nicholas. *Scofield Thayer and The Dial*. Carbondale: Southern Illinois University Press, 1964.

Josephson, Matthew. Rev. of *Harmonium*. *Broom* 5 (1923): 236–37.
Kees, Weldon. "Parts: But a World." Rev. of *Parts of a World*. *New Republic* 107 (1942): 387–88.
Kenner, Hugh. "The Making of the Modernist Canon." In *Canons*, edited by Robert von Hallberg, 363–75. Chicago: University of Chicago Press, 1984.
———. *The Pound Era*. Berkeley: University of California Press, 1971.
Kerfoot, J. B. Remarks on *Others*. *Life* 66 (1915): 568.
Kermode, Frank. *History and Value*. Oxford: Clarendon Press, 1988.
———. *The Sense of an Ending*. New York: Oxford University Press, 1967.
———. *Wallace Stevens*. London: Oliver & Boyd, 1960.
Koch, Vivienne. "The Necessary Angels of Earth." *Sewanee Review* 59 (1951): 664–77.
———. "Poetry in World War II." Rev. of *Esthétique du Mal*. *Briarcliff Quarterly* 3 (1946): 3–24.
Kramer, Hilton. Rev. of *Letters of Wallace Stevens*. *New Leader*, December 5, 1966, 18.
Kreymborg, Alfred. "As Others See Us." *Poetry* 12 (1918): 214–24.
———. "An Early Impression of Wallace Stevens." *Trinity Review* 8 (May 1954): 12–16.
———. *Our Singing Strength*. New York: Coward, McCann, 1929.
———. *Troubador*. New York: Boni & Liveright, 1925.
———, ed. *Lyric America, 1630–1930*. New York: Coward, McCann, 1930.
Krieger, Murray. *The New Apologists for Poetry*. 1956. Reprint. Bloomington: University of Indiana Press, 1963.
———. *Theory of Criticism*. Baltimore: Johns Hopkins University Press, 1976.
Kroll, Jack. "Imagination's Prince." Rev. of *Letters of Wallace Stevens*. *Newsweek*, November 28, 1966, 114.
Kronick, Joseph. Rev. of *The Dance of the Intellect*, by Marjorie Perloff. *American Literature* 59 (1987): 139–40.
Kunitz, Stanley. "The Hartford Walker." Rev. of *Letters of Wallace Stevens*. *New Republic*, November 12, 1966, 26.
Laros, Fred. "Wallace Stevens Today." *Bard Review* 2 (1947): 8–15.
Larsson, Raymond. "The Beau as Poet." Rev. of *Harmonium*. *Commonweal* 15 (1932): 640–41.
Lauter, Paul. "Race and Gender in the Shaping of the American Literary Canon: A Case Study from the Twenties." In *Feminist Criticism and Social Change: Sex, Class, and Race in Literature and Culture*, edited by Judith Newton and Deborah Rosenfelt, 19–44. New York: Methuen, 1985.
Leary, Lewis. *Articles on American Literature, 1900–1950*. Durham: Duke University Press, 1954.
———. *Articles on American Literature 1950–1967*. Durham: Duke University Press, 1970.
Lechlitner, Ruth. "Creative Imagination." Rev. of *Parts of a World*. *New York Herald-Tribune Books*, November 8, 1942, 26.

———. "Imagination as Reality." Rev. of *Ideas of Order* and *Owl's Clover*. *New York Herald Tribune Books*, December 6, 1936, 40.

———. "Wallace Stevens' Poetry." Rev. of *The Man With the Blue Guitar*. *New York Herald Tribune Books*, November 14, 1937, 2.

Leggett, B. J. *Wallace Stevens and Poetic Theory: Conceiving the Supreme Fiction*. Chapel Hill: University of North Carolina Press, 1987.

Lensing, George. *Wallace Stevens: A Poet's Growth*. Baton Rouge: Louisiana State University Press, 1986.

———. "Wallace Stevens in England." In *Wallace Stevens: A Celebration*, edited by Frank Doggett and Robert Buttel, 130–48. Princeton: Princeton University Press, 1980.

Lentricchia, Frank. *After the New Criticism*. Chicago: University of Chicago Press, 1981.

———. *Ariel and the Police*. Madison: University of Wisconsin Press, 1988.

———. "Lyric in the Culture of Late Capitalism." *American Literary History* 1 (1989): 63–88.

Levin, Harry. Rev. of *The Necessary Angel*. *Yale Review* n.s. 41 (1952): 615–16.

———. Untitled statement. *Wallace Stevens Number, Harvard Advocate* 127, no. 3 (December 1940): 30.

Lindsay, Robert O. *Witter Bynner: A Bibliography*. Albuquerque: University of New Mexico Press, 1967.

Litz, A. Walton. "Wallace Stevens: Books and a Sonnet." Rev. of *Letters of Wallace Stevens*. *Nation* 204 (1967): 85–87.

———. "La poésie pure, the New Romantic, and the Pressure of Reality: Wallace Stevens's Defense of Poetry." In *Romantic and Modern: Evaluations of Literary Tradition*, edited by George Bornstein, 111–32. Pittsburgh: University of Pittsburgh Press, 1977.

Loeb, Harold. "Comment—*Broom*, 1921–23." *Broom* 5 (1923): 56.

Lowell, Amy. *A Critical Fable*. Boston: Houghton Mifflin, 1922.

Lowell, Robert. "Imagination and Reality." Rev. of *Transport to Summer*. *Nation* 164 (1947): 400–402.

McGann, Jerome J. *The Beauty of Inflections: Literary Investigations in Historical Method and Theory*. New York: Oxford University Press, 1985.

McLeod, Glen G. *Wallace Stevens and Company: The Harmonium Years, 1913–1923*. Ann Arbor: UMI Research Press, 1983.

McNeil, Helen. "Double Indemnity." Rev. of *Letters of Wallace Stevens*. *Partisan Review* 34 (1967): 635–38.

Mariani, Paul. *William Carlos Williams: A New World Naked*. New York: McGraw-Hill, 1981.

Martin, Mildred. *A Half-Century of Eliot Criticism, 1916–1965*. Lewisburg, Pa.: Bucknell University Press, 1972.

Martz, Louis. "Recent Poetry." Rev. of *Transport to Summer*. *Yale Review* n.s. 37 (1947): 333–41.

———. "Wallace Stevens: The World as Meditation." *Yale Review* n.s. 47 (1958): 517–36. Reprint. In *The Achievement of Wallace Stevens*, edited by Ashley Brown and Robert S. Haller, 211–31. Philadelphia: Lippincott, 1962.
Matthiessen, F. O., ed. *The Oxford Book of American Verse*. New York: Oxford University Press, 1951.
———. "Society and Solitude in Poetry." Rev. of *Ideas of Order*. *Yale Review* n.s. 25 (1936): 605–7.
———. Untitled statement. *Wallace Stevens Number, Harvard Advocate* 127, no. 3 (December 1940): 31.
———. "Wallace Stevens at 67." Rev. of *Transport to Summer*. *New York Times Book Review*, April 20, 1947, 4, 26.
Meyer, Gerard Previn. "Actuary Among the Spondees." Rev. of *Collected Poems*. *Saturday Review of Literature*, December 4, 1954, 26–27.
———. "Bollingen Winner." Rev. of *The Shaping Spirit*, by William Van O'Connor. *Saturday Review of Literature*, July 1, 1950, 19.
———. "Mystic & Classic." Rev. of *The Necessary Angel*. *Saturday Review of Literature*, December 29, 1951, 11–12.
———. "Wallace Stevens: Major Poet." *Saturday Review of Literature*, March 23, 1946, 7.
Michelson, Max. "Arensberg and the New Reality." *Poetry* 8 (1916): 208–11.
———. "The Radicals." *Poetry* 8 (1916): 151–55.
Miles, Josephine. *The Continuity of Poetic Language*. Berkeley: University of California Press, 1951.
Miller, J. Hillis. "The Function of Rhetorical Study at the Present Time." *ADE Bulletin* 62 (1979): 10–18.
———. *Poets of Reality*. Cambridge: Harvard University Press, 1965.
Monroe, Harriet. "A Cavalier of Beauty." Rev. of *Harmonium*. *Poetry* 23 (1924): 322–27.
———. "The Free Verse Movement in America." *English Journal* 13 (1924): 691–705.
———. "The Motive for the Magazine." *Poetry* 1 (1912): 26.
———. "Mr. Yeats and the Poetic Drama." *Poetry* 16 (1920): 21–28. Partial reprint. In *The Achievement of Wallace Stevens*, edited by Ashley Brown and Robert S. Haller, 19–20. Philadelphia: Lippincott, 1962.
———. "Notes on Contributors." *Poetry* 5 (1914): 97.
———. "Others Again." *Poetry* 16 (1920): 150–59.
———. *A Poet's Life*. New York: Macmillan, 1938.
———. "These Five Years." *Poetry* 11 (1917): 33–41.
———. "Wallace Stevens." In *Poets and Their Art*, 39–45. New York: Macmillan, 1932.
———, and Alice Corbin Henderson, eds. *The New Poetry*. New York: Macmillan, 1917, 1923.
Moore, Geoffrey. "Wallace Stevens: A Hero of Our Time." Reprint. In *The Achievement of Wallace Stevens*, edited by Ashley Brown and Robert S. Haller, 249–70. Philadelphia: Lippincott, 1962.

Moore, Marianne. Rev. of *Ideas of Order*. *Criterion* 15 (1936): 307–9.
―――. "Unanimity and Fortitude." Rev. of *Ideas of Order* and *Owl's Clover*. *Poetry* 49 (1937): 268–72.
―――. "Well Moused, Lion." Rev. of *Harmonium*. *Dial* 76 (1924): 84–91. Reprint. In *The Achievement of Wallace Stevens*, edited by Ashley Brown and Robert S. Haller, 21–28. Philadelphia: Lippincott, 1962.
Morgan, Frederick. "Six Poets." *Hudson Review* 6 (1953): 131–34.
Morse, Samuel French. "Agenda: a Note on Some Uncollected Poems." *Trinity Review* 8 (May 1954): 34.
―――. "Introduction." *Opus Posthumous*, by Wallace Stevens, xiii–xxxviii. New York: Knopf, 1957.
―――. Rev. of *Collected Poems*. *New York Times Book Review*, October 3, 1954, 3.
―――, Jackson R. Bryer, and Joseph N. Riddel. *Wallace Stevens: Checklist and Bibliography of Stevens Criticism*. Denver: Alan Swallow, 1963.
Munson, Gorham B. *The Awakening Twenties*. Baton Rouge: Louisiana State University Press, 1985.
―――. "The Dandyism of Wallace Stevens." *Dial* 79 (1925): 413–17. Reprint. In *The Achievement of Wallace Stevens*, edited by Ashley Brown and Robert S. Haller, 41–45. Philadelphia: Lippincott, 1962.
―――. "Hart Crane: Young Titan in the Sacred Wood." In *Destinations*, 160–77. New York: Sears, 1928.
―――. "Interstice Between Scylla and Charybdis." *Secession* no. 2 (1922): 30.
―――. "The *Others* Parade." *Guardian* 1 (1925): 226–32.
Nash, Ralph. "Wallace Stevens and the Point of Change." *Perspective* 7 (1954): 113–21.
Nelson, Cary. *Repression and Recovery: Modern American Poetry and the Politics of Cultural Memory, 1910–1945*. Madison: University of Wisconsin Press, 1989.
Nemerov, Howard. "The Poetry of Wallace Stevens." *Sewanee Review* 65 (1957): 1–14.
Newcomb, John Timberman. "Archibald MacLeish and the Poetics of Public Speech: A Critique of High Modernism." *Journal of the Midwest Modern Language Association* 23 (1990): 9–26.
―――. "Canonical Ahistoricism vs. Histories of Canons: Towards Methodological Dissensus." *South Atlantic Review* 54 (1989): 3–20.
―――. "Life Anywhere But on a Battleship: Stevens's Wartime Poetry and the Apolitics of Postwar Criticism." *Criticism* 32 (1990): 101–28.
North, Michael. *The Final Sculpture: Public Monuments and Modern Poets*. Ithaca: Cornell University Press, 1985.
O'Connor, William Van. "He Dared to Speak for the Imagination." Rev. of *The Necessary Angel*. *New York Times Book Review*, December 2, 1951, 7, 22.
―――. Rev. of *The Auroras of Autumn*. *Poetry* 77 (1950): 109–12.
―――. *The Shaping Spirit: A Study of Wallace Stevens*. Chicago: Regnery, 1950.
Ohmann, Richard. "The Shaping of a Canon: U.S. Fiction, 1960–1975." In *Canons*, edited by Robert von Hallberg, 377–401. Chicago: University of Chicago Press, 1984.

Ostriker, Alicia Suskin. *Stealing the Language: The Emergence of Women's Poetry in America*. New York: Beacon Press, 1986.
Pack, Robert. *Wallace Stevens: An Introduction to His Poetry and Thought*. New Brunswick: Rutgers University Press, 1958.
Pearce, Roy Harvey. *The Continuity of American Poetry*. Princeton: Princeton University Press, 1961.
Pearson, Norman Holmes. "Like Rare Tea." Rev. of *Letters of Wallace Stevens*. *New York Times Book Review*, November 6, 1966, 53.
Perloff, Marjorie. *The Dance of the Intellect*. New York: Cambridge University Press, 1986.
―――. "Pound/Stevens: Whose Era?" *New Literary History* 13 (1982): 485–514.
―――. "Revolving in Crystal: The Impasse of Modernist Lyric." In *Wallace Stevens: The Poetics of Modernism*, edited by Albert Gelpi, 41–64. New York: Cambridge University Press, 1985.
"The Poetry of Wallace Stevens." Rev. of *Selected Poems*. *Times Literary Supplement*, June 19, 1953, 397. Reprint. In *Trinity Review* 8 (May 1954): 46.
Poirier, Richard. *A World Elsewhere: The Place of Style in American Literature*. New York: Oxford University Press, 1966.
Powys, Llewellyn. "The Thirteenth Way." *Dial* 77 (1924): 45–50. Reprint. In *The Achievement of Wallace Stevens*, edited by Ashley Brown and Robert S. Haller, 29–34. Philadelphia: Lippincott, 1962.
"Prize Announcement." *Poetry* 8 (1916): 160.
"Prize Pies." Rev. of *The Auroras of Autumn*. *Time*, September 25, 1950, 106, 108, 110.
Ransom, John C. "Criticism, Inc." In *The World's Body*, 327–50. 1938. Reprint. New York: Kennikat Press, 1964.
―――. "The Planetary Poet." *Kenyon Review* 26 (1964): 233–64.
―――. "Poets Without Laurels." *The World's Body*, 55–75. 1938. Reprint. New York: Kennikat Press, 1964.
"Recent Books in Brief Review." Rev. of *Harmonium*. *Bookman* 58 (1923): 483.
Reising, Russell. *The Unusable Past: Theory and the Study of American Literature*. New York: Methuen, 1986.
Rev. of *Harmonium*. *Boston Evening Transcript*, September 2, 1931, sec. 4: 3.
Rev. of *Harmonium*. *Springfield Republican*, October 28, 1923, 7a.
Rev. of *Others for 1916*. *Springfield Republican*, June 11, 1916, 17.
Rev. of *Parts of a World*. *Time*, November 2, 1942, 103–4.
Review of Reviews 53 (1916): 761.
Rexroth, Kenneth. "Art of Compromise." Rev. of *Opus Posthumous*. *Nation* 185 (1957): 268–69.
―――. "The Influence of French Poetry On American." In *Assays*, 143–74. New York: New Directions, 1961.
"Richard Sir Vallienne." *Rogue* 1 (1915): 3.
Richardson, Joan. *Wallace Stevens: The Early Years, 1879–1923*. New York: Beech Tree, 1986.

———. *Wallace Stevens: The Later Years, 1923–1955.* New York: Beech Tree, 1988.
Riddel, Joseph N. *The Clairvoyant Eye: The Poetry and Poetics of Wallace Stevens.* Baton Rouge: Louisiana State University Press, 1965.
———. "The Contours of Stevens Criticism." *ELH* 31 (1964): 106–38.
———. Rev. of *Letters of Wallace Stevens. American Literature* 39 (1967): 421.
Riding, Laura, and Robert Graves. *A Survey of Modernist Poetry.* London: Wishart & Morgan, 1927.
Roethke, Theodore. Rev. of *Ideas of Order. New Republic* 84 (1936): 304.
———. "A Rouse for Stevens." *7 Arts* 3 (1955): 117.
Rosenfeld, Paul. "Wallace Stevens." In *Men Seen*, 151–62. New York: Dial Press, 1925. Reprint. In *The Achievement of Wallace Stevens*, edited by Ashley Brown and Robert S. Haller, 35–40. Philadelphia: Lippincott, 1962.
Sader, Marion, ed. *Comprehensive Index to Little Magazines.* Millwood, N.Y.: Kraus-Thomson, 1976.
Said, Edward W. "The Horizon of R. P. Blackmur." *Raritan* 6 (1986): 35–52.
Sanborn, Pitts. "Some Recent American Poetry." *The Trend* 6 (1914): 570–76.
Schaum, Melita. "Lyric Resistance: Views of the Political in the Poetics of Wallace Stevens and H. D." *Wallace Stevens Journal* 13 (1989): 191–205.
———. *Wallace Stevens and the Critical Schools.* Tuscaloosa: University of Alabama Press, 1988.
Schneider, Isidor. Rev. of *Ideas of Order. New Masses*, October 27, 1936, 24.
Schwartz, Delmore. "In the Orchards of the Imagination." Rev. of *Collected Poems. New Republic*, November 1, 1954, 16–18.
———. "Instructed of Much Mortality: A Note on the Poetry of John Crowe Ransom." *Sewanee Review* 54 (1946): 439–48.
———. "The Literary Dictatorship of T. S. Eliot." *Partisan Review* 16 (1949): 119–37. Reprint. In *Literary Opinion in America*, edited by Morton Dauwen Zabel, 573–87. 2 vols. 3rd ed. New York: Harper, 1962.
———. "New Verse." Rev. of *The Man With the Blue Guitar. Partisan Review* 4 (1938): 49–52.
———. Rev. of *Transport to Summer. Partisan Review* 14 (1947): 531–32.
———. "The Ultimate Plato With Picasso's Guitar." *Wallace Stevens Number, Harvard Advocate* 127, no. 3 (December 1940): 11–16.
———. "Wallace Stevens: An Appreciation." *New Republic*, August 22, 1955, 20–22.
Seiffert, Marjorie Allen. "The Intellectual Tropics." Rev. of *Harmonium. Poetry* 23 (1923): 154–60.
Shapiro, Karl. " 'Aristotle Is a Skeleton.' " Rev. of *Opus Posthumous. Prairie Schooner* 32 (1958): 245–47.
Shepard, Odell. Rev. of *Harmonium. Bookman* 74 (1931): 207–8.
Sherry, Vincent B. Rev. of *The Dance of the Intellect*, by Marjorie Perloff. *Journal of Modern Literature* 13 (1986): 426–27.
Simons, Hi. "The Humanism of Wallace Stevens." Rev. of *Parts of a World. Poetry* 61 (1942): 448–52.

———. "Vicissitudes of Reputation, 1914–40." *Wallace Stevens Number, Harvard Advocate* 127, no. 3 (December 1940): 8–10, 24–44.
Simpson, Eileen. *Poets in Their Youth: A Memoir.* New York: Vintage, 1982.
Simpson, Louis. Rev. of *Collected Poems. American Scholar* 24 (1955): 240.
Singal, Daniel Joseph. "Toward a Definition of American Modernism." *American Quarterly* 39 (1987): 7–26.
"The Situation in American Writing." *Partisan Review* 6, no. 4 (1939): 25–47.
Smith, Barbara Herrnstein. "Contingencies of Value." In *Canons*, edited by Robert von Hallberg, 5–39. Chicago: University of Chicago Press, 1984.
———. *On the Margins of Discourse: The Relation of Literature to Language.* Chicago: University of Chicago Press, 1978.
———. "Value/Evaluation." *South Atlantic Quarterly* 86 (1987): 448–53.
Smith, Harrison. "More Gold Medals." *Saturday Review of Literature*, March 17, 1951, 23.
Smith, William Jay. *The Spectra Hoax.* Middletown, Conn.: Wesleyan University Press, 1961.
Snow, Wilbert. *Codline's Child.* Middletown, Conn.: Wesleyan University Press, 1968.
Soule, George. Rev. of *Anthology of Magazine Verse*, edited by William S. Braithwaite. *New Republic* 6 (1916): 223.
Spencer, Theodore. "The Poetry of Wallace Stevens: An Evaluation." *Wallace Stevens Number, Harvard Advocate* 127, no. 3 (December 1940): 26.
Spiller, Robert et. al., eds. *Literary History of the United States.* New York: Macmillan, 1948.
Squire, J. C. Rev. of *Harmonium. London Mercury* 12 (1925): 656.
Stanford, Donald. "The Well-Kept Life: The Letters of Wallace Stevens." *Southern Review* n.s. 3 (1967): 757–63.
Stevens, Holly. *Souvenirs and Prophecies: The Young Wallace Stevens.* New York: Knopf, 1977.
Stevens, Wallace. *The Palm at the End of the Mind.* Edited by Holly Stevens. New York: Knopf, 1971.
———. *Sur Plusieurs Beaux Sujets.* Edited by Milton J. Bates. Stanford and San Marino: Stanford University Press, and Huntington Library, 1989.
———. Untitled statement. *T. S. Eliot Number, Harvard Advocate* 125 (December 1938): 41. Reprint. In *Opus Posthumous*, edited by Milton J. Bates, 240. 2nd ed. New York: Knopf, 1989.
———. and José Rodríguez-Feo. *Secretaries of the Moon: The Letters of Wallace Stevens and José Rodríguez-Feo.* Edited by Beverly Coyle and Alan Filreis. Durham: Duke University Press, 1986.
Swallow, Alan. "Some Recent Poetry." Rev. of *Transport to Summer. New Mexico Quarterly Review* 18 (1948): 456–65.
Symons, Julian. "Stevens in England." *Trinity Review* 8 (May 1954): 45.
Sypher, Wylie. "Connoisseur in Chaos: Wallace Stevens." *Partisan Review* 12 (1946): 82–94.

Tate, Allen. "American Poetry Since 1920." *Bookman* 38 (1929): 503–8. Reprint. In *The Poetry Reviews of Allen Tate, 1924–1944*, edited by Ashley Brown and Frances Neel Cheney, 78–88. Baton Rouge: Louisiana State University Press, 1983.
Tebbel, John. *A History of Book Publishing in the United States*. 3 vols. New York: Bowker, 1975.
Tejera, Victor. Rev. of *Transport to Summer*. *Journal of Philosophy* 45 (1948): 137–39.
Tindall, William York. "Literary Signposts." Rev. of *Parts of a World*. *American Mercury* 56 (1943): 119–20.
— — —. *Wallace Stevens*. Minneapolis: University of Minnesota Press, 1961.
Tompkins, Jane. *Sensational Designs*. New York: Oxford University Press, 1985.
Unterecker, John. "No Time for Poetry?" *New Leader*, December 17, 1951, 25.
Untermeyer, Louis. *American Poetry Since 1900*. New York: Holt, 1923.
— — —. "Among the New Books." Rev. of *Harmonium*. *Yale Review* n.s. 14 (1924): 159–60.
— — —. "Departure from Dandyism." Rev. of *Parts of a World*. *Saturday Review of Literature*, December 19, 1942, 11.
— — —. "The Ivory Tower II." *New Republic* 19 (1919): 58–61.
— — —. *Modern American Poetry: A Critical Anthology*. New York: Harcourt Brace, 1919.
Van Doren, Mark. "Poets and Wits." Rev. of *Harmonium*. *The Nation* 117 (1923): 400–401.
Van Ghent, Dorothy. "When Poets Stood Alone." *New Masses*, January 11, 1938, 41–46.
Van Vechten, Carl. "Rogue Elephant in Porcelain." *Yale University Library Gazette* 38 (1963): 41–50.
Vanderbilt, Kermit. *American Literature and the Academy*. Philadelphia: University of Pennsylvania Press, 1986.
Vendler, Helen. *On Extended Wings*. Cambridge: Harvard University Press, 1968.
— — —. *Wallace Stevens: Words Chosen Out of Desire*. Knoxville: University of Tennessee Press, 1984.
Viereck, Peter. "Some Notes on Wallace Stevens." *Contemporary Poetry* 7 (1948): 14–15.
— — —. "Stevens Revisited." Rev. of *Transport to Summer*. *Kenyon Review* 10 (1948): 154–57.
Von Hallberg, Robert, ed. *Canons*. Chicago: University of Chicago Press, 1984.
Wagner, C. Roland. "A Central Poetry." Rev. of *The Necessary Angel*. *Hudson Review* 5 (1952): 144–47.
Walcutt, Charles C. "Interpreting the Symbol." *College English* 14 (1953): 446–54.
Wald, Alan. *The New York Intellectuals*. Chapel Hill: University of North Carolina Press, 1987.
Wallace Stevens Number, Harvard Advocate 127, no. 3 (December 1940).
Walton, Eda Lou. "Beyond the Wasteland." *Nation* 133 (1931): 263.
— — —. Rev. of *Ideas of Order* and *Owl's Clover*. *New York Times Book Review*, December 6, 1936, 18.

———. "Wallace Stevens's Two Worlds." *New York Times Book Review*, October 24, 1937, 5.
Warren, Robert Penn. Untitled statement. *Wallace Stevens Number, Harvard Advocate* 127, no. 3 (December 1940): 32.
Wasserstrom, William. *The Time of "The Dial."* Syracuse: Syracuse University Press, 1963.
Waugh, Evelyn. *Brideshead Revisited.* New York: Little Brown, 1946.
Weatherhead, A. Kingsley. "Poetry: 1930 to the Present." In *American Literary Scholarship, 1969*, edited by J. Albert Robbins, 278–92. Durham: Duke University Press, 1971.
Weiss, Theodore. "The Nonsense of Winters' Anatomy." *Quarterly Review of Literature* 1 (1944): 212–34.
———. "Three in One." *Quarterly Review of Literature* 1 (1944): 326–29.
Williams, Ellen. *Harriet Monroe and the Poetry Renaissance.* Urbana: University of Illinois Press, 1977.
Williams, William Carlos. "Belly Music." *Others* 5, no. 6 (1919): 25–32.
———. "The Great Opportunity." *Egoist* 3 (1916): 137.
———. "Poet of a Steadfast Pattern." Rev. of *Opus Posthumous*. *New York Times Book Review*, August 18, 1957, 6.
———. "Poets' Corner." Rev. of *The Man With the Blue Guitar*. *New Republic* 93 (1937): 50.
———. "Prologue to *Kora in Hell*." In *Selected Essays*, 3–26. 1954. Reprint. New York: New Directions, 1969.
———. "Wallace Stevens." *Poetry* 87 (1956): 234–39.
Wilson, Christopher P. *The Labor of Words: Literary Professionalism in the Progressive Era.* Athens: University of Georgia Press, 1985.
Wilson, Edmund. "The All-Star Literary Vaudeville." In *A Literary Chronicle 1920–1950*, 84–92. New York: Doubleday, 1952.
———. "Wallace Stevens and E. E. Cummings." Rev. of *Harmonium*. *New Republic* 38 (1924): 102–3.
Winters, Yvor. "A Cool Master." *Poetry* 19 (1922): 278–88.
———. "Mina Loy." *Dial* 80 (1926): 496.
———. "Wallace Stevens, or The Hedonist's Progress." *Anatomy of Nonsense.* New York: New Directions, 1943. Reprint. In *In Defense of Reason*, 431–59. Chicago: Swallow Press, 1947.
Wohl, Robert. *The Generation of 1914.* Cambridge: Harvard University Press, 1979.
Wood, Clement. *Poets of America.* New York: Dutton, 1925.
Woodress, James. *Dissertations in American Literature, 1891–1966.* Durham: Duke University Press, 1968.
Woodward, Anthony. Rev. of *The Dance of the Intellect*, by Marjorie Perloff. *Review of English Studies* 38 (1987): 411–12.
Zabel, Morton Dauwen. "The *Harmonium* of Wallace Stevens." Rev. of *Harmonium*. *Poetry* 39 (1931): 148–54.

———. "Two Years of Poetry, 1937–1939." *Southern Review* 5 (1939): 569–605.
———. "Wallace Stevens and the Image of Man." *Wallace Stevens Number, Harvard Advocate* 127, no. 3 (December 1940): 19–23.
———, ed. *Literary Opinion in America.* 3rd ed. New York: Harper & Row, 1962.
Ziff, Larzer. *The American 1890's: The Life and Times of a Lost Generation.* 1966. Lincoln: University of Nebraska Press, 1979.
Zigrosser, Carl. *My Own Shall Come to Me.* Casa Laura, Calif.: n.p., 1971.
Zukofsky, Louis. "For Wallace Stevens." In *Prepositions: The Collected Critical Essays of Louis Zukofsky,* 24–38. Berkeley: University of California Press, 1981.

Index

Adams, Léonie, 170
Aiken, Conrad, 38, 39, 40, 47, 49, 50, 52, 59, 78, 87, 99, 126, 151, 205, 250n42, 254n18, 265n14
Alcestis, 98–99, 101–02
Aldington, Richard, 70
American Caravan, The, 45, 98
American Literature, 261n38
Ammons, A. R., 226
Anderson, Margaret, 248n22
Anderson, Sherwood, 27
Anthology of Magazine Verse, 35, 40
Arac, Jonathan, 19
Arensberg, Walter, 29, 32, 34, 38, 59, 248n13, 249n30
Arnold, Matthew, 124
Arvin, Newton, 255n25
Ashbery, John, 226
Atlantic Monthly, 31, 51
Auden, W. H., 191

Baker, Howard, 123, 124, 255n22
Bates, Milton J., 30, 242
Baudelaire, Charles, 179
Bauer, Paul, 256n4
Beecher, John, 134
Belitt, Ben, 82, 100, 103, 105, 106, 112, 115, 116
Bender, Thomas, 260n32
Benét, Stephen Vincent, 265n14
Benét, William Rose, 105, 117
Bennett, Joseph, 193
Berryman, John, 105
Bewley, Marius, 197–98, 220
Bishop, Elizabeth, 174
Bishop, John Peale, 151, 265n14

Blackmur, R. P., 12, 51, 82, 86–97, 112–14, 118, 126, 146–47, 243
Blake, William, 220, 222
Bloom, Harold, 7–9, 12–14, 17, 22, 67, 207, 219–26, 227, 228, 231, 234, 241, 243, 261n41
Bodenheim, Maxwell, 43, 44, 250n42, 265n14
Bogan, Louise, 51, 158, 178, 258n16, 263n1
Bok, Edward, 26
Bollingen Prize, 169–71
Boni, Albert and Charles, 29
Book Review Digest, 41
Borroff, Marie, 237
Bradley, Sculley, 157, 195
Braithwaite, William Stanley, 35, 40
Brazeau, Peter, 130, 242, 254n15
Brogan, Jacqueline Vaught, 253n6, 257n7, 259n22
Brooks, Cleanth, 19, 92, 96, 123, 124, 255n25, 259n24, 260n33
Brooks, Van Wyck, 123, 154–55, 158, 264n9
Broom, 30, 31, 39, 45, 47, 51, 248n22
Brown, Nicholas L., 41
Brown, Robert Carlton, 249n30
Bryer, Jackson, 206
Burke, Kenneth, 42, 71, 76, 95
Burney, William, 205
Burnshaw, Stanley, 100, 102, 105, 107, 114, 125, 255n20
Buttel, Robert, 205
Bynner, Witter, 30, 32, 99, 248n13, 255n20

Cain, William, 260n35
Camus, Albert, 216
Cannell, Skipwith, 249n30
Cargill, Oscar, 141–42, 148, 150

Carne-Ross, D. S., 10
Carrier, Warren, 150, 178
Carruth, Hayden, 131, 172, 179, 189–90, 202
Casillo, Robert, 263n48
Century, 51
Chapbook, 45, 70
Chase, Stanley P., 56
Church, Henry, 130–31
Ciardi, John, 174–75, 192
Coleridge, Samuel Taylor, 95
College English, 157
Colum, Mary, 163
Contact, 30–31
Contempo, 98
Cook, Howard Willard, 49
Corman, Cid, 237, 268n5
Cowley, Malcolm, 76, 247n5, 255n25
Crane, Hart, 49, 158, 205, 226, 260n28, 265n14
Crane, Stephen, 25, 231
Crapsey, Adelaide, 250n42
Cummings, E. E., 34, 86, 92–93, 97, 119–20, 158, 183, 250n40, 265n14
Cummington Press, 145–46
Cummins, Virginia Kent, 170

Dante, 78
Davidson, Michael, 253n8
Davie, Donald, 141–42
Deen, Rosemary, 176, 208–09
Dent, J. M., 99
Derrida, Jacques, 267n22, 267n28
Deutsch, Babette, 82, 189
Diacritics, 17
Dial, 34, 38, 42–43, 51, 69, 70, 71, 76, 158, 250n34, 265n14
Dickinson, Emily, 156
Dillon, George, 161–62, 164
Direction, 98
Donne, John, 19
Drew, Elizabeth, 142–43
Dryden, John, 77
Duchamp, Marcel, 252n9

Earle, Ferdinand, 29
Eberhart, Richard, 100, 161, 174, 254n15

ELH, 157
Eliot, T. S., 7–8, 13, 19, 41, 42, 56, 71, 77–80, 84–85, 86, 87, 91, 92, 93, 95, 97, 120, 124, 126, 158, 180–84, 188, 190, 191–92, 195–96, 199–200, 203–05, 206, 207, 209, 210, 212, 213, 234, 236, 240, 245n4, 247n3, 250n42, 252n11, 253n7, 260n28, 264n8, 264–65n13, 265nn14–17
Emerson, Ralph Waldo, 23, 223–25
Empson, William, 94
Enck, John, 164
Evans, Donald, 29, 105, 247n13
Evans, Oliver, 206
Explicator, 157, 261n36

Faulkner, William, 7
Fearing, Kenneth, 254n16
Feidelson, Charles, Jr., 262n45
Ficke, Arthur Davison, 30, 66
Filreis, Alan, 242, 268n2
Finch, John, 123
Fish, Stanley, 17
Fitzgerald, F. Scott, 206
Fitzgerald, Robert, 82, 105, 113, 115, 116, 117, 255n24
Fletcher, John Gould, 39, 45, 55, 58, 63, 66, 67, 68, 79, 100, 251n3, 254n18, 265n14
Flint, F. Cudworth, 258n18
Foucault, Michel, 267n22
Fowler, Alastair, 251n46
Fraser, Russell, 94
Freeman, 51
Frost, Robert, 26, 27, 43, 45, 78, 79, 97, 100, 107, 116, 119–22, 126, 156, 171, 173, 175, 180, 203, 205, 206, 236, 247n3, 255n26, 260n28, 265n14, 265n17
Frye, Northrop, 4, 5, 207–15, 217, 218–19, 220, 221, 226–28, 233, 235
Fuchs, Daniel, 186, 188, 205

Gibbs, Barbara, 185, 189–90, 208, 263n4
Gilder, Richard Watson, 247n7
Gioia, Dana, 24
Giotto, 181
Glebe, 33
Golding, Alan C., 20

INDEX 289

Graff, Gerald, 246n10
Graves, Robert, 70
Gregory, Horace, 82, 133, 135–36, 141, 150, 151, 162–63, 166, 169
Groff, Alice, 249n30
Gruen, John, 130
Guillory, John, 19

H. D., 58, 265n14
Hagedorn, Hermann, 30
Harcourt, Alfred, 29
Harkness Hoot, 98
Hartman, Geoffrey, 218–19
Harvard Advocate, 31, 118, 122–27, 147, 181, 263–64n5
Hawthorne, Nathaniel, 5
Hayakawa, S. I., 165
Hecht, Anthony, 186–87
Heidegger, Martin, 267n25
Henderson, Alice Corbin, 37, 40, 249n30
Heringman, Bernard, 130, 156
Herr, Michael, 262–63n47
Hoffman, Frederick, 158
Holden, Raymond, 74
Holmes, John, 82, 103, 114, 194
Hound and Horn, 86–87, 91, 94, 98
Howard, Richard, 237–38, 239–40
Howe, Irving, 177, 187, 189, 191–92, 195–96, 211, 217
Hoyt, Helen, 37–38, 44
Hubbell, Jay B., 206, 261n38
Huebsch, B. W., 29, 43
Hughes, Langston, 134
Hulme, T. E., 221
Humphries, Rolfe, 152
Husserl, Edmund, 216, 267n25
Hyman, Stanley Edgar, 95

Independent, 51
Ingalls, Jeremy, 161
Iser, Wolfgang, 17

James, Henry, 162
James, William, 262–63n47
Jameson, Fredric, 242
Jarrell, Randall, 12, 82, 105, 152–53, 163, 174, 176, 177, 188, 261–62n42

Jauss, Hans Robert, 16, 19
Jeffers, Robinson, 100, 107, 116, 119, 126, 255n26, 265n14
Johns, Orrick, 43, 250n42
Jones, Frank, 135, 136, 162
Joost, Nicholas, 70, 71
Josephson, Matthew, 47, 54, 76, 252n8
Journal of Aesthetics and Art Criticism, 157
Journal of Philosophy, 157
Joyce, James, 7, 8, 158, 245n4

Keats, John, 23, 220, 222
Kees, Weldon, 134–35, 136
Kenner, Hugh, 7–8, 12–14, 17, 19, 20, 22, 241
Kennerly, Mitchell, 29, 43
Kermode, Frank, 13, 20, 205, 207–08, 217–18, 220, 226, 235, 243
Kilmer, Joyce, 44
Kirstein, Lincoln, 87
Knopf, Alfred A., 29, 41, 43, 44, 47, 70, 81, 82–83, 99
Koch, Vivienne, 137, 154
Kramer, Hilton, 237, 239
Kreymborg, Alfred, 29, 30, 32, 33, 34–46, 50–52, 55, 66, 68–73, 76, 78, 99, 105, 118, 248n22, 249n30, 254n18, 265n14
Krieger, Murray, 206–08
Kroll, Jack, 238
Krutch, Joseph Wood, 255n25
Kunitz, Stanley, 239, 268n5

Laforgue, Jules, 75, 105
Latimer, J. Ronald Lane, 99–100
Lauter, Paul, 246n11
Lear, Edward, 7
Leary, Lewis, 203–04
Lechlitner, Ruth, 82, 115–16, 117, 133, 135, 138, 139
Lee, Peter, 100
Leggett, B. J., 261n41
Lensing, George, 205, 255n20
Lentricchia, Frank, 205, 207–08, 218, 242–43, 262–63n47
Levin, Harry, 123, 140
Lewis, Wyndham, 7, 267n23
Life, 35

INDEX

Lindsay, Vachel, 25, 27, 43, 44, 79, 247n5, 248n19, 265n14
Literary Digest, 35, 40, 41, 51
Little Review, 32–33, 36, 49, 248n22
Litz, A. Walton, 236, 238
Liveright, Horace, 29
Lodge, George Cabot, 25
Loeb, Harold, 39, 47, 76
London, Jack, 25
Long, Haniel, 107
Lowell, Amy, 4, 5, 25–27, 29, 39, 41, 44, 49, 51, 58, 68, 70, 79, 105, 126, 254n18
Lowell, Robert, 152, 174
Loy, Mina, 40, 254n18

McCarthy, Joseph, 170
McClure's, 32
McGann, Jerome J., 3, 16, 20–21
McGrath, Thomas, 134
MacLeish, Archibald, 205, 256–57n6, 261n39, 265n14
McLeod, Glen G., 31
McNeil, Helen, 239
Mallarmé, Stephane, 23
Marlowe, Christopher, 88
Martz, Louis, 153, 167, 187, 261n42
Masters, Edgar Lee, 25–27, 39, 43, 44, 79, 105, 111, 247n3, 248n19, 265n14
Matthiessen, F. O., 19, 76, 82, 107, 116, 117, 123, 124, 126, 151, 156, 243, 264n5
Measure, 30, 31, 51, 74, 76, 248n22
Melville, Herman, 4, 5, 19
Merrill, James, 226
Meyer, Gerard Previn, 82, 166, 170, 179–80, 183, 185, 189, 195
Michelson, Max, 249n30
Miles, Josephine, 183–84
Millay, Edna St. Vincent, 100, 105, 119–20, 126, 247n3, 265n14
Miller, J. Hillis, 5, 207–08, 219, 226–35, 236, 242–43
Milton, John, 19, 77, 93, 124, 179
Modern Philology, 157
Modern School, 36
Monroe, Harriet, 23, 27, 32–41, 44–45, 47, 50, 52, 56, 57, 58, 64, 66–69, 72, 78, 82, 84, 99, 105, 117, 122, 160, 248n19, 249n30, 252n8
Moody, William Vaughn, 25, 265n14
Moore, Geoffrey, 190
Moore, Marianne, 39, 40, 42, 47, 71, 75, 77, 105, 108, 117–18, 123, 158, 205, 265n14
Morgan, Frederick, 193, 256–57n14
Morse, Samuel French, 100, 130, 153, 156, 174, 179, 185, 188, 264n6
Munson, Gorham B., 47, 49, 51, 75–77, 79, 85, 86, 251n8

Nassar, Eugene, 205
Nation, 51, 250n38
Nelson, Cary, 268n3
Nemerov, Howard, 216–17
New Act, 98
New Masses, 107
New Republic, 35, 51, 59, 98, 250n34, 254n12
New York Times Book Review, 51, 250n38
New Yorker, 17
Norris, Frank, 25
North American Review, 51
North, Michael, 111–12
Norton, Allen, 29, 31, 69, 247–48n13

O'Connor, William Van, 12, 24, 153, 156–57, 160, 181, 183, 185, 264n8
Ohmann, Richard, 20
Ostriker, Alicia Suskin, 268n3
Others, 31–46, 50, 59, 70, 249n30, 250n38

Pach, Walter, 29
Pack, Robert, 177, 188, 196, 208
Patchen, Kenneth, 91
Pater, Walter, 23, 57, 64
Peanuts, 268n6
Pearce, Roy Harvey, 178, 194, 199–202, 208, 214, 217, 221, 226, 227, 228, 231, 243
Perloff, Marjorie, 9–14, 20, 243
Perspective, 174
Peterson, Margaret, 205
Phillips, David Graham, 25
Picasso, Pablo, 180
PMLA, 157
Poe, Edgar Allan, 148, 156

INDEX

Poetry, 27–28, 32–41, 44–45, 50–51, 55–58, 98, 122, 192, 249n30, 249n33, 250n38, 254n12
Poetry Journal, 38
Poirier, Richard, 197–99, 220
Poulet, Georges, 267n25
Pound, Ezra, 7–14, 18, 29, 33, 34, 39, 42, 43, 44, 58, 59, 70, 86, 92, 93, 97, 100, 126, 127, 134, 158, 159, 164, 169–71, 173, 183, 191, 203, 205, 206, 236, 247n3, 250n42, 252n11, 260n38, 265n14, 265–66n17, 267n23
Pound, Homer, 91
Powers, James, 100
Powys, Llewellyn, 71, 75, 77, 114
Pulitzer Prize, 175–76

Rahv, Philip, 255n25
Ransom, John Crowe, 91, 96, 148, 255n25, 259n24, 265n14, 266n19
Ray, Man, 250n39
Reedy, William Marion, 33
Reising, Russell, 198
Review of Reviews, 35, 40, 41
Rexroth, Kenneth, 183
"Richard Sir Vallienne," 31
Richardson, Joan, 242
Riddel, Joseph N., 205, 207–08, 239
Ridge, Lola, 42
Riding, Laura, 70
Rilke, Rainer Maria, 122
Rimbaud, Arthur, 87
Robinson, Edwin Arlington, 25–27, 43, 45, 53, 78, 105, 126, 205, 247n3, 260n28, 265n14, 266n17
Rocking Horse, 98
Rodríguez-Feo, José, 100, 130
Roethke, Theodore, 105, 174
Rogue, 31, 36, 69
Rolfe, Edwin, 134
Romanic Review, 261n36
Rosenfeld, Paul, 48, 53, 75–77, 92
Rousseau, Jean-Jacques, 169

Said, Edward W., 95, 96
Sanborn, Pitts, 29–31, 248n14

Sandburg, Carl, 25, 27, 43, 44, 78, 79, 105, 193, 247n3, 248n19, 265n14
Santayana, George, 106
Saturday Review of Literature, 51, 98
Schaum, Melita, 16, 254n10
Schneider, Isidor, 256n1
Schwartz, Delmore, 82, 85, 100, 105, 106, 112–14, 116, 123–25, 130, 176–83, 188–91, 241, 264n5
Scribners', 51
Secession, 30, 76
Seiffert, Marjorie Allen, 55–58, 64, 67, 160
Seldes, Gilbert, 69, 71
Shakespeare, William, 93, 117–18, 124, 179
Shapiro, Karl, 124, 186–87
Shelley, Percy Bysshe, 164, 222
Sidney, Sir Philip, 164
Simons, Hi, 100, 123, 125–26, 130, 138–40, 160, 165–66
Simpson, Eileen, 105
Simpson, Louis, 181, 195
Singal, Daniel Joseph, 20
Sitwell family, 183
Smith, Barbara Herrnstein, 4–5, 21, 46
Smith, Harrison, 170
Smoke, 98
Snow, Wilbert, 140
Soil, 36
Southern Review, 118–22, 254n12
Spectra, 30, 32
Spencer, Theodore, 123
Spender, Stephen, 136
Spenser, Edmund, 124
Spiller, Robert, 128, 159, 258–59n20
Squire, J. C., 54, 58, 60, 63
Stanford, Donald, 268n5
Stein, Gertrude, 254n16
Stern, Herbert, 205
Stevens, Elsie Kachel (wife), 27
Stevens, Garrett Barcalow (father), 27
Stevens, Holly (daughter), 98, 238
Stevens, Wallace, Works: "Adagia," 239; "Anecdote of the Jar," 56, 167–69, 195, 208, 216; "Angel Surrounded by Paysans," 257n15; "Anglais Mort a Florence," 111; "Another Weeping Woman," 140; "Architec-

ture," 187, 194, 198–99; "Asides on the Oboe," 149, 169, 200, 224, 260n26; *Auroras of Autumn, The,* 132, 152, 163, 170, 176, 193, 260n29, 263n3; "Auroras of Autumn, The," 141–42, 225, 226; "Bantams in Pine-Woods," 62, 64, 71, 88, 90, 254n17; "Botanist on Alp (I)," 110; "Carlos Among the Candles," 68; "Collect of Philosophy, A," 266n21; *Collected Poems,* 103, 132, 173–92, 202–03, 263n3; "Comedian as the Letter C, The," 3, 48, 51, 66, 67, 90–91, 93, 112, 132, 151, 188; "Dance of the Macabre Mice," 110–11; "Death of a Soldier," 254n17; "Depression Before Spring," 49; "Dezembrum," 137; "Disillusionment of Ten O'Clock," 94; "Doctor of Geneva, The," 254n17; "Domination of Black," 72, 110; "Earthy Anecdote," 110; "Emperor of Ice-Cream, The," 71, 90, 151, 254n17; "Esthétique du Mal," 129, 132, 153, 154, 165; "Examination of the Hero in a Time of War," 129; "Explanation," 64–65, 112, 116; "Fabliau of Florida," 57; "Farewell to Florida," 110; "Fugure of the Youth as Virile Poet, The," 140, 221; "Frogs Eat Butterflies. Snakes Eat Frogs. Hogs Eat Snakes. Men Eat Hogs," 63, 72; "God Is Good. It Is a Beautiful Night," 184; *Harmonium,* 31, 45, 46, 48–80, 81–85, 90, 97, 99, 101–02, 104, 107, 109–14, 116, 117, 132–33, 136, 147, 150–53, 157–60, 173, 176, 183, 260n29; "Idea of Order at Key West, The," 267n26; *Ideas of Order,* 76, 99, 101–18, 122, 134, 260n29; "Irrational Element in Poetry, The," 258n15; "Jack-Rabbit, The," 110; "Last Looks at the Lilacs," 254n17; "Latest Freed Man, The," 144–45; *Letters of Wallace Stevens,* 236–40; "Like Decorations in a Nigger Cemetery," 197; "Lions in Sweden," 111; "Man and Bottle," 137; "Man on the Dump, The," 261n42; *Man With the Blue Guitar, The,* 101–18, 121–22, 162, 231–32, 239; "Man With the Blue Guitar, The," 81, 96; "Mandolin and Liqueurs," 70; "Mechanical Optimist, The," 260n27; "Metaphors of a Magnifico," 64, 116; "Monocle de Mon Oncle, Le," 36, 65, 68, 90, 106, 117, 249n33; "Motive for Metaphor, The," 145; "Mozart, 1935," 109, 111; "Mrs. Alfred Uruguay," 139–40, 222; *Necessary Angel, The,* 132, 160n29; "Negation," 64–65, 112; "Noble Rider and the Sound of Words, The," 131, 137; "Not Ideas About the Thing But the Thing Itself," 232–33; *Notes Toward a Supreme Fiction,* 128–29, 131–32, 145–47, 153, 169, 236; "Nuances of a Theme by Williams," 116; "O Florida, Venereal Soil," 57; "Of Modern Poetry," 261n42; "On the Road Home," 143–44, 149, 216; *Opus Posthumous,* 123, 176–94, 202–03, 263n3; "Ordinary Evening in New Haven, An," 245n6, 267n27; "Ordinary Women, The," 90, 93; "Paltry Nude Starts On a Spring Voyage, The," 254n17; "Parochial Theme," 142–43; *Parts of a World,* 132, 134–45, 160–61, 260n29; "Pecksniffiana," 34, 38; "Peter Quince at the Clavier," 34, 36, 40–41, 53, 55, 116, 152, 249n33, 254n17; "Phases," 32, 35, 36, 38, 52, 251n5; "Plot Against the Giant, The," 64; "Ploughing on Sunday," 64; "Quiet Normal Life, A," 189; "Rock, The," 201; "Sad Strains of a Gay Waltz," 110–11; "Sailing After Lunch," 110; "Sea Surface Full of Clouds," 71–72, 148, 153, 160, 229; "Six Significant Landscapes," 37, 116; "Snow Man, The," 90; "So-and-So Reclining on Her Couch," 184; "Stars at Tallapoosa," 261n40; "Sunday Morning," 36, 53, 55, 65–66, 68, 71–72, 90–91, 96, 110, 116, 124–25, 147, 150–51, 222, 249n28, 249n33, 249n43; "Tea," 69, 116; "Thirteen Ways of Looking at a Blackbird," 96, 249n33; "Three Travelers Watch a Sunrise," 34, 36; "To the One of Fictive Music," 65, 116; *Transport to Summer,* 132, 140, 145, 148, 152–53, 176, 260n29; "Valley Candle," 189; "Waving Adieu, Adieu, Adieu," 110; "Wind Shifts, The," 73; "World as Meditation, The," 261n42

Stickney, Trumbull, 25
Sukenick, Ronald, 105

INDEX

Swallow, Alan, 148–49, 162
Swimming Pool Q's, The, 268–69n6
Symons, Julian, 100, 183
Sypher, Wylie, 149

Taggard, Genevieve, 91, 119
Tate, Allen, 12, 76, 91, 92, 93, 96–97, 123, 151, 254n15, 259n25, 265n14
Tennyson, Alfred Lord, 247n3
Thayer, Scofield, 31, 42, 70
thirtysomething, 269n6
Thomas, Dylan, 174
Thoreau, Henry David, 198–99
Tindall, William York, 136–38, 162–63, 193–94, 243
Tompkins, Jane, 5
Trend, 30–31
Trinity Review, 174

Untermeyer, Louis, 28, 39, 46, 54–55, 56, 58–63, 66, 68, 71, 73, 77, 78, 83–85, 88, 114, 117, 128, 141, 160–61, 243

Valery, Paul, 87, 124
Van Doren, Mark, 39, 54, 55, 58, 60, 63
Van Ghent, Dorothy, 126
Van Vechten, Carl, 29, 31, 44, 70, 106, 247–48n13
Vanderbilt, Kermit, 157, 210n34
Vendler, Helen, 67, 257n11, 262n43
Verlaine, Paul, 106
Viereck, Peter, 82, 140–41, 152, 157, 163–64, 168–69, 174

Wagner, C. Roland, 156
Walcutt, Charles C., 167–68
Wald, Alan, 260n33
Wallace, Henry, 157
Walton, Eda Lou, 82, 84, 87, 103, 115, 116, 180
Warren, Robert Penn, 96, 123, 125, 255n25, 260n33

Wasserstrom, William, 42, 71
Waste Land, The, 77–80, 84, 93, 174, 183, 184
Watson, James Sibley, 42, 71
Waugh, Evelyn, 79
Weatherhead, A. Kingsley, 206
Weiss, Theodore, 135, 144, 148, 150, 169
Westminster Magazine, 254n12
Wheelock, John Hall, 30
Whicher, Stephen, 224
Whitehead, Alfred North, 266n21
Whitman, Walt, 19, 23, 28, 45, 156, 174, 192, 196, 223–25, 247n3
Wilbur, Richard, 174
Williams, Ellen, 71
Williams, William Carlos, 27, 31, 34, 39–40, 42, 44, 47, 50, 51, 70, 77, 99, 105, 119–21, 123, 127, 134, 158, 170, 185–87, 205, 206, 219, 230, 232–34, 238, 249n26, 252n16, 254n16, 265n14
Wilson, Christopher P., 28
Wilson, Edmund, 55, 58–59, 63, 79, 82, 117, 180, 251n46, 255n25
Winters, Yvor, 12, 40, 47, 51, 53, 55, 91, 96, 113, 124, 147–48, 150, 156, 168–69, 210, 255n22, 255n25, 255n26, 261n40
Wohl, Robert, 248n3
Wood, Clement, 40
Woolf, Virginia, 7
Wordsworth, William, 220, 222, 224
Wylie, Elinor, 265n14

Yale Review, 51
Yeats, William Butler, 7, 120–22, 124, 127, 265n15, 267n23

Zabel, Morton Dauwen, 76, 82, 84–87, 100, 116, 118–27, 255n22
Zaturenska, Marya, 151
Zigrosser, Carl, 29, 36, 69, 76
Zorach, William, 250n39
Zukofsky, Louis, 45, 47, 51, 250n44

www.ingramcontent.com/pod-product-compliance
Lightning Source LLC
Chambersburg PA
CBHW030335240426
43661CB00052B/1646